MCAT Chemistry and Organic Chemistry

CONTENT REVIEW AND PRACTICE PASSAGES

NextStep

TEST PREP nextsteptestprep.com

Printed in the United States of America

Second Printing, 2017

ISBN 978-1-944-935-19-1

Next Step Test Prep, LLC
4256 N Ravenswood Ave
Suite 207
Chicago IL 60613

www.nextsteptestprep.com

MCAT is a registered trademark of the American Association of Medical Colleges (AAMC). The AAMC has neither
reviewed nor endorsed this work in any way.

Revision: 1.02 (2017-12-01)

FREE ONLINE FULL LENGTH MCAT

Want to see how you would do on the MCAT
and understand where you need to focus your prep?

TAKE OUR FREE MCAT DIAGNOSTIC EXAM
and **FREE FULL LENGTH**
Timed practice that simulates Test Day and provides
comprehensive analysis, reporting, and in-depth explanations.

Included with this free account is the first lesson
in Next Step's online course, a free sample
from our science QBank, and more!

All of these resources are provided free to students who have
purchased a Next Step book. Register for your free account at:

http://nextsteptestprep.com/mcat-diagnostic

This page left intentionally blank.

STOP! READ THIS FIRST!

The book you're holding is one of Next Step's six MCAT review books and contains both concise content review and questions to practice applying your content knowledge. In order to get the most out of this book, we strongly recommend that you follow a few simple steps:

1. Register for a free MCAT bundle at http://nextsteptestprep.com/mcat-diagnostic and begin your prep by taking the MCAT Diagnostic and Science Content Diagnostic to assess your strengths and weaknesses.

2. Begin working through the Next Step Review set starting with the Verbal, Quantitative, and Research Methods book. Complete this entire book at the start of your prep.

3. Use the Study Plan generator in your free account at nextstepmcat.com to generate a day-by-day study plan to take you through the rest of the Next Step Books.

4. Begin working through the rest of the Next Step MCAT review books, including this one. To get the most value out of these books, use spaced repetition to ensure complete mastery of the material. A spaced repetition approach would look something like this:

    I. Begin by skimming through the chapter to familiarize yourself with the key terms and content in the book. Then go back and read the chapter carefully.

    II. Sleep on it! Solidifying those long term memories requires sleep.

    III. Come back to the chapter *the next day*, re-skim it and then *complete the questions at the end of the chapter*. Carefully read all of the explanations, even for the questions you got right.

    IV. Take notes in your Lessons Learned Journal from the chapter. For a full explanation on what a Lessons Learned Journal is, watch Lesson 1 included in the free online bundle at nextstepmcat.com.

    IV. Sleep on it!

    V. Two days later, come back, briefly re-skim the chapter, re-do the questions at the end of the chapter, and review your Lessons Learned Journal.

Mastering the MCAT requires more than just a good set of books. You'll want to continue your prep with the most representative practice tests available. Your free bundle includes Next Step Full Length #1. After you've completed that, you can upgrade your account to include additional practice exams.

Finally, if you would like more extensive help, including daily live office hours with Next Step's senior faculty, contact us for more information about our online course. You can reach us at 888-530-NEXT or mcat@nextsteptestprep.com.

Group→	1	2	3	4	5	6	7	8	9	10	11	12	13	14	15	16	17	18
Period ↓																		
1	1 H																	2 He
2	3 Li	4 Be											5 B	6 C	7 N	8 O	9 F	10 Ne
3	11 Na	12 Mg											13 Al	14 Si	15 P	16 S	17 Cl	18 Ar
4	19 K	20 Ca	21 Sc	22 Ti	23 V	24 Cr	25 Mn	26 Fe	27 Co	28 Ni	29 Cu	30 Zn	31 Ga	32 Ge	33 As	34 Se	35 Br	36 Kr
5	37 Rb	38 Sr	39 Y	40 Zr	41 Nb	42 Mo	43 Tc	44 Ru	45 Rh	46 Pd	47 Ag	48 Cd	49 In	50 Sn	51 Sb	52 Te	53 I	54 Xe
6	55 Cs	56 Ba	57 La *	72 Hf	73 Ta	74 W	75 Re	76 Os	77 Ir	78 Pt	79 Au	80 Hg	81 Tl	82 Pb	83 Bi	84 Po	85 At	86 Rn
7	87 Fr	88 Ra	89 Ac **	104 Rf	105 Db	106 Sg	107 Bh	108 Hs	109 Mt	110 Ds	111 Rg	112 Cn	113 Nh	114 Fl	115 Mc	116 Lv	117 Ts	118 Og

*	58 Ce	59 Pr	60 Nd	61 Pm	62 Sm	63 Eu	64 Gd	65 Tb	66 Dy	67 Ho	68 Er	69 Tm	70 Yb	71 Lu
**	90 Th	91 Pa	92 U	93 Np	94 Pu	95 Am	96 Cm	97 Bk	98 Cf	99 Es	100 Fm	101 Md	102 No	103 Lr

TABLE OF CONTENTS

This page left intentionally blank.

Atomic Structure and Periodic Trends

CHAPTER 1

0. Introduction

The study of matter is the foundation of all chemistry. Matter is composed of atoms, which interact with other atoms in generally predictable but still fascinating ways. In this chapter, we will first answer the question: *What is the substance of life?* (Hint: it's atoms.) We will then discuss how atoms are characterized and the trends we can use to predict their behavior. These may seem like easy concepts, and you almost certainly learned them first in your college or even high school chemistry courses. For this reason, you might be tempted to rush through this chapter to save time for more traditionally intimidating concepts, such as electrochemistry or optics. However, MCAT chemistry—like the exam in general—requires a knowledge of basic concepts above all else, and a thorough understanding of the material in this chapter will help you draw connections to later topics or even separate subjects.

1. Atomic Structure and Identity

All matter is composed of atoms, which are the building blocks of molecules. Matter that is composed entirely of one atomic type is called an element, such as gold or helium. When two or more atoms join together, they become a molecule; examples include O_2 and S_8. Some molecules include atoms of multiple different elements. This earns them the distinction of being a compound, such as ammonia (NH_3) or carbon dioxide (CO_2). Atoms are composed of subatomic particles, which constitute a large and complex field of study in advanced physics. (Have you ever heard of quarks? How about bosons or leptons?) For the MCAT, however, you should understand only three types of subatomic particles: protons, neutrons, and electrons.

Protons carry a positive charge and have a mass of 1 atomic mass unit (amu) or 1 dalton (Da). The actual charge on a single proton is approximately 1.6×10^{-19} coulombs (C), a magnitude that is termed the elementary charge (e). However, while this value is used in some calculations, we simplify it in most situations by saying that each proton has a charge of + 1. Protons exist in the nucleus, or central core of the atom. All atoms must contain at least one proton.

Neutrons are neutral in charge, from which their name derives. The mass of one neutron is larger than that of one proton, but only very slightly; for the sake of the MCAT, neutrons can thus be thought of as weighing the same as protons (1 amu). Neutrons also reside in the atomic nucleus. As such, both neutrons and protons can be termed "nucleons."

MCAT STRATEGY > > >

As you build your chemistry foundation, you will become very familiar with the fact that 1 amu corresponds to a mass of 1 g/mol. In this way, the number of protons and neutrons in an atom can be used to determine its molar mass. Don't worry, however; you will be given access to a periodic table on the exam, where the mass of each element in amu is given.

Finally, electrons carry a negative charge and have a mass so small as to be considered negligible. The approximate charge on an electron is -1.6×10^{-19} C. Sound familiar? In fact, this is the same magnitude as the charge on a proton, except with the sign reversed, and is typically simplified as -1. This brings us to a concept that you will see repeatedly throughout chemistry, physics, and even biochemistry and biology: opposite charges attract. For this reason, electrons are held close to the nucleus even though they are not themselves nucleons. Specifically, electrons exist in an electron cloud around the nucleus (Figure 1). You may have seen descriptions of electrons as existing in regularly-spaced spherical orbitals, or shells, surrounding the center of the atom. While this model is useful to conceptualize the atom, it is now somewhat outdated. The electron cloud model, proposed by Erwin Schrödinger, is more modern. This model states that we cannot know *exactly* where an electron is located at any given time, but it is more probable that it exists in certain locations, or clouds, rather than others. The farther away an electron is from the nucleus, the higher the energy of the electron. The electrons in the shell farthest from the nucleus are called valence electrons and play a vital role in chemical bonding, as you will see in Chapter 2.

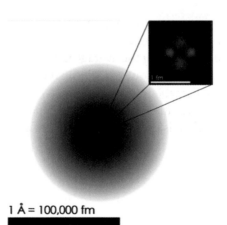

1 Å = 100,000 fm

Figure 1. Atomic structure of helium.

MCAT STRATEGY > > >

Do not get too caught up in high-level chemical theories, as fascinating as they are. The MCAT is not designed to quiz you on the history of chemistry, and it similarly is usually not trying to trick you on the minute points of theoretical chemistry. Instead, focus on the basics: what are protons and electrons, and how do they affect how an atom behaves?

Now that we are familiar with subatomic particles, let's think about how this information can be used to determine the unique identity of any given atom. The atoms of each element are associated with a certain number of protons, termed the atomic number (Z). The atomic number gives each element its unique identity. For example, every nitrogen atom (Z = 7) contains 7 protons. If an atom contains more or fewer than 7 protons, it cannot possibly be a nitrogen atom.

In contrast, the mass number (A) of an atom is the total number of neutrons and protons contained in the nucleus. Recall that the mass contributed by electrons is negligible, so they are excluded in this calculation. Atomic number and mass number are usually represented as shown in Figure 2.

$$\text{mass number} \rightarrow {}^{4}_{2}\text{He} \leftarrow \text{element symbol}$$
$$\text{atomic number} \rightarrow$$

Figure 2. The mass and atomic number of helium (He).

While no two atoms of the same element can have different numbers of protons, they certainly can vary in their number of neutrons. Atoms of the same element that have different numbers of neutrons are called isotopes. For example, carbon-12 and carbon-13 are isotopes: these possess 6 protons plus 6 and 7 neutrons, respectively. Even hydrogen has several isotopes. As you likely know, hydrogen is the lightest element; it contains only a single proton. The form of hydrogen with which we are most familiar is protium (^{1}H), which contains no neutrons and thus has a mass number of 1. Deuterium (^{2}H, or D) is a hydrogen isotope with one proton and one neutron, and tritium (^{3}H) contains one proton and two neutrons. Deuterium in particular may appear on the MCAT for the purpose of labeling hydrogens and tracking their movement through the course of an organic reaction. If you see "D" on an organic molecule, this is what that refers to; note that deuterium will behave similarly to a regular protium atom.

Two concepts that are related to mass number are the atomic mass and the atomic weight. Atomic mass is virtually synonymous with atomic number; the only difference relates to the binding energy of the nucleus, another concept that you will encounter in physics. But the atomic mass refers only to the mass of one particular atom of an element. A concept termed "atomic weight" goes one step further, giving the average mass of *all possible isotopes* of an element, weighted to account for abundance. This is the value that is shown on the periodic table; after all, it would become rather cumbersome to show the different atomic mass of each possible isotope on the table separately. The atomic weight of carbon is 12.01 amu, which tells us that the majority of carbon atoms that exist in the universe have a mass of 12 amu, and a small proportion have a mass greater than 12 amu.

> > **CONNECTIONS** < <

Chapter 10 of Physics

Knowing what we know now about protons, neutrons, and electrons, we are now well equipped to predict the charge on a particular atom. Neutral atoms have an equal number of protons and electrons, but they can gain or lose electrons to become ions, which carry a net charge. The two main types of ions are cations, which carry a net positive charge, and anions, which carry a net negative charge. For example, a calcium (Ca) atom that contains 20 protons and 20 electrons is considered neutral. By losing two electrons, calcium will become a cation with a charge of + 2, which is expressed as Ca^{2+}.

Let's say an atom contains eight protons, seven neutrons, and nine electrons. What is the charge on its nucleus? Well, remember that the nucleus contains only protons (+1 charge) and neutrons (uncharged). The nucleus of this atom thus has a charge of +8. What about the charge on the entire atom? Now, we do factor in electrons, which have a combined charge of −9. The overall charge on the atom is thus (+ 8) + (−9) = −1. In general, when you see negative species (anions), you should think "electron-rich," and when you see positive species (cations), you should think "electron-deficient" or "proton-rich."

Polyatomic ions containing multiple atoms follow a few simple nomenclature rules. If several differently-charged ionic forms of an element exist, the positive charge value can be represented by Roman numerals. Furthermore, the ion with the lesser charge will use the suffix *-ous*, and the ion with the greater charge will use the suffix *-ic*.

Fe^{2+}	Iron (II)	Ferrous ion
Fe^{3+}	Iron (III)	Ferric ion

Monatomic ions use the suffix *-ide*.

H^-	Hydride	O^{2-}	Oxide

Oxyanions—polyatomic anions that contain oxygen—use the suffix *-ite* and *-ate* for compounds with fewer and greater numbers of oxygen atoms, respectively. The prefix *hypo-* is added for oxyanions with one fewer oxygen than *-ite* ions, and *per-* is added for ions with one more oxygen than *-ate* ions.

ClO^-	Hypochlorite		
NO_2^-	Nitrite	ClO_2^-	Chlorite
NO_3^-	Nitrate	ClO_3^-	Chlorate
ClO_4^-	Perchlorate		

If the polyatomic anion includes a hydrogen (H^+) ion, *hydrogen* or *dihydrogen* is added to the name of the parent anion.

CO_3^{2-}	Carbonate	HCO_3^-	Hydrogen carbonate
PO_4^{3-}	Phosphate	$H_2PO_4^-$	Dihydrogen phosphate

2. The Bohr Model

We're about to step into the realm of some of the more conceptually difficult topics in MCAT chemistry, so hold on tight. In particular, let's go back to 1913, when Niels Bohr and Ernest Rutherford introduced their revolutionary model of the atom, building on Rutherford's earlier work. The Bohr model helps explain the electronic structure of the hydrogen atom; this is a useful, albeit simplified model, since hydrogen is the simplest element.

MCAT STRATEGY > > >

Throughout both general and organic chemistry, it will be very helpful if you constantly remind yourself that energy and stability are inversely correlated. A high-energy molecule, for example, is typically very unstable, while a low-energy molecule is expected to be stable.

As mentioned previously, electrons exist in "clouds" that denote the probability of finding them in a given location. However, the earlier view of electrons (as exemplified by the Bohr model) held that they orbit the nucleus in spherical shells that vary in their distance from the nucleus. Positively-charged protons in the nucleus exert an attractive force on electrons, preventing them from straying, although they remain in constant motion with quantized angular momentum. As you can imagine, the electrons closest to the nucleus experience the greatest attractive force, and thus the closer an electron is to the nucleus (and the smaller the orbital radius), the greater its stability and the lower its energy level. On the other hand, an electron located farther from the nucleus will have a higher energy and will be less stable.

Each shell is numbered by its proximity to the nucleus (n = 1, 2, 3…) and is associated with a unique energy level. The lowest possible energy level is closest to the nucleus and is termed the ground state (n = 1 for the single electron in hydrogen). For larger atoms with multiple electrons, the ground state refers to the lowest possible energy level for the electron in question, which is not necessarily n = 1.

Interestingly, an electron in its ground state is not limited to remaining there forever. Each shell is characterized by a certain amount of energy, and if a ground-state electron absorbs energy equal to the difference between a higher shell's energy level and the ground state's energy level, it can jump to the higher-energy shell. This electron is no longer in the ground state, so it is now termed "excited." If energy absorption can cause an electron to move to a higher level, what happens if the electron then drops back down to the ground state? As we might expect, that excess energy must go somewhere, so it will be emitted in the form of a photon, the subatomic particle that makes up light. Since the gaps between energy levels are set at certain values, the photons emitted are "quantized," meaning that they can only contain certain discrete amounts of energy.

We have stated that energy is emitted in the form of photons, which can be conceptualized as light particles. But this is not an entirely comprehensive description. More accurately, energy is emitted and absorbed in the form of electromagnetic radiation, which is radiation that includes both electric and magnetic fields. The electromagnetic spectrum includes visible light, radio waves, gamma rays, X-rays, and more.

> > CONNECTIONS < <

Chapter 9 of Physics

The many forms of electromagnetic radiation differ in their energies, frequencies, and wavelengths. The energy of electromagnetic radiation is given by Equation 1, which was proposed by the physicist Max Planck.

Equation 1.
$$E = hf$$

Here, h is Planck's constant (approximately 6.63×10^{-34} J·s) and f is the frequency of the light. Since the frequency of a wave (f) is equal to the speed of light (c, or 3.00×10^8 m/s in a vacuum) divided by its wavelength (λ), the energy of a photon can also be expressed as the following (Equation 2).

Equation 2.
$$E = hf = \frac{hc}{\lambda}$$

As mentioned earlier in this chapter, the work of chemists Ernest Rutherford and Niels Bohr showed that the energy is emitted and absorbed in discrete amounts called quanta. The emission or absorption of electromagnetic radiation results in a characteristic atomic emission spectrum and atomic absorption spectrum that are unique for each element.

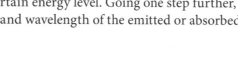

Figure 3. The atomic emission spectrum of iron (Fe).

These spectra contain distinct lines that represent quantized energy levels. Equation 3, below, shows how to calculate the energy held by an electron at a certain energy level. Going one step further, the Rydberg formula (Equation 4) can be used to determine the energy and wavelength of the emitted or absorbed radiation as an electron moves between two energy levels.

Equation 3.
$$E = -\frac{R}{n^2}$$

Equation 4.
$$\Delta E = \frac{hc}{\lambda} = R\left(\frac{1}{n_f^2} - \frac{1}{n_i^2}\right)$$

In both equations, R denotes the Rydberg constant (2.18×10^{-18} J). In Equation 3, n denotes the energy level at which the electron is present. In Equation 4, n_f and n_i represent the final and initial energy states of the electron, respectively.

Let's try an example. Say you are asked to calculate the energy of the emitted photon when an electron transitions from the $n = 4$ to the $n = 2$ energy level. As the electron transitions from a higher-energy to a lower-energy state, electromagnetic radiation will be emitted in the form of a photon. Let's plug in $n_i = 4$ and $n_f = 2$ and solve:

$$\Delta E = R\left(\frac{1}{n_f^2}-\frac{1}{n_i^2}\right)$$

$$\Delta E = (2.18 \times 10^{-18}\,J)\left(\frac{1}{4^2}-\frac{1}{2^2}\right) = (2.18 \times 10^{-18}\,J)\left(-\frac{3}{16}\right) = -4.09 \times 10^{-19}\,J$$

Of course, this math is somewhat more difficult than you might usually see on the MCAT, as you will not be allowed to use a calculator. However, you certainly should be very familiar with the fact that going from a higher to a lower energy level is associated with emission, while moving from a lower level to a higher one requires energy absorption.

3. Quantum Numbers and Electron Configuration

As mentioned earlier, the Bohr model of the atom is now considered outdated, although it provided us with an enormously useful foundation to build upon. Interestingly, the scientific advances related to this area of study have shown us, in part, that we cannot be fully certain where an electron is and how it is behaving at a certain point in time. Specifically, the Heisenberg uncertainty principle posits that the more we understand about the position of an electron, the less we must know about its momentum, and vice versa. In fact, it is impossible to accurately know *both* the exact position and the momentum of a given electron at once.

The system of quantum numbers does help us describe electrons to a certain extent. To understand this concept, first note that electrons exist in orbitals, or areas of space in which an electron is likely to be located, as described by mathematical functions. A given orbital can hold a maximum of two electrons. Each electron in an atom is associated with four quantum numbers that describe its position, the shape of its orbit, its orientation, and its angular momentum. Quantum numbers narrow down exactly which electron within an atom is being described. In fact, the Pauli exclusion principle states that no two electrons in a given atom can have the exact same values for all four quantum numbers.

The first quantum number is the principal quantum number, or *n*. This denotes the energy level of the electron. This number can theoretically take any integer value, as long as it is 1 or greater. As mentioned earlier, higher principal quantum numbers ($n = 2$ rather than $n = 1$) have greater energy, and they are also associated with a greater distance from the nucleus. The periodic table is a topic of discussion later in this chapter, but for now, it is important to know that the principal quantum number relates to the row of the table in which the element in question is found. For example, consider the valence (outermost) electron in sodium (Na). Consulting the periodic table tells us that sodium is displayed in the third period, or row. This valence electron will thus have a principal quantum number of $n = 3$. (Note that this rule does not always hold true quite so perfectly, as we will discuss.)

The azimuthal, or angular momentum, quantum number (*l*) describes the subshell of the principal quantum number in which the electron is found. The possible *l* values for a given principal quantum number range from 0 to $n - 1$, where $l = 0$ is the s subshell, $l = 1$ is the p subshell, $l = 2$ is the d subshell, and $l = 3$ is the f subshell. For example, if we are dealing with an electron in the $n = 1$ shell, the only possible value for the l quantum number is $(1 - 0) = 0$, and the electron must be located in an s subshell. This makes sense, as the only subshell with $n = 1$ is the 1s subshell. The azimuthal quantum number is sometimes described as denoting the shape of the orbital, which in effect is the same as describing the subshell. Each type of subshell has its own characteristic orbital shape(s); s orbitals are spherical, p orbitals are dumbbell-shaped, and d and f orbitals have shapes that are more complex.

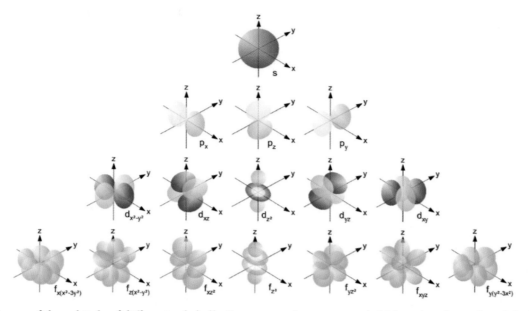

Figure 4. Shapes of the orbitals of different subshells. From top to bottom: s, p, d, f. Note that the p, d, and f subshells have multiple possible shapes.

Next, the magnetic quantum number (m_l) describes the spatial orientation of the orbital in question *within* its subshell. Notice how we are becoming increasingly specific! Potential values of the m_l number range from $-l$ to $+l$. Thus, the s subshell, with its $l = 0$ value, holds only one orbital ($m_l = 0$). The p subshell ($l = 1$) holds 3 orbitals ($m_l = -1$, 0, and +1), the d subshell ($l = 2$) holds 5 orbitals ($m_l = -2, -1, 0, +1$, and + 2), and the f subshell holds 7 orbitals ($m_l = -3, -2, -1, 0, +1, + 2$, and + 3). Since each orbital can hold a maximum of two electrons, this means that an s subshell can contain up to two electrons, a p subshell can hold up to six electrons, a d subshell can contain up to 10, and an f subshell can hold up to 14.

Finally, the spin quantum number (m_s) describes the spin orientation of the electron, which relates to its angular momentum. Angular momentum is a vector quantity, which means that it accounts for both magnitude and direction; for this reason, the spin quantum number can be either positive or negative. The two possible spin orientations are $m_s = -\frac{1}{2}$ and $m_s = + \frac{1}{2}$. Two electrons in the same orbital (and thus with the same m_l value) are said to be paired and must have opposite spin.

In this way, we can see that quantum numbers serve as a sort of "street address" for an electron. The principal quantum number is analogous to the city in which a person lives, while the azimuthal quantum number represents their street. The magnetic quantum number narrows down the person's possible location to their house, and the spin quantum number finally points out *exactly which person* within the house we are referring to.

Let's try a quick example to solidify this information. What is the maximum number of electrons that can exist at the energy level $n = 3$? Well, remember that n is the principal quantum number. We can begin by identifying how many subshells can exist with this n value. Within $n = 3$, there are three possible subshells: $l = 0$ (s), $l = 1$ (p), and $l = 2$ (d). The s subshell ($l = 0$) holds one orbital ($m_l = 0$), the p subshell ($l = 1$) holds three orbitals ($m_l = -1, 0$, and + 1), and the d subshell ($l = 2$) holds five orbitals (m_l = −2, −1, 0, +1, and + 2). Each orbital can hold two electrons (m_s = −½ or +½). Therefore, the maximum number of electrons at the third energy level is:

$$(1 + 3 + 5) \times 2 = 18 \text{ electrons}$$

We can also represent this with a branching diagram:

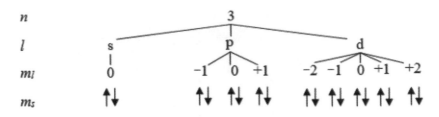

Figure 5. The maximum number of electrons possible with a principal quantum number of $n = 3$.

But how do we know which subshells or orbitals will contain electrons? That is to say, for a given atom, which subshells will become filled with electrons first? And how can we denote this in numbers or words? The answers to these questions can be found in a related topic: electron configuration. The electron configuration of an atom describes the arrangement of electrons in subshells around the atomic nucleus. The notation consists of a series of terms, each of which contains a number, a letter, and a superscript. For example, the lowest-energy subshell is 1s; if this subshell were filled with two electrons, its corresponding term in the electron configuration would be $1s^2$. A 3d subshell that contains eight electrons would be denoted as $3d^8$, and so on. According to the Aufbau principle, electrons fill lower-energy orbitals first to create the most stable electron configuration. Subshells usually, but not always, increase in energy by increasing the principal and azimuthal quantum numbers. Electrons fill orbitals in order of increasing energy level, as depicted in Figure 6.

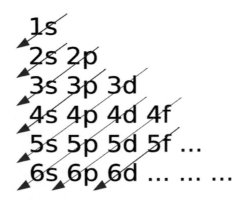

Figure 6. Order of orbital filling. Begin with 1s and follow each consecutive arrow from tail to tip (1s, then 2s, 2p, 3s, 3p, etc.).

Let's give it a try. What is the electron configuration of a neutral chlorine (Cl) atom? Begin by finding the total number of electrons. A neutral Cl atom has 17 protons, according to the periodic table, and thus must have 17 electrons to cancel out the positive charge. We know that each s subshell can hold 2 electrons, and each p subshell can hold 6 electrons. Electrons will fill orbitals from lower to higher energy levels, filling low-energy orbitals first. The first two electrons will fill the 1s subshell, the next two will fill the 2s subshell, and so forth, until all 17 electrons have found a place in an orbital. This gives us an electron configuration of $1s^2 2s^2 2p^6 3s^2 3p^5$, which is shown in Figure 7 with a common form of arrow notation.

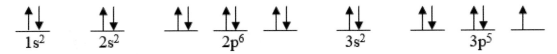

Figure 7. The electron configuration of a neutral chlorine atom.

Another important principle to remember when dealing with electron configuration is Hund's rule. Recall that each orbital can hold up to two paired electrons with opposite spin. If possible, however, one electron will "prefer" to exist in an orbital by itself, rather than be squeezed in with another electron. According to Hund's rule, then, one electron will fill each orbital of a given subshell until each is half-filled, and only then do they begin sharing orbitals, or pairing, with additional electrons.

MCAT STRATEGY > > >

Notice that the exponents on the full electron configuration must add up to equal the total number of electrons in the species. When presented with an electron configuration question, quickly eliminate any answer choices that do not do this!

We can easily illustrate Hund's rule with an example. A neutral nitrogen atom has seven electrons. The first four of these electrons fill the 1s and 2s orbitals. For the next three, note the diagram below; each exists in its own separate orbital, and all three have parallel spins. We should never see two paired electrons in the same orbital until all orbitals are half-filled.

Figure 8. The electron configuration of neutral nitrogen.

A shortcut for determining the electron configuration of an atom is to divide the periodic table into blocks by azimuthal momentum number (Figure 9). The s-block consists of the first two columns (or groups) on the left (along with helium), while the p-block includes the last six groups on the right. The d-block contains transition metals, and the f-block contains the lanthanide and actinide series, which are often shown at the bottom of a periodic table diagram.

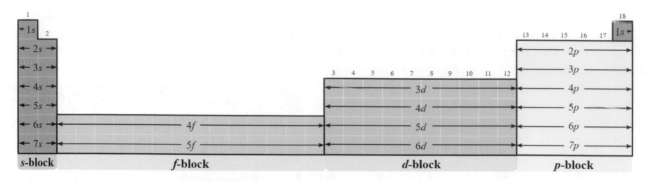

Figure 9. Element blocks of the periodic table.

For a given atom, the electron configuration can be abbreviated by placing the noble gas from the prior row in brackets to represent its electron configuration, then adding the configuration of the valence electrons from the periodic table. Valence electrons are the outermost electrons of an atom and exist in the highest energy levels. For elements in the s and p blocks, it is easy to determine which electrons are valence electrons. For s elements, only their s electrons with the highest principal quantum number are valence electrons. For example, potassium (located in the fourth period, or row, of the table in the s block) contains only a single valence electron, and it is found in the 4s subshell. The abbreviated electron configuration of potassium, then, is [Ar] $4s^1$. For p elements, their s and p electrons with the highest principal quantum number are valence electrons. Oxygen is found in the p-block of the second period of the periodic table, and its shortened electron configuration is [He] $2s^2 2p^4$.

For elements found in the d or f blocks, this gets slightly trickier. Let's consider the transition metal iron (Fe). In iron, the electrons with the highest principal quantum number are its two 4s electrons. However, it also has six 3d electrons, and these are valence electrons as well, even though their principal quantum number is lower. The periodic table makes remembering this easy; both the 4s and 3d segments of the table are found in the same period (row) as iron, so they should be included as valence electrons. Finally, for elements found in the f block, their valence electrons include the electrons in both the s and f blocks with the highest principal quantum numbers.

> ## MCAT STRATEGY > > >
>
> Valence electrons play a key role in chemical bonding. This will be discussed in much more depth in Chapter 2 of this book; for now, just know that they are particularly important.

What if we want to determine the electron configuration of an ion, or charged species? Remember, negative ions (anions) have an excess of electrons, while positive ions, or cations, are electron-deficient. Let's learn through example. Imagine that you are asked to determine the electron configuration of the Ca^{2+} ion. First, write out the configuration of neutral Ca: $1s^2 2s^2 2p^6 3s^2 3p^6 4s^2$. Now, since Ca^{2+} has a +2 charge, we must remove two electrons. We remove them from the highest-energy subshell, which is 4s, as it has the highest principal quantum number. This leaves us with $1s^2 2s^2 2p^6 3s^2 3p^6$, which, in shortened form, is simply [Ar].

This is fairly simple, but one point of confusion is worth noting. According to the Aufbau principle, the 4s subshell fills before the 3d subshell. We previously said that lower-energy orbitals fill first; thus, we would think that 4s is lower-energy than 3d, or conversely, that 3d is higher-energy than 4s. We also just learned that, when forming cations, we should remove electrons from the highest-energy subshells first. Wouldn't we then think that we should remove from 3d before 4s? The answer to this question is no, although the scientific explanation is not necessary to understand for the MCAT. Simply remember that electrons must always be removed from the subshell with the highest principal quantum number first, and thus, we must remove from 4s before starting to remove from 3d.

Finally, it can be very helpful to ask yourself one question whenever you learn a new chemistry concept: *do any exceptions exist?* Unfortunately, the answer is often "yes," and electron configuration is no different. The notable exceptions to the classic rules of electron configuration stem from the idea that half-filled and fully-filled subshells are more stable than subshells filled with some other number of electrons. For a p subshell, then, it is energetically favorable to contain either three or six electrons; similarly, a d subshell will be especially stable if it contains either five or ten electrons.

The exceptions to understand for the MCAT are the transition metals in the same groups, or columns, as chromium (Cr) and copper (Cu). Specifically, these constitute exceptions to the Aufbau principle. We would expect the shortened configuration of chromium to be $[Ar] 4s^23d^4$. However, if the 3d orbital "steals" one electron from the 4s orbital, it will achieve that coveted half-filled state, with five total 3d electrons. The electron configuration of chromium is thus $[Ar] 4s^13d^5$. Similarly, we might use the Aufbau principle to predict the electron configuration of copper as $[Ar] 4s^23d^9$. In reality, however, it is $[Ar] 4s^13d^{10}$. Remember these exceptions on Test Day!

> **MCAT STRATEGY >>>**
>
> Just as it is helpful to remember exceptions to the rules of chemistry, it can also be productive to make note of concepts that have no exceptions—in other words, for the sake of the MCAT, they always follow the same rule. Throughout this book, we will try to point out cases like this whenever they are relevant.

4. Structure of the Periodic Table

The periodic table, the initial version of which was proposed by Dmitri Mendeleev in 1869, is an elegant system for organizing an enormous amount of information. The modern periodic table arranges the known chemical elements by atomic number, although Mendeleev sorted his table according to atomic weight. Mendeleev's table positioned elements with similar properties in the same column, leaving some gaps where no known elements yet existed. Interestingly, Mendeleev was able to use his table to predict information about these then-unknown elements, and when they were subsequently discovered, his predictions largely held true. This is but one example of the tremendous utility of the periodic table.

The rows of the periodic table are called periods, while the columns are called groups or families. Across a period, the number of valence electrons increases until the valence shell is full. For example, in the second period, lithium has one valence electron, beryllium has two, boron has three, carbon has four, and so on. Since elements belonging to the same group (or column) have the same number of valence electrons, they tend to share physical and chemical properties. Atoms may donate or gain electrons to obtain a full 8-electron valence shell, which confers stability.

> **MCAT STRATEGY >>>**
>
> You will be able to click to access a periodic table on the MCAT, so there is no need to memorize the place of every element. However, we recommend regular chemistry practice until the location of certain common elements becomes second nature.

Groups have been named according to several different conventions throughout history. In the old IUPAC naming system, groups were designated by Roman numerals and the letter A or B. The group number corresponded to the number of valence electrons possessed by a neutral atom within that group, with the exception of Groups IB-VIIIB (the transition metals). In contrast, the current IUPAC system numbers the groups from 1 to 18, without distinguishing the transition metals separately. Note that the lanthanide and actinide series (the *f*-block elements) are not given group numbers.

Group 1 (previously IA) elements are commonly referred to as alkali metals, which include lithium (Li), sodium (Na), potassium (K), and others. A natural follow-up question might be, "What's a metal?" Metals are good electrical conductors and are typically solid under standard conditions, although exceptions such as mercury exist. They are shiny, or lustrous, and they exhibit ductility, or the property of being easily stretched into wires. They are opaque, rather than transparent, and they can be made to form other shapes or sheets, a property termed malleability. Some—but not all—metals have multiple oxidation states, which will be discussed further in Chapter 8 of this book. To return to alkali metals, all share these metallic properties, with the exception of hydrogen (H). The lone valence electron (ns^1) makes alkali metals highly reactive, as they will readily donate their valence electron to other atoms and form cations with a + 1 charge or oxidation number. In fact, some alkali metals, in particular sodium and potassium, are so reactive that they explode in water if exposed to it in their solid metal forms.

Group 2 (previously IIA) elements, or alkaline earth metals, have a metallic character and include magnesium (Mg), calcium (Ca), and more. Alkaline earth metals have two valence electrons (ns^2), which they will donate to form +2 cations. In their solid states, they are reactive, a property they share with alkali metals.

The elements in groups 3-12 are the transition metals. Transition metals include some of our most prized elements, such as gold (Au) and platinum (Pt), which are valued for their luster and other unique properties. Transition elements are hard, durable metals that readily conduct electricity, and they often take on vivid colors due to electronic transitions between d orbitals. The number of electrons a transition metal can lose varies, so most have multiple oxidation states. For example, iron (Fe) is most commonly found with oxidation numbers of +2 or +3, although states from −2 to +6 are possible.

MCAT STRATEGY > > >

The individual characteristics of each element can get overwhelming, so note that you do *not* need to memorize most of them. Instead, pay special attention to those elements that play a biologically relevant role.

Now that we have discussed the alkali metals, alkaline earth metals, and transition metals, we will begin to describe elements that are *not* metallic in nature. In particular, the nonmetals (found at the far right of the periodic table) have many traits that are opposite of those of metals. Nonmetals are not lustrous (shiny); as examples, consider oxygen gas or solid carbon. Nonmetals are also poor electrical conductors. Some elements share some traits of both metals and nonmetals; these are the semimetals, or metalloids. The metalloids you are most likely to see on the MCAT are boron and silicon, a major component of Earth's crust. Metalloids vary in their characteristics, but in general, they are brittle, are poor to decent electrical conductors, and tend to act like nonmetals in chemical reactions, although even this can vary.

Group 13 (formerly IIIA) elements include boron (B), aluminum (Al), and others. Boron is a semimetal, while the rest of the elements in this group are categorized as metals. Some form + 3 cations, as they have three valence electrons.

> > CONNECTIONS < <

Chapter 7 of Chemistry

Group 14 (formerly IVA) elements belong to the carbon family. These elements also have properties of both metals and nonmetals and are capable of forming oxides (CO_2, SiO_2, etc.). The study of organic chemistry can be thought of as the study of carbon-containing compounds, so pay close attention whenever you see carbon in your MCAT prep! Group 14 elements have four valence electrons, which explains quite a bit about organic chemistry, most notably the principle that carbon overwhelmingly prefers to form four bonds. As a final note regarding carbon, you should know that this element can take many forms, including that of diamond (a very hard solid), although carbon in its standard state exists as a gray mineral termed graphite. Next, Group 15 (previously known as Group VA) elements belong to the nitrogen family. These elements have five valence electrons and display properties of both metals and nonmetals.

Group 16 (VIA) elements are the chalcogens, which include oxygen (O) and sulfur (S). Chalcogens have mostly non-metallic characteristics. Their nearly filled valence shell (ns^2np^4) causes them to react with other atoms to gain two electrons, forming -2 anions. These elements, especially oxygen, are enormously important components of organic molecules, so you will encounter them regularly in biochemistry, biology, and of course chemistry.

Group 17 (formerly VIIA) elements are called halogens, which are reactive species with a nearly-filled valence shell (ns^2np^5). In other words, an uncharged halogen atom contains seven valence electrons, so it will readily accept one electron from an alkali metal or other species to form an anion with a -1 charge. The halogens include fluorine (F) and chlorine (Cl), which exist as diatomic gases (F_2, and Cl_2), bromine (Br), which exists as a diatomic liquid (Br_2), and iodine (I), which exists as a diatomic solid (I_2), at room temperature. Note that the halogens are nonmetals.

> **MCAT STRATEGY > > >**
>
> You will see halogens regularly throughout this book, whether as components of several strong acids (HCl, etc.) or as participants in common organic chemistry reactions. When you encounter them, think about how their position within the periodic table relates to their chemical properties.

Finally, Group 18 (or VIIIA) elements are the inert or noble gases, including helium (He), neon (Ne), argon (Ar), krypton (Kr), and more. Noble gases have a non-metallic character and are very unreactive due to their filled valence shell (ns^2np^6). The exception is helium, whose electron configuration is ns^2. As you may have guessed from the term "gas," these elements have low boiling points, causing them to exist in the gaseous state under standard conditions. (Contrast this with most metals and even nonmetals, such as carbon, which exist in the solid form at room temperature.)

5. Periodic Trends

We've now discussed the organization of the periodic table by group (or column) and by larger region (metals, nonmetals, etc.). However, this is only a small amount of the information the table gives us. Let's say we want to compare an alkali metal (located on the far left of the table) with a chalcogen (found in the same group as oxygen). Can we predict at least some relationships between the two, even without having memorized the specific parameters of these groups? Of course we can! This is where periodic trends come into play.

The periodic trends you should be familiar with for the MCAT are atomic/ionic radius, electronegativity, electron affinity, and ionization energy. Luckily, these four trends follow an overarching pattern. Ask yourself this: why do chemists spend so much time talking about the positioning of electrons? Well, these electrons, and more specifically the attractive force of the nucleus on the electrons, determine the nature of the atom's behavior. The attractive force of the positively-charged nucleus on the atom's valence electrons is termed the effective nuclear charge (Z_{eff}). As the number of protons in the nucleus increases from left to right across a period, Z_{eff} also increases, since each additional proton adds positive charge to the nucleus. However, Z_{eff} is not synonymous with the number of protons held by an atom. Moving down a group, the principal quantum number of the outermost energy level increases, which effectively means that more shells of electrons are added between the nucleus and the outermost, or valence, electrons. These layers of core electrons partially shield the valence electrons from the effects of the positive charge in the nucleus. Thus, Z_{eff} decreases as one moves down a group.

Periodic trends in Z_{eff} help explain other trends on the periodic table. Atomic size, or radius, is inversely related to Z_{eff}. Atomic radius decreases from left to right across a period as Z_{eff} increases and the addition of protons pulls the valence electrons closer to the nucleus. In contrast, atomic radius increases down a column as more electron shells are added and electron shielding decreases the attractive force of the nucleus on valence electrons. To summarize this trend, the atoms with the largest radii are found nearest the bottom left of the periodic table.

A concept that relates closely to atomic radius is *ionic* radius, or the radius of a charged species (for example, F⁻). The exact details of ionic radius fall beyond the scope of the MCAT, especially since this characteristic can vary based on the ion's surroundings. However, it is important to understand that *cations* (positive ions) tend to have smaller ionic radii than the atomic radii of their corresponding uncharged elements. Consider Na^+, which has an electron configuration of $1s^22s^22p^6$. In contrast, the electron configuration of uncharged Na (s) has a configuration of $1s^22s^22p^63s^1$—giving the uncharged atom an extra electron shell. As a result, we can say that the atomic radius is larger, or conversely that the ionic radius is smaller. On the other hand, for *anions* (negative ions), the ionic radius is typically larger than the corresponding atomic radius, since these species must gain electrons, and thus become slightly larger, to take on their negative forms.

MCAT STRATEGY >>>

It can be easier to retain information about chemistry concepts if you pair each concept with an example. Here, we could say that Mg^{2+} has a smaller radius than Mg (s), while Cl^- has a larger radius than uncharged Cl.

Moving on, ionization energy is the energy required to remove one valence electron from a neutral atom in the gaseous state. Ionization energy (IE) is positive, since it requires a positive amount of energy input to pull an electron away from the nucleus. As you might imagine, the first ionization energy (the energy required to remove one electron from a neutral species) is always smaller than the second ionization energy (the energy required to remove a second electron), and so on, as the atom becomes more resistant to giving up its electrons. Ionization energy is directly related to Z_{eff}, as atoms with a greater Z_{eff} hold their electrons tightly and are more reluctant to donate them. Thus, in general, IE increases as one moves up and to the right along the periodic table. One important point, however, is that this trend does not hold true perfectly. For example, one might assume that oxygen would have a higher first IE than nitrogen, as oxygen is found to the right of nitrogen in the second period. In reality, nitrogen has the higher first IE of the two. Remember what you have learned about electron configuration; nitrogen has a half-filled 2p subshell, which is particularly stable. It is thus more difficult to remove a valence electron from nitrogen than from oxygen, which has an additional 2p electron. Thinking about relationships between seemingly-distinct general chemistry concepts will be immensely helpful on the MCAT!

Our next periodic trend is electron affinity. This quantity denotes the amount of energy released when an electron is *added* to an atom. Atoms that can more readily accept an electron, such as halogens, have higher electron affinities. Note that the sign convention for electron affinity can be confusing, so let's clear it up now. For most species, the addition of an electron is an exothermic process, meaning that energy is lost or released. However, since electron affinity by convention refers to the quantity of energy released, electron affinity is generally positive. (In some rare cases, where the addition of an electron actually requires energy input, electron affinity will be negative.) Like ionization energy, electron affinity is directly related to Z_{eff}, because atoms with a more positive nuclear charge have a greater affinity for electrons. This causes atoms closer to the top right of the periodic table to have higher electron affinity values. A key exception to this trend is the noble gases, which, in spite of their position on the far right of the table, have near-zero electron affinities as they already possess a stable octet.

>> CONNECTIONS <<

Chapter 4 of Chemistry

Finally, electronegativity refers the tendency of an atom to attract electrons that are shared in a chemical bond between two atoms. Since atoms with high electron affinities will naturally attract electrons more strongly, electronegativity is also directly related to Z_{eff}. (In fact, students often confuse electronegativity with electron affinity, but the only difference to know for the MCAT is that electronegativity directly relates to behavior *within a chemical bond*.) Electronegativity increases from left to right along a period and decreases as one moves down a group; an easy way to remember this trend is to commit to memory that fluorine, near the top right of the table, is the most electronegative element. Figure 10 summarizes these trends; be sure to understand them as well as memorize them if you want to ensure that your chemistry foundation is strong for the coming chapters!

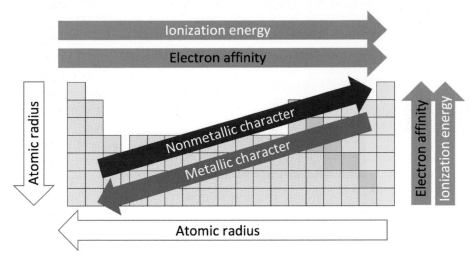

Figure 10. Periodic trends.

6. Must-Knows

> All matter is composed of atoms, which in turn are composed of subatomic particles.
  – Protons have a charge of $+1e$ and a mass of 1 amu.
  – Neutrons are uncharged and have a mass of approximately 1 amu. Both protons and neutrons are found in the nucleus.
  – Electrons are nearly massless and have a charge of $-1e$.
> Atomic number (Z): number of protons in an atom, which determines chemical identity.
> Mass number (A): total number of protons and neutrons in the nucleus.
> Isotope: same number of protons, different number of neutrons (different mass number).
> Cations = positively-charged ions, while anions = negatively-charged ions.
> Bohr model of the hydrogen atom: electrons orbit the nucleus in spherical shells.
  – When energy is absorbed: electrons can "jump" to higher-energy levels, farther from the nucleus.
  – When energy is released/emitted: electrons fall from higher- to lower-energy levels, closer to the nucleus.
> 4 quantum numbers describe each electron in an atom: n, l, m_l, and m_s.
  – n = principal quantum number; denotes size of electron shell.
  – l = azimuthal quantum number; denotes shape and subshell identity (s, p, d, or f)
  – m_l = magnetic quantum number; denotes orbital within subshell (orientation)
  – m_s = describes angular momentum/spin ($+\frac{1}{2}$ or $-\frac{1}{2}$)
> Pauli exclusion principle: no two electrons in the same atom can have the same set of four quantum numbers.
> Aufbau principle: lower-energy orbitals fill first.
  – Watch out for exceptions: Cr, Cu, and other elements in their groups.
> Hund's rule: within a subshell, each orbital will fill with one electron before any fill with a second.
> Periodic table: periods = rows, groups = columns (elements in same group often share properties)
> Periodic trends:
  – Atomic radius increases moving down and to the left along the table.
  – Ionization energy, electron affinity, and electronegativity increase moving up and to the right.

Practice Passage

There are two types of covalent bonds found in biologically important molecules, nonpolar and polar covalent bonds. The distinction between these bond types is based on differences in electronegativity between the nonmetal atoms involved in sharing pairs of electrons. Differences less than 0.5 result in nonpolar bonds while differences greater than 0.5 and less than 2.0 result in polar bonds. If the difference in electronegativity is greater than 2.0, the bond is no longer considered covalent. Of particular interest to biochemists are the properties of elements found in period two of the periodic table.

Table 1. Electronegativity of Select Period Two Elements

ATOMIC SYMBOL	ELECTRONEGATIVITY (PAULING SCALE)
H	2.2
C	2.6
N	3.0
O	3.4
F	4.0

Unequal sharing of electrons in a covalent bond, due to differences in electronegativity, imparts a degree of ionic character to the bond. Specifically, the more electronegative atom will gain a partial negative charge ($-\delta$) and the atom that is less able to attract the shared electrons will gain an equal amount of partial positive charge ($+\delta$). Electronegativity differences greater than 2.0 are generally classified as ionic. Having polar covalent bonds is a necessary requirement, but not sufficient, for a molecule to have a molecular dipole moment. Table 2 lists the experimentally determined molecular dipole moments for select compounds.

Table 2. Molecular Dipole Moments

MOLECULAR FORMULA	MOLECULAR NAME	MOLECULAR DIPOLE (D)
CH_4	Methane	0.00
NH_3	Ammonia	1.47
H_2O	Water	1.85
H_2CO	Methanal	2.33
CO_2	Carbon dioxide	0.00
CH_3COH	Ethanal	2.72
$(CH_3)_2CO$	Propanone	2.91
C_2H_6	Ethane	0.00
N_2H_4	Hydrazine	1.85
H_2O_2	Hydrogen peroxide	2.26
CH_3NH_2	Methyl amine	1.31
CH_3OH	Methanol	1.69
$(CH_3)_2O$	Dimethyl ether	1.30

1. Of the elements listed in Table 1, which has the highest electron affinity?
   A. Carbon
   B. Nitrogen
   C. Oxygen
   D. Fluorine

2. Which of the following electron configurations represents an element that would be likely to form an ionic bond?
   A. $1s^2 2s^2 2p^6 3s^1$
   B. $1s^2 2s^2 2p^2$
   C. $1s^2 2s^2 2p^6 4s^2 4p^6$
   D. $1s^2 2s^2 2p^6$

3. An element is discovered with the following properties: unfilled *d*-orbitals, high thermal conductivity, and high malleability. Where on the periodic would this most likely be found?
   A. Alkali metals
   B. Alkaline earth metals
   C. Transition metals
   D. Noble gases

4. Which of the following elements from Table 1 has the lowest first ionization energy?
   A. Carbon
   B. Nitrogen
   C. Oxygen
   D. Fluorine

5. Which of the following is the best estimate of an O-H bond dipole moment in water? Note that sin 109° = 0.95; sin 55° = 0.82; cos 109° = -0.33; and cos 55° = 0.57.
   A. 0.97 D
   B. 1.13 D
   C. 1.50 D
   D. 3.24 D

6. According to the passage, which bond will be characterized as nonpolar?
   A. C-F
   B. C-N
   C. C-O
   D. O-F

7. Students performed an experiment to measure ionization energies of an unknown element.

IONIZATION NUMBER	ENTHALPY (KJ/MOL)
1st	652
2nd	1,380
3rd	2,416
4th	3,300

Which element have the students identified?

A. Cs
B. Ra
C. Nb
D. Y

This page left intentionally blank.

19

Practice Passage Explanations

There are two types of covalent bonds found in biologically important molecules, non-polar and polar covalent bonds. The distinction between these bond types is based on differences in electronegativity between the nonmetal atoms involved in sharing pairs of electrons. Differences less than 0.5 result in nonpolar bonds while differences greater than 0.5 and less than 2.0 result in polar bonds. If the difference in electronegativity is greater than 2.0, the bond is no longer considered covalent. Of particular interest to biochemists are the properties of elements found in period two of the periodic table.

Key terms: 2 types of covalent bonds, electronegativity, period 2

Cause and effect: ΔEN < 0.5 → nonpolar; 0.5 < ΔEN < 2.0 → polar

Table 1. Electronegativity of Select Period Two Elements

ATOMIC SYMBOL	ELECTRONEGATIVITY (PAULING SCALE)
H	2.2
C	2.6
N	3.0
O	3.4
F	4.0

Table 1 shows the trend of increasing EN across the period; higher EN indicates the atom will draw electrons more strongly

Unequal sharing of electrons in a covalent bond, due to differences in electronegativity, imparts a degree of ionic character to the bond. Specifically, the more electronegative atom will gain a partial negative charge (-δ) and the atom that is less able to attract the shared electrons will gain an equal amount of partial positive charge (+δ). Electronegativity differences greater than 2.0 are generally classified as ionic. Having polar covalent bonds is a necessary requirement, but not sufficient, for a molecule to have a molecular dipole moment. Table 2 lists the experimentally determined molecular dipole moments for select compounds.

Key terms: ionic character, bond dipole, molecular dipole

Cause and effect: unequal e⁻ sharing / ΔEN > 2 → ionic bonding; bond dipoles required but not sufficient to cause molecular dipoles

Table 2. Molecular Dipole Moments

MOLECULAR FORMULA	MOLECULAR NAME	MOLECULAR DIPOLE (D)
CH_4	Methane	0.00
NH_3	Ammonia	1.47
H_2O	Water	1.85
H_2CO	Methanal	2.33
CO_2	Carbon dioxide	0.00
CH_3COH	Ethanal	2.72
$(CH_3)_2CO$	Propanone	2.91
C_2H_6	Ethane	0.00
N_2H_4	Hydrazine	1.85
H_2O_2	Hydrogen peroxide	2.26
CH_3NH_2	Methyl amine	1.31
CH_3OH	Methanol	1.69
$(CH_3)_2O$	Dimethyl ether	1.3

Table 2 shows the relationship between ΔEN and molecular dipole; note that molecular shape will also influence overall molecular dipole

1. D is correct. Remember that electron affinity increases as one moves towards the upper-right corner of the periodic table. Fluorine is the element with the highest electronegativity, ionization energy, and electron affinity of the elements listed.

2. A is correct. This is the electron configuration for Na, which is very likely to form an ionic bond by giving up its single outer valence electron to become Na^+.

   B: This is the electron configuration for carbon. As a nonmetal, carbon tends to form covalent bonds.
   C: This is not a valid electron configuration as it skips past the n = 3 level.
   D: This is the electron configuration for neon. As a noble gas, it tends not to form bonds.

3. C is correct. The giveaway here is the unfilled *d*-orbitals. This is a characteristic trait of transition metals.

   A, B: The alkali metals and alkaline earth metals have filled *d*-orbitals and outer valence electrons in *s*-orbitals.
   D: Noble gases have all of their orbitals filled.

4. A is correct. Remember that ionization energy increases as you move from left to right across the periodic table. Thus, carbon, the element to the left of the other answer choices on the periodic table, would have the lowest ionization energy of the elements listed.

5. C is correct. From Table 2, the molecular dipole of water is 1.85 D. To calculate the dipole moment of a single O-H bond, you must recognize that the direction of the molecular dipole in water bisects the H-O-H angle, which is approximately 109°. The O-H bond represents the hypotenuse of a right triangle where the side adjacent to the 55° angle is 1.85/2 = 0.925 D. Therefore:

$$\cos 55° = 0.925/H$$
$$H = 0.925/\cos 55°$$
$$H = 0.925/0.57$$
$$H \approx 1.66 \text{ D}$$

This actual bond dipole moment of O-H is slightly less than the value calculated above because the actual H-O-H angle in water is 104.5°, not an idealized tetrahedral angle of 109°, because the lone pairs of electrons on the oxygen actually occupy more space around the oxygen atom than the O-H bonding pairs of electrons.

6. B is correct. According to paragraph 1, electronegativity differences less than 0.5 are nonpolar. According to Table 1, the electronegativity difference between C and N is 3 – 2.6 = 0.4.

    A, C, D: The respective electronegativity differences for these choices are 1.4, 0.8, and 0.6, respectively.

7. C is correct. Examining the table, we can see that the atom loses all 4 electrons with equal requirements of energy. Thus, we would expect that each loss of the 4 electrons impacts the overall stability of the valence shell equally. Only Niobium, element 41, found in Group 5 of Period 5 would explain this since each loss of an electron brings the valence shell closer to an empty of half-filled subshell.

    A: Being in Group 1, we would expect cesium to have a much larger 2nd IE compared to its 1st IE, since losing the 1st electron gives it a full octet.
    B: Being in Group 2, we would expect radium to have a much larger 3rd IE compared to its 2nd IE, since losing the 2nd electron gives it a full octet.
    D: Being in Group 3, we would expect yttrium to have a much larger 4th IE compared to its 3rd IE, since losing the 3rd electron gives it a full octet.

Independent Questions

1. Which quantum number describes the spatial orientation of a specific orbital within a given electronic subshell?
   A. Principal quantum number
   B. Spin quantum number
   C. Magnetic quantum number
   D. Angular momentum quantum number

2. Which of the following, together with a neutral carbon atom, would comprise an isoelectronic pair?
   A. O^{2-}
   B. C^+
   C. B^-
   D. N^-

3. Consider two atoms in the gas phase. Compared to Ne, one would expect O^{2-} to have:
   A. a larger radius.
   B. a greater atomic mass.
   C. a different electron configuration.
   D. the same nuclear charge.

4. Which of the following pure substances is a poor conductor of electricity?
   A. Mercury
   B. Lead
   C. Aluminum
   D. Iodine

5. The unusually low melting point of mercury is partially due to the relatively minimal extent to which its valence electrons participate in metallic bonding. Which of the following, if true, would best explain this unique characteristic?
   A. Mercury's 4f electrons are relatively ineffective at nuclear shielding.
   B. Mercury has a high ratio of neutrons to protons in its nucleus.
   C. Like cadmium and zinc, mercury has a full d subshell.
   D. In solution, mercury tends to exist as the cation Hg_2^{2+}.

6. The Bohr model's insistence on well-defined orbits and predictable positions in space for electrons is most *incompatible* with:
   A. the Aufbau principle.
   B. the quantized nature of electronic transitions.
   C. the concept of effective nuclear charge.
   D. the Heisenberg uncertainty principle.

7. Within a hemoglobin subunit, diatomic oxygen binds a coordinated Fe^{2+} ion, temporarily oxidizing it to Fe^{3+}. In this case, oxygen acts as:
   A. an electron acceptor, because it is more electronegative than Fe^{2+}.
   B. an electron acceptor, because it is less electronegative than Fe^{2+}.
   C. an electron donor, because it is more electronegative than Fe^{2+}.
   D. an electron donor, because it is less electronegative than Fe^{2+}.

8. Which of the following atoms is expected to have the greatest first ionization energy?
   A. Calcium
   B. Bromine
   C. Sodium
   D. Copper

Independent Question Explanations

1. C is correct. However, subshells may contain more than one orbital with the same angular momentum quantum number. The magnetic quantum number distinguishes between different orbitals in a given subshell and describes their orientation in space. Since this question mentions the orientation of an orbital within a subshell, the best answer here is choice C.

   A: The principal quantum number denotes the energy of an electron by assigning it to a certain shell.
   B: The spin quantum number describes the momentum or direction of electron spin in the shell, either plus or minus one half.
   D: The angular momentum (or azimuthal) quantum number then specifies the electronic subshells (s, p, d, f) that exist within a given shell.

2. C is correct. An uncharged carbon atom has six electrons in the configuration $1s^2 2s^2 2p^2$. Neutral boron has the configuration $1s^2 2s^2 2p^1$. The addition of one electron to a neutral boron atom will confer upon it the same electronic configuration as neutral carbon, making the pair isoelectronic. This is not true of any of the other options.

3. A is correct. Although they have the same number of electrons in the same configuration, O^{2-} has a smaller nuclear charge (number of protons) than Ne. This causes its electrons to be more loosely attracted to the nucleus, which gives it a larger atomic radius than Ne. Choice B is incorrect because O^{2-} has a smaller atomic mass than Ne.

4. D is correct. Metals are good conductors of electricity because their outer electrons can freely move between atoms. This movement of electrons is referred to as electrical current. Lead, mercury, and aluminum are all metals, while iodine is a nonmetal.

5. A is correct. The state of ionic mercury in solution is not relevant to the melting point of the pure metal (eliminate choice D). Electrons, not protons or neutrons, determine bonding behavior (eliminate choice B). Mercury, like cadmium and zinc, does have a full d subshell; however, those two other metals are not known for their low melting points, and they do have valence electrons which participate in metallic bonding, so choice C does not explain the given statement. Unlike cadmium and zinc, however, mercury has a full 4f subshell. If the 4f electrons were ineffective at shielding the valence electrons from the nuclear charge, the valence electrons would be held more tightly by the nucleus and less able to participate in metallic bonding.

6. D is correct. The Bohr model depicts electrons orbiting the nucleus in discrete energy levels. Electrons preferentially fill less energetic shells first (according to the Aufbau principle), and the release or absorption of quantized amounts of energy is required to transition between these levels. The Bohr model also explains effective nuclear charge, since electrons farther away from the nucleus are shielded from the nuclear charge by the more interior electrons. However, the Bohr model suggests that electrons have well-defined, predictable orbits and positions, which is inconsistent with the Heisenberg uncertainty principle.

7. A is correct. The increased oxidation state of the iron ion reflects a loss of electron density, which must have been accepted by the oxygen molecule. The tendency of an atom to attract electron density towards itself is associated with electronegativity.

8. B is correct. Ionization energy refers to the energy that must be expended to completely remove an electron from an atom. In general, ionization energy increases from left to right along the periodic table. Bromine is a halogen and belongs to Group 17 in the periodic table, while calcium, sodium, and copper are metals; thus, bromine is the farthest to the right and is expected to have the highest first ionization energy. Alternatively, one might consider that bromine could achieve a full octet configuration if it were to gain just one electron. Therefore, the *loss* of an electron would be unfavorable.

Bonding, Molecules, and Intermolecular Forces

CHAPTER 2

0. Introduction

If atoms are the building blocks of molecules, chemical bonds are the glue that holds these molecules together. The components of your own body contain countless such bonds, which are broken and re-formed in very specific ways to keep your physiological functions intact. And many more interactions take place outside of chemical bonds, such as the interactions between distinct molecules in close physical proximity. In this chapter, we will discuss molecules in general, then cover intra- and intermolecular attractions. This portion of the book also includes some classic topics that you may remember from your early undergraduate years, such as formal charge and VSEPR theory.

1. Molecules

As mentioned in Chapter 1, a molecule consists of multiple atoms—either like or unlike—bonded together. When atoms combine to form a molecule, the masses of the individual atoms combine to form the molecular weight of the overall species. For example, the molecular weight of water (H_2O) is the sum of the masses of two hydrogen atoms and one oxygen atom: $1 + 1 + 16 = 18$ amu.

> **MCAT STRATEGY > > >**
>
> You may see periodic tables give more numerically exact values for atomic weight, such as 15.999 amu for oxygen. On the MCAT, it is virtually always acceptable to round values to make math faster and easier. Of course, be sure to check to ensure that the available answer choices are sufficiently far apart before rounding.

You probably have seen the term "moles" in reference to the amount of a substance present. Chemists define one mole as the number of molecules contained in 12 grams of carbon-12, but it easier to consider a mole as a unit of measurement used to communicate about a large number of items (atoms, molecules, electrons, etc.). A mole contains a number of items equal to Avogadro's number, which is approximately 6.022×10^{23}. A mole of elephants is thus equal to 6.022×10^{23} elephants, and a mole of glucose molecules is equal to 6.022×10^{23} glucose molecules. The mass of one mole of a substance is its molar mass. Calculations associated with these values will be discussed in much more depth in Chapter 3; for now, knowledge of the general concepts is sufficient.

Again, molecules are held together by chemical bonds. But what, exactly, *is* a bond? Before we can answer this question, we must outline some fundamental concepts that were alluded to in Chapter 1. First, the electrons in an element's outermost shell are termed valence electrons, and it is these electrons that are involved in the formation of chemical bonds. (Inner layers of electrons are called core electrons, and these play no direct role in bonding.) Atoms tend to follow a principle known as the octet rule, which posits that each atom will act in such a way as to obtain eight electrons in its valence shell—a highly stable state. Each lone pair of electrons surrounding an atom counts as two electrons, and each single bond participated in also counts as two electrons. (Double bonds count as four, while triple bonds count as six.)

As an example, consider the diatomic oxygen (O_2) molecule below. On its own, an oxygen atom possesses six valence electrons. However, if it forms a chemical bond as pictured here, each oxygen atom will have four electrons from its lone pairs and four from the double bond, for a total of eight. As such, the formation of O_2 is favorable, as it leads to a state of stability. In fact, bond formation is generally exothermic, or energy-releasing, for this very reason.

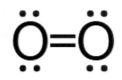

Figure 1. A molecule of O_2, in which both oxygen atoms possess a full octet.

Like most concepts in chemistry, however, the octet rule is not without exceptions. For an obvious example, consider hydrogen (H). One neutral hydrogen atom contains only one electron, meaning that a molecule of H_2 will contain a total of only two. In fact, two valence electrons is the *maximum* number that a hydrogen atom will have, and as such, an H atom will be stable with a single bond and no lone pairs. This ability to exist in a stable bonded state with fewer than eight valence electrons is termed an incomplete octet. Other atoms that form incomplete octets are helium (which has a maximum of two valence electrons), lithium (also a max of 2), beryllium (max of 4), and boron (max of 6).

MCAT STRATEGY > > >

The incomplete octet of a central boron atom allows this atom to act as an electron acceptor, or Lewis acid. Lewis acids will be discussed in more detail in Chapter 7.

What about the opposite scenario—*more than eight* valence electrons? This, too, is possible. For example, consider the compound phosphorus pentafluoride (PF_5). Each fluorine atom is attached to the central phosphorus atom by a single bond. Since each single bond constitutes two electrons, this central P atom has a total of $2 \times 5 = 10$ valence electrons. This ability to hold excess valence electrons in a bonded state is termed an expanded octet. Phosphorus is not the only atom that can accomplish this; in fact, atoms in the third period ($n = 3$) and below tend to form expanded octets readily.

A final case in which atoms can violate the octet rule is in the case of odd-electron molecules. As a classic example, nitric oxide (NO) possesses five valence electrons from nitrogen and six from oxygen. With a total of eleven valence electrons, a distribution of eight around each component atom is impossible.

2. Bond Types

Now that we have a solid understanding of what bonds are and why they form, we can move on to the types of chemical bonds you are nearly certain to see on the MCAT. The two main forms of *intra*molecular bonds—that is to say, bonds that hold a single molecule together—are ionic bonds and covalent bonds. (You may have heard of other types of "bonds," such as hydrogen bonds. These will be covered when we discuss *inter*molecular attractions later in this chapter.)

Ionic bonds are strong chemical bonds that hold together ions, or specifically that attract species that tend to become positively charged (cations) to those that tend to become negatively-charged (anions). In an ionic bond, electrons are completely transferred from the cation to the anion, leaving the cation positively charged and the anion negatively charged. Ionic bonds occur when the two species involved have a large difference in electronegativity such that one will readily accept electrons from the other. Electronegativity is most commonly measured using the Pauling scale, which assigns fluorine (the most electronegative element, as you learned in Chapter 1)

> **MCAT STRATEGY > > >**
>
> A similar situation exists for free radicals, reactive compounds that contain one unpaired electron. As with all MCAT content, we want to stop and think: what does this mean? How is a single unpaired electron different from a lone pair? And would a radical be considered electron-rich or electron-deficient? (It's electron-deficient. You will learn more about electron-rich and -deficient compounds in organic chemistry.)

an electronegativity value of 4.0. In contrast, the alkali metals on the other side of the periodic table have Pauling electronegativity values close to 1.0. An oft-cited rule is that ionic bonds only form when the difference between the Pauling electronegativities of the two species is 1.7 or greater. However, you are not given an electronegativity table for the MCAT, and it is not worthwhile to attempt to memorize these values for the entire range of chemical elements. Instead, use the rule of thumb that metals (especially alkali and alkaline earth metals) tend to form ionic bonds with nonmetals (especially halogens). For example, table salt used to season food is made of sodium chloride (NaCl), which is an ionic salt formed by Na^+ cations and Cl^- anions. Ionic compounds tend to take on a highly-ordered crystal lattice structure and have high melting points due to strong electrostatic forces. When an ionic compound dissociates in aqueous solution, the resulting solution tends to conduct electricity, which explains why such ionic compounds are often termed "electrolytes."

In contrast to ionic bonding, covalent bonding involves the sharing of an electron pair between two atoms. The electrons within a covalent bond are attracted to the positive nuclei of both atoms. Compared to ionic compounds, the electronegativity difference between covalently bonded atoms is small, such that the bond strengths and melting and boiling points of covalent compounds are lower than those of ionic compounds. Since the two atoms taking part in a covalent bond both "want" to share electrons, they do not form ions. (Remember, ions result from the complete donation or acceptance of electrons by an atom.)

> **MCAT STRATEGY > > >**
>
> You'd be surprised at just how many MCAT concepts revolve around the simple idea of "opposite charges attract." It is generally beneficial to keep this principle in mind when studying topics from ionic bonding to polar protic solvents to protein folding.

Covalent bonds exist on a spectrum according to the electronegativity difference between the two bonded atoms. Nonpolar covalent bonds form between atoms that have very similar or identical electronegativity values, such that the electrons are shared equally. For example, the two chlorine atoms in a molecule of Cl_2 obviously have equal electronegativity values, so the Cl_2 bond is nonpolar covalent. In contrast, atoms with a moderate electronegativity difference—greater than nonpolar covalent but less than ionic—form polar covalent bonds. The more electronegative atom will attract the shared electrons more strongly, gaining a partial negative charge ($\delta-$), while the less electronegative atom will gain a partial positive charge ($\delta+$). An example of this convention is shown in Figure 2.

$$\overset{\delta+}{H}\text{---}\overset{\delta-}{Cl}$$

Figure 2. The polarity displayed by a molecule of hydrochloric acid (HCl). The bond between hydrogen and chlorine is polar covalent.

This polarity, termed a dipole moment, is often represented by an arrow with a plus sign near the atom with the $\delta+$ charge, pointing in the direction of the pull of electrons towards the electronegative atom.

> > CONNECTIONS < <

Chapter 1 of Biology

Finally, a coordinate covalent bond, sometimes called a dative bond, forms when the shared electrons are derived from a lone pair on only one of the bonded atoms. For example, when ammonia (NH_3) bonds with boron trifluoride (BF_3), the lone pair on the nitrogen atom contributes both electrons to the bond (Figure 3). This is actually a Lewis acid-base reaction, which will be discussed further in Chapter 7.

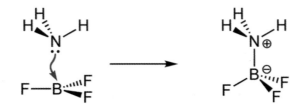

Figure 3. Coordinate covalent bond formation between NH_3 and BF_3.

Finally, we must discuss a few concepts that can be used to compare covalent bonds. First, bond order describes the number of bonds between two atoms. Until now, our discussion has remained centered on single bonds, which arise from the sharing of one electron pair. However, double and triple bonds can form as well: double bonds from the sharing of two electron pairs (or four total electrons) and triple bonds from the sharing of three electron pairs (or six electrons).

When reading about single and multiple bonds, you may encounter the terms sigma (σ) and pi (π). These are designations used to describe the symmetry of molecular orbitals, or the mathematical functions that arise from the combination of atomic orbitals in a bonded atom. A σ bond, or σ molecular orbitals, forms due to end-to-end overlap of the two atomic orbitals along the internuclear axis. (You can picture a σ bond as consisting of two clouds, each pointing directly from one nucleus to the other, and overlapping.) In contrast, a π bond forms when the atomic orbitals point above and below the atoms in question, making them parallel to each other but perpendicular to the axis that connects the two nuclei. If this seems difficult to visualize, note that a π bond is pictured in Figure 4.

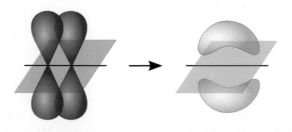

Figure 4. A π bond, formed from parallel orbitals that extend up and down from the atomic nuclei.

The first bond to form between two nuclei is always a σ bond; thus, single bonds can be characterized as sigma, but not pi, bonds. Additional bonds are always π in nature. As such, a double bond contains one σ and one π bond, while a triple bond includes one σ and two π bonds. Singly-bound atoms that are not in a cyclic structure can rotate around the single bond because σ bonds allow free rotation. In contrast, rotation cannot occur around double or triple bonds.

Two other characteristics of covalent bonds are bond length and bond energy. As one would expect, bond length refers to the distance between the bonded atoms. More specifically, bond length is the average distance between the two nuclei involved in the covalent bond. Bond length is inversely related to bond order; single bonds are longer than double bonds, which are longer than triple bonds. Finally, bond energy is the energy required to break the covalent bond(s) between two atoms. The higher the bond energy, the stronger the bond, and as it is more difficult to break a double or triple bond than to break a single bond, bond energy can be said to increase as bond order increases.

3. Intermolecular Forces

Earlier, we mentioned hydrogen bonding, but we did not discuss it along with ionic and covalent bonding. You may be asking yourself, "Why?" The simple answer to this question is that hydrogen bonding is not a form of intramolecular chemical bonding, nor are hydrogen bonds actually bonds, in the classic chemical sense, at all. Instead, hydrogen bonds, along with the other main forms of intermolecular chemical forces, are attractions between positive or partially positive and negative or partially negative regions of different molecules.

Intermolecular forces are attractive forces between molecules that are notably weaker than intramolecular bonds. For this reason, it is typically fairly easy to disrupt these attractions using common lab techniques, such as heating. (Imagine boiling a pot of water. As heat is added, the *inter*molecular attractions between separate water molecules break, releasing these molecules as water vapor. However, the *intra*molecular bonds are undisrupted; after all, boiling water does not separate the H_2O molecules into many H and O atoms.) There are three main categories of intermolecular forces to know for the MCAT: hydrogen bonding, dipole-dipole interactions, and van der Waals forces.

Hydrogen bonding is an attractive force between an electronegative atom (oxygen, nitrogen, or fluorine) and a hydrogen atom in a nearby molecule that is covalently bonded to an electronegative atom. For hydrogen bonding to take place, one of the molecules present must contain one or more O-H, N-H, or F-H bonds. The hydrogen bond in question is *not* the same as the O-H, N-H, or F-H bonds themselves, all of which are covalent and thus intramolecular. Instead, the hydrogen

> > **CONNECTIONS** < <

Chapter 2 of Biochemistry

"bond" is the attraction between the positive dipole of that covalent bond and the O, N, or F position on a different molecule. Examples of hydrogen bonding include between H_2O molecules in water and between nitrogenous bases in complementary DNA strands.

Of the three main types of intermolecular attractions, hydrogen bonds are the strongest. This can be explained simply by the strength of the O-H, N-H, or F-H dipole. O, N, and F are three of the most electronegative atoms on the periodic table, so they pull a large proportion of electron density toward themselves, leaving the hydrogen end of the bond significantly partially positive. The resulting attraction is similar to a weak version of an ionic bond. Interestingly, the other types of intermolecular forces are really the same force, only with weaker dipoles. For example, interactions that occur between polar molecules that do *not* contain O-H, N-H, or F-H bonds are called dipole-dipole interactions. These attractive forces draw the negative end of one dipole closer to the positive end of another. If this sounds like hydrogen bonding, it should! Dipole-dipole interactions are the same electrostatic force, only weaker, as the dipoles in question do not display quite so large a difference in electronegativity.

Finally, we are left with the weakest of the three forms of intermolecular attraction: London dispersion forces. All molecules experience these attractions, which can be thought of as synonymous to van der Waals forces for the sake of the MCAT. As you may have predicted, London dispersion forces are *also* fundamentally similar to hydrogen bonds and dipole-dipole forces, but are simply weaker due to the presence of weaker dipoles. (Specifically, London dispersion forces stem from instantaneous dipoles, which are transient dipoles created by the random movement of electrons. Even nonpolar molecules display these instantaneous dipoles, so even they will experience London dispersion forces. In fact, polar molecules that display hydrogen bonding or dipole-dipole attraction will not be affected by London dispersion forces to a significant extent, since those other attractions are much stronger; MCAT students thus often learn to associate London forces with nonpolar molecules.) These weak intermolecular forces increase in strength as the length of the molecule increases, like a long strip of Velcro.

4. Lewis Structures

The intramolecular bonds that we have discussed in this chapter involve the transfer or sharing of electrons. Specifically, these shared electrons are valence electrons, which reside in the outermost and highest-energy electron shell of the atom and are thus the farthest away from the nucleus. (The exception to this rule lies in the transition metals; for example, the transition metal cobalt has valence electrons in the 3d subshell, even though its outermost shell holds 4s electrons.) The location of valence electrons, coupled with the comparatively weak pull on them by the nucleus, allows them to interact with the electrons of other atoms, which is why valence electrons play such an important role in predicting atomic behavior.

How are valence electrons represented on paper? The Lewis dot structure system, first depicted by Gilbert Lewis in 1916, is a method used to diagram the relationships between atoms and their valence electrons. In a Lewis structure, valence electrons are represented by dots in pairs surrounding the element symbol. Recall that the number of valence electrons is equal to the group number in the periodic table, with the exception of transition elements.

Figure 5. The Lewis structure of monoatomic chlorine, which has seven valence electrons.

Figure 5 shows only a single atom, but Lewis structures are also used to depict chemical bonding. Covalent bonds are indicated by a line that represents two shared electrons connecting two atoms. Multiple lines may be used to signify double and triple bonds.

Figure 6. The Lewis structure of water (H_2O).

How do we count valence electrons in a Lewis structure? Let's use Figure 6 as an example. While a single bond counts as two electrons when determining whether a bonding arrangement satisfies the octet rule, it counts as only one when considering valence electrons. (After all, in a covalent single bond, each atom contributes only one electron to the bond.) In Figure 6, then, we can see that each hydrogen atom contains a single valence electron. The central oxygen atom has two valence electrons from each lone pair (four overall), plus one from each bond, for a total of six. In contrast, if we were determining whether oxygen followed the octet rule, we would count two electrons from each lone pair, plus *two* from each single bond, for a total of eight.

When drawing the Lewis structure of a molecule, be certain to adhere to the following rules. We'll use carbon dioxide (CO_2) as an example, as it is a common organic molecule that you will see often throughout your MCAT prep.

1. Draw the atoms of the molecule in the proper positioning. For a diatomic molecule like O_2, this is easy; simply draw two oxygen atoms next to each other. Molecules with more than two atoms can be more difficult, since the bonding pattern may not be obvious. For these compounds, you should determine which atom is the central atom, then arrange the other atoms around it. Carbon is a common central atom; hydrogen, with its inability to form more than one bond, is never a central atom. When in doubt, note that the atom with the lowest electronegativity is nearly always central. Carbon will be the central atom of CO_2.

$$O \quad C \quad O$$

2. Determine how many valence electrons must be present in the entire molecule. Remember, you can find the number of valence electrons associated with a certain atom by using the periodic table. Here, carbon has four valence electrons, while oxygen has six, yielding a total of $(4) + (2 \times 6) = 16$ valence electrons.

3. The atoms must be connected by at least one bond, so draw single bonds to connect them.

$$O-C-O$$

4. Determine how many valence electrons are yet to be assigned. We know the compound has a total of 16; subtract two for each single bond, and we see that we need to assign an additional 12 electrons. Assign these in lone pairs to the peripheral atoms (those which are *not* the central atom), in an attempt to give each a full octet. (Recall that certain atoms can exist with an incomplete or expanded octet, as described earlier in this chapter. Carbon and oxygen cannot, so we do not need to worry about these exceptions.)

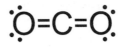

5. Uh-oh—we have a problem. Our compound has the proper number of electrons, and the two oxygen atoms have complete octets, but the central carbon atom only contains four electrons. (Remember, when assessing whether an atom has an octet, you must count each single bond as two electrons.) When this occurs, start erasing lone pairs on the peripheral atoms and replace each with a multiple bond to the central atom. Do this until all atoms have proper octets. The final Lewis structure of CO_2 is shown below.

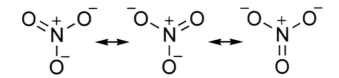

Compounds that have more than one possible Lewis structure are said to have resonance. Resonance structures must have the same positioning and connectivity of atoms, but they differ in the distribution of electrons across the molecule. As one simple example, consider the nitrate, or NO_3^-, anion, below. Note that the separate resonance structures are separated by a double-headed arrow, as is conventional.

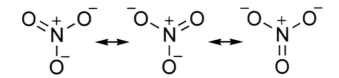

Figure 7. Resonance structures of the nitrate ion.

To determine whether two structures are resonance forms of each other, be certain to clarify a few points. First, the forms must have the same number of *total* electrons, whether these are held as bonds or lone pairs. Second, when converting one resonance structure into another, shift lone pairs or π electrons to adjacent atoms, as opposed to atoms more distant on the molecule. Finally, remember that atoms themselves cannot change position if two structures are to be categorized as resonance forms.

The "true" Lewis structure of such a compound is ultimately a hybrid of all possible resonance structures, with the most stable resonance structure predominating. For example, ozone (O_3) has two resonance structures with equal stability, so the resonance hybrid will contain two partial double bonds with an even distribution of electrons (Figure 8). The bond order of each of these bonds will be

1.5, halfway between that of a single and that of a double bond. (Yes, it is possible to have a bond order that is not a whole number!) Finally, note that delocalization of electrons increases the stability of molecules with resonance.

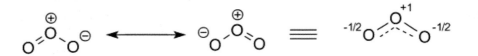

Figure 8. Resonance structures of ozone.

If you look at the resonance forms in Figure 8, you may notice something interesting. Consider the first structure, on the far left. Although lone pairs are not shown, note that the central oxygen atom must have one lone pair to have a full octet. This gives that oxygen atom two valence electrons from the lone pair and one from each of the three bonds, for a total of five. But wait—doesn't the periodic table say that oxygen should have six electrons? This brings us to the concept of formal charge, or the disparity between the number of valence electrons an atom "should" have (according to the periodic table) and the number it actually has. Formal charge can be calculated according to Equation 1.

Equation 1.   Formal charge = VE − ½ BE − LPE

Here, VE refers to the number of valence electrons held by the neutral atom, according to the periodic table. BE denotes the number of bonding electrons (two per bond), and LPE refers to the number of electrons present on the atom in the form of lone pairs. A simple way to remember this equation is as "'should' minus 'actually has'." VE is the number of valence electrons the atom "should" have, while the combination of ½ BE and LPE gives the number that it actually has in the molecule in question.

Let's attempt an example. What is the formal charge of nitrogen in NH_3? The first step is to draw the Lewis structure of the molecule in question.

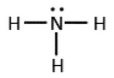

Figure 9. The Lewis structure of ammonia (NH_3).

Next, recall that formal charge = valence electrons − ½ bonding electrons − lone pair electrons. Here, then, the formal charge of the central nitrogen atom must be 5 − ½ (6) − 2 = 0. This fits with the prediction we may have made using logic, as nitrogen "prefers" to have five valence electrons and does have five in the compound shown above. Note that atoms that have fewer valence electrons than the periodic table would predict have positive formal charges, and atoms that have extra valence electrons when compared to the periodic table have negative formal charges.

5. Orbital Hybridization and VSEPR Theory

In section 2 of this chapter, we briefly discussed molecular orbitals in the context of σ and π bonds. Let's dive into the details a little bit more, so we can introduce a related concept: orbital hybridization. First, recall from Chapter 1 that electrons exist in the regions around atoms in characteristic shapes depending on the angular momentum quantum number of their subshell: s, p, d, or f. Most commonly, you will encounter the s subshell, which is spherical, and the p subshell, which has two lobes and a central node.

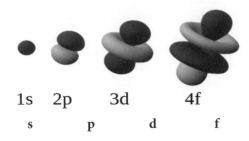

1s   2p   3d   4f

s   p   d   f

Figure 10. Examples of atomic orbital shapes. Note that p, d, and f orbitals can take on shapes distinct from those shown here.

When atoms combine to form a molecule, their atomic orbitals overlap to produce molecular orbitals. A single bond—again, consisting of two electrons—between two atoms will form a sigma (σ) bond, which has an overlapping region of electron density. Pi (π) bonds occur between two parallel p orbitals and are weaker than σ bonds. Double bonds consist of one π bond and one σ bond, while triple bonds include two π bonds and one σ bond.

This is largely information you've seen before, so what's the point? Well, an understanding of σ and π bonds, as well as subshells and orbitals, is helpful for understanding how these orbitals *actually* work in a real-life molecule. For example, on paper, the central carbon in methane (CH_4) has four valence electrons and would appear to have one s orbital and three p orbitals. In reality, however, these orbitals combine, or hybridize, to produce four equal sp^3 orbitals.

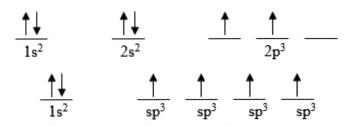

Figure 11. Electron configuration of CH_4 (top) and its molecular orbital hybridization (bottom).

Hybridization between one s orbital and two p orbitals may also occur to produce three sp^2 orbitals, or between one s orbital and one p orbital to produce two sp orbitals. A quick guide to identifying the orbital hybridization of a molecule is to determine the number of regions of electron density around the atom. A region of electron density is defined as either a bond (single, double, or triple) or a lone pair of electrons. Two regions yields a hybridization of sp (common in cases of triple bonds or central atoms with two double bonds). Having three regions of electron density is associated with an sp^2 hybridization, and having four regions yields an sp^3 hybridization.

> > CONNECTIONS < <

Chapter 1 of Chemistry

Again, let's solidify this concept by working through a simple example. Let's say we are asked to identify the orbital hybridization of the carbon atom in CO_2. To solve, we should first draw the Lewis structure of CO_2, which we have done earlier in this chapter and which is also shown below.

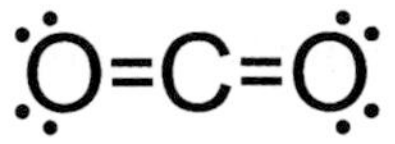

$$\ddot{O}=C=\ddot{O}$$

The central carbon atom is bonded to two other atoms and has no lone pairs, so there are only two regions of electron density. The carbon atom in CO_2 thus has sp hybridization. See—it's that easy!

This knowledge equips us to build molecules and predict their shapes using the valence shell electron pair repulsion (VSEPR) theory. The VSEPR theory uses Lewis structures and electronic relationships to determine the shapes of molecules, assuming that the distance between electron-rich regions will be maximized due to electronic repulsions. As discussed earlier, the number of regions of electron density is determined by the number of bonds and lone pairs around the central atom. Lone pairs of electrons take up more space than bonded atoms because electron pairs generate the strongest repulsive force. The number of lone pairs and bonded atoms associated with a central atom can be used to predict its bond angles and molecular shape, as shown in Table 1.

ELECTRON-RICH REGIONS	BONDED ATOMS	LONE PAIRS	MOLECULAR SHAPE	BOND ANGLE	EXAMPLE	SHAPE
2	2	0	Linear	180°	CO_2	
3	3	0	Trigonal planar	120°	BF_3	
4	4	0	Tetrahedral	109.5°	CH_4	
4	3	1	Trigonal pyramidal	107°	NH_3	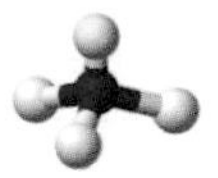
4	2	2	Bent	104.5°	H_2O	
5	5	0	Trigonal bipyramidal	90°, 120°, 180°	PCl_5	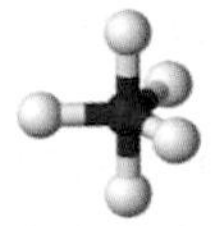
6	6	0	Octahedral	90°, 180°	SF_6	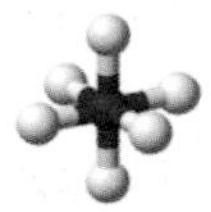

Table 1. VSEPR geometries.

Note that the shape of a molecule can be described by two closely-related terms: molecular shape and electronic geometry. Electronic geometry takes into account lone pairs as well as bonded atoms when predicting shape. In contrast, molecular shape or molecular geometry (which is given in Table 1) considers only bonded atoms, although those atoms are still repelled by any lone pairs present on the central atom. Take ammonia (NH_3) as an example. Its central nitrogen atom is attached to three bonded atoms and one lone pair, giving it four regions of electron density. As such, its electronic geometry is tetrahedral, as electronic geometry considers lone pairs as well as bound atoms. However, its molecular shape is trigonal pyramidal; the lone pair pushes the bonded atoms into a pyramid-like shape, but it is not itself considered part of the shape.

Let's delve into a few specific molecular shapes. Tetrahedral molecular geometry is common among carbon-containing molecules, such as methane (CH_4). To maximize the separation of hydrogen atoms, the bond angle between each hydrogen angle is 109.5°.

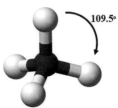

Figure 12. The bond angle between atoms in a tetrahedral molecule.

Phosphine, or phosphorus trihydride (PH_3), is a molecule with three bonded atoms and one lone pair, so it also possesses four regions of electron density. Because the lone pair generates stronger repulsive forces, the bond angle between the hydrogen atoms will be slightly smaller (107°), resulting in trigonal pyramidal geometry.

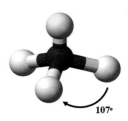

Figure 13. A trigonal pyramidal molecule, with a lone pair pushing the three bonded atoms slightly closer together than expected.

Water (H_2O) also has four regions of electron density—two bonded atoms and two lone pairs—but the bond angle between hydrogen atoms is even smaller due to (you guessed it!) the strong repulsive forces from both electron pairs. The bond angle between hydrogen atoms is 104.5° in the bent shape.

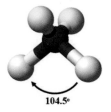

Figure 14. The bond angle between the two hydrogen atoms in water (H_2O).

Now that you have built a foundation of understanding of molecules, bonding, intermolecular forces, and VSEPR theory, you are ready to move on to the next phase of chemistry: chemical reactions and stoichiometry.

6. Must-Knows

> Molecular weight = sum of masses of individual atoms in the molecule
> 1 mole = 6.022×10^{23} atoms or molecules (Avogadro's number)
> Valence (outermost shell) electrons participate in chemical bonding
> The octet rule: states that atoms tend to prefer a state of having eight valence electrons, and will form bonds to achieve this
> Exceptions to the octet rule:
  – Incomplete octet: stable with < 8 valence electrons
    • H (max 1 electron), He (max 2), Li (max 2), Be (max 4), B (max 6)
  – Expanded octet: stable with > 8 valence electrons
    • Elements from the third period and below
  – Molecules with odd #s of electrons
> Types of intramolecular bonds (strong, hold an individual molecule together)
  – Ionic (large electronegativity difference, dissociate into ions)
  – Covalent (smaller electronegativity difference, do not dissociate)
    • Nonpolar covalent = no or virtually no electronegativity difference
    • Polar covalent = moderate electronegativity difference; dipole moment
    • Coordinate covalent = one atom donates both electrons
> Types of intermolecular forces (weaker, attract different molecules together); all based on positive-negative attraction
  – Hydrogen bonding = relatively strong; requires F-H, N-H, or O-H
  – Dipole-dipole forces = weaker than H-bonding; seen between polar molecules
  – London dispersion forces = weakest; arise from instantaneous dipoles (in nonpolar molecules)
    • AKA Van der Waals forces
> Lewis structures: depict valence electrons/bonds/lone pairs of atoms and molecules
> Formal charge = VE – ½ BE – LPE
> Orbital hybridization
  – Central atom attached to 2 regions of electron density: sp
  – …3 regions of electron density: sp^2
  – …4 regions of electron density: sp^3
> VSEPR theory: uses # of bonded atoms and lone pairs to predict shape
> Bond angles to know:
  – Bent (water): 104.5°
  – Trigonal pyramidal: 107°
  – Tetrahedral: 109.5°
  – Trigonal planar: 120°
  – Linear: 180°

MCAT STRATEGY > > >

At this point, ask yourself whether you truly feel comfortable with the information in this chapter. Students often move quickly past "simple" topics like bonding and hybridization, but these are foundational concepts. Each hour you spend on understanding them may save you multiple hours in the future as you learn complex topics built upon the very same principles.

Practice Passage

Valence bond (VB) theory allows chemists to explain bonding in simple molecules. It is assumed that the direct overlap of hybridized atomic orbitals results in the formation of σ-type covalent bonds, and that multiple bonding result from the sideways overlap of pure p-type atomic orbitals and the formation of π-type bonds. VB theory has struggled to explain the properties of molecular oxygen. VB theory predicts that molecular oxygen should have a double bond and be diamagnetic. While O_2 contains a double bond, it is known to be paramagnetic.

Molecular orbital (MO) theory exceeds VB theory in explaining physical properties. Atomic orbitals are proposed to have wave properties, so they can interfere constructively and destructively. When two atomic orbitals interact, there will always be two molecular orbitals that result, one an energetically stabilized bonding interaction and the other a destabilized out-of-phase anti-bonding interaction. MO theory takes advantage of the directionality of atomic orbitals and symmetry to predict the resulting energy differences between molecular orbitals. Molecular orbitals are obtained by combining the atomic orbitals in the molecule. For example, in H_2 one of the molecular orbitals is constructed by adding the mathematical functions for the two 1s orbitals that come together, while another orbital is formed by subtracting one function from the other. However, the molecular orbital diagram for an O_2 molecule would ignore the 1s electrons on both oxygen atoms and concentrate on the interactions between the 2s and 2p valence orbitals. Using MO diagrams, as shown in Figure 1, chemists have succeeded at explaining spectroscopic properties and chemical reactivity.

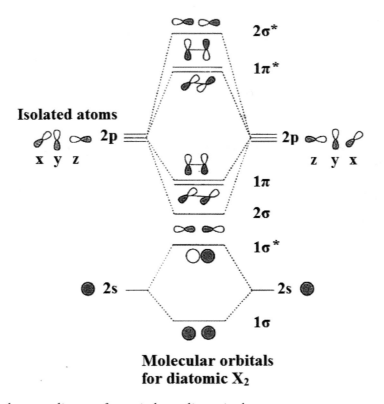

Figure 1. Molecular orbital energy diagram for period two diatomic elements

The MO energy diagram can be used to predict the bonding of the second period diatomic elements. The bond order between the diatomic elements can be determined as well.

1. Place the total number of valence electrons in the various orbitals in order of increasing energy, following Hund's rules for degenerate orbitals.

2. Subtract the number of electrons in anti-bonding orbitals from the number of electrons in bonding type orbitals.

3. Divide by two and note that in certain cases, it is possible to have fractional bond orders.

This model uses a second order mixing of the 2s and 2p orbitals to form the sigma-bonding (σ) and anti-bonding (σ^*) type orbitals. Shaded portions of atomic orbitals are considered to have positive amplitudes while un-shaded portions are considered to have negative amplitudes.

1. Based on the MO energy diagram in Figure 1, what is the bond order between oxygen atoms in O_2?
   A. 1.5
   B. 2
   C. 2.5
   D. 3

2. The superoxide anion, shown below, is a highly reactive species which has been implicated in the aging process of human cells.

   Superoxide dismutase enzymes rapidly convert superoxide into elemental oxygen and peroxide. Which of the following sets of distances would be consistent with the bond orders in elemental oxygen, superoxide, and peroxide?

   A. 1.21 Å, 1.32 Å, and 1.49 Å, respectively
   B. 1.49 Å, 1.32 Å, and 1.21 Å, respectively
   C. 1.21 Å, 1.49 Å, and 1.32 Å, respectively
   D. 1.49 Å, 1.49 Å, and 1.21 Å, respectively

3. Based on the MO energy diagram in Figure 1, which of the following diatomic elements would have unpaired electrons?
   A. Nitrogen
   B. Oxygen
   C. Fluorine
   D. Chlorine

4. Which of the following does NOT have π-type bonds?
   A. Acetic acid
   B. Propanol
   C. Propanal
   D. Propanone

5. Which of the following would be isoelectronic with elemental nitrogen?
   I.   Carbon monoxide
   II. Hydrogen peroxide
   III. Acetylene

   A. I only
   B. I and II only
   C. II and III only
   D. I and III only

6. According to the passage, how can the MO theory be used to explain why stable He_2 cannot exist?
   A. The total energy of the molecule is greater than the energy of a pair of isolated He atoms.
   B. Formation σ bonding and σ^* antibonding orbitals result in insufficient energy to hold the atoms together.
   C. An imbalance occurs with the 1s electrons, resulting in only the σ orbital forming.
   D. The total energy of the molecule is less than the energy of a pair of isolated He atoms.

7. The Bohr model, in combination with the Rydberg constant (R), allows for the rough approximation of the energy level of an electron.

$$E_n = - R_E / n^2$$

   Which of the following electrons will have the greatest energy?

   A. $n = 2; l = 1; m_l = 1$
   B. $n = 3; l = 0; m_l = 0$
   C. $n = 3; l = 2; m_l = -2$
   D. $n = 4; l = 3; m_l = -1$

Practice Passage Explanations

Valence bond (VB) theory allows chemists to explain bonding in simple molecules. It is assumed that the direct overlap of hybridized atomic orbitals results in the formation of σ-type covalent bonds, and that multiple bonding result from the sideways overlap of pure p-type atomic orbitals and the formation of π-type bonds. VB theory has struggled to explain the properties of molecular oxygen. VB theory predicts that molecular oxygen should have a double bond and be diamagnetic. While O_2 contains a double bond, it is known to be paramagnetic.

Key terms: valence bond theory, covalent bonds, σ-type, p-type, diamagnetic, paramagnetic

Contrast: VB explains bonding properties of simple molecules, but fails to accurately predict the number of unpaired electrons in O_2 (para = unpaired e⁻; dia = no unpaired e⁻)

Molecular orbital (MO) theory exceeds VB theory in explaining physical properties. Atomic orbitals are proposed to have wave properties, so they can interfere constructively and destructively. When two atomic orbitals interact, there will always be two molecular orbitals that result, one an energetically stabilized bonding interaction and the other a destabilized out-of-phase anti-bonding interaction. MO theory takes advantage of the directionality of atomic orbitals and symmetry to predict the resulting energy differences between molecular orbitals. Molecular orbitals are obtained by combining the atomic orbitals in the molecule. For example, in H_2 one of the molecular orbitals is constructed by adding the mathematical functions for the two 1s orbitals that come together, while another orbital is formed by subtracting one function from the other. However, the molecular orbital diagram for an O_2 molecule would ignore the 1s electrons on both oxygen atoms and concentrate on the interactions between the 2s and 2p valence orbitals. Using MO diagrams, as shown in Figure 1, chemists have succeeded at explaining spectroscopic properties and chemical reactivity.

Key terms: molecular orbital theory, wave interference, symmetry, spectroscopic properties

Cause and effect: MO better predicts orbitals and ensuing properties of molecules by combing atomic orbitals, will always get 2

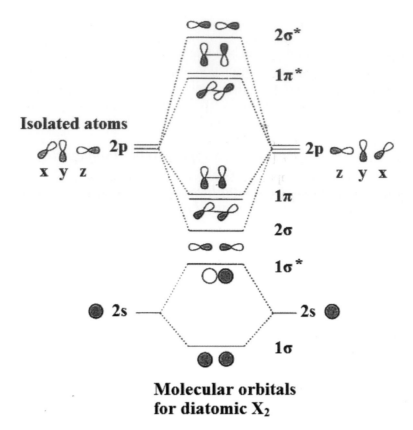

Figure 1. Molecular orbital energy diagram for period two diatomic elements

Figure 1 includes the shapes of the atomic and resulting molecular orbitals for the σ and σ*-type orbitals; in-phase combinations are bonding and out-of-phase combinations are anti-bonding (*)

The MO energy diagram can be used to predict the bonding of the second period diatomic elements. The bond order between the diatomic elements can be determined as well.

1. Place the total number of valence electrons in the various orbitals in order of increasing energy, following Hund's rules for degenerate orbitals.

2. Subtract the number of electrons in anti-bonding orbitals from the number of electrons in bonding type orbitals.

3. Divide by two and note that in certain cases, it is possible to have fractional bond orders.

This model uses a second order mixing of the 2s and 2p orbitals to form the sigma-bonding (σ) and anti-bonding (σ*) type orbitals. Shaded portions of atomic orbitals are considered to have positive amplitudes while un-shaded portions are considered to have negative amplitudes.

Key terms: predict bonding, bond order, mixing of orbitals, shaded, amplitudes

Cause and effect: 3 steps allow bond order calculation for period 2 diatomic elements (N, F, O)

1. B is correct. The MO diagram predicts a double bond based on the fact that there are twelve valence electrons, with eight of these electrons being in bonding type MOs and the remaining four electrons in anti-bonding MOs. As stated in the last paragraph of the passage, subtracting the number of anti-bonding electrons from the bonding electrons and dividing by 2, gives the bond order, BO = (8-4)/2 = 2. Therefore O_2 has a double bond, consistent with the Lewis dot structure.

2. A is correct. Molecular oxygen (O_2) has a double bond and should be shorter than the single bond shown in the superoxide Lewis structure. Superoxide has a total of thirteen valence electrons, with eight in bonding MOs and five in anti-bonding MOs. According to the passage, BO = (8-5)/2 = 1.5 meaning superoxide has a bond order of 1.5 (the passage tells us it is possible to have fractional bond orders). Peroxide has a total of 14 valence electrons, with 8 in bonding MOs and 6 in anti-bonding MOs. BO = (8-6)/2 = 1. Since the higher the bond order the shorter the bond length, superoxide should be longer than oxygen but shorter than peroxide.

3. B is correct. O_2 has a total of 12 valence electrons. Placing these electrons in the MO diagram gives two electrons in the σ^* orbitals, which are energetically degenerate, so following Hund's rules, putting one electron in each of the two σ^* type orbitals, results in two unpaired electrons. This is consistent with the statement in the passage that "molecular oxygen is known to be paramagnetic", which results from oxygen having unpaired electrons.

    A, C, D: Nitrogen, fluorine and chlorine (14, 16, 32 electrons) will have no unpaired electrons according to the MO model.

4. B is correct. Propanol is an alkyl alcohol and does not have a multiple bonds, making it the correct answer.

    Multiple bonds between second period elements will have π-bonds. Acetic acid has a C=O and therefore has a π-bond, eliminating choice A. Propanal and propanone are an aldehyde and a ketone respectively and have C=O bonds, and therefore also have π-bonds, eliminating choices C and D. Propanol is an alcohol and does not have a multiple bond.

5. D is correct. Isoelectronic compounds have the same number of electrons. Elemental nitrogen, N_2, has a total of 14 electrons.

    I: CO has 6 + 8 = 14 electrons as well, eliminating choice C.
    II: H_2O_2 has, 2(1) + 2(8) = 18 electrons and is not isoelectronic with N_2, eliminating choice B.
    III: C_2H_2 has 2(6) + 2(1) = 14 electrons and is isoelectronic with N_2, eliminating choice A.

6. B is correct. According to paragraph 2, combining a pair of He atoms (each with a $1s^2$ e^- configuration) would produce a molecule with a pair of electrons in both the σ bonding and the σ^* antibonding molecular orbitals. This would mean the total energy of the molecule would be the same as the energy of a pair of isolated helium atoms, and there would be nothing to hold the helium atoms together to form a molecule. If a He_2 molecule is neither more nor less stable than a pair of helium atoms means that the central orbitals on an atom make no contribution to the stability of the molecules that contain this atom. The only orbitals that are important in MO theory are the ones formed when valence-shell orbitals are combined.

7. D is correct. Using the equation provided in the question, we can determine that E_n increases (i.e. becomes less negative) as n increases. Therefore the greatest energy will have the greatest n value. For choice D, $E_n = - R_E /4^2 = - R_E /16$.

    A: $E_n = - R_E /2^2 = - R_E /4$
    B: $E_n = - R_E /3^2 = - R_E /9$
    C: $E_n = - R_E /3^2 = - R_E /9$

Independent Questions

1. Which of the following exhibits trigonal planar molecular geometry?
   A. Ammonia (NH_3)
   B. Methanol (CH_3OH)
   C. Aluminum chloride ($AlCl_3$)
   D. Acetylene (C_2H_2)

2. Which of the following pure substances is expected to have the highest boiling point?
   A. Hydrogen sulfide
   B. Carbon tetrachloride
   C. Ammonia
   D. Water

3. Which of the following covalent bonds is the shortest?
   A. The C-O bond in ethanol
   B. The P-O bond in phosphoric acid
   C. The C-H bond in methanol
   D. The C-Cl bond in carbon tetrachloride

4. The structure of guanine is shown below.

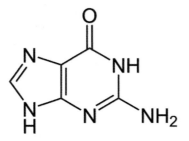

   How many of the atoms in the guanine molecule exhibit sp³ hybridization?

   A. 0
   B. 1
   C. 2
   D. 6

5. Which of the following atoms are most likely to participate in ionic bonding with one another?
   A. Carbon and oxygen
   B. Carbon and iodine
   C. Chlorine and aluminum
   D. Calcium and bromine

6. Which of the following molecules exhibits a permanent dipole moment?
   A. Diatomic nitrogen
   B. Carbon dioxide
   C. Sulfur dioxide
   D. Heavy hydrogen (D_2)

7. The H-C-H bond angle in dichloromethane (DCM) is expected to be:
   A. greater than 109.5°, but less than 120°.
   B. equal to 109.5°.
   C. less than 109.5°.
   D. equal to 120°.

8. The Lewis dot structure of carbon monoxide features a carbon-oxygen triple bond. How many lone pairs of electrons are present on the carbon and oxygen atoms, respectively?
   A. 1, 1
   B. 1, 2
   C. 2, 2
   D. 2, 1

Independent Question Explanations

1. C is correct. Aluminum is an exception to the octet rule. It exists in a stable state with an open-shell configuration. Therefore, the central aluminum atom in aluminum chloride does not have a lone pair of electrons, and VSEPR theory dictates it will have a trigonal planar molecular geometry. In contrast, nitrogen cannot violate the octet rule. The central nitrogen atom in ammonia has a lone pair of electrons and exhibits a trigonal pyramidal molecular geometry (eliminate option A). Methanol has a tetrahedral molecular geometry around the carbon and a bent molecular geometry around the oxygen (eliminate option B). Acetylene has a linear molecular geometry (eliminate option D).

2. D is correct. Of the given choices, only water and ammonia are capable of intermolecular hydrogen bonding, one of the strongest intermolecular reactions. Hydrogen sulfide and carbon tetrachloride molecules are attracted only by dipole-dipole interactions and London dispersion forces. Covalent bonds between oxygen and hydrogen are more polarized than covalent bonds between nitrogen and hydrogen, because oxygen is more electronegative than nitrogen. Consequently, the intermolecular hydrogen bonds between water molecules are stronger than those between ammonia molecules. Alternatively, you could eliminate choice C if you knew that ammonia (unlike water) is a gas at room temperature, meaning that it must have a boiling point lower than room temperature.

3. C is correct. Bond length is primarily determined by the atomic radii of the bonded atoms. Therefore, bonds formed with hydrogen atoms tend to be shorter than bonds formed with any other atom.

4. A is correct. Atoms can only adopt sp^3 hybridization states if they do not participate in π bonds. Furthermore, if an atom appears to exist in more than one hybridization state depending on the resonance structure drawn, the lowest possible hybridization state is always assigned. All carbon and oxygen atoms in the given structure participate in π bonds and are sp^2 hybridized. All nitrogen atoms participate in π bonds or have lone pairs of electrons that can be delocalized into a π system in a resonance structure, making them sp^2 as well.

5. D is correct. Ionic bonding occurs between atoms that differ substantially in electronegativity. Of the choices given, calcium and bromine lie on opposite ends of the periodic table and, therefore, have the greatest difference in electronegativity of the choices given. Note that options A and B each consist of two nonmetals, meaning they will not participate in ionic bonding at all. Choice C can form an ionic bond, but the electronegativity difference between chlorine and aluminum is less than that between calcium and bromine.

6. C is correct. Molecular nitrogen and molecular hydrogen (whether in the form of H_2 or D_2) do not have any polarized bonds that could produce permanent dipole moments. Since carbon dioxide displays linear geometry, the two opposing dipoles produced by the carbon-oxygen double bonds cancel each other out, yielding no overall dipole moment. Since sulfur dioxide exhibits a bent geometry, its sulfur-oxygen dipoles do not cancel and it does display a net dipole moment.

7. C is correct. The bond angles in an ideal tetrahedral geometry are equal to 109.5°. This value applies to cases in which the central atom is bonded to four identical atoms. Here, however, the two large chlorine atoms in DCM will be forced apart by steric clashing between their electron clouds. This will cause the Cl-C-Cl bond angle to be greater than the ideal 109.5° and force the two hydrogen atoms closer together than they would be in an ideal case.

8. A is correct. If the carbon and oxygen atoms participate in a triple bond with one another, each cannot have more than one lone pair of electrons without violating the octet rule.

This page left intentionally blank.

Reactions and Stoichiometry

CHAPTER 3

0. Introduction

In the previous chapter, we discussed the fundamentals of chemical bonds—what they are, which types exist, and the properties of the bonds of each type. However, Chapter 2 was largely limited to describing bonds that already existed between the atoms of a molecule. But how did these bonds form in the first place? And can they break, allowing the component atoms to form new bonds and construct new molecules? The answer to this second question is an emphatic yes. The process of bond breaking and formation to create novel products takes place through chemical reactions. In this chapter, we will begin with a brief discussion of some basic foundational chemical concepts, such as empirical and molecular formulas. We will then describe the various types of chemical reactions that you are likely to see on the MCAT. Finally, the latter chunk of this chapter will enter the realm of chemistry-related math, including stoichiometry, a form of mathematical comparison used to predict the quantity of products formed or reactants required for a chemical process.

Before diving into new material, we must first briefly return to some basic concepts that were introduced in Chapter 2 but remain highly relevant here. Recall that a mole of any chemical substance is a quantity that contains 6.022×10^{23} particles (molecules, ions, or atoms). This value is termed Avogadro's number and should be committed to memory. A related concept, molar mass, refers to the mass of exactly one mole of a species. Molar mass has units of grams per mole (g/mol). Interestingly, the molar mass of a compound has the same numerical value as the compound's molecular weight, or the mass of one molecule in atomic mass units (amu). As a simple example, diatomic hydrogen (H_2) has a molecular weight of approximately 2.0 amu, and one mole of diatomic hydrogen gas has a molar mass of about 2.0 g/mol. This is no accident, but it is certainly fortunate for MCAT students, as you will have access to a periodic table on Test Day. Practice using the atomic weight listed on the table for each element to calculate the molar mass of a larger compound. In practice, this simply involves adding up the atomic weights of each atom in the compound, but every second counts!

MCAT STRATEGY > > >

Note that some MCAT questions will provide molar mass values, so check before beginning any calculation. In fact, it is a good idea to double-check any relevant given information before beginning a math-heavy question. You don't want to waste time calculating a value that is already staring you in the face in the passage text.

As you progress through this text, do not rush! Stoichiometry and its related concepts are often perceived as "easy" or basic chemistry, since you likely learned about them for the first time in the early weeks of an introductory chemistry class. However, the vast majority of MCAT students harbor at least some major misconceptions about stoichiometry. The MCAT tends to focus heavily on foundational concepts, so your best bet for success on Test Day is to understand the material in this chapter inside and out. Good luck!

1. Chemical Formula and Percent Composition

From the very first pages of this book, you have been repeatedly presented with the terms "molecule," "compound," and "element." Chapter 1 defined these concepts; recall that an element is matter composed of atoms that share the same number of protons, or atomic number. A molecule, then, is a species that consists of two or more connected atoms, and a compound is a special form of molecule in which these connected atoms are of at least two different types of element. Let's consider a simple example of a compound: sulfur hexafluoride. With the knowledge that this compound consists of one sulfur atom attached to six fluorine atoms, we can write out its molecular formula: SF_6. The molecular formula is exactly what you might expect it to be: it gives the number of atoms of each element present in a single molecule.

An alternative way to express the constitution of a compound is to use its empirical formula. The empirical formula of a molecule consists of the ratio of atoms of each element present, simplified to the lowest whole numbers possible. In our previous example, SF_6, only a single sulfur atom is present, so SF_6 already represents a simplified whole-number ratio of elements. As such, the molecular formula of SF_6 is identical to its empirical formula. For other compounds, however, these two formulas can be dramatically different. Consider glucose, one molecule of which contains six carbon atoms, twelve hydrogen atoms, and six oxygen atoms. The molecular formula of glucose must then be $C_6H_{12}O_6$, which directly reflects the number of each type of atom present. Contrast this with the empirical formula! Since the ratio of carbon to hydrogen to oxygen atoms in a molecule of glucose is 1:2:1, the empirical formula of glucose is CH_2O. In summary, if the molecular formula is not already simplified—if the numbers for each type of atom share a common factor—the empirical formula will differ from the molecular formula.

Another concept you will likely encounter when dealing with molecules is percent composition by mass. Percent composition refers to the percent of the total mass of a compound that a particular element contributes. Finding this value requires only a simple calculation; take the combined mass of all atoms of the element in question and divide it by the mass of the entire molecule. For a quick example, let us return to glucose, with its empirical formula of CH_2O. The percent composition by mass of oxygen is equal to the mass contributed by oxygen divided by the total mass of the molecule. Here, that value would be (16 g) / (12 g + 2 g + 16 g) = about 53%.

MCAT STRATEGY > > >

Notice how we used the empirical formula rather than the molecular one? We could have calculated the same value using the molecular formula, but that would require more addition (unless we were already familiar with the molecular weight of glucose, which you will be by Test Day—it's approximately 180 amu). Becoming familiar with ways to lower your mathematical workload will help you enormously on the MCAT.

Let's try a variation on this problem type. What is the empirical formula of a compound that contains 54.5% carbon, 9.15% hydrogen, and 36.3% oxygen by mass? To solve this, first take stock of what information we are and are not given. We are not told the mass of compound present, nor are we given the compound's molar mass. Luckily, we do not need this information; our answer will be the same regardless of whether we have 2 grams, or 10 grams, or 1000 grams of the compound, since chemical compounds are consistent in their composition. (The scientific principle behind this is known as the law of constant composition.) The easiest way to solve this problem, then, is to assume that the compound's mass is some number that makes calculations as simple as possible. A good choice for that number is 100 grams.

Now, we need to calculate the number of moles of each element present, assuming that we have 100 grams of the compound.

$$\text{carbon: } \frac{54.5 \text{ g}}{12 \frac{\text{g}}{\text{mol}}} = \text{approximately 4.5 mol}$$

$$\text{hydrogen: } \frac{9.15 \text{ g}}{1 \frac{\text{g}}{\text{mol}}} = \text{approximately 9 mol}$$

$$\text{oxygen: } \frac{36.3 \text{ g}}{16 \frac{\text{g}}{\text{mol}}} = \text{approximately 2.25 mol}$$

Finally, we must determine the smallest whole-number ratio of these elements. We have about twice as many moles of carbon as we do moles of oxygen, and we have twice as many moles of hydrogen as moles of carbon. Thus, carbon, hydrogen, and oxygen atoms exist in a 2:4:1 ratio, and the empirical formula must be C_2H_4O. This intuitive approach is more than sufficient for the MCAT, but you may have also heard of a slightly more formal method of working out the empirical formula. Of the three values above (4.5, 9, and 2.25), you can choose the smallest value (2.25). Now, divide each of the mole values by this number. 4.5 moles of carbon divided by 2.25 is 2, giving us 2 carbon atoms in the formula. 9 moles of hydrogen divided by 2.25 is 4, meaning that our empirical formula should contain 4 carbon atoms. Of course, 2.25 moles of oxygen divided by 2.25 yields 1, so our empirical formula must be C_2H_4O—just as we found above.

> **MCAT STRATEGY > > >**
>
> As we have mentioned, you will be given a periodic table on the MCAT, but it can save time to memorize the approximate atomic weight of some common elements. In particular, the weights of hydrogen (1 amu), carbon (12 amu), and oxygen (16 amu) should be at the forefront of your memory.

2. Chemical Reaction Types

By definition, a chemical reaction is a process by which one or more chemical species (reactants) are converted into one or more chemically different species (products). This typically occurs via the breaking and re-forming of chemical bonds. Note that in most cases, the atoms themselves do not change; if the reactants contain only carbon and hydrogen, the products will consist of only C and H as well.

Not *all* processes that involve a visible change to a chemical compound are chemical reactions. For example, imagine that you place a block of ice on a hot sidewalk. Before long, the ice is transformed into a puddle of liquid water. Although the ice did experience a change, no intramolecular bonds were broken; the H_2O molecules that formed the block of ice are still H_2O molecules in the liquid phase. Indeed, phase changes are physical processes, not chemical reactions. However, even once we exclude such physical transitions, *millions* (or more) of processes remain within the category of chemical reactions. Luckily, for the sake of MCAT general chemistry, these can be sorted into only seven large reaction classes. The seven reaction types are synthesis, decomposition, single displacement, double displacement, neutralization, combustion, and oxidation-reduction, or redox reactions. (Many processes fit into multiple categories, such as a decomposition that is also an oxidation-reduction.)

> **MCAT STRATEGY > > >**
>
> One exception to the above statement is radioactive decay, in which atomic nuclei of one element can be transformed into atomic nuclei of another. This concept is discussed in detail in Chapter 10 of our physics book.

Let's begin with synthesis reactions, which are also known as combination reactions. In a synthesis reaction, two or more reactants (elements, molecules, or ions) combine to form a single product. Most commonly, these reactions involve two reactants, but more can be observed as well. As a simple example, note that hydrogen gas and nitrogen gas react to form ammonia according to the reaction below.

$$3\ H_2 + N_2 \rightarrow 2\ NH_3$$

MCAT STRATEGY > > >

In a biochemical context, synthesis reactions often appear as part of anabolic pathways. Anabolic processes involve the formation of larger macromolecules from multiple smaller reactants.

If a certain process exists in MCAT chemistry, it's a decent bet that its opposite exists, too, and this chapter is no exception. Specifically, decomposition reactions are the reverse of synthesis reactions. A decomposition reaction involves the breakdown of one reactant into multiple smaller products, as in the decomposition of potassium chlorate ($2\ KClO_3 \rightarrow 2\ KCl + 3\ O_2$). The breaking of chemical bonds is typically endothermic, meaning that it requires the input of energy, and as such, most decomposition reactions are endothermic overall. This will seem logical if you have ever seen a description of a chemical that decomposes at high temperatures. The abundant thermal energy present allows the decomposition to progress.

The next two reaction types are displacement reactions, or processes in which at least one element or group replaces another within a compound. If only one element or group does this, it is termed a single displacement reaction, while if two groups from different compounds "trade places," the reaction is a double displacement. A single displacement is shown in the example below, in which elemental potassium (K) replaces the zinc (Zn) ion in zinc chloride ($ZnCl_2$) to produce potassium chloride (KCl).

$$2\ K\ (s) + ZnCl_2\ (aq) \rightarrow 2\ KCl\ (s) + Zn\ (s)$$

In reality, this reaction would likely not be feasible due to potassium's explosive reactivity with water, but it exemplifies a single displacement well. As in most displacements, the species that trade places are metals; in other displacement reactions, a halogen may displace another halogen. The species that does the displacing (here, K) is typically more reactive than the species that is displaced (Zn).

How about double displacement reactions? The same rules largely apply; for example, the species that trade places are typically metals or halogens. Unlike in single displacements, however, both reactants usually begin and end as charged species within ionic compounds, as opposed to one solid metal and one ionic form on each side. Double displacement reactions are also called metathesis reactions, a nomenclature that is most commonly used when an insoluble (solid) product is formed. In the double displacement reaction below, barium (Ba) and magnesium (Mg) cations exchange places to generate two new ionic compounds.

$$BaCl_2\ (aq) + MgSO_4\ (aq) \rightarrow BaSO_4\ (s) + MgCl_2\ (aq)$$

MCAT STRATEGY > > >

In the reaction above, note that both reactions are in the aqueous phase, which means that they are dissolved in water. The barium sulfate product, however, is a solid. Keeping track of phases may seem unhelpful now, but try to do so anyway, as it will be helpful later when you review phase changes and solutions.

The next major type of chemical reaction is the neutralization reaction. In such a process, an acid and a base react with each other to produce a salt and water. The actual neutralization that takes place can be thought of as a "canceling out" of each proton from the acid with one hydroxide ion from the base, forming a molecule of H_2O. Despite the name, neutralizations do not always result in a solution of neutral pH (pH = 7 under standard conditions), since the product salt may be acidic or basic. An example of an acid-base neutralization reaction between an acid (HCl) and a base (NaOH) is shown below. We'll leave it at that, since you will learn a great deal more about acids and bases in Chapter 7.

$$HCl\ (aq) + NaOH\ (aq) \rightarrow NaCl\ (aq) + H_2O\ (l)$$

Almost done! Only two reaction categories remain: combustion and oxidation-reduction. Combustion is a unique reaction in which a compound reacts, or burns, in the presence of elemental oxygen (O_2). The non-oxygen compound is termed the fuel, and it is converted to gaseous products as it reacts with the oxygen. You have almost certainly seen these reactions many times before—for example, any time you have attended a bonfire or struck a butane lighter. Combustion reactions are highly exothermic, meaning that they release a large amount of heat. Students are often confused by this idea; after all, starting a fire must *require* heat, or we would see trees and wooden structures suddenly catch fire wherever oxygen was present. Indeed, heat is needed to overcome the activation energy (or initial energy barrier) of a combustion process, as you will see in Chapter 6. Once this barrier is crossed, however, much more thermal energy can then be released. On the MCAT as in real life, the fuel in most combustion reactions is an organic compound that contains carbon and hydrogen. Burning such a hydrocarbon reactant produces carbon dioxide and water, as seen below in the combustion of octane.

$$C_3H_8\ (g) + 5\ O_2\ (g) \rightarrow 3\ CO_2\ (g) + 4\ H_2O\ (g)$$

By Test Day, the process of "hydrocarbon plus oxygen produces carbon dioxide and water vapor" should be etched into your memory as a classic combustion reaction. However, not all combustion fuels are hydrocarbons. In chemistry class or lab, you may have observed the combustion of sulfur, a reaction which produces striking blue flames. This reaction is written below. The takeaway is that you should have combustion in mind whenever seeing *any* compound or element burn in oxygen to produce one or more gaseous products.

> > **CONNECTIONS** < <

Chapter 12 of Biochemistry

$$S\ (s) + O_2\ (g) \rightarrow SO_2\ (g)$$

Finally, we have oxidation-reduction, or redox reactions. We devote an entire chapter of this book (Chapter 8) to these processes, so we will discuss them here only briefly. Redox reactions involve a transfer of electrons from one species to another. The species that gives up electrons is said to become oxidized, while the species that gains electrons becomes reduced. Both reactants experience a change in oxidation state, which we will not delve into here, although for now it can be conceptualized as something like the electronic charge on an atom. Note that oxidation and reduction always go hand in hand; you will never see a complete reaction where only one of the two occurs. Redox reactions are vital to our physiological function and are thus a favorite topic of the MCAT test-makers.

MCAT STRATEGY > > >

This section of the book is a great place to start practicing finding overlap between pieces of MCAT content. Ask yourself this: which reactions can fit into multiple categories? The combustion of sulfur, for example, is also a synthesis or combination reaction, and all combustions are redox reactions. Don't just memorize discrete chunks of information; thinking actively is essential to MCAT success!

3. Balancing Equations and Stoichiometry

You may have noticed that some of the examples in the previous section included numbers before some or all of the species involved. For example, the reaction of potassium was written as 2 K + $ZnCl_2$ → 2 KCl + Zn, *not* as K + $ZnCl_2$ → KCl + Zn. (We omitted phase designations for the sake of simplicity.) To understand why these numbers are needed, we must transition into our next topic: balancing chemical reactions. You already know that elements can carry different charges depending on their location on the periodic table. Sodium, an alkali metal, forms an Na^+ ion, oxygen usually exists as an O^{2-} ion, and so on. When ions of different charges combine to create an ionic compound, they do so in a way that makes the compound electrically neutral. Sodium oxide, then, is not NaO, as this would have a net charge of (+ 1) + (−2) = −1. Instead, it exists as Na_2O, with a net charge of (2)(+ 1) + (−2) = 0. The small "2" is termed a subscript and denotes the presence of two sodium ions in the compound.

Let's now imagine that we place our Na_2O in water (H_2O), and sodium hydroxide (NaOH) forms. We can initially write this reaction as Na_2O (*s*) + H_2O (*l*) → NaOH (*aq*). While this reaction contains the correct compounds, it violates an important law of chemistry and physics: the law of conservation of mass. Apart from extreme circumstances like nuclear reactions, mass cannot be created from nothing or destroyed out of nowhere. Furthermore, in basic chemistry, elements do not change identities over the course of a reaction, so the mass of an element on the reactant side of a process must equal that of the same element on the product side. In the reaction above, the reactant side includes two sodium ions while the products include only one. We call such an equation "unbalanced," and the process required to correct it is termed "balancing" the reaction.

To balance a reaction, we must change the numbers of certain products or reactants present so that the two sides of the reaction have the same number of each atom. However, we cannot use subscripts to do this, as we did with the 2 in Na_2O. Instead, we can place a number, called a coefficient, in front of the compound. Try this with our sodium oxide reaction. Since the reactant side of the unbalanced reaction has twice the sodium atoms of the product side, place a coefficient of 2 in front of NaOH, as shown below.

$$Na_2O \ (s) + H_2O \ (l) → 2 \ NaOH \ (aq)$$

Now, count each atom. We have two sodium atoms, two oxygen atoms, and two hydrogen atoms on each side, so we're done—the reaction is balanced! One quick note on our process: it was no accident that we began with sodium rather than oxygen. A key strategy in general chemistry is to start simple whenever possible. When balancing reactions, then, you should begin with the element present in the fewest compounds. This way, you can get these atoms out of the way early, and you may find that the atoms present in more species become balanced along the way. Of course, when two elements "tie," you can choose to begin with either. Here, we could have begun with hydrogen instead of sodium, as both exist in only one reactant and one product.

While you will not see it as often, note that a properly-written chemical reaction must be balanced with regard to charge as well as atoms. This stems from another law of physics: the law of conservation of charge. In an isolated system, positive and negative charges do not simply appear and disappear. As such, the *net* charge of the reactant side of a reaction should be identical to the net charge of the product side.

With this discussion complete, we now turn to *why* balancing reactions is so important. After all, if we are simply looking at what happens in a process, the exact number of each reactant or product molecule does not

MCAT STRATEGY > > >

Never assume a reaction is already balanced unless you are told so! The MCAT can, and will, present equations in unbalanced form, causing students who rush to miss easy points.

> > CONNECTIONS < <

Chapter 6 of Physics

really matter. These numbers become important, however, when we need to use a chemical reaction mathematically. In the introduction to this chapter, we mentioned stoichiometry, which is a special set of tools that allows us to calculate the amounts of reactants or products involved in a balanced reaction. Stoichiometry may be a source of bad memories from chemistry class, but the processes involved are simple. Each mathematical step relies on a basic principle: that we can begin with a piece of given information and manipulate it to find another piece using known relationships. To do this most effectively, keep track of units at all times! The main units involved in stoichiometry are grams, moles, and grams per mole (g/mol).

> ## MCAT STRATEGY > > >
>
> This idea of "units are important" is a common theme throughout MCAT science. Many physics and chemistry questions can be answered with only an understanding of units and a level head! As you read these chapters, pay close attention to any units you see, and think critically about their relationships with each other.

Let's introduce this set of tools through example. Suppose that 88 grams of propane (C_3H_8) are completely combusted in the presence of abundant oxygen gas. How many moles of CO_2 will be produced? First, write out the unbalanced chemical reaction. Because this is a combustion reaction, propane must react with O_2 to produce CO_2 and H_2O.

$$C_3H_8 + O_2 \rightarrow CO_2 + H_2O$$

Next, balance the reaction. Both carbon and hydrogen are present in only one species on each side, so we can begin with either. Let's start with carbon, of which we have three atoms on the reactant side and only one in the products. To correct this, add a coefficient of 3 before carbon dioxide:

$$C_3H_8 + O_2 \rightarrow 3\ CO_2 + H_2O$$

Hydrogen is also unbalanced, which we can fix by placing a 4 in front of H_2O:

$$C_3H_8 + O_2 \rightarrow 3\ CO_2 + 4\ H_2O$$

Finally, we turn to oxygen. The reactant side contains two oxygen atoms, while the product side contains $(3)(2) + (4)(1) = 10$. Our reaction will thus be balanced if we add a coefficient of 5 in front of O_2 on the reactant side:

$$C_3H_8 + 5\ O_2 \rightarrow 3\ CO_2 + 4\ H_2O$$

Once the balanced reaction is written, return to the question and locate any quantitative (number-based) information given. Here, this information is the 88 grams of propane that reacted. The question wants us to use this value to find the amount of carbon dioxide produced. This is where the balanced reaction becomes so valuable; it directly tells us that for every atom of propane on the reactant side, we can expect 3 atoms of carbon dioxide on the product side. Remember, atoms directly correlate with moles, so every *mole* of propane reacted should create 3 moles of CO_2. We call this relationship the mole ratio. Importantly, this ratio does not carry over to grams! We cannot multiply our 88 grams of propane by 3 to find grams of CO_2. Instead, we must first convert grams of propane to moles. This is a vital step in a stoichiometry procedure—after writing out the balanced reaction, you *must* convert the given mass of product or reactant to moles.

Luckily, this is a simple step. Propane has a formula of C_3H_8. According to the periodic table, carbon has an atomic weight of 12 amu and thus a molar mass of 12 g/mol. Hydrogen, as we should remember, has a molar mass of 1 g/mol. (Using approximate values is fine.) The molar mass of propane, then, is $(3)(12\ \text{g/mol}) + (8)(1\ \text{g/mol}) = 44\ \text{g/mol}$. Here is where we begin to see the importance of units. Stoichiometry utilizes an incredibly helpful method called dimensional analysis, in which a quantity with certain units is converted to another quantity with different units by taking advantage of the fact that multiplying a value by one does not alter it. During this process, a unit in the numerator of a fraction can be canceled if multiplied by a fraction with the same unit in the denominator, and vice versa. Let's give it a try here.

$$88 \text{ \sout{g propane}} \left(\frac{1 \text{ mol propane}}{44 \text{ \sout{g propane}}} \right) = 2 \text{ mol propane}$$

Pay close attention to what happened here. We began with grams of propane, which we needed to convert to moles. We found the conversion rate between the two units: 1 mole of propane is equal to 44 grams. Since these quantities are equal, we could place them in a fraction that is effectively equivalent to one. By placing the unit that we *want* in the numerator of this fraction and the unit that we need to *cancel* in the denominator, we could multiply to get our answer.

Now that we have the amount of propane in moles, we can use the mole ratio from the balanced reaction to find moles of carbon dioxide produced. Recall that this ratio is 3 moles of carbon dioxide for every mole of propane, or 3:1. Again, these quantities are equivalent, so we can set up a fraction in which the unit that we *want* (moles of CO_2) is in the numerator:

$$2 \text{ \sout{mol propane}} \left(\frac{3 \text{ mol } CO_2}{1 \text{ \sout{mol propane}}} \right) = 6 \text{ mol } CO_2$$

This is the essence of stoichiometry: start with a quantity, progressively multiply by conversion factors to cancel unwanted units, and end with the quantity that we are asked to find.

MCAT STRATEGY > > >

Be sure to include units in your written-out work when completing stoichiometry problems. Cross out any units that cancel, and double-check that the units that remain are those that you want your answer to have. If your units differ from those in the answer choices, it's likely that you made a mistake.

Now that we understand the basics, let's cover the remaining stoichiometric math the MCAT will expect you to understand. In particular, one concept that gives many students migraines is limiting reagent. To define this term, let's deviate from chemistry for a moment. Imagine that you are baking cupcakes that require two cups of flour, one cup of sugar, and four tablespoons of salt per dozen. You check your kitchen and see that you have four cups of flour, two cups of sugar, and four tablespoons of salt. How many cupcakes can you bake? Looking at your flour, you have enough to make two dozen cupcakes, and the same is true of your sugar. However, four tablespoons of salt can only make one dozen. If you want to follow the recipe and not have salt-less cupcakes, then, you'll need to bake only one dozen cupcakes. Here, salt was your limiting reagent.

For all the stress it causes students, limiting reagent works just as simply with chemical reactions as it does with cupcakes. A balanced chemical reaction tells us exactly how much of each reactant we need to make a certain amount of each product. If we have enough of one reactant, but not enough of another, this latter reactant limits the amount of product we can make. The amount of product is thus solely determined by the limiting reagent. The other, non-limiting reactant is said to be in excess, and no matter how much of this excess reactant we add, we will not make any more product. For this reason, a crucial first step of any stoichiometry problem is identifying the

> > CONNECTIONS < <

Chapter 4 of Chemistry

limiting reagent. (You'll remember that we did *not* do this in our earlier example with propane—this is because that scenario directly told us that oxygen was in excess, so we knew that propane was limiting right off the bat.) Finally, note that the concept of limiting reagent carries with it the assumption that *any* species reacts to completion. In real-life chemistry, reactants are rarely completely "used up," and the end of the reaction instead consists of an equilibrium between reactants and products. When dealing with limiting reagent, however, you can assume that the limiting species reacts completely and only the excess reactants remain at the end.

Numerous so-called shortcuts exist for finding the limiting reagent, but these tend to confuse more often than they save time. The safest way to identify the limiting species is to calculate the amount of product that would form from the complete reaction of each reactant. The limiting reagent is the species predicted to produce the smallest amount of product. As an example, say that 50.6 grams of chromium (III) oxide is reacted with 24.0 grams of aluminum, as shown below. Which reactant is limiting, noting that the approximate molar masses of Cr_2O_3 and Al are 152 g/mol and 27 g/mol, respectively?

$$Cr_2O_3 + 2\ Al \rightarrow 2\ Cr + Al_2O_3$$

To solve, let us compare the quantity of product generated from the complete reaction of Cr_2O_3 to that formed from the complete reaction of Al.

$$50.6\ \text{g}\ \cancel{Cr_2O_3}\left(\frac{1\ \text{mol}\ \cancel{Cr_2O_3}}{152\ \text{g}}\right)\left(\frac{2\ \text{mol Cr}}{1\ \text{mol}\ \cancel{Cr_2O_3}}\right) = 0.66\ \text{mol Cr}$$

$$24.0\ \text{g}\ \cancel{Al}\left(\frac{1\ \text{mol}\ \cancel{Al}}{27\ \text{g}}\right)\left(\frac{2\ \text{mol Cr}}{2\ \cancel{\text{mol Al}}}\right) = 0.88\ \text{mol Cr}$$

If this math looks intimidating without a calculator, don't worry—rounding and shortcuts make it much easier. For example, for the Cr_2O_3 calculation, we know that 50 is one-third of 150, and one-third multiplied by 2 is two-thirds, or 0.66. For the Al calculation, 24/27 simplifies to 8/9, which is less than 9/10 (or 0.9), but not by much—and which is certainly larger than 0.66. Since the complete reaction of Cr_2O_3 forms the smaller molar amount of product, Cr_2O_3 is our limiting reagent and will react completely, while Al is present in excess and will remain to some extent at the end of the reaction.

Let's review this process in an attempt to prevent a few *extremely* common mistakes students make with limiting reagent. In the example above, we used both the mole ratios we obtained from the balanced reaction *and* the amount of each reactant that we actually had in our calculations. Neither of these pieces of information is sufficient on its own! Many students mistakenly think, for example, that since 50.6 g of Cr_2O_3 was present and only 24 g of Al, that Al must be limiting because we have less of it. As we saw above, this is incorrect, for multiple reasons—first and foremost that we cannot compare grams directly, only moles. Even if we converted these values to moles, however, we would also need to consult the balanced reaction to find the relative molar amounts needed of each species. If 3 moles of reactant X are required to react with species Y, and we have 2 moles of X and 1 mole of Y, then X will be limiting despite its larger molar quantity, because we need *even more* of X to react with Y in the proper stoichiometric ratio.

> ## MCAT STRATEGY > > >
>
> Our Cr_2O_3/Al example is a good example of the impact of molar mass. We had fewer grams of Al to begin, and more moles of Al than Cr_2O_3 were required to form one mole of product. With this information alone, we might think that Al was our limiting reagent. However, since Al has such a *lower* molar mass than Cr_2O_3, the amount we had constituted a much larger molar amount, leading to the formation of more product.

4. Yield

We've almost wrapped up our discussion of reactions and stoichiometric principles, but until this point, we have stayed within the realm of theory ("how many moles of product do we predict will form?") Calculations like these are great at telling us what will happen if the experiment proceeds perfectly, but this virtually never happens in a real-life lab setting. Some reactant sticks to the side of the flask, a side reaction reduces the number of moles of product formed, or our starting mixture was weighed improperly due to the presence of contaminants . . . the list of ways an experiment can go wrong is a very long one. Chemists even have a way to quantify the extent to which our actual results resemble the calculated predictions we make using stoichiometry. This is done by calculating the percent yield of the reaction. Percent yield can be calculated according to Equation 1.

Equation 1.
$$\text{percent yield} = \left(\frac{\text{actual mass of desired product}}{\text{theoretical mass of desired product}} \right) \times 100\%$$

Let's attempt a practice question. Consider the reaction $2\,H_2O \rightarrow H_2 + 2\,O_2$, which is often performed using electrolysis. What is the percent yield of this reaction if 1.31 grams of hydrogen gas were produced from 30 grams of water? If you are unsure where to begin, use Equation 1 as a guide. The actual mass of desired product (or actual yield) was given as 1.31 grams. In fact, actual yield *must* be given, since we cannot possibly guess the amount of product formed in this particular experiment, in which any number of things may have gone wrong. The only quantity left to be calculated, then, is the theoretical yield, which we can determine using classic stoichiometry:

$$\text{theoretical yield} = 30\ \cancel{\text{g }H_2O}\ \left(\frac{1\ \cancel{\text{mol }H_2O}}{18\ \text{g}}\right)\left(\frac{1\ \cancel{\text{mol }H_2}}{2\ \cancel{\text{mol }H_2O}}\right)\left(\frac{2\ \text{g}}{1\ \cancel{\text{mol }H_2}}\right) = 1.67\ \text{g }H_2$$

Now, it is a simple matter to plug in our two known values and calculate the percent yield:

$$\text{percent yield} = \frac{1.31\ \text{g }H_2}{1.67\ \text{g }H_2} \times 100\% = 78.4\%$$

Of course, no calculator is provided on the MCAT, so you would not need to pinpoint the answer quite so exactly. Instead, our reasoning may go something like this: 1.31 divided by 1.67 is similar to 13 divided by 17. This quantity is around 14/18, which can be reduced to 7/9, or 77.7%. So our right answer is somewhere between 70 and 80%, which is close enough for the MCAT.

Congratulations—now that you have covered atoms and reactions, bonding, and chemical reactions and stoichiometry, you have made it through the chemistry topics considered most foundational to the MCAT. In the remaining chapters, you will begin to learn about more advanced and specific areas of chemistry, from phases and solutions to acid-base chemistry. Good luck!

5. Must-Knows

> Chemical formulas:
  – Molecular formula: gives number of each atom present in a single molecule
  – Empirical formula: reduces molecular formula to smallest whole-number ratio
> Percent composition by mass = (mass contributed to molecule by element in question) / (total mass of molecule) × 100
> Chemical reactions involve one or more reactants changing into one or more products through the breaking and forming of bonds.
  – The atoms stay the same—only the bonding changes.
> Types of chemical reaction:
  – Synthesis: two or more reactants → one product
  – Decomposition: one reactant → two or more products
  – Single replacement: one element/group replaces another in a compound
  – Double replacement: two elements/groups of two different compounds switch places
  – Neutralization: acid + base → water + salt

- – Combustion: fuel (generally a hydrocarbon) burns in oxygen; highly exothermic
  - For a hydrocarbon fuel: $C_?H_? + ? \ O_2 \rightarrow ? \ CO_2 + ? \ H_2O$ (details of coefficients depend on the hydrocarbon)
- – Reduction-oxidation (redox): involves transfer of electrons
> Balancing reactions
  - – According to law of conservation of mass: same # of each type of atom must be present on reactant and product sides
  - – According to law of conservation of charge: net charge must be the same on both sides
> Stoichiometry: set of tools for chemical reactions that allows us to use given quantities to find unknown ones
  - – Dimensional analysis allows progressive canceling of units until desired quantity is found
  - – One common set of steps: given grams of reactant → convert to moles → use mole ratio from reaction to find moles of desired product → convert to grams
> Limiting reagent = the reagent that is fully used in a reaction
  - – Must take into account amount present *and* balanced reaction
> Percent yield = $\dfrac{\text{actual mass of desired product}}{\text{theoretical mass of desired product}} \times 100\%$
  - – Measures how close results were to those predicted by calculation

Practice Passage

A group of students were tasked with the study of reactions that produce precipitates when aqueous solutions are combined. Students were given nine unique solutions in dark brown glass bottles and told to mix equal portions of any two of these solutions in reaction wells, using pipets. Students observed the products of their combinations, and noted the formation of precipitates, bubbling, color changes or any other relevant changes to the mixture. Select observations are presented in Table 1.

All experiments were performed in a fume hood to prevent exposure to potentially noxious fumes. In order to prevent the formation of insoluble hydroxides from the Cu^{2+} or Fe^{3+} ions found in two of the solutions used, a small amount of acid was added to these solutions. The professor noted that the dark brown bottles can help prevent light-solution reactions common to transition metals in the fifth period and below.

Table 1. Observations in Mixes of Aqueous Solutions (Note: NR means no reaction occurred)

	NaCl	NaOH	Na$_2$S	Na$_2$CO$_3$
KNO$_3$	NR	NR	NR	NR
AgNO$_3$	White ppt.	Beige ppt.	Black ppt.	White ppt.
Ca(NO$_3$)$_2$	NR	White ppt.	White ppt.	White ppt.
Cu(NO$_3$)$_2$ (blue)	NR	Pale, blue gel	Black ppt.	Blue-green ppt.
Fe(NO$_3$)$_3$ (orange)	NR	Orange gel	Black ppt.	Orange ppt.

Finally, two students were presented with 2 different unknown mixtures, and told that the mixtures each contained a solution used in their earlier experiment. Mass spectroscopy revealed that both unknown mixtures contained sodium sulfate, but the other species in the mixture was determined by reacting the unknown mixture with the known solutions and comparing the results to the previous experiment.

Student A was given 20 mL of a colorless unknown mixture. After testing with all nine solutions, the calcium nitrate solution was the only one to cause the formation of a precipitate upon addition to the unknown. As a result, they were able to correctly report the ions present in the unknown mixture.

Student B was given 20 mL of an orange unknown mixture. The student reacted the unknown with a small amount of only one of the known solutions and found that no precipitate formed. Student B was able to identify the ions present in the unknown mixture correctly from this one test.

1. What is the most likely identity of the precipitate formed by combining the iron (III) nitrate and sodium sulfide solutions?
   A. FeS
   B. FeS$_2$
   C. Fe$_2$S$_3$
   D. Fe$_3$S$_2$

2. In aqueous solution Fe^{3+} will undergo a hydrolysis reaction to form an orange gelatinous precipitate. Which of the following reactions best describes the formation of this precipitate?
    A. Fe^{3+} (aq) → $FeOH_2^+$ (s) + H^+ (aq)
    B. Fe^{3+} (aq) + 3 H_2O → $Fe(OH)_3$ (s) + 3 H^+ (aq)
    C. Fe^{3+} (aq) + NO_3^- (aq) + 2 H^+ (aq) → $Fe(OH)_2$ (s) + NO (g)
    D. Fe^{3+} (aq) + 2 H_2O (l) → $Fe(OH)_2$ (s) + H_2 (g)

3. When the copper (II) nitrate and iron (III) nitrate solutions were reacted with the sodium carbonate solution, some bubble formation was observed by certain students. What was the most likely identity of the bubbles?
    A. Carbon dioxide
    B. Carbon monoxide
    C. Elemental nitrogen
    D. Nitrogen monoxide

4. Student C was given an unknown wrapped in aluminum foil. The student asked the professor why his unknown was the only one wrapped in aluminum foil and the professor responded, "To prevent light from causing an unwanted side reaction". Which of the following was most likely in the unknown solution, such that the professor wanted to keep it from being exposed to light?
    A. Copper (II) nitrate, because exposure to light causes the solution to turn blue.
    B. Silver nitrate, because exposure to light can cause the precipitation of elemental silver.
    C. Sodium sulfide, because exposure to light causes the formation of the smell of rotten eggs.
    D. Sodium carbonate, because exposure to produces carbon dioxide gas.

5. What was the most likely identity of the precipitate obtained by Student A?
    A. $AgSO_4$
    B. $CaNO_3$
    C. $CaSO_4$
    D. $NaNO_3$

6. Which of the following solutions is most likely to require a brown bottle for proper use in the experiment?
    A. Mn
    B. Cd
    C. Si
    D. Os

7. Which of the following reaction types most likely occurs when mixing NaCl and $AgNO_3$?
    A. Decomposition
    B. Neutralization
    C. Combustion
    D. Replacement

Practice Passage Explanations

A group of students were tasked with the study of reactions that produce precipitates when aqueous solutions are combined. Students were given nine unique solutions in dark brown glass bottles and told to mix equal portions of any two of these solutions in reaction wells, using pipets. Students observed the products of their combinations, and noted the formation of precipitates, bubbling, color changes or any other relevant changes to the mixture. Select recordings are produced in Table 1.

Key terms: precipitates, nine solutions, color changes

Cause and effect: 2-solution mixes → changes recorded in Table 1; insoluble mixture → ppt.

All experiments were performed in a fume hood to prevent exposure to potentially noxious fumes. In order to prevent the formation of insoluble hydroxides from the Cu^{2+} or Fe^{3+} ions found in two of the solutions used, a small amount of acid was added to these solutions. The professor noted that the dark brown bottles can help prevent light-solution reactions common to transition metals in the fifth period and below.

Key terms: noxious fumes, hydroxides, light-solution reactions

Cause and effect: adding acid to aqueous Cu/Fe solutions prevents the formation of insoluble Cu/Fe hydroxides

Table 1. Observations in Mixes of Aqueous Solutions (Note: NR means no reaction occurred)

	NaCl	NaOH	Na_2S	Na_2CO_3
KNO_3	NR	NR	NR	NR
$AgNO_3$	White ppt.	Beige ppt.	Black ppt.	White ppt.
$Ca(NO_3)_2$	NR	White ppt.	White ppt.	White ppt.
$Cu(NO_3)_2$ (blue)	NR	Pale, blue gel	Black ppt.	Blue-green ppt.
$Fe(NO_3)_3$ (orange)	NR	Orange gel	Black ppt.	Orange ppt.

Table 1 shows color/precipitate observations in combination of solutions shown

Finally, two students were presented with 2 different unknown mixtures, and told that the mixtures each contained a solution used in their earlier experiment. Mass spectroscopy revealed that both unknown mixtures contained sodium sulfate, but the other species in the mixture was determined by reacting the unknown mixture with the known solutions and comparing the results to the previous experiment.

Student A was given 20 mL of a colorless unknown mixture. After testing with all nine solutions, the calcium nitrate solution was the only one to cause the formation of a precipitate upon addition to the unknown. As a result, they were able to correctly report the ions present in the unknown mixture.

Student B was given 20 mL of an orange unknown mixture. The student reacted the unknown with a small amount of only one of the known solutions and found that no precipitate formed. Student B was able to identify the ions present in the unknown mixture correctly from this one test.

Key terms: mass spectroscopy, sodium nitrate, unknown mixture

Contrast: Student A vs. Student B; different unknowns, opposite approaches (trying all vs. trying only 1 solution); both obtained correct results

Cause and effect: Student A precipitation only with calcium nitrate suggests a Ca-based precipitate; Student B results too vague to pin down

1. C is correct. Iron (III), Fe^{3+}, and sulfide, S^{2-}, combine to give an equal number of positive and negative charges, hence there are two Fe^{3+} ions and three S^{2-} ions in the formula, Fe_2S_3. These molecules are Iron (II) sulfide, Iron disulfide/persulfide, which is arranged Fe-S-S, and Fe_3S_2 is formed in response to very high pressures, which are not described in this passage and is unlikely to form.

2. B is correct. The Fe^{3+} (aq) has water molecules acting as Lewis bases and that coordinate to the Fe^{3+} ion. The ion is electron withdrawing and makes the polar covalent bond of these coordinated water molecules, even more polarized, resulting is dissociation of hydrogen ions and producing iron (III) hydroxide as the "orange gelatinous precipitate." This precipitate is consistent with the observations observed in Table 1, when the iron (III) nitrate solution is combined with the sodium hydroxide solution.

   A, C, D: Choice A is not reasonable, since cations, such as $FeOH_2^+$, are unlikely to form solids at most temperatures, and must be associated with anions of equal charge to form species with no net charge in the solid state. The reactions in C and D are not balanced with respect to charge.

3. A is correct. Since the professor added a small amount of acid to the copper (II) nitrate and iron (III) nitrate solutions, when combined with the sodium carbonate solution, the acid reacted with the carbonate ion to generate carbon dioxide gas.

$$2 H^+ (aq) + CO_3^{2-} (aq) \rightarrow H_2O (l) + CO_2 (g)$$

   B, C, D: To produce these gases, the metal ions would have to be very good reducing agents. Both Cu^{2+} and Fe^{3+} are already in their highest commonly observed oxidations states, and are unlikely to be oxidized further under these conditions.

4. B is correct. One of the characteristic reactions of most silver salts is the production of finely divided silver metal when exposed to light. This formed the basis for the photographic industry for many years. The colloidal silver does not reflect light efficiently like crystalline silver metal and appears black, because it absorbs all of the wavelengths of visible radiation.

   A, C, D: Copper (II) solutions are blue because they absorb all other colors in the visible spectrum, due to electronic transitions of the Cu^{2+} ion. Choice A can be eliminated. Sodium sulfide, can produce the rotten egg smell of H_2S, if reacted with an acid, but will not undergo this reaction due to exposure to light. Choice C can be eliminated. Sodium carbonate will produce carbon dioxide gas if reacted with an acid, but not by exposure to light. Choice D can be eliminated.

5. C is correct. The passage tells us that a precipitate was only formed when Student A's unknown was combined with calcium nitrate, suggesting calcium and/or sulfate should be involved in the answer.

   A, B, D: While silver sulfate is insoluble, we have no evidence to indicate that silver is involved in the reaction which generated the precipitate. Solubility rules tell us that all nitrates are soluble.

6. D is correct. According to the 2nd paragraph, light-solution reactions are common to the transition metals in period 5 and below. Only osmium (Z = 76) is both a transition element and is found in period 6.

7. D is correct. In a replacement reaction, one or more elements replace other elements in a compound. Here, mixing these two salts to product a white precipitate likely involved silver or sodium replacing the other. That is, the precipitate is likely to be either $AgCl$ or $NaNO_3$.

A: Decomposition involves a single large molecule breaking down into multiple products. Here, we're starting with multiple reactants.
B: Neutralization would require an acid and a base. The question mentions two salts.
C: Combustion requires burning a compound in the presence of O_2. There is no O_2 mentioned in this reaction.

Independent Questions

1. Which of the following exemplifies a metathesis reaction?
   A. $2\ C_2H_6 + 7\ O_2 \rightarrow 4\ CO_2 + 6\ H_2O$
   B. $2\ Na + Cl_2 \rightarrow 2\ NaCl$
   C. $ZnBr_2 + Ni \rightarrow NiBr_2$
   D. $BaF_2 + Li_2SO_4 \rightarrow 2\ LiF + BaSO_4$

2. Sulfur dioxide reacts with diatomic oxygen to form sulfur trioxide. This reaction involves which of the following?
   I.   Oxidation
   II. Combination
   III. Substitution

   A. I only
   B. II only
   C. I and II only
   D. I, II, and III

3. Octane (C_8H_{18}) reacts with gaseous oxygen to form water vapor and carbon dioxide. When this reaction is written out and balanced, what will be the coefficient for the oxygen gas?
   A. 16
   B. 17
   C. 18
   D. 25

4. What is the percent oxygen by mass in deoxyribose ($C_5H_{10}O_4$)?
   A. 7%
   B. 36%
   C. 47%
   D. 64%

5. How many ions are expected to be present in a 1 L solution of 1.5 M NaCl? Assume ions present due to the dissociation of water are negligible.
   A. 3.0
   B. 1.806×10^{22}
   C. 9.03×10^{23}
   D. 1.806×10^{24}

6. Lithium hydroxide reacts with silver nitrate in a double displacement reaction. 48 g of lithium hydroxide and 85 g of silver nitrate are placed in a vessel and react to completion. If 50 g of silver hydroxide is obtained, what is the percent yield of silver hydroxide?
   A. 20%
   B. 40%
   C. 80%
   D. 125%

7. An organic compound known to contain only carbon and hydrogen is burned in the presence of excess oxygen. Quantitative analysis shows that this reaction produced 22 g CO_2 and 13.5 g H_2O. If the reaction went to completion, which of the following is the empirical formula of the organic compound?
   A. CH_3
   B. C_3H
   C. C_2H_5
   D. C_3H_9

8. Which of the statements below accurately describes the limiting reagent of a chemical reaction?
   A. It is always the reactant present in the smallest molar quantity.
   B. The amount of product expected to form when it reacts completely is termed the theoretical yield.
   C. The only information necessary to find it is the amount of each reactant present.
   D. It is the reactant present in the largest molar quantity at equilibrium.

Independent Question Explanations

1. D is correct. A metathesis reaction is synonymous with a double displacement reaction, in which two reactants exchange cations. (Alternatively, you can think of the two reactants switching anions.) In choice D, barium is initially paired with fluoride and lithium with sulfate. On the product side, we see that barium is now paired with sulfate, while lithium is paired with fluoride. The term "metathesis" is most commonly used when one of the products is insoluble, as is the case with barium sulfate. The other answers are incorrect; choice A is a combustion reaction, choice B is a combination reaction, and option C is a single displacement.

2. C is correct. The reaction described in the question stem is shown below:

$$2 SO_2 + O_2 \rightarrow 2 SO_3$$

The presence of large amounts of oxygen are an initial hint that oxidation may be taking place, but we can confirm this by the fact that the oxidation number of sulfur changes from +4 to +6. Oxidation is the loss of electrons, which is precisely what occurs when oxidation state becomes more positive. Thus, Roman numeral I is accurate. This reaction is also a combination reaction, since two reactants combine to form a single product. However, this is not a substitution, since no part of SO_2 is actually replaced.

3. D is correct. The unbalanced reaction can be written out as follows:

$$C_8H_{18} + O_2 \rightarrow CO_2 + H_2O$$

Let's begin by attempting to balance the carbon atoms, which requires multiplying the CO_2 on the right side by 8.

$$C_8H_{18} + O_2 \rightarrow 8 CO_2 + H_2O$$

Unfortunately, both hydrogen and oxygen are still present in different numbers on each side. Let's save oxygen for last, since it is present in more than one species on the right side. Balance the hydrogen atoms by multiplying the H_2O on the right by 9.

$$C_8H_{18} + O_2 \rightarrow 8 CO_2 + 9 H_2O$$

This leaves us with 2 oxygen atoms on the left and 25 on the right. We typically prefer whole-number coefficients in front of each species in a reaction, but the only value that 2 can be multiplied by to yield 25 is 12.5.

$$C_8H_{18} + 12.5 O_2 \rightarrow 8 CO_2 + 9 H_2O$$

To finish, multiply all species by 2 to remove the decimal, turning 12.5 into 25.

$$2 C_8H_{18} + 25 O_2 \rightarrow 16 CO_2 + 18 H_2O$$

4. C is correct. To solve this question, first find the total molar mass of the compound. Use the periodic table if you do not remember the masses of the component elements! Note that, since our answers are fairly far apart, we can round to the nearest whole number.

$$5 (12 \text{ g/mol}) + 10 (1 \text{ g/mol}) + 4 (16 \text{ g/mol}) = 134 \text{ g/mol}$$

Next, calculate how much of this value comes from oxygen.

$$4 (16 \text{ g/mol}) = 64 \text{ g/mol}$$

Finally, divide the mass of oxygen by the total mass.

$$(64 \text{ g/mol}) / (134 \text{ g/mol}) = 32/67 = \text{slightly less than } 50\%$$

Choice C is the closest answer available.

5. D is correct. To find the number of individual ions present, we must use Avogadro's number, as follows. Note that NaCl is soluble and dissociates into two ions (Na^+ and Cl^-) per NaCl molecule.

$$1.5 \frac{\text{mol NaCl}}{\text{L}} \times \frac{6.02 \times 10^{23} \text{ molecules}}{\text{mol NaCl}} \times \frac{2 \text{ ions}}{\text{molecule}} = 18.06 \times 10^{23} \text{ ions}$$

$$= 1.806 \times 10^{24} \text{ ions}$$

6. C is correct. The balanced chemical equation for the described reaction is below:

$$LiOH + AgNO_3 \rightarrow AgOH + LiNO_3$$

Percent yield is calculated by dividing the actual yield (50 g) by the theoretical yield, then multiplying by 100. First, then, let us find the theoretical yield. To do so, we must figure out which reagent is limiting. Consulting the periodic table allows us to discern that the molar masses of lithium hydroxide and silver nitrate are approximately 24 g/mol and 170 g/mol, respectively. We thus have 2 moles of LiOH and 0.5 moles of $AgNO_3$. Since the stoichiometric ratio of LiOH to $AgNO_3$ is 1:1, $AgNO_3$ is limiting. Finally, note that the molar mass of AgOH is approximately 125 g/mol.

$$\text{theoretical yield} = 0.5 \text{ mol } AgNO_3 \times \frac{1 \text{ mol AgOH}}{1 \text{ mol } AgNO_3}$$
$$\times \frac{125 \text{ g AgOH}}{1 \text{ mol}} = 62.5 \text{ g AgOH}$$

$$\text{percent yield} = \frac{50 \text{ g actual}}{62.5 \text{ g theoretical}} \times 100\% = 80\%$$

7. A is correct. Since this compound contains only carbon and hydrogen, the only products of its combustion will be CO_2 and H_2O. Thus, all of the carbon present in the initial reactant must be found in the form of CO_2 at the end of the reaction; similarly, all of the original hydrogen must be found in the form of H_2O. We can thus perform the following calculations:

$$22 \text{ g } CO_2 \times \frac{1 \text{ mol } CO_2}{44 \text{ g}} \times \frac{1 \text{ mol C}}{1 \text{ mol } CO_2} = 0.5 \text{ mol C}$$

$$13.5 \text{ g } H_2O \times \frac{1 \text{ mol } H_2O}{18 \text{ g}} \times \frac{2 \text{ mol H}}{1 \text{ mol } H_2O} = 1.5 \text{ mol H}$$

Note that we multiplied our moles of H_2O by 2 because each mole of H_2O contains two moles of hydrogen. From the calculations above, we can see that our compound contains three times as many hydrogen atoms as it does carbon. Choices A and D are the only options that fit this description, and choice D is not an empirical formula, leaving choice A as our answer.

8. B is correct. The limiting reagent is that which is used up first in a chemical reaction. Theoretical yield is defined as the amount of product expected to form from the complete reaction of the limiting reagent, assuming that the reaction goes perfectly (choice B is correct). The other options are false statements. Regarding choice A, the limiting reagent may be present in a larger molar quantity than the other reactant(s) in situations where the reaction stoichiometry indicates that more moles of the limiting reagent are required than are moles of the other reactant(s). Choice C is similarly false because the balanced chemical equation is generally required to determine which reactant is limiting. Finally, choice D is false; limiting reagent does not directly relate to equilibrium, and if anything, in many cases we would expect less of the limiting reactant to be present at equilibrium since it is the reactant that is used up first.

This page left intentionally blank.

Equilibrium and Thermodynamics

0. Introduction

In the previous chapters, we covered the fundamentals underlying chemical reactions: atoms, molecules, and the types of interactions in which they take part. However, discussions of these basic concepts often oversimplify what *actually* happens when molecules react. For example, our review of stoichiometry generally assumed that the reactions involved went to completion, meaning that one or more reactants was fully converted to products. In this chapter, we will see why this is usually not the case. In doing so, you will learn about the concept of chemical equilibrium, a topic with far-reaching implications. For this reason, don't rush your review of this information! A thorough understanding of equilibrium will help you conceptualize enzyme function and bioenergetics, described in Biochemistry Chapters 3 and 12, respectively. The other topic covered in this chapter—thermodynamics—will also give you a chemistry context for the concepts you will encounter in Chapter 4 of your physics book.

> **> > CONNECTIONS < <**
>
> **Chapters 3 and 12 of Biochemistry and Chapter 4 of Physics**

1. Equilibrium

Let's jump right in with a natural follow-up question from this chapter introduction. If most chemical reactions do not go to completion, what happens instead? To answer this, we must introduce the concept of reversibility. A reversible chemical reaction is one in which products are converted to reactants at the same time that reactants are converted to products. Consider the generic reaction below, where the letters X, Y, and Z represent reactants and products, and the numbers 3, 2, and (implicitly for reactant X) 1 represent their stoichiometric coefficients.

$$X\,(g) + 3\,Y\,(g) \rightleftharpoons 2\,Z\,(g)$$

Note that the reactants and products are separated by a double-headed arrow ($\rightleftharpoons$), which denotes reversibility. Imagine that we begin with only reactants X and Y in a closed container. At first, the reaction proceeds only in the forward direction, since no Z is even present to act as a reactant in the reverse reaction. As the process progresses, however, and some Z is made, the reverse reaction will start to take place simultaneously with the forward reaction. The rate of a chemical reaction is dependent on the concentration(s) of its reactant(s) (with the exception of zero-order reactions, which you will learn about in Chapter 6), so as X and Y are converted to Z, the reverse rate will

MCAT STRATEGY > > >

When reviewing equilibrium, be very careful to identify exactly what is taking place, while avoiding making unfounded assumptions. For example, some students wrongly assume that the *concentrations* of reactants and products must be equal at equilibrium. This is not true—they can differ wildly! It is only the forward and reverse *rates* that must be equal.

increase as the forward rate slows. Eventually, a state will be reached in which the forward and reverse reactions are proceeding at the same rate, and this is termed equilibrium. Note that neither reaction has stopped entirely—both continue to occur! But since the forward and reverse rates are equal, once equilibrium is reached, there will be no net change in concentrations of reactants or products. A special name exists for this steady-state system in which products and reactants are still interconverting: it is a system in dynamic equilibrium. Most reactions on the MCAT are reversible and thus reach a dynamic equilibrium, although irreversible reactions (those which proceed in only one direction and fully consume the limiting reagent) do appear in the context of stoichiometry. Any other inclusion of an irreversible reaction would have to be made clear in passage or question context.

Let's return to our generic reversible reaction, shown again below for convenience:

$$X\ (g) + 3\ Y\ (g) \rightleftharpoons 2\ Z\ (g)$$

At equilibrium, the rate at which X and Y are converted to Z must be equal to the rate at which Z is converted to X and Y. We can thus say that the rate law of the forward reaction must equal the rate law of the reverse reaction. You have not covered rate laws or chemical kinetics yet, so you do not need to worry too much about this concept. Suffice it to say that the rate law for the forward reaction is rate = $k_{forward}[X][Y]^3$, while that of the reverse reaction is rate = $k_{reverse}[Z]^2$. Since the rates are equal, we can say that $k_{forward}[X][Y]^3 = k_{reverse}[Z]^2$. Rearranging this equation leads to the following:

$$\frac{k_{forward}}{k_{reverse}} = \frac{[Z]^2}{X[Y]^3}$$

Since both k values are constants, we can combine them into a single constant that denotes the relative tendency for the reaction to progress forward compared to in reverse. This constant is termed the equilibrium constant, or K_{eq}. As shown above, K_{eq} is equal to the concentration(s) of the product(s) (each raised to the power of its respective coefficient) divided by the concentration(s) of the reactant(s), each of which is also raised to the power of its coefficient. A reaction that favors the products—in other words, that has a numerator greater than its denominator—will have a large K_{eq}, while a reaction that favors the reactants will have a small K_{eq}. Note that the concentrations used *must* be equilibrium concentrations; you cannot just plug any old concentrations into a K_{eq} expression and expect them to magically equal the equilibrium constant of the process.

Additionally, note that solids and pure liquids should not be included in the equilibrium expression. For example, if reactant X in our previous example had been in the solid phase, the denominator of the expression would have included $[Y]^3$ alone. The explanation for *why* this is true is beyond the scope of the MCAT, but do note that by "pure liquids," we typically mean water, which is often written as H_2O (*l*) in chemical reactions. This convention, then, saves us the trouble of having to calculate the concentration of water at equilibrium for any reaction in which it takes part.

What about the K_{eq} expression for the reverse reaction—how does it compare to the expression for the forward reaction? We can use the same example as above, only this time, we must use the reverse process: $2\ Z\ (g) \rightleftharpoons X\ (g) + 3\ Y\ (g)$. K_{eq} is still equivalent to product concentrations over reactants, with each product or reactant raised to its respective coefficient, so our $K_{eq\ reverse}$ is as follows:

$$K_{eq} = \frac{X[Y]^3}{[Z]^2}$$

You may notice that this is simply the reciprocal of the K_{eq} for the forward process. This holds true in general: since only the identities of the products and reactants switch places, the K_{eq} for a reverse reaction will always be equal to $\frac{1}{K_{eq}}$ for the forward reaction. Finally, note that since concentrations (usually given in units of moles/liter, or molarity) cannot be negative, K_{eq} cannot take on a negative value either. It can, however, have either a very large value (for example, 4×10^{17}, which denotes an equilibrium heavily leaning toward the product side) or a very small value (for example, 2×10^{-21}, which corresponds to a reaction in which barely any products are formed). The term "constant" in "equilibrium constant" is a bit of a misnomer, as the K_{eq} for a given process is not *always* the exact same value. Instead, it is important to note that K_{eq} is temperature-dependent. For this reason, textbooks that give select K_{eq} values generally do so with the stipulation that the temperature is 25°C, or standard (room) temperature.

> ## MCAT STRATEGY > > >
>
> Throughout this book, you will see both standard conditions (which stipulate a temperature of 25°C, among other conditions) and standard temperature and pressure, or STP (which assumes a temperature of 0°C, or about 273 K). Do not confuse the two! Standard temperature is typically used with thermodynamic parameters, while STP is used when dealing with gases.

Let's use what we have learned to write the K_{eq} expression for an actual chemical reaction, shown below:

$$SnO_2\ (s) + 2\ CO\ (g) \rightleftharpoons Sn\ (s)\ + 2\ CO_2\ (g)$$

First, check to ensure that the reaction is balanced, as an unbalanced reaction would have incorrect coefficients. The equation above is already balanced, so we can move on. Next, remember to exclude SnO_2 (s) and Sn (s), pure solids, from the expression. Then, simply raise the remaining species to their respective coefficients and place products over reactants:

$$K_{eq} = \frac{[CO_2]^2}{[CO]^2}$$

Just be certain that you do not confuse *subscripts* (the small numbers written after atoms to denote their number within a molecule, like the "2" in CO_2) with *coefficients* (the large numbers placed before compounds to represent their stoichiometric ratios.

Earlier, we mentioned that only equilibrium concentrations can be plugged in to the K_{eq} expression. But what if the reaction is not at equilibrium? Is there even a way to discern whether a reaction is at equilibrium if we are not explicitly told so? The answer lies in a concept called the reaction quotient (Q). The equation for the reaction quotient is the same as the equation used for K_{eq}, but the concentrations used can be from any moment in time, not necessarily at equilibrium. As with K_{eq}, the Q expression should not include solids or pure liquids. For our reaction between tin oxide and carbon monoxide, the equation for the reaction quotient is as follows:

$$Q = \frac{[CO_2]^2}{[CO]^2}$$

The reactant quotient can be used to predict the direction in which the reaction will proceed to reach equilibrium. When $Q < K_{eq}$, the ratio of products to reactants is *lower* than it would be at equilibrium, so the reaction will proceed in the forward direction to increase the product concentrations and thus move toward equilibrium. The reverse is also true: when $Q > K_{eq}$, the ratio of products to reactants is *greater* than it would be at equilibrium, so the reaction will proceed in the reverse direction to increase the reactant concentrations. Finally, if we plug in values and notice that Q is actually equal to K_{eq}, we know our reaction must already be at equilibrium. We can thus think of Q as "where the reaction actually is" and K_{eq} as "where it wants to be." This information is summarized in Table 1.

RELATIONSHIP	DIRECTION OF REACTION PROGRESSION
$Q < K_{eq}$	The reaction will proceed forward.
$Q = K_{eq}$	The reaction is at equilibrium.
$Q > K_{eq}$	The reaction will proceed in reverse.

Table 1. Predicted reaction progress based on the relationship between Q and K_{eq}.

Let's try an example. The components of the reaction shown below are present at the following concentrations: $[I_2]$ = 2 M, $[H_2]$ = 0.1 M, and [HI] = 4 M. Will the reaction proceed in the forward or reverse direction, or is it already at equilibrium? The K_{eq} of the reaction is approximately 50.

$$H_2 \,(g) + I_2 \,(g) \rightleftharpoons 2\,HI\,(g)$$

To find the direction in which this reaction will proceed, we must first solve for Q:

$$Q = \frac{[HI]^2}{[H_2][I_2]} = \frac{[4]^2}{[0.1][2]} = \frac{16}{0.2} = 80$$

Since $Q > K_{eq}$ (80 > 50), the ratio of products to reactants is higher than it "wants to be," and the reaction will proceed in reverse to increase the concentration of reactants until $Q = K_{eq}$.

2. Le Châtelier's Principle

If a reversible reaction is allowed to reach equilibrium, it will tend to remain in that state. But what if the experimenters make a drastic change to the reaction conditions, such that the mixture deviates from equilibrium? The results of such a change can be predicted using a phenomenon termed Le Châtelier's principle. The core of this principle is simple: if an equilibrium mixture is disrupted, it will shift to favor the direction of the reaction that best facilitates a return to equilibrium. As an MCAT student, you can think of this concept as simply "a reaction will shift in the direction that relieves the stress put on the system." Here, "stress" can refer to a change in reactant or product concentration, temperature, pressure, or volume.

The response to changes in concentration is usually the easiest to grasp, so we'll begin there. Consider the following reaction:

$$2\,SO_2 \,(g) + O_2 \,(g) \rightleftharpoons 2\,SO_3 \,(g)$$

A closed vessel contains SO_2, O_2, and SO_3 gases at equilibrium concentrations. If a chemist then decides to pump in excess SO_2, what will happen? The first thing to note is that the reaction previously was at equilibrium—in other words, we had the perfect concentrations necessary to keep the forward rate equal to the reverse rate. Adding SO_2, then, will disrupt this balance, resulting in too many reactant molecules. To compensate, the system will shift to the *right*—toward the product side—to use up some of the excess SO_2 and restore our perfect balance. Note that this shift will also decrease the concentration of O_2, leading to an O_2 concentration lower than we had at equilibrium. Even so, we can still regain equilibrium! Recall the concept of the equilibrium constant (K_{eq}), discussed in the previous section. To exist at equilibrium, the K_{eq} for the above reaction must be equal to $\frac{[SO_3]^2}{[SO_2]^2[O_2]}$, where current concentration values are used. We can thus see that we can regain equilibrium even with a reduced concentration of O_2 as long as our increased concentration of SO_2 balances it out. This is the gist of Le Châtelier's principle: the system shifts to relieve a stress and eventually regains equilibrium, albeit not necessarily with the exact same reactant and product concentrations as before the disruption.

Knowing that adding SO_2 to this equilibrium mixture will cause a rightward shift, what might we expect if we added SO_3? The same main idea holds true. Our system had reached equilibrium, but the subsequent addition of SO_3 results in an overabundance of product molecules. The reaction will thus shift to the *left*—toward the reactants—to use up the extra SO_3. In fact, whenever the concentration of a species in an equilibrium mixture is increased, the system always shifts in the opposite direction to consume the excess species.

What about the opposite: removing a reactant or product? Imagine our same old equilibrium mixture of SO_2, O_2, and SO_3. Suddenly, we use a device to selectively remove a large amount of O_2. Our "stress" has caused the system to lack O_2 (a reactant), so the system will shift to the left, toward the reactant side, to restore O_2 and increase our concentration of SO_2. Alternatively, the removal of a product would cause a shift toward the right to regenerate more product molecules.

Le Châtelier's principle can be used to maximize the yield of a reaction procedure. One common experiment that you may have done in organic chemistry lab is the synthesis of acetylsalicylic acid, commonly known as aspirin. Acetic anhydride is combined with salicylic acid to form the desired aspirin product along with acetic acid. To maximize the yield of our product, we have two options: either add one or both reactants in excess or remove products as they form. In fact, an excess of acetic anhydride (a reactant) is often used to push the system toward the products, forming more aspirin (and acetic acid). Alternatively, aspirin can be removed as soon as it forms; this removal of a product predictably shifts our system toward the product side, maximizing aspirin production.

Until now, we've only discussed the effects of changing concentration on a system at equilibrium. Next, let's talk about what happens when we change the volume and pressure. To make the most of this discussion, you must understand one concept that has not yet been discussed in this book: the idea that the pressure and the volume of a flexible gas-containing vessel are inversely proportional, assuming other factors remain constant. When volume increases, pressure decreases; conversely, if volume is made to decrease, pressure will increase. This relationship is outlined by Boyle's law, which you will review in more depth in the next chapter of this book.

> > CONNECTIONS < <

Chapter 5 of Chemistry

Back to Le Châtelier's principle: considering the same equilibrium mixture as before (shown again for convenience), what will happen if we then increase the volume of the container?

$$2\ SO_2\ (g) + O_2\ (g) \rightleftharpoons 2\ SO_3\ (g)$$

All three species involved are in the gas phase, and gases adjust to fit the container in which they are held. As such, an increase in volume means that our gas molecules will spread out, and less pressure will be exerted on the walls of the container. We might already be able to predict what happens next: the system will shift in such a way as to regenerate our "lost" pressure. But this isn't the most scientifically accurate description; instead, a change in pressure for the above reaction results in a change in the *partial pressures* of the reactants and products. In effect, this is similar to changing concentration. If it is easier to conceptualize a need to regenerate the lost pressure, however, that is perfectly fine. What needs to happen for this to take place? To increase the pressure inside the vessel, we need to shift toward the side of the reaction that contains *more moles* of gas. The production of more gas molecules will exert our much-needed pressure on the walls of the container. Here, this means that we will shift toward our reactant side, which includes 2 + 1 = 3 moles of gas compared to the product side's 2 moles.

As we may predict, the opposite will happen if we reduce the volume of the container, packing more gas molecules into a smaller area and increasing the pressure. To relieve this stress, the system will shift toward the side containing *fewer* moles of gas, which is the product side in the reaction above. Note that while this reaction took place entirely in the gas phase, this may not be true for other reactions on the MCAT! As a matter of habit, be certain to only count moles of *gas*. Solid or liquid products or reactants do not impact the direction of the shift; in fact, solids and pure liquids are not even included in the equilibrium expression.

The final variant of Le Châtelier's principle that we must be aware of is the change in the temperature of an equilibrium mixture. Unlike concentration, pressure, or volume, temperature changes have results that cannot be predicted without additional information. In particular, we need to know whether the reaction in question is endothermic (meaning that it requires heat input) or exothermic (meaning that it releases heat). This will typically be given, but it may not be in the form of a direct statement ("This reaction is exothermic!") Instead, keep a lookout for clues, such as ΔH values (negative means exothermic, while positive means endothermic) or reaction type (combustion reactions, for example, are well-known examples of exothermic processes).

Let's say you are given the generic reaction below, along with its ΔH value. This highly negative ΔH means that the reaction is exothermic. The reaction mixture is allowed to reach equilibrium, at which point the temperature is sharply increased. What will happen?

$$A\ (g) + B\ (g) \rightleftharpoons C\ (g) + D\ (g) \qquad \Delta H = -100\ \text{kJ/mol}$$

As with many MCAT concepts, it's a good idea to stop and think about what we already know. We have already reviewed the effects of changing the reactant or product concentration of an equilibrium mixture. If we simply treat "heat" as a reactant or product, we can follow the same rules we've already mastered. Exothermic reactions release heat, so heat should be written as a product, as shown:

$$A\ (g) + B\ (g) \rightleftharpoons C\ (g) + D\ (g) + \text{heat}$$

Now, a sharp increase in temperature is effectively identical to increasing the concentration of a product (heat). This will shift the system toward the reactants, or leftward. If this had instead been an endothermic reaction, we would have written "heat" as a reactant, meaning that an increase in temperature would shift the mixture toward the products. Decreases in temperature, then, must function exactly like decreases in product or reactant concentration. With all of this in mind, take a look at Table 2, which summarizes our discussion of Le Châtelier's principle.

DEVIATION FROM EQUILIBRIUM	EFFECT
Increased [reactant]	Shift toward products
Decreased [reactant]	Shift toward reactants
Increased [product]	Shift toward reactants
Decreased [product]	Shift toward products
Increased volume (↓ pressure)	Shift toward side w/more gas moles
Decreased volume (↑ pressure)	Shift toward side w/fewer gas moles
Increased temperature	If ΔH > 0, shift toward products; if ΔH < 0, shift toward reactants
Decreased temperature	If ΔH > 0, shift toward reactants; if ΔH < 0, shift toward products

Table 2. Direction of shifts expected after certain deviations from equilibrium.

As with nearly all chemistry topics, it is also worth noting the "exceptions"—here, changes that can be made to an equilibrium mixture *without* provoking a shift. The first such change is the addition of a catalyst. You may have read about enzymes, or biological catalysts, in Chapter 3 of your biochemistry book; regardless, you will review catalysts in depth later in this book. For now, just note that a catalyst increases the rate of a reaction, causing it to reach equilibrium more quickly. When a catalyst is added to a reaction already *at* equilibrium, however, no disruption takes place, since catalysts do not change the relative amounts of products or reactants and thus do not promote a deviation in either direction. As a result, the system will remain at equilibrium.

> **MCAT STRATEGY** > > >
>
> Le Châtelier's principle applies only to cases in which equilibrium has *already been established* and is later disturbed. If a change is made to the reaction conditions before equilibrium is reached, we cannot rely on the predictions of this principle.

The other such example is the addition of an inert (unreactive) gas at constant volume. Let's return to our recent gas-phase example: $2 SO_2 (g) + O_2 (g) \rightleftharpoons 2 SO_3 (g)$. After this reaction is allowed to run its course, we have all three components in a 1-liter flask at equilibrium. What happens if we add 0.5 moles of nitrogen gas? Well, nitrogen is not involved in this reaction (and is relatively unreactive in general). Its addition will increase the total pressure inside the flask, but this occurs due to the added pressure from the nitrogen, *not* to any changes in the partial pressures of the reactants or products. As such, equilibrium will not be disturbed.

> > > **CONNECTIONS** < <
>
> Chapter 3 of Biochemistry and Chapter 6 of Chemistry

3. Introduction to Thermodynamics

Now that we have wrapped up our introduction to equilibrium, we can move on to the second main topic of this chapter: thermodynamics. Note that we call the first portion of this chapter an "introduction" to equilibrium because equilibrium is a concept that will arise countless times during your review of MCAT content. Equilibrium is closely tied to thermodynamics (broadly, the study of heat and its connections to work and energy), so we will even continue to discuss it as this chapter continues. Note that our coverage of thermodynamics will remain rooted in general chemistry; for a review of the physics side of thermodynamics, consult Chapter 4 of your physics book.

> > > **CONNECTIONS** < <
>
> Chapter 4 of Physics

As we described in that physics chapter, an understanding of thermodynamics rests on a grasp of several foundational—albeit highly nuanced and potentially confusing—concepts. The first of these is a concept we have mentioned many times in this book already: temperature. Temperature is a property of the average kinetic energy of the particles under study and is in fact directly proportional to average kinetic energy. (This will be discussed further in the context of gases in Chapter 5.) Objects with a high temperature are perceived as hot, while those with a low temperature feel cold to the touch. Temperature can be measured using a thermometer along multiple distinct scales, the most MCAT-relevant of which are the Celsius and Kelvin scales. The conversion between Celsius and Kelvin temperatures is shown in Equation 1. For the sake of the MCAT, the lowest temperature possible is 0 K, termed absolute zero, which is the temperature at which virtually all motion of particles stops entirely.

Equation 1. $K = °C + 273.15$

In contrast, heat refers to the *transfer* of energy, specifically thermal energy, between objects of different temperatures. This brings us to another foundational topic: the laws of thermodynamics, which are again discussed in more detail in your physics book. The zeroth law

> > > **CONNECTIONS** < <
>
> Chapter 5 of Chemistry

MCAT STRATEGY > > >

If you are up-to-date on your knowledge of theoretical physics, you may have read about the potential of temperatures below absolute zero. This is *well* outside the scope of MCAT chemistry or physics. For best results, constantly remind yourself that the MCAT tests fundamentals, and avoid worrying about advanced/theoretical concepts unless told otherwise.

of thermodynamics describes the thermal relationship between systems. Specifically, it states that if one system (let's call it "System A") is in thermal equilibrium with another (we'll say that one is "System B"), and System B is in thermal equilibrium with System C, then System A must *also* be in thermal equilibrium with System C. By "thermal equilibrium," we generally mean that the systems have the same temperature. Thinking in terms of the familiar concept of temperature can make this law very clear—if Object A has the same temperature as Object B, and Object B has the same temperature as Object C, then *of course* Objects A and C have the same temperature. Relationships like this (where if A is related to B, and if B is related to C, then A is related to C) are termed transitive relations. What does this have to do with heat? Well, it introduces the question of what it actually means for two systems to have the same temperature (or in other words, to exist in thermal equilibrium). When this is the case, no heat transfer will take place between the systems. In contrast, if one system has a different temperature than another and thermal energy is allowed to move between the two, then heat transfer will take place. Imagine dropping an ice cube at −5°C into a glass of water at 25°C; heat will immediately begin to transfer from the water to the ice.

While the zeroth law can be thought of as the transitive property of thermal equilibrium, the first law of thermodynamics goes beyond the discussion of heat to involve work as well. To conceptualize this law, we must first touch upon the definition of a system, which is discussed in much more detail in Chapter 4 of your physics book. In scientific study, a system is whatever we are observing, while its surroundings consist of everything outside the system. This may seem broad, but it allows our concept of a system to vary depending on the circumstances. For example, if a chemical reaction is occurring between two solids immersed in water, the solids may be considered the system and the water molecules part of the surroundings. In other situations, the entire contents of the container may be thought of as the system, while the surroundings would include the container and its environment. On the MCAT, you may see three types of systems: open, closed, and isolated systems. Open systems are those which can exchange both matter and energy (namely work and heat) with their surroundings. For example, imagine that you conduct a chemical reaction in an open beaker. Heat is free to leave the beaker, as is matter in the form of evaporated reactants or solvent molecules. In contrast, in a closed system, energy can be exchanged with the surroundings, but matter cannot—as would be the case if we covered the beaker. Finally, isolated systems do not exchange matter *or* energy with their surroundings and are thus perfectly insulated.

Back to the first law of thermodynamics, which is most relevant to closed systems. In such a system, the change in the internal energy of the system (ΔU) is equal to the heat transfer into the system (Q) minus the work performed by the system on its surroundings (W). This is shown in equation form in Equation 2, below.

Equation 2.
$$\Delta U = Q - W$$

It is worth spending some time thinking about the sign conventions used in this equation, as you may have seen sources differ on this topic. The sign on Q is fairly straightforward: if the system is being heated, it is positive, while if heat is being lost from the system, it is negative. Work is somewhat trickier. Since Equation 2 subtracts work from heat, when work is done *by* the system on its surroundings, it is positive. This is true because work done by the system causes the system's internal energy to decrease. In contrast, work done *on* the system should be negative if you are using the equation above. When work is done on a system, its internal energy increases, as would be reflected by subtracting a negative quantity and thus effectively adding it.

We must wrap up our introduction to thermodynamics with a brief mention of a technique used to measure heat exchange: calorimetry. You may have performed this technique in chemistry lab with a coffee-cup calorimeter, which is as simple as it sounds: a Styrofoam coffee cup, tightly covered, with a thermometer extending down into the cup's contents. If a chemical reaction is performed inside the cup, the resulting temperature change can be measured and used as an estimate for the heat required or released by the reaction. We say "estimate" because calorimeters—especially simple ones like coffee-cup calorimeters—are difficult to completely insulate, so some heat virtually always escapes into the surroundings. Efforts should be taken to minimize this, such as making certain that no holes are present in the container or adding extra insulation with a second cup. The equation most often used for calorimetry-related calculations is Equation 3, below, where Q represents heat, m is the mass of the substance under observation, c is a substance-specific constant termed the specific heat capacity (which will be discussed further in Chapter 5), and ΔT is the measured temperature change.

> **MCAT STRATEGY >>>**
>
> For MCAT chemistry, the most common example of work done by a system is the expansion of gas against a flexible container or piston. Predictably, then, the most common case of work done on a system is gas compression.

Equation 3.
$$Q = mc\Delta T$$

4. Enthalpy and Entropy

With some basics of thermodynamics out of the way, we can now shift our focus to two conceptually difficult concepts: enthalpy and entropy. Although countless MCAT students have struggled with these ideas, you can master all you need to know for the exam by focusing on the basics ("What does this really mean for me, and how might I be asked about it?") rather than the advanced underlying chemistry and physics. Let's begin with enthalpy.

Broadly, enthalpy is a thermodynamic measurement of heat, with typical units of joules (J) or kilojoules (kJ). You might notice that these are also the units for energy, and this is no accident—enthalpy is typically used to describe changes to a system, in particular changes that involve the gain or loss of thermal energy. Enthalpy is described by Equation 4, below, where H represents enthalpy, U is the internal energy of the system, and PV is the product of pressure and volume.

Equation 4.
$$H = U + PV$$

On the MCAT, you typically will not be dealing with H, or the enthalpy of a static system. Instead, you will be presented with *changes* in enthalpy, which are described using the term ΔH. We can easily modify Equation 4 to include this quantity, as shown below in Equation 5.

Equation 5.
$$\Delta H = \Delta U + P\Delta V$$

Recall from the previous section the equation used to calculate changes in the internal energy of a system: $\Delta U = Q - W$. Consider that the W (work) that we deal with most often in this context is pressure-volume work, which is equal to $P\Delta V$. We can thus rewrite our internal energy equation as $\Delta U = Q - P\Delta V$. Finally, plugging this quantity into Equation 5 for the ΔU term yields $\Delta H = (Q - P\Delta V) + P\Delta V$, or $\Delta H = Q$. From this relation, we can clearly see that enthalpy change (ΔH) is equal to Q, or the heat lost or gained from the system. This relation is true under constant pressure, which will be the case for the vast majority of MCAT questions asked about this topic. In fact, for the sake of the MCAT, it is perfectly acceptable to think of enthalpy as an approximation of the total heat contained in a system. Since we most often deal with enthalpy *change*, we need special terms that denote whether a ΔH value is positive or negative. We have mentioned these terms in passing before: endothermic and exothermic. Specifically, endothermic processes require heat input and thus have positive ΔH values. Exothermic processes, which release heat, are associated with negative ΔH values.

While these terms may seem simple, we need to be careful when using them. Let's consider an example. A reaction occurs between two aqueous reactants in water. After the reaction, the temperature of the water is 1.2°C lower than it was before the reaction. Is this reaction endothermic or exothermic? To answer questions like this, consider the temperature change of the surroundings, or the immediate environment in which the reaction takes place. Since the temperature of the surrounding water decreased, the reaction must have "sucked" heat from the water to acquire the heat energy needed for the reaction to occur. As such, this reaction is endothermic.

On the MCAT, you are quite likely to see multiple variations of the ΔH term. Often, this term is presented with what looks like a degree symbol on its right side ($\Delta H°$). This symbol denotes standard conditions, which are 1 atm and 25°C. (Thermochemistry uses 25°C rather than 0°C in the standard state because most reactions are performed near room temperature.) $\Delta H°$, then, refers to the enthalpy change that occurs for a process when it is held at these conditions. This notation is not limited to enthalpy; you may also see $\Delta G°$, $\Delta S°$, or $E°_{cell}$, in reference to the change in Gibbs free energy, the change in entropy, or the potential of an electrochemical cell under standard conditions. The first two of these will be discussed later in this chapter, while $E°_{cell}$ will be covered in Chapter 8.

> > CONNECTIONS < <

Chapter 8 of Chemistry

Returning to enthalpy, we soon see that even more designations are possible. The standard enthalpy of formation ($\Delta H°_f$) of a compound is the change in enthalpy associated with the formation of one mole of the compound from its component elements, under standard conditions. These elements must be in their standard states: that is, the phase they exist in at 1 atm and 25°C. For example, carbon dioxide can be formed from carbon, which exists in the solid form of graphite under standard conditions, and oxygen gas. This reaction, along with its $\Delta H°_f$, is shown below. Note that the $\Delta H°_f$ of any element in its standard state is zero, so (for example) the $\Delta H°_f$ of O_2 (g) is 0 kJ. Standard enthalpy of formation is often used interchangeably with the term "standard *heat* of formation."

$$O_2 \ (g) + C \ (graphite) \rightarrow CO_2 \ (g) \qquad \Delta H°_f = -393 \text{ kJ (meaning 393 kJ released per mole } CO_2)$$

MCAT STRATEGY > > >

In addition to $\Delta H°_f$ and $\Delta H°_{rxn}$, you may see terms that relate to other specific enthalpy changes. One common example is $\Delta H°_{combustion}$, or the standard enthalpy of combustion. This represents the enthalpy change associated with the burning of a fuel, often an organic compound. It is helpful to understand that the more exothermic (negative) the heat of combustion, the more unstable the original reactant must have been, since it must have been carrying a large amount of energy in its bonds.

$\Delta H°_f$ applies only to reactions in which a compound forms from standard-state elements, but the enthalpy change of other reactions can be calculated as well. Broadly, the enthalpy change that takes place over the course of a reaction is denoted as $\Delta H°_{reaction}$, which is typically abbreviated as $\Delta H°_{rxn}$. Since the Δ term simply denotes a change, $\Delta H°_{rxn}$ can be calculated by finding the total enthalpy of the reactants and subtracting that amount from the total enthalpy of the products, as shown below in Equation 6.

Equation 6. $\qquad \Delta H°_{rxn} = \Delta H°_{products} - \Delta H°_{reactants}$

Equation 6 aligns with the categorization of enthalpy as a state function, meaning that only the starting and final states matter, not the pathway by which reactants turn into products. Let's attempt to use this equation to calculate the standard enthalpy change for the combustion of two moles of benzene (C_6H_6), given the information below.

molecule	$\Delta H°_f$
C_6H_6 (l)	49.0 kJ/mol
CO_2 (g)	–393.5 kJ/mol
H_2O (l)	–285.8 kJ/mol

$$2\ C_6H_6\ (l) + 15\ O_2\ (g) \rightarrow 12\ CO_2\ (g) + 6\ H_2O\ (l)$$

Note that the enthalpy of formation of O_2 (g) is not given, but never fear: we know that this value must be zero, because oxygen is a pure element in its standard state. The remaining $\Delta H°_f$ values that we need are given, which will be the case on the MCAT as well. For this reason, don't waste time trying to memorize any $\Delta H°_f$ values!

$$\Delta H°_{rxn} = \Delta H°_{products} - \Delta H°_{reactants}$$

$$\Delta H°_{rxn} = [12\ (\Delta H°_f(CO_2)) + 6\ (\Delta H°_f(H_2O))] - [2\ (\Delta H°_f(C_6H_6)) + 15\ (\Delta H°_f(O_2))]$$

$$\Delta H°_{rxn} = [12\ (-393.5\ kJ) + 6\ (-285.8\ kJ)] - [2\ (49.0\ kJ) + 0\ kJ] = -6534.8\ kJ$$

Two things to note about this process: first, on the MCAT exam, you would not need to calculate nearly this exact of a value. Your thought process might instead go something like this: we can round –393.5 to about –400, and we can round –285.8 to about –300. 49.0 is very close to 50. Plugging in these estimations yields the calculation below. We must just keep in mind that since we rounded our first two numbers in a way that made them considerably more negative, our estimated value will be more negative than the actual value. As you can see, even this heavy-handed rounding yields a value that is within 200 kJ of the exact answer—certainly close enough for the sake of the MCAT!

$$\Delta H°_{rxn} = [12\ (-400\ kJ) + 6\ (-300\ kJ)] - [2\ (50\ kJ) + 0\ kJ] = -6700\ kJ$$

The second thing to note is that this is the enthalpy change for the combustion of *two* moles of benzene, since the chemical reaction we used has a coefficient of 2 in front of the C_6H_6 (l) term. If we were asked to find the $\Delta H°_{rxn}$ for the combustion of *one* mole of C_6H_6, we'd need to divide our calculated value by two. Note that our answer was negative, meaning that this must be an exothermic reaction. In fact, combustion reactions are usually highly exothermic, giving off large amounts of heat!

Students often confuse the $\Delta H°_{rxn} = \Delta H°_{products} - \Delta H°_{reactants}$ equation with the concept of bond dissociation energy. The bond dissociation energy is the enthalpy change associated with the breaking (technically homolysis, or splitting where electrons are divided equally) of a particular bond. Bond enthalpies can be used to calculate $\Delta H°_{rxn}$, but in this case, the relevant equation is Equation 7, below.

Equation 7. $\qquad\qquad \Delta H°_{rxn} = \Delta H \text{ (bonds broken)} - \Delta H \text{ (bonds formed)}$

Why do we take the bonds broken (which are associated with the reactants) and subtract the bonds formed (which are associated with the products)? After all, isn't the other enthalpy equation in the opposite order: products minus reactants? The explanation for this relates to the nature of bond breakage and formation. The formation of bonds is by nature exothermic, since the bonded species is more stable, and thus lower-energy, then the separate component atoms. Bond breakage, then, is endothermic. Thus, our "bonds broken—bonds formed" equation can be conceptualized as the energy required by the endothermic part of the reaction minus the energy *released* by the exothermic part. This will yield a positive $\Delta H°_{rxn}$ if the overall reaction is endothermic and a negative $\Delta H°_{rxn}$ if the overall process is exothermic, which is exactly what we want.

Again, since enthalpy is a state function, its value depends only on the initial and final states rather than the path taken. However, sometimes you will be presented with multiple steps of a reaction procedure and asked to calculate the ΔH for the overall process. In these cases, you can use a very convenient concept known as Hess's law, which states that the enthalpy changes of the individual steps of a chemical reaction can be added together to equal the overall enthalpy change of the reaction. To illustrate this, we will use the made-up reaction A (s) + 2 B_2C (g) → AC_2 (g) + 2 B_2 (g). This reaction is a combination of multiple steps. Imagine that you are given the following information:

$$A\ (s) + C_2\ (g) \rightarrow AC_2\ (g) \qquad \Delta H = -393 \text{ kJ}$$
$$2\ B_2\ (g) + C_2\ (g) \rightarrow 2\ B_2C\ (g) \qquad \Delta H = -484 \text{ kJ}$$

How can we find the ΔH for the overall reaction given in the previous paragraph? Well, according to Hess's law, if we can arrange the two reactions above in a way that sums to the overall reaction, we can simply add the individual ΔH values to obtain the overall ΔH. The overall reaction includes A (s) on the reactant side, as does the top reaction listed above. For this reason, we should keep the top reaction written as-is. However, the bottom reaction has 2 B_2C (g) listed on the product side, while it exists as a reactant in the overall process. We thus need to reverse the bottom reaction. The reverse of a process will always have the same magnitude of ΔH as the forward process, but an opposite sign, as shown below:

$$2\ B_2C\ (g) \rightarrow 2\ B_2\ (g) + C_2\ (g) \qquad \Delta H = +484 \text{ kJ}$$

Adding these two reactions together yields A (s) + C_2 (g) + 2 B_2C (g) → AC_2 (g) + 2 B_2 (g) + C_2 (g), and removing the C_2 (g) that is present on both sides gives us A (s) + 2 B_2C (g) → AC_2 (g) + 2 B_2 (g). This is our overall reaction, so we are good! Since we added the two individual components to obtain the overall reaction, we must add the individual ΔH values to obtain the overall ΔH: -393 kJ $+484$ kJ = 91 kJ. Note that in this example, we left one reaction as written and reversed the other. In some cases, you may need to multiply one or more reactions by an integer value, most often 2, to get the steps to properly sum to the overall reaction. When you do this, be certain to multiply *all* reactant and product coefficients as well as the ΔH value for that step by the integer in question.

A term often discussed in tandem with enthalpy is entropy, which is an important, but often misunderstood, concept in chemistry. Entropy is at times oversimplified as the amount of disorder present in a system. A more complete definition is that entropy is related to the number of configurations a system can possibly have, with more potential configurations corresponding to greater entropy. Solids, with their energy packed into rigid crystalline structures, have low entropy; gases, consisting of individual molecules able to move unhindered, have higher entropy, and liquids typically fall in between. Similarly, a large compound has less entropy than it would if broken into multiple smaller molecules. As you can see, these examples basically consist of the "spreading out" of molecules and their energy along with them, and this is an acceptable way to conceptualize an entropy increase. This brings us back to the laws of thermodynamics, the zeroth and first of which we discussed in the previous section. But another law exists and should be understood for the MCAT: the second law of thermodynamics. According to this second law, the entropy of an isolated system will never decrease, and the entropy of the universe is always increasing. A reaction may decrease in entropy provided it is paired with processes that increase in entropy so that the overall entropy of the system increases.

As with enthalpy, we generally care about the change in entropy (ΔS) rather than entropy itself. An entropy increase

> > **CONNECTIONS** < <

Chapter 2 of Biochemistry

($+\Delta S$) is associated with favorable reactions, while an entropy decrease ($-\Delta S$) is associated with less favorable ones—although we cannot deduce whether a reaction is favorable or unfavorable from ΔS alone, as we shall soon see. Note also that typical units for entropy are joules per Kelvin (J/K) or joules per Kelvin per mole (J/K·mol). Unsurprisingly (given our existing knowledge about enthalpy), standard *entropy* is described as $\Delta S°$, the entropy of an overall reaction is termed $\Delta S°_{rxn}$, and $\Delta S°_{rxn} = \Delta S°_{products}$

$- \Delta S°_{reactants}$. Entropy plays a very important role in nearly every chemical process; for the MCAT, one particularly relevant example is protein folding, which depends on the entropy differences associated with both the protein and adjacent solvent molecules in the folded versus the unfolded state.

5. Gibbs Free Energy

To wrap up our discussion of thermodynamics, we must address a foundational concept that combines quite a bit of what we have learned so far. This concept is Gibbs free energy. Technically, Gibbs free energy is the maximum amount of work that can be performed by a system consisting of one or more reversible chemical reactants. More informally, however, we can think of it as a quantity that tells us whether a chemical reaction is spontaneous. Like enthalpy and entropy, Gibbs free energy is typically described in the form of a change, specifically the change in Gibbs free energy between products and reactants (ΔG). Enthalpy, entropy, and temperature all impact ΔG, which can be calculated using Equation 8, below. Note that ΔH is typically given in units of kJ, entropy in units of J/K, and temperature in units of K (Kelvin).

> ### MCAT STRATEGY > > >
>
> Note that the units for ΔH (kJ) and those for ΔS (J/K) do not align—kilojoules are one thousand times larger than joules! Whenever you see dissimilar units for quantities of the same type (here, we see dissimilar units for energy), you must convert one to match the other. For ΔG calculations, it is often easiest to convert ΔH to units of joules.

Equation 8. $$\Delta G = \Delta H - T\Delta S$$

Before attempting to perform any calculations, let us first solidify our understanding of ΔG with some visual help. In your chemistry classes, you were probably shown graphs called reaction coordinates diagrams, which depict the energy changes associated with a reaction over time. Examine the reaction coordinate displayed in Figure 1 as an example.

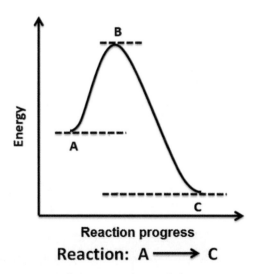

Figure 1. Reaction coordinate for the conversion of reactant A to product C.

Here, the reactants are represented by the label "A," while the products are denoted by "C." The reactants begin with a certain amount of energy. For the reaction to take place, an energy barrier termed the activation energy must be overcome; this will be discussed further in Chapter 6 of this book. Overcoming this barrier produces a transient species termed the transition state ("B"), which is so unstable and high-energy that it is only present instantaneously. From there, the products are formed. In Figure 1, we can clearly see that the products contain less energy than the reactants. This difference in energy—represented by the vertical distance between A and C along the y-axis—is the ΔG of the reaction. Again, pay special attention to the fact that the final state is lower than the initial state; this means that our ΔG value must be negative. In fact, a negative ΔG corresponds to a spontaneous reaction. If we were instead considering the reverse process, where C is converted back to A, the opposite would be true. ΔG would be positive, and the reaction would be nonspontaneous. For the MCAT, be certain to know some additional terminology: reactions with negative ΔG values are termed exergonic, while those with positive ΔG values are endergonic.

MCAT STRATEGY >>>

You can easily remember that a negative ΔG corresponds to a spontaneous reaction by considering the idea of stability. Stable molecules contain relatively low amounts of energy, and stability is a favorable characteristic. As such, a process in which higher-energy reactants are transformed into lower-energy products would logically "want" to occur.

We now know how to use a reaction's ΔG value to predict whether it will proceed spontaneously. But what exactly do we mean by "spontaneous"? A spontaneous reaction is one that can proceed without the help of some additional, external force. Importantly, spontaneity does not relate to the *rate* of the reaction, or the speed at which it progresses. Rate is a kinetic parameter and is determined largely by the activation energy, while spontaneity is a thermodynamic parameter and relates to ΔG. (Throughout your MCAT studies, you will repeatedly see the idea that kinetic and thermodynamic parameters are entirely different things!) Spontaneous reactions, then, can proceed either quickly or slowly.

Some spontaneous biochemical reactions actually proceed so slowly that without help, they would not occur to any measurable extent in the body. These reactions typically need the assistance of enzymes, or biological catalysts. Catalysts increase the rate of reaction by lowering the activation energy. Does this alter ΔG? No! Again, rate is a kinetic parameter, not a thermodynamic one, and altering the activation energy does not change the vertical distance between reactants and products along the reaction coordinate. Remember this for your exam: adding an enzyme or other catalyst does *not* change ΔG, nor can it make a nonspontaneous reaction spontaneous.

>> CONNECTIONS <<

Chapter 6 of Chemistry and Chapter 3 of Biochemistry

We can now return to ΔG calculations, which involve the previously mentioned equation $\Delta G = \Delta H - T\Delta S$. On the MCAT, you will most often only need to discern whether, or under what conditions, a reaction is spontaneous. This means that we care about the *sign* of ΔG more than the actual value. Spontaneity ($-\Delta G$) tends to be favored by exothermic ($-\Delta H$) reactions and reactions that increase in entropy ($+\Delta S$). However, an endothermic ($+\Delta H$) reaction can be spontaneous at high temperatures if ΔS is sufficiently positive. Likewise, reactions that decrease in entropy ($-\Delta S$) can be spontaneous at low temperatures if ΔH is negative. These guidelines are summarized in Table 3 and are extremely helpful to memorize, although you can always opt to plug given values into the Gibbs free energy equation and identify the conditions under which ΔG will be negative.

ΔH	ΔS	SPONTANEOUS?
+	−	Never
−	+	Always
+	+	Only at high T
−	−	Only at low T

Table 3. Signs of ΔH and ΔS and their relationship to reaction spontaneity.

Let's attempt an example. For a given reaction, $\Delta H = +14$ kJ and $\Delta S = +100$ J/K. Within what temperature range will this reaction be spontaneous? Since the signs given are both positive, we must plug the values provided into the Gibbs free energy equation. As usual, enthalpy is given in units of kJ while entropy uses J in its numerator, so let's convert ΔH from $+14$ kJ to $+14000$ J. We also should set ΔG equal to 0 because temperatures above this point will make ΔG negative (spontaneous), while temperatures below this point will make ΔG positive (nonspontaneous).

$$\Delta G = \Delta H - T\Delta S$$
$$0 = 14000 \text{ J} - (T)(100 \text{ J/K})$$
$$(100 \text{ J/K})(T) = 14000 \text{ J}$$
$$T = (14000 \text{ J}) / (100 \text{ J/K}) = 140 \text{ K}$$

Therefore, this reaction will be spontaneous at $T > 140$ K.

Like ΔH and ΔS, ΔG can be further specified to refer to certain quantities. Until this point, we have used ΔG to refer to the change in Gibbs free energy that occurs during a chemical reaction. Alternatively, you could see ΔG_{rxn} in reference to that same quantity. If the reaction occurs under standard conditions (1 atm, 25°C, and 1 M concentrations of any aqueous reaction components), it can be described using $\Delta G°$ or $\Delta G°_{rxn}$. The Gibbs free energy change for the formation of any compound from its standard-state elements is ΔG_f, and like enthalpy, the Gibbs free energy of formation of a standard-state element is zero. With these similarities to enthalpy, we can easily predict the equation for $\Delta G°_{rxn}$, shown here in Equation 9.

> ## MCAT STRATEGY > > >
>
> If you have trouble memorizing the information in Table 3, just think about the ΔG equation. In this equation, ΔS is multiplied by temperature, so the higher the temperature, the greater the effect of ΔS. If ΔS is negative (which is unfavorable), then, a low temperature would minimize its effect. If ΔS is positive (which is favorable), a high temperature would increase its impact on reaction spontaneity.

Equation 9.
$$\Delta G°_{rxn} = \Delta G°_{products} - \Delta G°_{reactants}$$

Finally, we can discuss ΔG in terms of its close relationship with equilibrium. Recall from earlier in this chapter that reversible chemical reactions tend to move toward equilibrium, a state in which the rates of the forward and reverse reactions are the same. This occurs because at equilibrium, the Gibbs free energy of the reaction system is at a minimum. In fact, if equilibrium concentrations of reactants and products are combined in a container, the reaction will not progress in either direction, meaning that the ΔG of a reaction at equilibrium is zero. Even if a reaction is not at equilibrium, we can use its ΔG to derive other useful pieces of information. Equations 10 and 11, below, relate ΔG to the concepts of K_{eq} and Q, both of which were discussed earlier in this chapter. In these equations, R denotes the gas constant, which is 8.314 J/mol·K or 0.008314 kJ/mol·K, depending on whether you are using joules or kilojoules. As in the typical ΔG equation, T is the temperature in Kelvin.

Equation 10.
$$\Delta G°_{rxn} = -RT\ln K_{eq}$$

Equation 11.
$$\Delta G_{rxn} = \Delta G°_{rxn} + RT\ln Q$$

If you started to panic at the sight of these terms, never fear—it is unlikely that the MCAT will ask you to use them in complex calculations. Instead, simply be certain to understand what they mean. The "ln" term stands for the natural logarithm, and the natural logarithm of 1 is 0. For this reason, if K_{eq} is equal to 1 (implying that neither products nor reactants are favored over the other), then $\Delta G°_{rxn}$ will be equal to 0, implying that the reaction is already at equilibrium. This is exactly what we would expect! Note also the negative sign in front of the right side of Equation 10. This means that a K_{eq} of greater than 1 (meaning that products are favored) corresponds to a *negative* ΔG value (a spontaneous reaction). In contrast, a K_{eq} that is less than 1 (implying that reactants are favored) yields a positive ΔG, meaning the reaction is nonspontaneous in the forward direction.

What about Equation 11? This equation includes Q (the reaction quotient) instead of K_{eq}. It also calculates ΔG_{rxn} instead of $\Delta G°_{rxn}$, meaning that it can be used to assess a reaction under non-standard conditions—in particular, a reaction that has already started to progress. Recall the relationship between Q and K_{eq}. If Q is smaller than K_{eq}, not enough products have formed, and the reaction will continue forward. This is reflected perfectly by Equation 11! If Q is sufficiently small, the RTln Q term will result in a negative ΔG_{rxn}. (The natural log of any number smaller than 1 will be a negative number.) This means that when Q < K_{eq}, the reaction is spontaneous. In contrast, when Q > K_{eq}, the reaction has proceeded too far in the direction of the products. The large Q term will result in a positive ΔG_{rxn} and a nonspontaneous reaction in the forward direction. Finally, when Q = K_{eq}, the reaction is already at equilibrium, and $\Delta G_{rxn} = \Delta G°_{rxn}$.

> > CONNECTIONS < <

Chapter 12 of Biochemistry

To finish our discussion of ΔG, note that Gibbs free energy plays an enormous role in biochemical reactions, most often encountered on the MCAT in the form of metabolic processes. For more information on ΔG in a biochemical context, consult Chapter 12 of your Biochemistry book.

6. Kinetic vs. Thermodynamic Control of Reactions

With our newfound understanding of thermodynamics, we may feel an urge to apply it to every additional concept we see in chemistry. This is good—thermodynamics is enormously important! However, other factors impact chemical reactions as well. For example, consider an organic reactant that can proceed through one of two different reaction pathways. We might assume that the reactant will always take the pathway that leads to the most stable product—in other words, the pathway with the more negative ΔG. Interestingly, this is not always the case. In such situations, where one reactant can form two different products, the concept of kinetic versus thermodynamic control is often relevant. Chemical kinetics will be discussed later (in Chapter 6), but thermodynamic and kinetic *control of reactions* will be discussed here, while our understanding of thermodynamics is still fresh.

> > CONNECTIONS < <

Chapter 6 of Chemistry

Let's explain this concept through an example. In the reaction in Figure 2, a carbonyl compound (technically 2-methylcyclohexanone, but that's a matter for the organic chemistry chapters) is converted to two different enolate products in a reaction that involves a base (B⁻). The more stable product arises from the pathway labeled 1, since its double bond is more substituted. However, the product made by the pathway labeled 2 is less sterically hindered, so it is able to form more quickly.

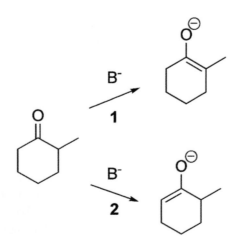

Figure 2. Thermodynamic (1) and kinetic (2) products of an organic reaction.

In this example, product 1 is the thermodynamic product, since it is more stable. The ΔG between the reactant and this product is more negative than that of the kinetic product. However, formation of the thermodynamic product is slowed by a high activation energy. (Activation energy will be described further in Chapter 6, but for now, it can be thought of as an energy barrier that must be overcome for a reaction to take place.) Here, the steric hindrance associated with the formation of the thermodynamic enolate increases the activation energy.

> > CONNECTIONS < <

Chapter 11 of Chemistry

Since a large amount of energy is required to facilitate this reaction pathway, the thermodynamic product is not favored at low temperatures. When temperatures are high, however, sufficient energy is present to surmount the activation energy barrier, and the thermodynamic product is favored due to its stability.

In contrast, product 2 is the kinetic product. The term "kinetic" broadly means "rate," and as such, the kinetic product is the product which forms at a faster rate. This rapid rate is a result of a relatively low activation energy, which allows for quick formation of the kinetic product in spite of the fact that it is less stable than the thermodynamic product. The kinetic product is favored at low temperatures, when available energy is scarce. Table 4 summarizes the characteristics of the thermodynamic and kinetic products. These are certainly good to remember, although perhaps more important is the idea that kinetics and thermodynamics are very different concepts, which we will elaborate on later.

KINETIC PRODUCT	THERMODYNAMIC PRODUCT
Forms more quickly	Forms more slowly
Less thermodynamically stable	More thermodynamically stable
Lower activation energy	Higher activation energy
Favored at low temperatures	Favored at high temperatures

Table 4. Characteristics of the kinetic versus the thermodynamic product of a reaction in which the two products compete.

The kinetic and thermodynamic products of a reaction can also be represented on a reaction coordinate, such as the generic example shown in Figure 3. In this diagram, the reactant is shown in the middle along the x-axis. Traveling to the left along this coordinate yields the kinetic product, which has the lower activation energy. In contrast, moving to the right yields the thermodynamic product, which exhibits the higher activation energy but ends at a lower point along the y-axis, representing stability (or a more negative ΔG)

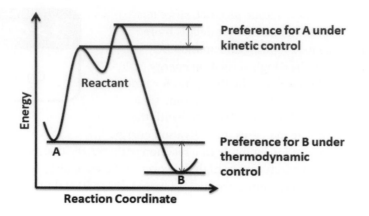

Figure 3. The reaction coordinate for a reactant that can undergo two competing pathways. A represents the kinetic product, while B is the thermodynamic product.

7. Must-Knows

> Chemical reactions may be reversible or irreversible.
  – Irreversible reactions go to completion (limiting reagent is entirely consumed).
  – Reversible reactions (marked by ⇌) proceed both forward and backward simultaneously and end with equilibrium.
> Equilibrium: a state where forward and reverse rates are equal
> Equilibrium constant = $\frac{[\text{products}]^{\text{coefficients}}}{[\text{reactants}]^{\text{coefficients}}}$
  – This expression should not include solids or pure liquids!
  – Favors products: large K_{eq} ($K_{eq} > 1$)
  – Favors reactants: small K_{eq} ($K_{eq} < 1$)
  – K_{eq} = temperature-dependent; temperature at standard conditions is 25°C.
> Reaction quotient (Q) uses same equation as K_{eq}, but can include non-equilibrium concentrations
  – $Q < K_{eq}$: reaction will proceed forward; $Q = K_{eq}$: reaction is already at equilibrium; $Q > K_{eq}$: reaction will proceed in reverse
> Le Châtelier's principle: if disturbed, an equilibrium mixture will shift to relieve stress
  – Shifts can result from changing concentrations, temperature, or pressure/volume
  – No shift results from adding a catalyst or inert gas
> Temperature ≠ heat; on MCAT, temp. is measured in Celsius, Kelvin (K = °C + 273.15)
> Zeroth law of thermodynamics: for thermal equilibrium, if A = B and B = C, then A = C
> First law of thermodynamics: $\Delta U = Q - W$
> Enthalpy (H): we usually discuss change, or ΔH; under constant pressure, $\Delta H = Q$
  – Endothermic: $+\Delta H$, heat input is required; exothermic: $-\Delta H$, heat is released
  – Be familiar with standard enthalpy change ($\Delta H°$), standard enthalpy of formation ($\Delta H°_f$), and standard enthalpy of reaction ($\Delta H°_{rxn}$)
    • $\Delta H°_{rxn} = \Delta H°_{products} - \Delta H°_{reactants}$
    • $\Delta H°_{rxn} = \Delta H \text{ (bonds broken)} - \Delta H \text{ (bonds formed)}$
    • Hess's law: enthalpies are additive
> Entropy (S): relates to # of possible configs/"spreading out"; we also typically discuss ΔS
  – $+\Delta S$ is favorable according to the second law of thermodynamics
> Gibbs free energy (G): $-\Delta G$ = spontaneous; $+\Delta G$ = non-spontaneous; $\Delta G = \Delta H - T\Delta S$

> Reactants that can proceed through more than one reaction pathway may display thermodynamic vs. kinetic control
>   — Thermodynamic: forms more stable product but may have higher E_a (and thus form more slowly); favored at high temperatures
>   — Kinetic: has lower E_a (and thus forms more quickly) but may be less stable; favored at low temperatures

Practice Passage

Air pollution is a major public health issue for people living in urban regions. Burning coal for electricity produces sulfur dioxide, which can contribute to particulate matter, and combines with water to produce acid rain. Internal combustion engines, which break down hydrocarbon fuels, also contribute to air pollution via the release of volatile organic compounds, as well as the production of oxides, both of which contribute to the production of photochemical smog which can produce dangerous concentrations of ground-level ozone.

Nitrogen oxides, both nitrogen monoxide and nitrogen dioxide, are formed when air is used as the source of oxygen in high temperature combustion reactions, such as in the internal combustion engine. The reaction between elemental nitrogen and elemental oxygen, Reaction 1, is thermodynamically favorable, but kinetically hindered.

Reaction 1 $$N_2 (g) + O_2 (g) \leftrightarrow 2 NO (g)$$

Nitrogen monoxide reacts further with elemental oxygen to form nitrogen dioxide. This reaction is thought to occur in a two-step mechanism, in which two nitrogen monoxide molecules combine in a relatively fast pre-equilibrium, forming an intermediate, dinitrogen dioxide, which then reacts in a slow step with an equivalent of elemental oxygen to form two nitrogen dioxide molecules.

Reaction 2 $$2 NO (g) \leftrightarrow N_2O_2 (g) \quad fast$$

Reaction 3 $$N_2O_2 (g) + O_2 (g) \rightarrow 2 NO_2 (g) \quad slow$$

Nitrogen dioxide is a brown colored gas and establishes equilibrium with the colorless gas dinitrogen tetroxide, (Reaction 4). The gas is manifested as seasonal smog episodes in cities such as Los Angeles and Beijing.

Reaction 4 $$2 NO_2 (g, brown) \leftrightarrow N_2O_4 (g, colorless) \quad \Delta H_{fwd} = -57 \text{ kJ}$$

1. Which of the following best describes the thermodynamic changes associated with the equilibrium in smog formation?
   A. The enthalpy change is positive and the entropy change is negative.
   B. The enthalpy change is negative and the entropy change is positive.
   C. Both the enthalpy and entropy changes are positive.
   D. Both the enthalpy and entropy changes are negative.

2. Which of the following best describes the season during which air above a city will be brown?
   A. Air has a brown color in the summer due to the increased amounts of nitrogen dioxide formed at high temperatures, because the reaction is exothermic.
   B. Air has a brown color in the summer due to the increased amounts of dinitrogen tetroxide formed at high temperatures, because the reaction is endothermic.
   C. Air has a brown color in the winter due to the increased amounts of nitrogen dioxide formed at low temperatures, because the reaction is exothermic.
   D. Air has a brown color in the winter due to the increased amounts of dinitrogen tetroxide formed at low temperatures, because the reaction is endothermic.

3. Which of the following energy diagrams best describes Reaction 1?

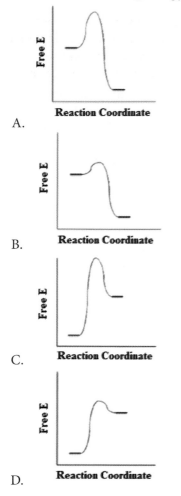

A.

B.

C.

D.

4. According to the passage, what is the most likely cause of the elevated hydrogen ion concentration in acid rain?
   A. Sulfonic acid
   B. Sulfurous acid
   C. Sulfuric acid
   D. Hydrosulfuric acid

5. In a given reaction vessel, the concentrations of NO_2 and N_2O_4 are measured. Researchers find that the calculated reaction quotient is significantly lower than the expected K_{eq} for this system. This indicates that the:
   A. measurements were in error since this is impossible.
   B. reaction will proceed forward.
   C. reaction will proceed in reverse.
   D. temperature in the reaction vessel is very low.

6. In reaction 4, the shift in color of the reagents involved indicates which of the following?
   A. Entropy increased.
   B. Entropy decreased.
   C. Entropy change was zero.
   D. Color change indicates nothing about entropy change.

7. A researcher investigating a reaction mechanism for nitrogen gases finds that the reaction is endothermic and displays a large increase in entropy. From this, the researcher can conclude that the reaction will be spontaneous under which of the following conditions?
   A. High temperature
   B. Low temperature
   C. Always
   D. Never

Practice Passage Explanations

Air pollution is a major public health issue for people living in urban regions. Burning coal for electricity produces sulfur dioxide, which can contribute to particulate matter, and combines with water to produce acid rain. Internal combustion engines, which break down hydrocarbon fuels, also contribute to air pollution via the release of volatile organic compounds, as well as the production of oxides, both of which contribute to the production of photochemical smog which can produce dangerous concentrations of ground-level ozone.

Key terms: sulfur dioxide, acid rain, nitrogen oxides, photochemical smog, ozone

Cause and effect: hydrocarbon combustion/coal burning → volatile organic compounds, oxides, photochemical smog, ozone (O_3)

Nitrogen oxides, both nitrogen monoxide and nitrogen dioxide, are formed when air is used as the source of oxygen in high temperature combustion reactions, such as in the internal combustion engine. The reaction between elemental nitrogen and elemental oxygen, Reaction 1, is thermodynamically favorable, but kinetically hindered.

Key terms: nitrogen oxides

Cause and effect: combustion of air/O_2 = therm. favored, but kin. hindered (stable but high E requirements); air/O_2 rxns → NO, NO_2

Reaction 1 $N_2 (g) + O_2 (g) \leftrightarrow 2\ NO\ (g)$

Reaction 1 shows the kinetically slow (large E_{act}) production of N-oxides; if collisions have enough energy to get over E_{act} hump, produce thermo-stable products

Nitrogen monoxide reacts further with elemental oxygen to form nitrogen dioxide. This reaction is thought to occur in a two-step mechanism, in which two nitrogen monoxide molecules combine in a relatively fast pre-equilibrium, forming an intermediate, dinitrogen dioxide, which then reacts in a slow step with an equivalent of elemental oxygen to form two nitrogen dioxide molecules.

Key terms: mechanism, pre-equilibrium, intermediate, slow step

Cause and effect: step 1 fast due to low E_{act}; step 3 = rate-limiting step; equilibrium indicates E_{free} of the reactants and products are similar

Reaction 2 $2\ NO\ (g) \leftrightarrow N_2O_2 (g)$ *fast*

Reaction 3 $N_2O_2 (g) + O_2 (g) \rightarrow 2\ NO_2 (g)$ *slow*

Nitrogen dioxide is a brown colored gas and establishes equilibrium with the colorless gas dinitrogen tetroxide, (Reaction 4). The gas is manifested as seasonal smog episodes in cities such as Los Angeles and Beijing.

Cause and effect: NO_2 production → smog, brown haze in sky in cities

Reaction 4 $2\ NO_2 (g, brown) \leftrightarrow N_2O_4 (g, colorless)$ $\Delta H_{fwd} = -57\ kJ$

Reaction 4 establishes an equilibrium that is exothermic; brown color of NO_2 is due to low E electronic transitions involving the partially-filled sp^2 orbital; color disappears in N_2O_4 because all of the bonding orbitals are now completely filled

1. D is correct. Smog was mentioned in relation to Reaction 4. As seen in Reaction 4, heat is a product and hence the reaction is exothermic, with a negative enthalpy. Since there are fewer gas molecules as products than reactants, the system becomes more ordered, entropy decreases and the entropy change would be negative.

2. A is correct. Based on Le Châtelier's principle, since heat is a product of Reaction 4, increasing the temperature would shift the reaction towards the reactants, increasing the amount of the brown NO_2 gas. Choices C and D can be eliminated. The temperatures in Los Angeles are on average higher in the summer than in the winter. Choice B can be eliminated because dinitrogen tetroxide, N_2O_4, is not the molecule in question.

3. A is correct. We are told in the second paragraph that Reaction 1 is thermodynamically favorable, but kinetically hindered. This would mean we expect a large activation energy, but with the products being more stable than reactants (i.e. lower free energy).

   B, C, D: Choices C and D are not thermodynamically favorable, because the free energy change is positive. Reactions with high activation energies would cause a reaction to be "kinetically hindered". The activation energy in choice A is higher than the activation energy in choice B.

4. B is correct. Acid rain was mentioned in paragraph 1. We are told sulfur dioxide is the major oxide of sulfur initially formed when coal is burned, and reacts with water to form acid rain. The reaction between sulfur dioxide (SO_2) and water (H_2O), produces H_2SO_3, known as sulfurous acid, because the anion is sulfite.

   A, C, D: Sulfuric acid is H_2SO_4, which has the sulfate anion. Sulfuric acid is the product of the reaction between water and sulfur trioxide. Hydrosulfuric acid exists as H_2S in aqueous solution, with the anion being sulfide, S^{2-}. Sulfonic acid is a class of organic acids with the general formula of RSO_3H.

5. B is correct. Both Q and K_{eq} are calculated as [products]/[reactants] and thus a low reaction quotient indicates a high concentration of reactants and a low concentration of products. With lots of reactants in the reaction vessel, the reaction will proceed forward.

   A: It is possible for Q and K_{eq} to be different numbers.
   C: This would happen when $Q > K_{eq}$.
   D: The relationship between Q and K_{eq} indicates which direction the reaction will proceed, not the current temperature of the reaction.

6. D is correct. While color changes are associated with changes in the electronic structures of the various reagents involved, these shifts in electronic structure do not directly correlate with shifts in entropy. When analyzing entropy changes on the MCAT, look for changes in phase, not color.

7. A is correct. From the reaction $\Delta G = \Delta H - T\Delta S$ we know that a reaction with an increase in entropy will be more likely to be spontaneous at high temperature. We also know from Le Châtelier's principle that an endothermic reaction will prefer to proceed forward when energy is put into the system in the form of high temperature.

Independent Questions

1. The chemical equation for the dissociation of hypochlorous acid in water is shown below.

$$HClO + H_2O \rightarrow ClO^- + H_3O^+$$

   Which of the following will be true of this reaction mixture at equilibrium?

   A. The rate of conversion of reactants to products will be zero.
   B. The concentrations of HClO and ClO⁻ will be equal.
   C. $[HClO] = [ClO^-][H_3O^+]$.
   D. HClO and H_3O^+ will form at equal rates.

2. A mixture of reactants and products is held at equilibrium in an inflexible container. What effect will adding 2 moles of an inert gas have on this mixture?
   A. It will disrupt equilibrium by increasing the pressure, favoring the side of the reaction with fewer moles of gas.
   B. It will disrupt equilibrium by increasing the pressure, favoring the side of the reaction with more moles of gas.
   C. It will disrupt equilibrium by increasing the pressure, but its effect cannot be predicted without knowing whether the reaction is endo- or exothermic.
   D. It will not disrupt equilibrium, and the reaction will not shift to either side.

3. A biochemist is conducting a thermodynamic analysis of a biologically-relevant reaction. The K_{eq} for this reaction is 5.06×10^{-11}. At one moment in time, the biochemist calculates that Q (the reaction quotient) is 7.69×10^{-14}. Which of the following statements is true at this moment?
   A. The reaction will proceed in a manner that favors the formation of the products.
   B. The reaction will proceed in a manner that favors the formation of the reactants.
   C. The reaction is already at equilibrium.
   D. Once equilibrium is reached, product concentrations will be much higher than reactant concentrations.

4. A certain reaction has a $\Delta H°$ of −14.0 kJ and a $\Delta S°$ of −70 J/K. Under what temperature conditions will this reaction be spontaneous, assuming standard pressure?
   A. It will be spontaneous at all temperatures.
   B. It will be spontaneous at temperatures above 0.2 K.
   C. It will be spontaneous at temperatures below 200 K.
   D. It will not be spontaneous regardless of the temperature.

5. The addition of a catalyst to a reaction mixture:
   A. makes the ΔG of the reaction more negative.
   B. increases the rate of the reverse reaction.
   C. shifts the reaction toward the products if the mixture was previously at equilibrium.
   D. can cause the reaction to become exothermic.

6. Consider the following reaction, where A represents an unknown element.

$$2 A_3 (g) \leftrightarrow A_6 (g)$$

   If $K_p = 2.0$ and the partial pressure of A_6 is 0.72 atm at equilibrium, what is the mole fraction of A_3 at equilibrium?

   A. 0.33
   B. 0.45
   C. 0.54
   D. 2.2

7. Which of the following would NOT be expected to appear in an equilibrium constant expression?
   A. AgCl (s)
   B. HF (aq)
   C. H_2O (l)
   D. Both A and C

8. A given reaction is spontaneous in the forward direction. Which of the following statements must be true?
   I. K_{eq} for the forward reaction is larger than 1.
   II. K_{eq} for the reverse reaction is smaller than 1.
   III. K_{eq} for the forward reaction is positive.

   A. I only
   B. I and II only
   C. II and III only
   D. I, II, and III

Independent Question Explanations

1. D is correct. At chemical equilibrium, the forward and reverse reaction rates are equal. This means that reactants are still being converted to products (and vice versa), but their concentrations remain unchanged. For this to occur, reactants (like HClO) and products (like H_3O^+) must form at equal rates. Choice A is a common misconception; in reality, however, reactions do not slow to zero at equilibrium. Choice B can also be eliminated because equilibrium does not require the concentration of any one product/reactant to be equal to that of any other product/reactant. Finally, option C would only be true if $K_{eq} = 1$; this is unlikely in itself, and you will learn in Chapter 7 that it is not possible for a weak acid such as HClO.

2. D is correct. Adding moles of an inert gas (that is to say, one that does not react and is not involved in the reaction at hand) will increase the pressure, but it will not change the relative *partial* pressures of the reactants and products. As such, it will not disrupt equilibrium.

3. A is correct. Remember, K_{eq} is equal to the product concentrations (raised to their respective coefficients) divided by the reactant concentrations (also raised to their coefficients). The reaction quotient, Q, is calculated in the same manner as K_{eq}, but it can be found for a reaction at any stage, not just at equilibrium. Here, Q is significantly smaller than K_{eq} (be careful with negative exponents!). This means that at this moment, we have fewer products present than we would "want" to have at equilibrium, and the reaction will proceed in the forward direction to generate more products. Note that choice D is false because the given K_{eq} is smaller than 1, which means that the reactants are favored.

4. C is correct. This reaction has a negative ΔH, which is favorable, but its ΔS is negative, which is not; thus, it will be spontaneous at some, but not all, temperatures (eliminate choices A and D). Thus, to solve this problem, we need to use the equation $\Delta G = \Delta H - T\Delta S$. Be careful, however—the units for ΔH and ΔS are not the same! We can address this by converting -14.0 kJ into $-14,000$ J.

$$\Delta G = -14,000 \text{ J} - T(-70 \tfrac{J}{K})$$

We can plug in 0 for ΔG, as that is the point at which the reaction switches between being nonspontaneous and spontaneous.

$$0 \text{ J} = -14,000 \text{ kJ} - T(-70 \tfrac{J}{K})$$

$$14,000 \text{ kJ} = - T(-70 \tfrac{J}{K})$$

$$14,000 \text{ kJ} = T(70 \tfrac{J}{K})$$

$$\frac{14,000 \text{ kJ}}{70 \tfrac{J}{K}} = T = 200 \text{ K}$$

5. B is correct. You will read more about catalysts throughout this book and others, but it is important to understand that a catalyst lowers the activation energy of its associated reaction. By nature, this increases the rate of both the forward and the reverse reaction. This makes choice B a true statement. Catalysts affect the kinetics of a reaction, not the thermodynamics; as such, they do not alter thermodynamic parameters such as the ΔG or the endo- or exothermic nature of the reaction. Finally, addition of a catalyst to a mixture at equilibrium will not shift the reaction in either direction.

6. B is correct. To find mole fraction, we must first find the partial pressure of A_3, then divide it by the pressure of both gases combined. K_p is an equilibrium constant in which partial pressure (rather than molarity) is used. The K_p expression can be set up just like a K_{eq} expression, as shown below:

$$K_p = 2.0 = \frac{P_{A_6}}{P_{A_3}^2}$$

Plugging in our known partial pressure of A_6, 0.72 atm, yields:

$$2.0 = \frac{0.72}{P_{A_3}^2}$$

$$P_{A_3}^2 = \frac{0.72}{2.0} = 0.36$$

$$P_{A_3} = 0.6 \text{ atm}$$

From this value, we know that the mole fraction of compound A_3 is (0.6 atm) / (0.6 atm + 0.72 atm) = (0.6 atm) / (1.32 atm), or slightly less than 0.5. This is closest to choice B.

7. D is correct. Solids, like solid AgCl, and pure liquids, most notably H_2O (l), should not be included in an equilibrium constant expression. Aqueous reactants or products are included.

8. D is correct. K_{eq} is equal to the concentration of products (each raised to their respective coefficients and multiplied together) divided by the concentration of reactants (also raised to their respective coefficients and multiplied together).

Since concentration is always positive, K_{eq} must be positive as well (statement III is accurate). Additionally, note that a spontaneous reaction has a negative ΔG and a K_{eq} that is greater than 1 (statement I is correct). Finally, if a forward direction has a K_{eq} greater than 1, it favors the products; the corresponding reverse reaction must have a K_{eq} that is less than 1, as it will favor the reactants (statement II is correct).

This page left intentionally blank.

Phases, Gases, and Solutions

CHAPTER

5

0. Introduction

Envision holding a cup of your favorite fizzy beverage and taking a sip. Imagine the heaviness of the cup in your hand, the cool liquid hitting your tongue, and the bubbles of carbon dioxide gas. The cup is formed out of a solid substance that gives it a durable shape, the liquid (even if it is just water) almost certainly contains some ions or other chemicals in solution, and the gas bubbles out into the air. This example illustrates the theme of this chapter: phases, gases, and solutions.

These are general chemistry topics that may initially seem familiar, but don't neglect them! The concept of phases has some important interconnections with thermodynamics, so developing a solid understanding of phases and phase changes can help support your success in multiple areas of general chemistry. When it comes to gases, the MCAT likes to go beyond asking you to just 'plug and chug' with equations, and may test you on the theoretical assumptions underlying kinetic gas theory as well, so this is another area that is important to review carefully. Finally, solutions and solubility are core content areas because the entire body, with its thousands of intricate physiological processes, can in some sense be understood as one big subdivided aqueous solution stuffed into a bag of skin. What this means is that even though solution chemistry may not be emphasized in biochemistry textbooks, it is still essential for understanding why our bodies work the way they do, and therefore it is regularly tested on the MCAT.

1. Phases and Phase Changes

Let's start with phases and phase changes. There are three basic phases of matter: solid, liquid, and gas. In addition to this, there are two other phases of matter, plasma and Bose-Einstein condensate, but those go beyond the scope of the MCAT—this may be one of the rare instances where you can legitimately say that the MCAT is keeping it simple! When thinking about phases and phase changes, it's important to focus your attention on intermolecular forces—that is, the forces that exist *between* molecules. Intermolecular forces are what help determine which phase of matter a substance will be in. As we will see, stronger intermolecular forces tend to be associated with solids, weaker intermolecular forces with gases, and liquids are in between.

A solid is a structure with a rigid, tightly-packed organization of atoms, such as ice, sodium chloride (table salt), and most metals, like iron. Solids are characterized by a fixed volume, meaning that they do not expand and are not compressible to any significant degree, as well as a fixed shape. Solids also do not flow, although their particles do vibrate in place.

A solid may be either crystalline or amorphous in nature. Crystalline solids exhibit a regular arrangement of atoms. In solid sodium chloride (NaCl), for example, each Na^+ ion is surrounded by six Cl^- ions, and each Cl^- ion is in turn surrounded by six Na^+ ions. This structured arrangement is termed a lattice structure, as illustrated in Figure 1. This lattice is extremely difficult to disrupt, although it can be broken if the NaCl is dissolved in water, in which case polar H_2O molecules will "solvate," or separate and surround, the individual ions. The lattice energy of an ionic solid refers to the amount of energy required to separate the solid into its component cations and anions. As you might guess, this is typically a very large amount of energy! In contrast to crystalline solids, amorphous solids are solids that do not have a regular crystal structure. The classic example is glass, a solid typically composed of silica (SiO_2).

Figure 1. Lattice structure of sodium chloride.

Like solids, liquids have a fixed volume, meaning that they are not compressible. Unlike solids, however, liquids do not have a fixed shape, instead assuming the shape of their container. This tendency allows liquids to flow, or move continuously through a container in the form of a stream. Another important property of liquids is viscosity, or the resistance of the liquid to deformation by certain forces. Molasses has a higher viscosity than water, so it is thicker and flows much more slowly. Viscosity is discussed in more depth in Chapter 5 of the Physics textbook, which covers fluids.

> > CONNECTIONS < <

Chapter 5 of Physics textbook

The third phase of matter that we will discuss is the gas phase. Gas, unlike solids and liquids, is not a condensed phase, as gas particles are relatively spread out and not in contact with one another. Gases lack a fixed shape and volume. The lack of a fixed volume—or compressibility— is especially important because it means that the density of a given gas is not constant. Rather, if the gas is forced into a smaller container, its density will increase as its particles pack more closely together.

Now, let's step back and think about how to relate phases of matter to intermolecular forces. How can we predict what phase a substance will be under various conditions? The key point here is to understand the contrast between solids and gases, which represent the two extreme ends of this spectrum. In solids, the constituent atoms are all up in each other's business. They stick close to each other, which is why solids do not flow and are not compressible. In gases, in contrast, the constituent atoms don't really want anything to do with each other. They're all flying around in space, and don't interact with each other much. With this in mind, we can identify how intermolecular forces, temperature, and pressure can combine to favor certain phases.

Intermolecular forces, which include ionic bonds, ion-ion interactions, permanent dipole interactions, and London dispersion forces (in descending order of strength), provide an indication of how much molecules will want to interact with each other. All things being equal, at a given temperature and pressure, stronger intermolecular forces will make a substance more likely to be a solid than a liquid, or a liquid than a gas. A classic example is provided by contrasting ethane and ethanol. Ethane only has weak London dispersion interactions, because it is a hydrocarbon; therefore, it has a very low boiling point of −88.5°C. In contrast, ethanol has a much higher boiling point of 78.37°C. (Ethanol does have a larger molecular weight than ethane, which contributes to this effect to some extent, but intermolecular forces explain most of this discrepancy). Ionic bonds are extremely strong, so ionic substances not in solution tend to have very high melting points—for instance, the melting point of pure sodium chloride (NaCl; table salt) is 801°C.

Higher temperatures mean that the particles in a substance will have more kinetic energy and therefore will be able to move around more. Thus, heating a solid can turn it into a liquid or a gas, and heating a liquid can turn it into a gas. In contrast, higher pressures force particles to interact with each other more closely within a confined space, so increasing the pressure can turn gases into liquids or solids, and can turn liquids into solids.

When a substance transitions from one phase to another, that is known as a phase change. We can observe up to six types of phase changes, assuming that each phase can transition directly into every other phase. For the MCAT, be sure to remember all six!

1. Melting, or fusion, is the transition from solid to liquid.

2. Freezing is the transition from liquid to solid.

3. Evaporation, or boiling, is the transition from liquid to gas.

4. Condensation is the transition from gas to liquid.

5. Sublimation is the transition from solid directly to gas.

6. Deposition is the transition from gas directly to solid.

These six processes are also summarized in Figure 2.

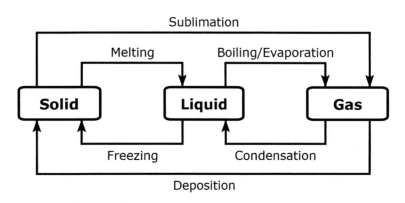

Figure 2. The six phase transitions.

The endothermic phase changes—melting, evaporation, and sublimation—require the input of heat, while the exothermic phase changes—condensation, freezing, and deposition—release heat into the environment. Endothermic processes involve the breaking of bonds or intermolecular interactions, which require a source of heat energy. As you might expect, exothermic processes typically involve bond formation or an increase in intermolecular forces.

Let's now take a closer look at how heat transfer can be used to make a substance undergo phase changes. Suppose that we are heating a block of ice. At first, the heat simply raises the temperature of the ice until the temperature reaches the melting point of ice (0°C for H_2O under 1 atm of pressure). At this point, the added heat no longer increases the temperature of the ice, but instead is diverted towards disrupting the intermolecular interactions holding the solid together. The amount of heat that was used solely to disrupt these interactions and melt the ice is the heat of fusion.

Once our sample is in the form of liquid water, adding heat will increase the temperature of the water until it reaches the boiling point (100°C for water at 1 atm). Again, the heat will then cease raising the water temperature and instead will break the intermolecular attractions that keep water in liquid form. The heat required to convert the liquid to gas at constant temperature is the heat of vaporization. Once our sample is water vapor, any additional heat will simply increase the temperature of the gas. These concepts are illustrated in Figure 3.

MCAT STRATEGY > > >

If you're faced with a calculation problem on Test Day involving heat of fusion, heat of vaporization, or specific heat, be sure to check your units carefully! This is a common source of avoidable mistakes. In particular, watch out for units of heat energy (J, kJ, or cal) and whether the units are per mass or per mole.

As always, it's important to be careful about the units that we use to describe these parameters. The specific heat of fusion, which describes how much heat energy is necessary to melt a substance, and the specific heat of vaporization, which describes how much heat energy is necessary to boil a substance, are both given in units of energy per unit of mass or per mole.

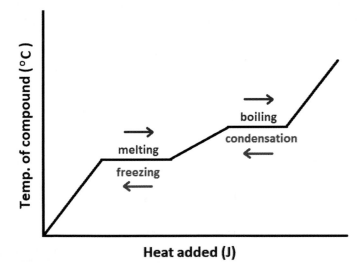

Figure 3. Phase changes as heat is added.

You should also be aware of some specialized terminology used to describe how substances respond to the addition of heat. In particular, specific heat capacity is the amount of heat required to raise the temperature of one unit mass (typically one gram or kilogram) of a substance by one degree. The specific heat capacity of water is 4.184 J/g·°C. This is an unusually high heat capacity, and is due to hydrogen bonding. The high specific heat capacity of water is why the temperature of the ocean does not vary much over the course of the day, even though the sand will cool at night and burn your feet under the hot sun. Due to the fact that water can "hold" a large amount of heat without experiencing a dramatic change in temperature, it is often used to cool extremely hot objects, perhaps to cool a hot pan from the stove, or in nuclear technology applications.

Specific heat capacity can be used in the following equation that relates the heat applied to (or released by) a system to the temperature change.

> ### MCAT STRATEGY > > >
>
> It's absolutely key to understand that adding heat to a substance does not necessarily change its temperature. At a phase change, that energy goes towards breaking intermolecular attractions, *not* to increasing the kinetic energy of the particles, which is what temperature measures.

Equation 1.
$$Q = mc\Delta T$$

In this equation, Q is the heat (usually in joules) applied to or released by the system, m is mass, c is the specific heat capacity of a substance (note that this value varies across different phases), and ΔT is the change in temperature. In this equation, temperature is usually measured in degrees Celsius, because we are concerned with *changes* in temperature, not absolute temperature; however, nothing would stop you from using degrees Kelvin here.

Students often experience confusion about when to use which quantities and equations, so to summarize:

> > At phase changes, use heat of fusion or vaporization. A separate equation is not usually given for this, because heats of fusion and vaporization are simple conversion factors relating energy to mass or moles. Dimensional analysis does the trick. Temperature remains constant.
> > Between phase changes, heat will be related to temperature change. Use $Q = mc\Delta T$.

Let's work through an example to illustrate this workflow in practice. Imagine that we want to take 250 g of ice from a –20°C freezer and turn it into water at 30°C under standard conditions. How much heat will this process require? We need to break it up into three steps, which you can check by referring to Figure 3. The first step is heating the ice to the melting point (0°C), the second step is applying enough heat to fully melt it into water, and the third step is to heat the water to 30°C. We will need three quantities, one for each step: the specific heat capacity of ice (c_{ice} = 2.03 J/g·°C), the heat of fusion of water (334 J/g), and the specific heat capacity of water (c_{water} = 4.18 J/g·°C).

1. Step 1: heating the ice. We can use $Q = mc\Delta T$, and approximate c_{ice} as 2 J/g·°C to make the mental math easier. Thus, Q = (250 g)(2 J/g·°C)(20°C) = 10,000 J.

2. Step 2: melting the ice. Here, we need the heat of fusion of water. Q = (250 g)(334 J/g) = 83,500 J. (Note that we could crudely approximate this by rounding 334 J/g down to 300 J/g. If we understand that the corresponding result of 75,000 J is an underestimate, we still may be able to get the right answer).

3. Step 3: heating the water. Again, we need to use $Q = mc\Delta T$, and we can estimate c_{water} as 4 J/g·°C, although we should keep in mind that this will lead to an underestimation of the real value. Thus, Q = (250 g)(4 J/g·°C)(30°C) = 30,000 J.

4. Step 4: totaling up the results. 10,000 J + 83,500 J + 30,000 J = 123,500 J. This is likely to be a slight underestimation of the real value because of how we rounded down the specific heat capacity values to make the calculations easier, so we should look for an answer choice somewhere in the range of 125,000 J. If, in step 2, we rounded down the heat of fusion of water to 300 J/g, then we would have more significantly underestimated the real value, so we'd want to correct accordingly when choosing an answer choice.

As discussed above, the phase of a substance is affected by temperature and pressure. These relationships are illustrated using phase diagrams, which are usually drawn with pressure on the y-axis and temperature on the x-axis. A general phase diagram is shown in Figure 4.

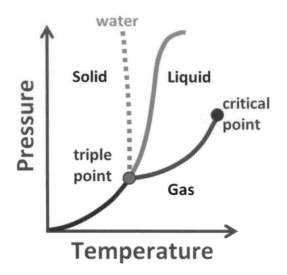

Figure 4. Phase diagram.

In phase diagrams, phase changes occur across the solid lines. An increase in pressure or decrease in temperature can convert gas to solid (deposition), gas to liquid (condensation), or liquid to solid (freezing), depending on the temperature. A decrease in pressure or increase in temperature can promote the opposite processes: sublimation (solid to gas), boiling (liquid to gas), and melting (solid to liquid).

MCAT STRATEGY > > >

In phase diagrams, you can remember the orientation as follows: solid → liquid → gas (SLUG) in clockwise order.

MCAT STRATEGY > > >

Be certain to memorize which phases correspond to each region of the diagram—they likely won't be labeled on Test Day. Although you could *theoretically* derive which region is which based on an understanding of which phases are favored by increased/decreased temperature or pressure, you don't want to waste precious time on Test Day trying to figure this out (and risking the possibility of error).

Where phase diagrams become interesting is the transition between the solid and liquid phases, depicted by green lines in Figure 4. For most substances, the solid phase is denser than the liquid, so an increase in pressure causes liquids to form solids. Ice, however, is less dense than liquid water due to its unique crystal structure. (This is how icebergs float!) Therefore, increasing pressure can melt ice into liquid water, so the phase change line between solid and liquid tilts to the left for water. Study Figure 4 carefully to understand how this concept affects the diagram.

As shown above, phase diagrams include a triple point, the point at which solid, liquid, and gas are in equilibrium, and a critical point, the point that represents the end of the liquid–gas interface. Above this point, matter exists as supercritical fluid, which possesses properties of both liquid and gas.

An important concept known as vapor pressure describes what happens when a vapor, or gas, is in thermodynamic equilibrium with the liquid phase (or, theoretically, the solid phase as well). The idea here is that there is always some interchange between the liquid and gas phase at the boundaries of a liquid. The vapor pressure is defined as the pressure exerted by the molecules of that substance that are in gas form in a closed system at a given temperature. Vapor pressure increases with temperature, and the point at which the vapor pressure of a liquid is equal to that of the surrounding atmospheric pressure corresponds to the boiling point of a substance.

Now that we've reviewed phases of matter in general, we're in a good position to focus more closely on gases and solutions.

2. Gases

The gas phase is particularly important for the MCAT, not least because gases play a major role in physiology, most notably in the form of oxygen and carbon dioxide gas, which are central to the cycle of respiration. Additionally, some gases, such as nitric oxide (NO), are important signaling molecules.

Since gases are compressible, their density is affected by pressure and temperature. This means that we have to specify certain pressure and temperature conditions in order to be able to compare density (or any related parameter) in a meaningful way. In general, for the MCAT, questions about gases will specify conditions of standard temperature and pressure (STP), at which the temperature is equal to 0°C (273 K), and pressure is 1 atmosphere (1 atm = 760 mmHg = 760 torr). For a more detailed discussion of pressure, including a formal definition and a review of the various units that are used for pressure, see Chapter 5 of the Physics textbook.

> > CONNECTIONS < <

Chapter 5 of Physics

At STP, one mole of any gas has a volume of 22.4 L. In general, one mole of any gas at a given temperature and pressure will have a constant volume, as we will see in more detail in the equations presented later in this section. Thus, equal volumes of any two gases under the same conditions will always contain the same number of gas molecules. This generalization is sometimes known as Avogadro's law, which states that the volume divided by the number of moles is constant.

When studying the behavior of gases, certain assumptions are used to model gases more elegantly. In particular, on the MCAT, you will generally encounter ideal gases, unless specified otherwise. An ideal—or theoretical—gas follows the parameters of kinetic molecular theory, which states that:

> The average kinetic energy of the gas molecules is directly proportional to temperature.
> The gas particles have no volume.
> Gas particles do not exert attractive forces on each other, although they do exert force on the walls of the container. All collisions with the walls of the container are elastic.

In reality, no gases obey these rules. This is why they are called ideal! However, these parameters allow us to predict the behavior of gas molecules and ascertain the extent to which a gas deviates from ideal behavior. Gases deviate from ideal behavior at high pressures and low temperatures and behave most ideally at low pressures and high temperatures.

There's an easy way to remember these relationships. Imagine cooling and compressing a gas, forcing it into the liquid form. You can therefore conceptualize liquids as the "ultimate non-ideal gas" where intermolecular forces become significant. Thus, the parameters that tend to favor condensation into a liquid also favor real, or non-ideal, gas behavior. Conversely, the more spread out gas molecules become—at high temperatures and low pressures—the less they interact and the more likely they are to conform to ideal behavior.

The relationships between the pressure, volume, and temperature of an ideal gas are described by several important equations. Note that you should *always* express temperature in Kelvin for gas equations. To convert temperature in Celsius to the Kelvin (K) scale, simply add 273. Freezing of water occurs at 0°C and 273 K, and boiling occurs at 100°C or 373 K. The relationship between Celsius and Fahrenheit is: $F = \left(\frac{9C}{5}\right) + 32$. For more details about temperature scales, see Chapter 4 of the Physics textbook. As discussed in that chapter, you may want to memorize

> > **CONNECTIONS** < <

Chapter 4 of the Physics textbook

the conversion equation, but it is more useful to be aware of the Fahrenheit and Celsius values of some important values (e.g., freezing point of water = 0°C and 32°F, boiling point of water = 100°C and 212°F, body temperature = 37°C and 98.6°F, room temperature = 20-25°C or 68-77°F).

Boyle's law states that the pressure and volume of a gas are inversely proportional at a constant temperature.

Equation 2A. $P_1V_1 = P_2V_2$

Equation 2B. $PV = \text{constant}$

In Equation 2A, P_1 and V_1 represent the pressure and volume of the gas in one state, and P_2 and V_2 represent the pressure and volume in another. This makes logical sense: by shrinking the volume of the container, the pressure of the gas inside will increase since gas particles must be packed more closely together. Alternatively, if we increase the volume of the container, the pressure will decrease as particles have more space and collide with the walls of the container less frequently. Equation 2B provides another way of thinking about this generalization, which is to say that the pressure of a gas multiplied by its volume forms a constant at a certain temperature. Be sure to understand that Equation 2A and 2B are two ways of formulating the same insight.

Charles' law states that the volume and temperature of a gas are directly proportional under constant pressure:

Equation 3A. $\dfrac{V_1}{T_1} = \dfrac{V_2}{T_2}$

Equation 3B. $\dfrac{V}{T} = \text{constant}$

As with Boyle's law, Charles' law can be written in the two equivalent forms shown in Equations 3A and 3B. Again, this relationship should make logical sense: if we heat a gas-filled balloon, the gas molecules gain kinetic energy and collide more frequently, increasing the internal pressure. If pressure increases, the balloon will certainly expand. To put it simply, increasing temperature will increase volume, and decreasing temperature will decrease volume.

Synthesizing these relationships yields one of the most important equations in all of chemistry, the ideal gas law:

Equation 4. $PV = nRT$

In this equation, n is the number of moles of a gas and R is the universal gas constant (0.08206 L·atm/K·mol or 8.314 J/K·mol). The ideal gas law accounts for the addition or removal of molar amounts of gas. The ideal gas law can be tested on the MCAT in two major ways. One way is numerically, much like the "plug and chug" variety you may have seen in chemistry class. If you encounter such a problem on Test Day, you have two basic tasks. First, ensure that the units of each parameter in the ideal gas law match the units of R that you use (typically 0.0826 L·atm/K·mol), and second, you must carry out the calculation quickly and accurately, using scientific notation and/or estimations to facilitate speed and accuracy. The second way the ideal gas law can be tested is conceptually or proportionally. For example, such a problem might ask what would happen to the temperature of a gas if its volume were tripled and pressure halved.

The ideal gas law can be modified to model the behavior of non-ideal gases, in a modified form known as the Van der Waals' equation. There are two basic factors that we need to account for: (1) the volume taken up by the molecules of the gas, and (2) the attractive forces experienced among the gas molecules. The first factor is easy; we can just subtract a certain quantity from the V term, modifying it to $V_m - b$, where V_m is the molar volume of the gas (at a given temperature and pressure) and b is the volume occupied by the molecules per mole. The second factor is a little bit more complicated. The way we account for it is by adding a/V_m^2 to the P term, where a is a constant that is different for every gas and V_m is the molar volume of the gas. The Van der Waals' equation can be written in two ways, depending on how we handle the variable of moles: either we can use Vm as we've done so far in this paragraph, which yields a simpler equation (Equation 5A) or we can incorporate n into the equation and use a simple

term V for volume, resulting in an equation (Equation 5B) that looks scarier than Equation 5A but has the advantage of being more similar to the ideal gas law.

Equation 5A.
$$\left(P + \frac{a}{V_m^2}\right)(V_m - b) = RT$$

Equation 5B.
$$\left(P + \frac{an^2}{V_2}\right)(V - nb) = nRT$$

All the above material on gases has been based on the assumption that we're dealing with just a single gas. However, in real life, it is very common for gases to be mixed together, as in the air that we breathe, which is made up of about 78% nitrogen and 21% oxygen, with small amounts of other gases and water vapor. There is some terminology relating to such situations that you need to be aware of for the MCAT. The first is the mole fraction (X_{gas}), which just refers to the number of moles of a given gas divided by the total moles of gas in the mixture:

Equation 6.
$$X_{gas} = \frac{n_{gas}}{n_{total}}$$

Now, the work that we've done so far in this chapter tells us that when we have a relationship defined in terms of moles of a gas, we can easily relate that to other quantities, such as pressure, volume, or temperature, using the ideal gas law. Such a derivation is shown in Equation 7.

Equation 7.
$$X_{gas} = \frac{n_{gas}}{n_{total}} = \frac{P_{gas}V/RT}{P_{total}V/RT} = \frac{P_{gas}}{P_{total}}$$

A useful point to understand regarding Equation 7 is that the volume and temperature terms are the same for the gas we're interested in and for the mixture as a whole. However, each gas in a mixture only contributes to part of the pressure of the whole. Based on this realization, we can define partial pressure as the pressure that a gas in a mixture would exert if it took up the same volume by itself; this corresponds to P_{gas} in Equation 7.

The relationship between the mole fraction and the partial pressure we derived in Equation 7 can be rearranged more typically as follows:

Equation 8.
$$P_{gas} = \frac{X_{gas}}{P_{total}}$$

This equation states that the partial pressure of a gas is equal to the total pressure of the mixture multiplied by the mole fraction of that gas. Implicit in this is a relationship known as Dalton's law, which states that the total pressure of a mixture of gases is equal to the sum of the partial pressures of its components.

3. Solutions and Solubility

In the final section of this chapter, we'll explore solutions. Solutions are homogenous mixtures containing particles that are evenly distributed throughout the solution. Gases, liquids, solids—and even multiple phases!—can be in solution. From a theoretical point of view, this is an important point to recognize. Technically speaking, the gas mixtures we talked about in section 2 were solutions, and metallic alloys (such as steel) can be thought of as solutions made up of solids. However, on the MCAT, solutions almost always contain solid molecules dissolved in liquids.

Dissolution occurs when particles, called solutes, are dissolved in another substance, usually a fluid, called a solvent. How can we predict whether one substance will dissolve in another? Solute-solvent interactions are one part of the answer. For example, hydrophilic substances are molecules that contain polar or charged groups and are capable of dissolving in water and other hydrophilic solvents, whereas hydrophobic substances are nonpolar molecules that are capable of dissolving in nonpolar, hydrophobic solvents. An easy way to remember this phenomenon is recognizing that "like dissolves like"—solutes will dissolve in solvents that they share similar properties with.

As solute is added to a solvent, the solution is considered saturated when the maximum amount of solute that can be dissolved has been added. Upon heating, more solute can be dissolved in the solution, and then upon slowly cooling the solution, the same concentration of solute will remain dissolved in what is now considered a supersaturated solution. Crystals can form in supersaturated solutions with the addition of a small amount of solute, which creates a nucleation site for solute to precipitate and form a crystal. This process is called crystallization.

The concentration of a solution can be expressed in multiple ways. Solute concentrations are frequently expressed in terms of molarity (M), which is the number of moles of solute per liter of solution:

Equation 9.
$$\text{molarity (M)} = \frac{\text{moles of solute}}{\text{liters of solution}} = \frac{\text{mol}}{\text{L}}$$

In biological processes, it is often the case that very small amounts of a substance are present in a solution, so you may encounter millimolar (mmol), micromolar (μm), and nanomolar (nm) concentrations, which simply refer to 1×10^{-3} M, 1×10^{-6} M, and 1×10^{-9} M concentrations, respectively. In contrast, molality (m) is a measure of concentration that represents the number of moles of solute per kilogram of solvent:

Equation 10.
$$\text{molality (m)} = \frac{\text{moles of solute}}{\text{kilograms of solvent}} = \frac{\text{mol}}{\text{kg}}$$

Molality is less common on the MCAT than molarity, but you should be aware of it anyway. Interestingly, for aqueous solutions with relatively small amounts of solute, molality and molarity values tend to be similar. This is because one liter of water weighs one kilogram, and therefore the difference between "liters of solution" and "kilograms of water" only becomes meaningful when there is enough solute present to materially affect the volume of the solution.

The normality (N) of a solution is the number of equivalents of reactive species per liter of solution, for which we must define the reactive species. Normality is often used to express the concentration of H^+ or OH^- ions produced in acid-base reactions. For example, hydrochloric acid (HCl) generates one equivalent of H^+ ions and one equivalent of Cl^- ions per mole, while sulfuric acid (H_2SO_4) generates two equivalents of H^+ ions and one equivalent of SO_4^{2-} ions per mole. Acids and bases that can produce more than one H^+ or OH^- equivalent are polyvalent species.

Equation 11.
$$\text{normality (N)} = \frac{\text{equivalents of solute}}{\text{liters of solution}} = \frac{\text{eq}}{\text{L}}$$

An easy way to remember how to deal with normality for acids (where it most often shows up) is to use the simple equation:

Equation 12.
$$\text{normality (N)} = \text{molarity M} \times \text{\# of H's in the acid}$$

On a conceptually similar note, there are some important properties of solutions that are related to the total number of solute molecules present in the solution (regardless of whether they are the same or different compounds). These are known as colligative properties. There are four basic colligative properties that you must be familiar with for the MCAT: (1) vapor pressure reduction, (2) boiling point elevation, (3) freezing point reduction, and (4) osmotic pressure.

The addition of solutes reduces the vapor pressure of a solvent in a relationship proportional to molal solute concentration. In other words, the presence of solute decreases the concentration of solvent that exists in the gas phase and reduces evaporation. Vapor pressure lowering is expressed by Raoult's law:

> ### MCAT STRATEGY > > >
>
> Normality is basically just a version of molarity that accounts carefully for the total number of solute molecules in solution. It is highly unlikely that the MCAT will explicitly test you on its definition; the most important thing is to be able to apply this concept in problem-solving and to correctly be able to relate the concentration of a polyprotic acid like H_2SO_4 to the concentrations of H^+ and SO_4^{2-}.

Equation 13.
$$P = X_A P_A^\circ$$

In Raoult's law, P is the vapor pressure of the solution, X_A is the mole fraction of the solvent, and P_A° is the vapor pressure of the pure solvent. Note the similarity to Dalton's law, which we discussed above in section 2. The same basic insight that the pressures of components of a solution are additive is at the foundation of both laws. Raoult's law often feels obscure to students, but the underlying idea is fairly intuitive. Imagine the surface of an aqueous solution with a lot of solutes in it. Some of the solutes will be at the surface of the solution, and the space they take up is unavailable for the liquid-gas phase transition that is at the core of vapor pressure.

Reducing the vapor pressure of a solution is equivalent to increasing the boiling point, since the boiling point is defined as the temperature at which the vapor pressure equals the ambient pressure and vapor point increases with temperature. Boiling point elevation can therefore be calculated as follows:

Equation 14.
$$\Delta T_b = iK_b C_m$$

In this equation, ΔT_b is the boiling point elevation, i is the ionization factor (also known as the van 't Hoff factor; this is a measure of how many particles are generated when a substance is placed into solution, similarly to how we thought about normality), K_b is the boiling-point depression constant (which is specific for each substance), and C_m is the molal solute concentration.

Nonvolatile solutes also decrease the freezing point of solutions. Freezing point depression can be calculated as follows:

Equation 15.
$$\Delta T_f = iK_f C_m$$

In this equation, ΔT_f is the freezing point depression, i is the van't Hoff ionization factor, K_f is the freezing-point depression constant, and C_m is the molal solute concentration. A key point to note here is that the equation for freezing point depression is basically the same as that for boiling point elevations, with different subscripts. The formal similarity between equations 14 and 15 works in your favor to some extent, but also be sure to know that boiling point is *elevated* and freezing point is *depressed*.

Our final colligative property, osmotic pressure, relates to the principle of osmosis, the flow of solvent through a semipermeable membrane. Let's consider, for example, the movement of water across a porous membrane that divides a beaker into two partitions (Figure 5). If one partition contains a high concentration and the other side a low concentration of NaCl, water will diffuse through the membrane from the dilute solution to the more concentrated solution via osmosis.

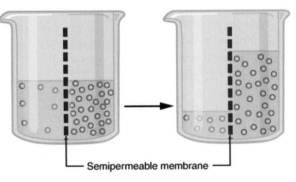

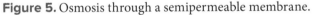
— Semipermeable membrane —

Figure 5. Osmosis through a semipermeable membrane.

Osmosis is important in biological contexts, because the plasma membrane of eukaryotic cells is a semipermeable membrane through which osmosis can take place. The entirety of Chapter 11 in the Biochemistry textbook is dedicated to biological membranes, which reflects the importance of membranes for physiology, and osmosis is also discussed there in a context more specific to physiological functioning.

> > CONNECTIONS < <

Chapter 11 of Biochemistry

As suggested by Figure 5, at some point, the flow of water through the semipermeable membrane will eventually stop, once the concentrations of solute have become more equalized. Osmotic pressure describes the pressure required to prevent osmosis, and is given by the following equation:

Equation 16.
$$\pi = MRT$$

Equation 16 is essentially a 'cousin' of the ideal gas equation, $PV = nRT$. If you were to take the ideal gas equation and divide through by V, the V term would disappear from the left side, and an (n/V) term would appear on the right side. Moles divided by volume is molarity, so we can represent this by M, the molar volume concentration. We then use π instead of P to indicate that this is the *osmotic* pressure, not the pressure of a real gas, and R is the ideal gas constant and T is the absolute temperature.

At this point, we've put a fair amount of effort into thinking about what happens when we have a solution, but we also need to explore the extent to which various substances will dissolve in a solvent. This is known as solubility. Solubility is an equilibrium process between the non-dissolved form of a substance (usually a solid in most MCAT contexts, but gases and liquids are also possible) and the dissolved form. For an ionic species that is dissolved in solution, the proportion that is in the dissociated state reaches equilibrium with the proportion that is in the undissociated state. In other words, for the dissociation reaction given by $MgCl_2(s) \rightleftharpoons Mg^{2+}(aq) + 2\ Cl^-(aq)$, we can define an equilibrium constant that is known as the solubility product constant (K_{sp}): $K_{sp} = [Mg^{2+}][Cl^-]^2$. Note that this is simply the equilibrium constant for the dissociation reaction; we give it a special name, but all the information presented about equilibrium constants in Chapter 4 holds true for K_{sp} as well.

> > **CONNECTIONS** < <

Chapter 4 of Chemistry/
Organic Chemistry

When the concentrations of the dissolved species are not at equilibrium, we refer to this expression (in our example, $[Mg^{2+}][Cl^-]^2$) as the ion product Q. Conceptually, this is the exact same idea as the reaction quotient Q that you saw in Chapter 4—that is, we're analyzing the relative concentrations of products and reactants in the same way that we do for K_{sp} or K_{eq}, but the reaction is not at equilibrium.

A high K_{sp} value means that a substance will readily dissolve in a solution (usually water, for the purposes of the MCAT), while a low K_{sp} value means that it is insoluble. K_{sp} values can vary tremendously; for example, magnesium chloride ($MgCl_2$) is highly soluble and has a K_{sp} of nearly 740, while that of aluminium hydroxide, $Al(OH)_3$, a highly insoluble compound, is 3×10^{-34}. An important point to understand here is that solubility is *actually a spectrum*, although we often talk about compounds as being 'soluble' or 'insoluble' as a shorthand. This point also applies to the conceptually linked question of whether biologically relevant compounds are hydrophilic or hydrophobic, because we can think of those categories as being equivalent to saying 'soluble in water' or 'insoluble in water.'

At this point, a natural question would be *why* we use solubility products. Why not just express solubility as mass per unit volume at a given temperature? In fact, we can do so. For instance, the solubility of CaF_2 (which is relatively insoluble) in water at 20°C is 0.0016 g/100 mL. However, using the solubility product allows us to capture some other important dynamics associated with solubility. One of the most important of these phenomena is known as the common-ion effect.

Consider silver chloride, AgCl, which is only very slightly soluble in water ($K_{sp} = 1.77 \times 10^{-10}$). Let's first consider what this value would imply for dissolving AgCl in pure water. We can write the solubility product as follows: $K_{sp} = 1.77 \times 10^{-10} = [Ag^+][Cl^-]$. Then, we can substitute x for the concentration of AgCl:

$$1.77 \times 10^{-10} = [x][x]$$
$$1.77 \times 10^{-10} = [x]^2$$
$$[x] = 1.77 \times 10^{-5}\,M$$

In words, what we have just found is that 1.77×10^{-5} M is the maximum concentration of AgCl that we can have suspended in solution before some will start to precipitate out. Now, let's imagine that we dissolve AgCl in a solution of 0.5 M NaCl. In this case, the $[Cl^-]$ term will automatically be [0.5 M]. We can neglect the amount of chloride ion that comes from AgCl to simplify our calculations, and carry out the following math:

$$K_{sp} = 1.77 \times 10^{-10} = [Ag^+][Cl^-]$$
$$1.77 \times 10^{-10} = [x][0.5]$$
$$[x] = 3.54 \times 10^{-10}\,M$$

This shows that *dramatically* less—to be precise, 50,000 times less—AgCl will dissolve now that we have flooded the reaction environment with $[Cl^-]$. This is the common ion effect in action! Theoretically, you could manipulate Le

Châtelier's principle to have the opposite effect; that is, if you found an effective way of removing Cl⁻ from solution, that would push the equilibrium of the dissociation reaction to favor the dissolution of AgCl.

It is important not to confuse solubility with ionization, although it can be easy to do so because examples like the dissolution of $MgCl_2(s)$ into its component ions are very common in discussions of solubility. Such substances are called electrolytes because charged cations and anions are capable of conducting electricity in solution. The more readily a substance ionizes in solution—for example, strong acids and ionic compounds with high K_{sp} values—the stronger the electrolyte. However, it is entirely possible for molecules composed of covalent bonds that do not readily ionize in solution to be very soluble. A classic example of this is glucose, although many biologically relevant molecules would fall into this category as well. These molecules are referred to as nonelectrolytes.

> > CONNECTIONS < <

Chapter 4 of Chemistry/ Organic Chemistry

MCAT STRATEGY > > >

The effects of temperature on the solubility of solids are yet another example of how Le Châtelier's principle appears again and again in chemistry. Recall that for endothermic reactions, heat can be thought of as a 'reactant,' while for exothermic reactions, heat is a 'product.' A hot environment can be thought of as having more heat on the reactant side, which will therefore favor endothermic reactions and disfavor exothermic reactions.

To some extent, it is possible to make predictions about whether a substance will be soluble in water under various circumstances. In particular, it's worth making a note of the effects of temperature and pressure. Some of the effects of temperature are familiar to anyone who's ever tried (unsuccessfully) to dissolve sugar in a cup of iced coffee—that is, higher temperatures generally favor the solubility of ionic compounds. There are some exceptions to this, though. On a fundamental level, this has to do with whether the dissolution reaction is exothermic or endothermic. Most dissolution reactions in water are endothermic, meaning that increased heat favors them, but some are exothermic, in which case the opposite effect can be expected.

Gases, in contrast, are more soluble at lower temperatures. This is because higher temperatures provide gases with more kinetic energy that they can use to escape the solution. Additionally, pressure favors the solubility of gases. A way you can think about this is that the ideal storage conditions for a bottle of soda (or your carbonated beverage of choice)—that is, cold and unopened (at high pressure)—are those that help carbon dioxide remain in solution.

Finally, there are some trends that help us predict whether ionic substances will be soluble in water. These are presented below in Table 1.

SOLUBLE IONIC COMPOUNDS
Alkali metals (Li^+, Na^+, K^+, Rb^+, Cs^+, Fr^+) and NH_4^+
Nitrates (NO_3^-) and chlorates (ClO_3^-)
Halides (Cl^-, Br^-, I^-) except compounds containing Ag^+, Pb^{2+}, or Hg_2^{2+}
Sulfates (SO_4^{2-}) except compounds containing Ca^{2+}, Sr^{2+}, Ba^{2+}, or Pb^{2+}

INSOLUBLE IONIC COMPOUNDS
Carbonates (CO_3^{2-}), phosphates (PO_4^{3-}), sulfides (S^{2-}), and sulfites (SO_3^{2-}) except compounds containing alkali metals or NH_4^+
Hydroxides (OH^-) and metal oxides (O^-) except compounds containing alkali metals, Ca^{2+}, Sr^{2+}, or Ba^{2+}

Table 1. Solubility rules for ionic substances.

MCAT STRATEGY > > >

It is unlikely that the MCAT will test you on the finer details of the solubility rules, but it is definitely a good idea to familiarize yourself with some of the general trends of the table, especially the fact that alkali metals are strongly soluble.

4. Must-Knows

> Phases of matter: solid (fixed volume and shape), liquid (fixed volume, flexible shape), gas (variable volume).
  - Strong intermolecular interactions favor solids (vs. liquids) and liquids (vs. gases). High temperature and low pressure favor gases (vs. solids/liquids); low temperature and high pressure favor solids.
> Adding heat changes the phase:
  - Heat of fusion = heat necessary to convert from solid to liquid
  - Heat of vaporization = heat necessary to convert from liquid to gas
  - At phase changes, temperature remains constant while heat is being added
  - Between phase changes, adding heat increases temperature ($Q = mc\Delta T$)
> Phase diagrams: generally, solid → liquid → gas in clockwise order (SLUG)
  - Triple point: solid, liquid, and gas are in equilibrium; critical point: end of liquid-gas interface (beyond critical point matter is a supercritical fluid)
> Assumptions of kinetic molecular theory for ideal gases: (1) average KE is proportional to T, (2) particles have no volume, (3) particles exert no forces on each other. Non-ideal behavior is found at low T and high P.
> Ideal gas law: $PV = nRT$. Avogadro's law: V/n is constant (1 mole occupies 22.4 L at STP). Boyle's law: $PV = $ constant ($P_1V_1 = P_2V_2$). Charles' law: V/T = constant ($V_1/T_1 = V_2/T_2$).
> Partial pressure: the pressure that a gas in a mixture would exert if it took up the same volume by itself
  - Dalton's law: partial pressures of components add up to form total pressure of a mixture; $P_{gas} = X_{gas}P_{total}$
> Solutions: units include molarity (mol/L), molality (mol/kg_{solv}), and normality (eq/L)
> Colligative properties: depend solely on number of solute particles in solution:
  - Vapor pressure reduction: Raoult's law ($P = X_AP_A°$)
  - Boiling point elevation: $\Delta T_b = iK_bC_m$
  - Freezing point depression: $\Delta T_f = iK_fC_m$
  - Osmotic pressure: $\pi = MRT$
> Solubility constant: for AB(s) → aA(aq) + bB(aq), $K_{sp} = [A]^a[B]^b$
  - High solubility constant: high solubility

- Solubility constant is an *equilibrium constant* (i.e., does not change, but defined relative to a given temperature); Q (ion product) is same expression when mixture is not at equilibrium.
> Common ion effect: presence of one ion already in solution will decrease the solubility of a compound containing that ion (i.e., very little AgCl will dissolve in a solution of NaCl because $[Cl^-]$ is already high).
> Key solubility rules: <u>Soluble</u>: Alkali metals (Li^+, Na^+, K^+, Rb^+, Cs^+, Fr^+) and NH_4^+; nitrates (NO_3^-) and chlorates (ClO_3^-); halides (Cl^-, Br^-, I^-) except compounds containing Ag^+, Pb^{2+}, or Hg_2^{2+}; sulfates (SO_4^{2-}) except compounds containing Ca^{2+}, Sr^{2+}, Ba^{2+}, or Pb^{2+}. <u>Insoluble</u>: Carbonates (CO_3^{2-}), phosphates (PO_4^{3-}), sulfides (S^{2-}), and sulfites (SO_3^{2-}) except compounds containing alkali metals or NH_4^+; hydroxides (OH^-) and metal oxides (O^-) except compounds containing alkali metals, Ca^{2+}, Sr^{2+}, or Ba^{2+}

This page left intentionally blank.

Practice Passage

To survive underwater, divers inhale highly compressed air in deep water, allowing more gases than normal to dissolve in their blood and tissues. If the diver returns to the surface too rapidly, the dissolved gas forms bubbles, much like what happens when the cap of a soda bottle is removed, causing pain and possibly death. This condition is commonly known as "the bends." To prevent this condition, a diver must return to the surface slowly, allowing the dissolved gases to slowly adjust to the changes in pressure. Rather than breathing compressed air, the diver may breathe a mixture of compressed helium and oxygen, known as heliox, thereby avoiding the bends. This is possible because helium is less soluble in water than nitrogen, the major gas found in air and nitrox mixtures (approximately 79%). The solubility of gas in aqueous solution is illustrated by Henry's Law, which reveals how the solubility (C, mol/L) of a gas is also affected by the pressure (P) of the gas on the surface of the liquid:

$$C = k\text{P}$$

where k represents the proportionality constant (Table 1), a property arising from the intermolecular and chemical interactions of the gas and the liquid, with similarities to the intermolecular forces generally favoring the formation of the solution. Experiments reveal an inverse relationship between gas solubility and solvent temperature for most gases.

Table 1. Henry's Law Constants at 25 °C in Aqueous Solution

Formula	k (M/atm)
N_2	6×10^{-4}
He	4×10^{-4}
Ne	5×10^{-4}
Ar	1×10^{-3}
CO	1×10^{-3}
CO_2	3×10^{-2}

Narcosis, an alteration in consciousness at depth, can also occur while scuba diving due to the anesthetic effect of certain gases at high pressure. All gases have this effect to varying degrees, with lipid solubility correlating positively with the degree of narcosis. The noble gases, aside from the apparent exception of helium, have been shown to alter human mental functions at various levels. This effect, which is different than that caused by hypoxia, is also observed with nitrogen and carbon dioxide gas. In fact, the heavy noble gases are more narcotic than nitrogen at a given pressure, and xenon has been used at standard pressures as a surgical anesthetic. The precise mechanism of this narcosis is not well understood, but appears to correlate to the solubility of the gas in neuronal membranes.

It is hypothesized that the noble gas narcotic effects may be similar to the mechanism of nonpolar anesthetics such as chloroform, diethyl ether and nitrous oxide. The production of these effects by the noble gases suggests a mechanism unrelated to chemical reactivity. A physical effect based on intermolecular forces may cause a change in membrane volume, thereby affecting the transport of ions through channels in axonal membranes.

1. Which of the following lipid-soluble compounds has a nonzero dipole moment?
   A. Argon
   B. Elemental nitrogen
   C. Chloroform
   D. Carbon dioxide

2. Based on information in the passage, which of the following best explains the increase in anesthetic properties of the noble gases as the atomic number increases?
   A. The polarizability of the atoms increases.
   B. The number of protons in the nucleus increases.
   C. The number of neutrons in the nucleus increases.
   D. The size of the atoms decreases.

3. Which of the following best describes the effect of increasing temperature on the value of the Henry's law constant for a gas?
   A. Since the solubility of gases generally decreases with an increase in average kinetic energy, the value of the Henry's law constant increases.
   B. Since the solubility of gases generally decreases with an increase in average kinetic energy, the value of the Henry's law constant decreases.
   C. Since the solubility of gases generally increases with an increase in average kinetic energy, the value of the Henry's law constant decreases.
   D. Since the solubility of gases generally increases with an increase in average kinetic energy, the value of the Henry's law constant increases.

4. Which of the following gas mixtures is LEAST likely to cause the bends for a scuba diver?
   A. Compressed air
   B. Nitrox
   C. Heliox
   D. Neonox

5. Which of the following gases is expected to have the highest average kinetic energy?
   A. 20 moles of Kr at 320 K
   B. 50 moles of Ar at 220 K
   C. 100 moles of Kr at 250 K
   D. 10 moles of Ar at 350 K

6. Which of the following is the formula for nitrous oxide?
   A. N_2O
   B. NO
   C. NO_2
   D. N_2O_5

7. Which of the following systems will have the lowest volume?

GAS	P (KPA)	T (K)	MOLES PRESENT
H_2	20	300	20
F_2	30	300	20
Br_2	40	300	30
O_2	50	300	40

A. H_2
B. F_2
C. Br_2
D. O_2

Practice Passage Explanations

To survive underwater, divers inhale highly compressed air in deep water, allowing more gases than normal to dissolve in their blood and tissues. If the diver returns to the surface too rapidly, the dissolved gas forms bubbles, much like what happens when the cap of a soda bottle is removed, causing pain and possibly death. This condition is commonly known as "the bends." To prevent this condition, a diver must return to the surface slowly, allowing the dissolved gases to slowly adjust to the changes in pressure. Rather than breathing compressed air, the diver may breathe a mixture of compressed helium and oxygen, known as heliox, thereby avoiding the bends. This is possible because helium is less soluble in water than nitrogen, the major gas found in air and nitrox mixtures (approximately 79%). The solubility of gas in aqueous solution is illustrated by Henry's Law, which reveals how the solubility (C, mol/L) of a gas is also affected by the pressure (P) of the gas on the surface of the liquid:

$$C = kP$$

where k represents the proportionality constant (Table 1), a property arising from the intermolecular and chemical interactions of the gas and the liquid, with similarities to the intermolecular forces generally favoring the formation of the solution. Experiments reveal an inverse relationship between gas solubility and solvent temperature for most gases.

Key terms: bends, heliox, solubility, Henry's Law

Cause and effect: diver under increased fluid P have more gas dissolved in blood, rapid ascent → P decreases → gas precipitates out as bubbles, causing damage; gas solubility ~ $1/T_{solvent}$

Equation 1 is a simple direct relationship between the pressure (P) of a gas on the surface of a liquid and the proportionality constant

Table 1. Henry's Law Constants at 25 °C in Aqueous Solution

Formula	k (M/atm)
N_2	6×10^{-4}
He	4×10^{-4}
Ne	5×10^{-4}
Ar	1×10^{-3}
CO	1×10^{-3}
CO_2	3×10^{-2}

Table 1 shows that the value for the noble gases increases as the size and polarizability associated with increases in the van der Waals forces of attraction

Narcosis, an alteration in consciousness at depth, can also occur while scuba diving due to the anesthetic effect of certain gases at high pressure. All gases have this effect to varying degrees, with lipid solubility correlating positively with the degree of narcosis. The noble gases, aside from the apparent exception of helium, have been shown to alter human mental functions at various levels. This effect, which is different than that caused by hypoxia, is also observed with nitrogen and carbon dioxide gas. In fact, the heavy noble gases are more narcotic than nitrogen at a given pressure, and xenon has been used at standard pressures as a surgical anesthetic. The precise mechanism of this narcosis is not well understood, but appears to correlate to the solubility of the gas in neuronal membranes.

Key terms: narcosis, noble gases, lipid solubility

Cause and effect: higher lipid solubility → gas passes through neuron membrane → narcotic effects

It is hypothesized that the noble gas narcotic effects may be similar to the mechanism of nonpolar anesthetics such as chloroform, diethyl ether and nitrous oxide. The production of these effects by the noble gases suggests a mechanism unrelated to chemical reactivity. A physical effect based on intermolecular forces may cause a change in membrane volume, thereby affecting the transport of ions through channels in axonal membranes.

Key terms: narcotic mechanism

Cause and effect: noble gases unreactive, so effect is due to physical mechanism, not chemical; noble gases interrupt ion transport across axons → impaired AP conduction

1. C is correct. To have a dipole, there must be polar covalent bonds and an asymmetric molecular structure. Chloroform ($CHCl_3$) has three polar covalent C-Cl bonds forming a pyramidal-like structure that does produce a net dipole moment.

   A, B, D: Argon can be eliminated because it is monatomic. Elemental nitrogen, N_2, does not have a polar covalent bond. Carbon dioxide does have polar covalent bonds, but the symmetrical linear structure does not produce a net dipole moment.

2. A is correct. The passage suggests that the anesthetic properties of the noble gases result from their degree of lipid solubility, which would be related to the van der Waals interactions. As the size of an atom or molecule increases, it becomes easier to create temporary dipoles, which increase the intermolecular forces associated with the interactions of molecules.

   B, C, D: While the number of protons and neutrons in the nucleus do increase with an increase in the atomic number, all of the noble gases have full octets and do not generally form covalent bonds. As the atomic number increases, the number of electron shells increases and the size of the atom increases. It is the size and polarizability of an atom or molecule that affects the Van der Waals intermolecular forces the most.

3. B is correct. Temperature is a measure of the average kinetic energy of a system. As stated at the end of the first paragraph, there is inverse relationship between gas solubility and solvent temperature for most gases. This explains why a soda will go flatter (i.e. the gas precipitates out) quicker on a hot day than a cold day. Increasing the temperature should therefore decrease the solubility of a gas in aqueous solution, which is directly related to the magnitude of the Henry's law constant, k.

4. C is correct. The first paragraph tells us that air is about 79% elemental nitrogen, with elemental oxygen representing about 20% and the remaining portion is made up of other gases. Nitrox is a synthetic mixture of elemental nitrogen (79%) and elemental oxygen. Likewise heliox and neonox are similar synthetic mixtures of oxygen, combined with helium and neon, respectively. The passage indicates that helium is much less soluble in aqueous solution than nitrogen, and based on the Henry's law constants in Table 1, helium is much less soluble than neon as well. Therefore, since there will be less dissolved gas in the blood and tissues of a diver that was

breathing heliox, this person is much less likely to experience the formation of bubbles and experience the bends when returning to the surface.

5. D is correct. The average kinetic energy of a gas is directly related to its temperature (KE ~ 3/2 NkT). Thus, the gas with the highest temperature will have the greatest average kinetic energy.

6. A is correct. Nitrous oxide is an alternative name for dinitrogen monoxide, N_2O. The suffix –ous indicates a lower oxidation state. Nitric oxide is the older name for nitrogen monoxide (NO), a potent neurotransmitter and vasodilator. Nitrogen dioxide is NO_2, and dinitrogen pentoxide is N_2O_5, the latter is sometimes called nitrogen pentoxide.

7. B is correct. According to the ideal gas law, PV = nRT where R is the universal gas constant. Since the question is asking for V, rearrange the equation.

$$V = nRT/P$$

Since the only values that differ are n and P, we can simply compare the relative values of n/P for each gas.

A: V = n/P = 20/20 = 1
B: V = n/P = 20/30 = 2/3 = 0.66
C: V = n/P = 30/40 = 3/4 = 0.75
D: V = n/P = 40/50 = 4/5 = 0.80

 different gas. If the two samples are held at the same temperature, which of the following must be true?
   A. The average kinetic energy of the molecules is the same for both samples.
   B. The two gas samples exert the same amount of pressure on the walls of their respective containers.
   C. The total kinetic energy of the gas molecules is the same for both samples.
   D. The average speed of the molecules is the same for both samples.

2. Which of the following gases is LEAST likely to behave in a manner consistent with that predicted for an ideal gas?
   A. Helium
   B. Nitrogen
   C. Hexane
   D. Propane

3. A sample of argon gas is initially contained in an 18-liter aluminum tank at a pressure of 90 atmospheres. If half of the gas molecules are allowed to slowly escape from the tank, such that temperature does not change significantly, what is the pressure of the remaining gas?
   A. 9 atm
   B. 18 atm
   C. 45 atm
   D. 90 atm

4. A container holds a mixture of 2 moles of hydrogen gas and 2 moles of nitrogen gas at a total pressure of 20 atm. If the two gases effuse from the tank into the ambient environment through a very small hole, what is the approximate ratio of the rate of effusion of hydrogen to that of nitrogen?
   A. 4:1
   B. 1:4
   C. 14:1
   D. 1:14

5. Cooking at high altitude often requires modification of temperatures and cook times compared to those used at altitudes close to sea level. These changes are necessary because at high altitude:

   A. the boiling point of water is higher than at sea level.
   B. the atmospheric pressure is higher than at sea level.
   C. the vapor pressure of water at any given temperature is higher than at sea level.
   D. the value of the vapor pressure of water is closer to that of atmospheric pressure than it is at sea level.

6. The walls of most blood vessels are impermeable to macromolecules, but somewhat permeable to water and small ions. Hydrostatic pressure drives the movement of water out of the vascular space and into the surrounding tissue. Which of the following would most likely increase the net movement of water out of the vasculature?
   A. An increase in plasma sodium ion concentration
   B. A decrease in plasma sodium ion concentration
   C. A decrease in plasma protein concentration
   D. An increase in plasma protein concentration

7. Which of the following accurately describes the melting of a pure substance in a closed system?
   A. The total energy of the system does not change during the melting process.
   B. The temperature of the system does not change during the melting process.
   C. The average kinetic energy of the molecules in the system increases during the melting process.
   D. The amount of heat input required for complete melting is independent of the amount of substance.

8. Consider a system at equilibrium consisting of an atmosphere of inert gas over an inert liquid. If the dissolution of the gas into the liquid is exothermic, which of the following accurately describes a change to the system that will reduce the concentration of dissolved gas?
   A. Decreasing the quantities of both liquid and gas by equimolar amounts
   B. Increasing the pressure of the system
   C. Increasing the temperature of the system
   D. Decreasing the temperature of the system

Independent Questions

1. Two separate containers are each filled with a

Independent Question Explanations

1. A is correct. The average kinetic energy of the molecules in a sample of gas is directly proportional to the temperature of the sample. If two gases have the same temperature, the molecules in each sample must have the same average kinetic energy. Since the two gases may consist of molecules with different masses, this does not necessarily imply that the molecules are traveling at the same speed. Total kinetic energy is an extrinsic property, as it depends on the number of molecules present; the question stem does not specify that the samples contain equal numbers of molecules.

2. C is correct. The ideal gas model does not account for attractive intermolecular forces or the volume of the gas molecules themselves. Therefore, this model is most applicable to real gases composed of small molecules that do not experience significant intermolecular interactions. Since hexane has the highest molecular weight of the choices given, it is most likely to deviate from the ideal gas model, assuming other conditions are constant.

3. C is correct. Since the number of moles of gas is halved but the volume of the container does not change, the ideal gas law may be simplified in order to determine the new pressure, such that:

$$\frac{P_1}{n_1} = \frac{P_2}{n_2} \rightarrow P2 = \frac{P_1 \times n_2}{n_1} \rightarrow P_2 = \frac{P_1 \times \frac{1}{2}n_1}{n_1} \rightarrow P_2 = \frac{1}{2}P_1 = 45\text{atm}$$

4. A is correct. Since the two gases are mixed together in the same container at the same temperature, their relative rates of effusion depend only on the molar mass of each gas molecule. This relationship is described by Graham's law:

$$\frac{\text{rate of effusion of H}_2}{\text{rate of effusion of N}_2} = \frac{\sqrt{\text{molar mass of N}_2}}{\sqrt{\text{molar mass of H}_2}} = \frac{\sqrt{28}}{\sqrt{2}} \approx 4$$

5. D is correct. Vapor pressure increases with increasing temperature until it equals the pressure of the atmosphere above the liquid, at which point the liquid boils. The relationship between vapor pressure and atmospheric pressure determines the boiling point of the liquid. Therefore, since atmospheric pressure at high altitude is lower than at sea level, the difference between the vapor pressure of water and the atmospheric pressure is smaller and the liquid boils at a lower temperature.

6. C is correct. Since the question stem suggests that small ions cross the vascular endothelium to a greater extent than plasma proteins, changes in plasma protein concentrations are more likely to influence the osmotic gradient. Decreased plasma protein concentration will reduce the osmotic pressure of the plasma, consequently reducing the movement of water back into the vascular space. The net movement of water *out* of the vasculature, then, must be increased.

7. B is correct. Temperature is constant during phase transitions, but the total energy continues to increase as heat enters the system. Since temperature directly reflects the average kinetic energy of the molecules in a system, the average kinetic energy is also constant during the transition.

8. C is correct. If the dissolution process is exothermic, an increase in temperature will disfavor the forward process. The result will be a shift in equilibrium to a state in which less gas is dissolved. This is consistent with the fact that gases are typically most soluble in liquids at low temperature.

This page left intentionally blank.

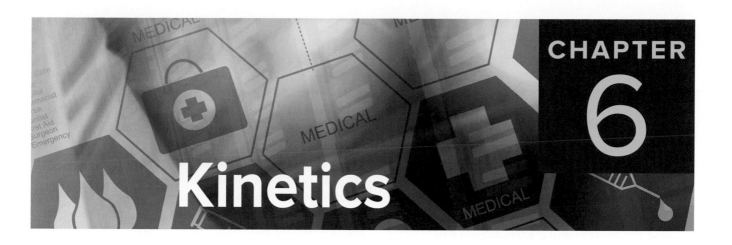

0. Introduction

Kinetics is the branch of chemistry that deals with the rate of reactions, which is a biologically relevant topic because an organism must complete metabolically important reactions quickly in order to function. This chapter will proceed through a review of the mechanisms of chemical reactions and discuss catalysts, before moving on to rates and rate laws and concluding with a comparison of kinetics and equilibrium, which is an essential distinction to master for the MCAT.

1. Mechanisms

Let's start our analysis of kinetics by thinking about what it means for a reaction to take place in the simplest possible terms. For a reaction to occur, the reactants must collide with each other in the correct spatial orientation and with sufficient kinetic energy for the reaction to happen, a threshold which is known as the activation energy (E_a) of a reaction. The rate of a reaction corresponds to how many such collisions take place over a given unit of time. This intuition is mathematically codified in the Arrhenius equation below, which defines k, the rate constant. The rate constant k can be thought of in this context as corresponding to the rate of a reaction, although, as we will see below, the rate constant and the rate are technically two distinct concepts.

Equation 1.
$$k = Ae^{-E_a/RT}$$

In this equation, k is the rate constant, and A is the frequency factor, which corresponds to the frequency of collisions between reactants in proper spatial orientations. E_a is the activation energy, R is the ideal gas constant, and T is the temperature in kelvins. Since A can be thought of as a constant, e is a mathematical constant, and R is a physical constant, the rate constant can only meaningfully be affected by the activation energy and the temperature. That is, if the quantity $-(E_a/RT)$ increases, the rate constant will increase, and if it decreases, the rate constant will decrease. Larger values of E_a make $-(E_a/RT)$ more negative, demonstrating an inverse relationship between the activation energy and the reaction rate. The idea that lower activation energies correspond to faster reaction rates is fundamental for kinetics on the MCAT. In contrast, temperature has a direct relationship with reaction rate; higher values of T make E_a/RT smaller, meaning that $-(E_a/RT)$ is less negative or larger. Chemically, higher temperatures have the effect of both increasing the overall collision rate and the proportion of those collisions that will have kinetic energy values exceeding the activation energy. The takeaway point here is that there are two ways to speed up a reaction: reduce the activation energy or increase the temperature. The body can't really raise the temperature that much, so as we will see in physiology and biochemistry, biological systems use enzymes (biological catalysts) to regulate reaction rates by reducing the activation energy.

MCAT STRATEGY > > >

Focus on understanding the concepts expressed by the Arrhenius equation before memorizing it. It is absolutely essential that you understand that a reaction will proceed faster if you lower the activation energy and/ or raise the temperature. Memorizing the equation itself is a much lower priority.

Although not indicated in the Arrhenius equation, which illustrates how the reaction rate is affected by activation energy and temperature, some other parameters can affect the reaction rate. The most important of these is the concentration of the reactants, which is incorporated into the rate law of a reaction and discussed below in Section 3. Additionally, the reaction rate of gaseous reactions can be affected by pressure; higher pressures increase the reaction rate for essentially the same reason that higher temperatures do (i.e., more pressure means more effective collisions). The rate of reactions in solution can be affected by properties of the solvent, but the details vary among reactions.

Reactants that collide with sufficient energy in the proper orientation form a short-lived transition complex. For example, in the reaction $H_2(g) + Cl_2(g) \rightarrow 2HCl(g)$, there is an extremely brief period in which the covalent bonds in the reactants begin to weaken and the bonds in the products begin to form, as illustrated in Figure 1. The activation energy refers to the energy necessary to reach the transition state. Transition complexes are not isolable and occur at the highest-energy point of the reaction.

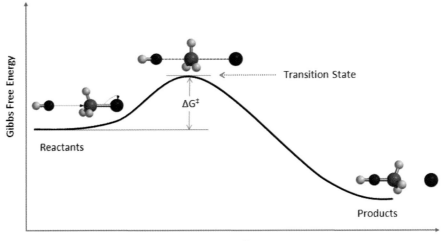

Reaction: $HO^- + CH_3Br \rightarrow [HO\text{-}\text{-}\text{-}CH_3\text{-}\text{-}\text{-}Br]^{\ddagger} \rightarrow CH_3OH + Br^-$

Figure 1. Transition complex.

Reactions may occur in multiple steps that are omitted when we consider only the overall reactants and products. For example, consider the reaction $NO_2(g) + CO(g) \rightarrow NO(g) + CO_2(g)$. This reaction proceeds in the following two steps:

$$\text{Step 1: } NO_2(g) + NO_2(g) \rightarrow NO(g) + NO_3(g) \qquad \text{(slow)}$$

$$\text{Step 2: } NO_3(g) + CO(g) \rightarrow CO_2(g) \qquad \text{(fast)}$$

Note that $NO_3(g)$ can be cancelled when combining these reactions. In this reaction, $NO_3(g)$ acts as a reaction intermediate. Step 1 is slow and step 2 is fast, which indicates that each of these steps can be considered to be a distinct reaction with its own individual reaction rate. A reaction with multiple steps can go forward no faster than its slowest step, which means that the slowest step is referred to as the rate-limiting step of a reaction.

Reaction coordinate diagrams are used to illustrate how the energy states of a reaction proceed over time, as shown for a single-step reaction in Figure 2. The x-axis of a reaction coordinate diagram indicates time and the y-axis indicates free energy. The difference between the initial energy and the energy of the transition-state complex is the activation energy (E_a) of the reaction, and the difference between the free energy of the initial reactants and the final products is known as ΔG. A reaction like that shown in Figure 2, in which the products are at a lower energy state than the reactants, has a ΔG value less than zero, which is referred to as exergonic, meaning that it is spontaneous and energy is released. If $\Delta G > 0$, the reaction is endergonic, meaning that it is not spontaneous and energy is absorbed.

> ## MCAT STRATEGY > > >
>
> Be able to distinguish reaction intermediates and transition states. It may be helpful to think of transitional states as being basically theoretical constructs that are used to explain how a reaction proceeds. As such, they're not a "real" substance—you can't isolate them. In contrast, reaction intermediates are "real" chemicals that are at least in principle isolable, although they may be quite reactive and therefore unstable.

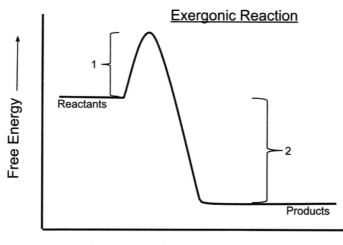

Figure 2. Single-step reaction coordinate diagram.

It is absolutely crucial for the MCAT to consistently distinguish kinetics and thermodynamics. ΔG is a thermodynamic constant for a reaction, and whether or not a reaction is spontaneous has nothing to do with its rate. For instance, the oxidation of iron in air (i.e., the formation of rust) is spontaneous but occurs quite slowly.

> ## > > CONNECTIONS < <
>
> Chapter 12 of biochemistry

Reaction coordinates can also be used to illustrate reactions that occur in multiple steps, as shown below in Figure 3. Such reaction diagrams can either be considered as a single whole, as when evaluating the ΔG of the combined reaction, or as two distinct reaction steps with individual kinetic parameters, as reflected by the presence of two transition states with two distinct E_a values.

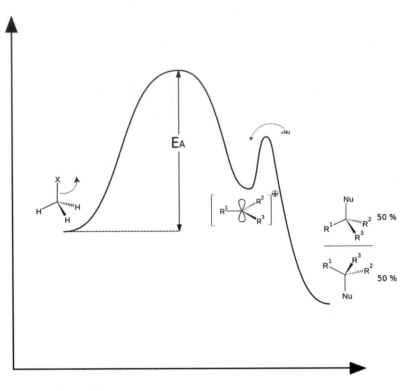

Figure 3. Two-step reaction coordinate diagram.

2. Catalysts

Catalysts are substances that increase the rate of a reaction by reducing its activation energy. The physical mechanisms through which catalysts accomplish this include stabilizing the transition state, weakening bonds within the reactants, changing the orientation of the reactants to facilitate effective collisions, increasing the frequency of collisions, and donating electron density to the reactants. Effectively, this means that catalysts provide an alternative reaction mechanism. The effect of a catalyst on an exergonic reaction is shown in Figure 4.

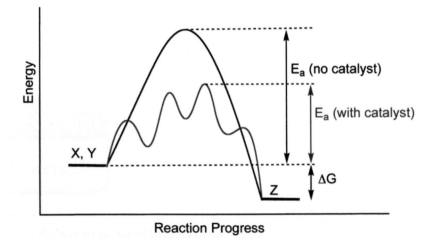

Figure 4. Reaction coordinates for a catalyzed versus uncatalyzed exergonic reaction.

Catalysts do not affect any thermodynamic parameters of the overall reaction; as can be seen in Figure 4, the ΔG values for the catalyzed and uncatalyzed reactions are identical (as are the ΔH and ΔS terms). This means that catalysts cannot make thermodynamically unfavorable and nonspontaneous reactions favorable and spontaneous. Moreover, catalysts are not consumed in the reaction.

It is useful to distinguish between heterogeneous and homogeneous catalysis. In heterogeneous catalysis, the catalyst is in a different phrase from the reactants; typically, the catalyst is a solid and the reactants are liquids or gases. In such cases, the reactants must adsorb onto the catalyst for it to be effective. Since this depends on the surface area of the catalyst, it may be necessary to grind it or to find other ways of optimizing the surface area. An example is the Haber synthesis of ammonia ($N_2(g) + 3 H_2(g) \rightarrow 2NH_3(g)$), which is performed in industrial contexts under high temperature and pressure with ground iron catalysts. Homogeneous catalysis occurs when the catalyst and reactants are in the same phase. Many biologically relevant reactions involve homogeneous catalysis in aqueous solution, with examples including any organic reactions in which H^+ or OH^- function as a catalyst.

The catalysis of biological reactions is crucial for the function of organisms because physiological functioning depends both on whether a reaction occurs at all and whether it occurs in a timely manner. Proteins that catalyze biological reactions are known as enzymes. Since enzymes play a fundamental role in regulating metabolic processes, they are one of the highest-yield biochemistry topics on the MCAT. Although enzymes are covered in more detail in Chapter 3 of the Biochemistry textbook, a thorough understanding of the fundamentals of kinetics is important for properly understanding enzyme function.

MCAT STRATEGY >>>

The fact that catalysts do not affect the thermodynamic parameters of a reaction is a perennial MCAT favorite. No matter how a question might be phrased, the *only* correct thing to say about the effects of a catalyst is that a catalyst increases the rate of a reaction by reducing its activation energy. Anything else is a trap.

>> CONNECTIONS <<

Chapter 3 of Biochemistry

MCAT STRATEGY >>>

Since enzymes are biological catalysts, all the points we made about MCAT strategy regarding catalysts apply to enzymes too. Enzymes never affect the thermodynamic constants of a reaction and can never turn a nonspontaneous reaction into a spontaneous one.

3. Rates and Rate Laws

The rate law of a reaction is given as a function of the rate constant k discussed above (see Equation 1 for the Arrhenius equation) and the concentration of some or all of the reactants. The rate law of a general reaction of the form $aA + bB \rightarrow cC + dD$ is given in Equation 2.

Equation 2. $$\text{rate} = k[A]^x[B]^y$$

The rate itself has units of M/s or mol/L·s. [A] and [B] are concentrations of the reactants in units of M or mol/L. The exponents x and y must be experimentally determined; they do *not* correspond to the stoichiometric coefficients a and b in the reaction formula. The order of a reaction is defined by the sum of the exponents in the rate law; here, these are given as x and y, although a third reactant $[C]^z$ could theoretically be present. If the exponents sum to zero, the reaction is zero-order. If the reactants sum to 1, the reaction is first-order. If they sum to 2, it is second-order, if they sum to 3 it is third-order, and so on. In principle, non-integer values are possible, as well as negative values for individual components of the rate law; however, in practice, the MCAT emphasizes zero-order, first-order, and second-order reactions, so you should mostly be aware of third- or higher-order rates as a possibility.

The rate law can be determined experimentally using the method of initial rates. In this method, multiple trials are run with variations in the concentration of individual reactants. The initial rate is then measured, with the goal of identifying how changes in the concentration of a reactant affect the rate. An example is given for the hypothetical reaction A + B → C + D.

Trial	Initial rate (mol/L·s or M/s)	Initial concentration of A (mol/L or M)	Initial concentration of B (mol/L or M)
1	1.0×10^{-5}	0.2	0.2
2	2.0×10^{-5}	0.4	0.2
3	4.0×10^{-5}	0.2	0.4
4	3.0×10^{-5}	0.6	0.2

Table 1. Method of initial rates.

MCAT STRATEGY > > >

The math in this example was as nice as it could be, making it easier to follow the logic of the process. However, on Test Day, you could be given a table with more challenging math. Trial 1 might not be the baseline trial, and the values could be given in more complex scientific notation, requiring you to recognize, for instance, that 3.588×10^{-3} is 4 times 5.99×10^{-4}. Alternatively, you could be asked to explore the effects of tripling or quadrupling reactant concentrations. These possibilities emphasize the importance of constant practice with scientific notation and estimation and of using a systematic approach to tackle these questions.

A systematic approach is key for analyzing a table like this. First, determine the effects of changing the concentration of A by looking for pairs of trials in which the concentration of A changes while the concentration of B remains constant. In this table, that is the case for Trials 1 and 2 and Trials 1 and 4. Using Trial 1 as a baseline, we see that in Trial 2 [A] was doubled and the initial rate was doubled, while in Trial 4 [A] was tripled and the rate tripled. This means that in the rate law for this reaction, the term for [A] is $[A]^1$, and that this reaction is first-order for A. Turning to B, we again use Trial 1 as a baseline and observe that in Trial 3, only the concentration of B was changed. In this trial, doubling [B] quadrupled the reaction rate, meaning that the term for [B] in the rate law of this reaction is $[B]^2$, and that this reaction is second-order for B. The rate law for this reaction is therefore rate = $k[A][B]^2$, meaning that it is third-order overall.

The rate constant k can be calculated from any of the trials in Table 1 after the exponents of the rate law have been established, and the units of k can be derived once those exponents are known. Given the general rate law equation of rate = $k[A]^x[B]^y$, the algebraic logic for calculating k, either numerically or in units, is presented in Equation 3.

Equation 3.
$$k = \frac{rate}{[A]^x[B]^y}$$

For a reaction with an overall order of z, the general form for the units of k is given in Equation 4.

Equation 4.
$$k = \frac{\frac{M}{s}}{M^z} = M^{1-z} \cdot s^{-1}$$

An important point to note about the units of k is that while the units of M (alternatively expressible as mol/L) vary according to the overall order of the reaction, the units of k must always involve inverse seconds. The units of k for the reaction orders most commonly encountered on the MCAT are presented in Table 2, but it is important to understand that they can easily be derived and presented in different ways depending on whether units of molarity or moles per liter are used, and whether inverse units are represented using a fraction or a negative exponent.

Order	Units of k (molarity, negative exponents)	Units of k (molarity, fractions)	Units of k (mol/L, negative exponents)	Units of k (mol/L, fractions)
Zero	$M \cdot s^{-1}$	M/s	$mol \cdot L^{-1} \cdot s^{-1}$	mol/(L·s)
First	s^{-1}	1/s	s^{-1}	1/s
Second	$M^{-1} \cdot s^{-1}$	1/(M·s)	$mol^{-1} \cdot L \cdot s^{-1}$	L/(mol·s)
Third	$M^{-2} \cdot s^{-1}$	$1/(M^2 \cdot s)$	$mol^{-2} \cdot L^2 \cdot s^{-1}$	$L^2/(mol^2 \cdot s)$

Table 2. Reaction order and the rate constant k.

Physiologically, zero-order reactions are exemplified by enzyme-catalyzed reactions in which the enzyme is saturated—that is, when concentrations of the reactant far exceed the available active sites on enzymes. In such a situation, the catalysis is the rate-limiting step and the concentration of the reactant is irrelevant. First-order reactions are exemplified by radioactive decay and S_N1 reactions that are dependent on carbocation formation. Second-order reactions physically involve collisions between two reactant molecules, as in S_N2 reactions.

The rate law formula tested on the MCAT refers to the initial rate of the reaction. It is also possible to plot the concentration of reactants over time as the reaction progresses, and the shape of such a graph differs depending on the order of the reaction. It is linear for zero-order reactions because the rate of the reaction never changes based on the concentration of the reactants. For a first-order reaction, such a graph is non-linear, but transforming the graph to be a plot of the natural logarithm of the reactant as a function of time results in a linear plot. For a second-order reaction in which the rate is dependent on one reactant (i.e., rate = $k[A]^2$), a graph of [A] versus time is again non-linear, but transforming the graph to 1/[A] versus time results in a linear graph.

MCAT STRATEGY > > >

Do not memorize Table 2. Instead, focus on understanding that each row contains four ways of expressing *the same thing*, make sure you understand the algebra and dimensional analysis necessary to interconvert between these various ways of representing the units of k, and review how they can be derived from the underlying rate law. MCAT questions about k can seem intimidating, but they are very doable if you invest the time in understanding the fundamentals, because there are only so many ways they can ask the question.

> > CONNECTIONS < <

Chapter 11 of Chem/Organic Chemistry

4. Must-Knows

> Activation energy refers to the energy necessary to reach the transition state.
> The rate of a reaction can be increased by increasing temperature or decreasing the activation energy (E_a).
> $\Delta G < 0 \rightarrow$ exergonic and spontaneous. $\Delta G > 0 \rightarrow$ endergonic and nonspontaneous.
> Be able to read a reaction coordinate diagram and identify the following features:
>   – ΔG
>   – E_a
>   – Transition state(s)
>   – Intermediates
>   – Is the reaction spontaneous (exergonic) or not?
> ΔG, ΔH, and ΔS are thermodynamic properties independent of rate.
> Catalysts increase reaction rate by reducing E_a.
> Enzymes are biological catalysts made of proteins.
> Catalysts (and therefore enzymes) *cannot* turn a nonspontaneous reaction into a spontaneous one, or change any thermodynamic parameters of a reaction (ΔG, ΔH, or ΔS).
> The rate law of $a\text{A} + b\text{B} \rightarrow c\text{C} + d\text{D}$ is rate $= k[\text{A}]^x[\text{B}]^y$.
>   – The exponents x and y **must** be experimentally determined. They do not reflect the stoichiometric coefficients a and b.
>   – This rate law reflects the initial rate.
>   – The units of the rate constant k can be determined algebraically. Rate is in M/s and concentration is in M.
>   – The overall order of this reaction is the sum of the exponents x and y.
> Be able to use the method of initial rates to determine the order of a reaction.
>   – Compare two trials where the concentration of only one reactant is changed and see how that change affects the rate. If doubling the reactant concentration doubles the rate, the reaction is first-order for that reactant. If doing so quadruples it, it is second-order for that reaction, etc.
>   – Repeat for all reactants.

This page left intentionally blank.

Practice Passage

In addition to producing nitrogen oxides, the incomplete combustion of hydrocarbon-based fuels also produces hydrocarbon radicals. Elemental nitrogen is the major gas in the earth's atmosphere (78%) and oxygen represents the majority of the remainder (20.8%). Elemental nitrogen is typically stable, and will not react with the oxygen in the air, but elevated temperatures inside an engine provide sufficient activation energy for toxic oxide production (Reaction 1). The rate of reaction between nitrogen monoxide and elemental oxygen (Reaction 2) has been studied using the method of initial rates and select data are presented in Table 1, with the initial rate being measured in terms of the change in the concentration of elemental oxygen.

Reaction 1. $\qquad\qquad\qquad\qquad N_2 (g) + O_2 (g) \rightarrow 2\ NO\ (g)$

Reaction 2. $\qquad\qquad\qquad\qquad 2\ NO\ (g) + O_2 (g) \rightarrow 2\ NO_2\ (g)$

Table 1. Initial Rate Data for Reaction 1

Trial	Initial Rate (M/s)	Initial [O2] (M)	Initial [NO] (M)
1	6.8×10^{-4}	6.5×10^{-3}	7.8×10^{-3}
2	2.1×10^{-3}	1.9×10^{-2}	7.8×10^{-3}
3	6.1×10^{-3}	6.5×10^{-3}	2.3×10^{-2}
4	5.4×10^{-3}	1.3×10^{-2}	1.6×10^{-2}

1. Which kinetic conclusions are most strongly supported by the data in Table 1?
    A. First order with respect to O_2, second order with respect to NO, first order overall.
    B. Second order with respect to O_2, first order with respect to NO, first order overall.
    C. First order with respect to O_2, second order with respect to NO, third order overall.
    D. Second order with respect to O_2, first order with respect to NO, third order overall.

2. Which of the following is the rate constant for the formation of nitrogen dioxide?
    A. 1.7×10^3 M/s
    B. 2.2×10^1 M/s
    C. 6.7×10^1 M/s
    D. 5.4×10^5 M/s

3. Which of the following is least likely to exist as a radical?
    A. $CH_3 (g)$
    B. $N_2 (g)$
    C. $NO (g)$
    D. $NO_2 (g)$

4. The following two-step mechanisms have been proposed for Reaction 2. Which of these mechanisms can be eliminated based on the data in Table 1?

    I. $2 NO (g) \rightleftharpoons N_2O_2 (g)$ (fast)
        $N_2O_2 (g) + O_2 (g) \rightarrow 2 NO_2 (g)$ (slow)

    II. II. $NO (g) + O_2 (g) \rightarrow NO_2 (g) + O (g)$ (slow)
        $NO (g) + O (g) \rightarrow NO_2 (g)$ (fast)

    III. $2 NO (g) + O_2 (g) \rightarrow 2 NO_2 (g)$ (slow)

A. I only
B. II only
C. II and III only
D. I and II only

5. The entropy change in Reaction 1 is:
A. positive.
B. negative.
C. unknown.
D. zero.

6. The kinetics of the reaction $A + B \rightarrow C$ was studied, and a plot of [A] vs. time was generated.

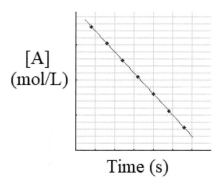

If the reaction is found to be zero order overall, which value is equivalent to the slope of the line?

A. [A]
B. [C]
C. k
D. -k

7. For a second order reaction with the mechanism A → C, which of the following represents the plot of 1/[A] vs. time?

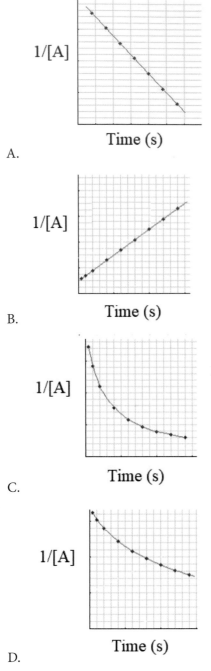

A.

B.

C.

D.

Practice Passage Explanations

In addition to producing nitrogen oxides, the incomplete combustion of hydrocarbon-based fuels also produces hydrocarbon radicals. Elemental nitrogen is the major gas in the earth's atmosphere (78%) and oxygen represents the majority of the remainder (20.8%). Elemental nitrogen is typically stable, and will not react with the oxygen in the air, but elevated temperatures inside an engine provide sufficient activation energy for toxic oxide production (Reaction 1). The rate of reaction between nitrogen monoxide and elemental oxygen (Reaction 2) has been studied using the method of initial rates and select data are presented in Table 1, with the initial rate being measured in terms of the change in the concentration of elemental oxygen.

Key terms: Combustion, radicals, activation energy, and initial rates

Reaction 1. $N_2 (g) + O_2 (g) \rightarrow 2\ NO\ (g)$

Reaction 1 has a high activation energy since it takes place typically only in a hot engine

Reaction 2. $2\ NO\ (g) + O_2 (g) \rightarrow 2\ NO_2\ (g)$

Reaction 2 suggests a rate law that is 1ˢᵗ order with respect to O₂, 2ⁿᵈ order with respect to NO

Table 1. Initial Rate Data for Reaction 1

Trial	Initial Rate (M/s)	Initial [O2] (M)	Initial [NO] (M)
1	6.8×10^{-4}	6.5×10^{-3}	7.8×10^{-3}
2	2.1×10^{-3}	1.9×10^{-2}	7.8×10^{-3}
3	6.1×10^{-3}	6.5×10^{-3}	2.3×10^{-2}
4	5.4×10^{-3}	1.3×10^{-2}	1.6×10^{-2}

Table 1 allows the general rate law for reaction 2 to be determined; but save the work for the Qs

Trials 1, 2: [O₂] is changed by 3x, [NO] is constant, rate increases by 210/68 ~ 3 or 3¹

Trials 1, 3: [O₂] is constant, [NO] increases by 3x, rate increases by 610/68 ~ 9 or 3²

Thus, rate will be k[O₂][NO]²

1. C is correct. The general rate law for reaction 2 can be determined from the initial rate data in Table 1.

    In comparing experiments number 1 and 2, it should be noted that the concentration of nitrogen monoxide does not change, whereas the concentration of oxygen is approximately tripled, resulting in a three-fold increase in the rate. This indicates that the reaction is first order in oxygen. Then comparing experiments 1 and 3, it should be noted that the concentration of oxygen remains constant, but the concentration of nitrogen oxide increases by a factor of three, causing the rate of the reaction to increase by a factor of 0.0061/0.00068 ~ 9. The reaction order in terms of nitrogen monoxide is second order. The overall order for this reaction is third order.

2. A is correct. From the data in Table 1, the rate law for Reaction 2 is:

$$\text{Rate} = k\,[O_2][NO]^2$$

Selecting the rate and concentrations for one of the experiments, i.e. number 1, inserting these values into the rate law and rearranging for the rate constant, gives:

$k = \text{Rate}/[O_2][NO]^2$
$k = (6.8 \times 10^{-4})/[6.5 \times 10^{-3}][7.8 \times 10^{-3}]^2$

Using approximate values gives:

$k \sim (7 \times 10^{-4}) / [7 \times 10^{-3}][8 \times 10^{-3}]^2$
$k \sim 1/64 \times 10^5 \rightarrow 1/6 \times 10^4 \rightarrow 0.15 \times 10^4 \rightarrow 1.5 \times 10^3$

An alternative method would be to insert the answer choices as the rate constant in the rate law, along with the rate and concentration values from one of the experiments and see which choice gives the equality.

3. B is correct. A radical is a species with one or more unpaired electrons. Generally for this to be true there needs to be an odd number of valence electrons. Elemental nitrogen has $2(5) = 10$ valence electrons. The Lewis dot structure indicates that there is a triple bond between the nitrogen atoms and no unpaired electrons.

A, C, D: The number of valence electrons in CH_3 is $4 + 3(1) = 7$. Six of the electrons are used to form the three single bonds between the carbon and hydrogens. The remaining electron on the carbon represents the unpaired electrons and CH_3 is a radical. Nitrogen monoxide has $5 + 6 = 11$ valence electrons. Drawing the Lewis dot structure, it can be concluded that the unpaired electron is on the nitrogen atom and NO is a radical. Nitrogen dioxide has $5 + 2(6) = 17$ valence electrons. Drawing the Lewis dot structure, it can be concluded that the unpaired electron is on the nitrogen atom and NO_2 is a radical.

4. B is correct. The data in Table 1 indicates that the Reaction 2 is first order for oxygen and second order for nitrogen monoxide. The rate law for this slow one step reaction, would be $k[O_2][NO]^2$. This rate law is consistent with the data in Table 1.

I: The rate of the forward and reverse reactions for the first step, which is a fast equilibrium, will be equal. Writing the rate law for both the forward and reverse reactions gives:

$$\text{Rate}_{fwd} = k_1\,[NO]^2$$
$$\text{Rate}_{rev} = k_{-1}\,[N_2O_2]$$

Setting the two equations equal to each other gives: $k_1[NO]^2 = k_{-1}[N_2O_2]$

Rearranging for the $[N_2O_2]$ gives: $[N_2O_2] = k_1/k_{-1}\,[NO]^2$

Writing the rate law for the second slow step, which is the rate determining step, gives: $\text{Rate} = k_2\,[N_2O_2][O_2]$ Combining these two equations gives:

$$\text{Rate} = k_2\,k_1/k_{-1}\,[NO]^2[O_2]$$
$$\text{Rate} = k\,[NO]^2[O_2]$$

This mechanism would be second order in nitrogen monoxide and first order for oxygen, which is consistent with the data in Table 1.

II: The rate law for mechanism II would be the rate law for the first slow step, Rate = k_1 [NO][O_2], which would be first order in both nitrogen monoxide and oxygen, which is not consistent with, the data in Table 1. This mechanism can be eliminated.

5. D is correct. When the MCAT asks you about entropy, simply look to phase changes and count up the number of moles of gas present in both the reactants and the products. More moles of gas means more entropy. Here, there are two moles of gas in both the reactants and the products, so the entropy change will be zero.

6. D is correct. For a zero order reaction, the rate law is just the rate constant (rate = k), and a plot of the reactant concentration over time will be a straight line with -k = slope of the line.

7. B is correct. For a 2nd order reaction, the plot of 1/[A] versus time is a straight line with k = slope of the line. Other graphs such as [A] vs. time or ln[A] vs. time will be curved for a second order reaction.

   A: Since [A] is consumed during the reaction, we would expect 1/[A] to increase as [A] decreases with time.
   C: This would be the plot of [A] vs. time for a 2nd order reaction.
   D: This would be the plot of ln[A] vs. time for a 2nd order reaction.

Independent Questions

1. Which of the following is true of the reaction represented by the reaction coordinate below, in the forward direction?

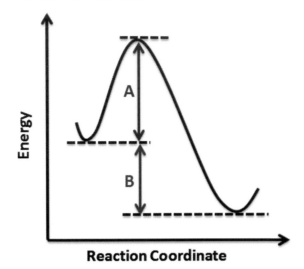

Reaction Coordinate

A. It is exergonic, and the addition of a catalyst would make it more exergonic.

B. It is endergonic, but the addition of a catalyst would make it less endergonic.

C. It is exergonic, and the addition of a catalyst would decrease the interval marked "A."

D. It is endergonic, and the addition of a catalyst would decrease the intervals marked "A" and "B."

2. A chemical reaction has a rate law in the format of rate = $k[X][Y]^2$. What are the units of the rate constant k for this reaction?

A. Ms^{-1}

B. s^{-1}

C. $M^{-1}s^{-1}$

D. $M^{-2}s^{-1}$

3. Catalytic hydrogenation involves the addition of hydrogen to alkenes or alkynes. One such reaction involves the bubbling of gaseous hydrogen through a liquid solution of alkene, in the presence of a solid palladium catalyst. In this reaction, the catalyst is:

A. homogenous, and it destabilizes the reaction transition state.

B. homogenous, and it stabilizes the reaction transition state.

C. heterogenous, and it destabilizes the reaction transition state.

D. heterogenous, and it stabilizes the reaction transition state.

4. What must be the overall order of a chemical reaction if it involves a single reactant (R) and if a plot of $\frac{1}{[R]}$ vs. time is linear?

A. Zero order

B. First order

C. Second order

D. Third order

5. The reaction $CO\ (g) + NO_3\ (g) \rightarrow CO_2\ (g) + NO_2\ (g)$ is an elementary reaction. Which of the following accurately gives the rate law for this process?

A. rate = $k[CO][NO_3]$

B. rate = $k[CO][NO]^3$

C. rate = $k\frac{[CO_2][NO_2]}{[CO][NO_3]}$

D. rate = $k\frac{[CO]^2[NO]^2}{[CO][NO]^3}$

6. A reaction is fourth order overall: first order with respect to reactant X and third order with respect to reactant Y. If the initial concentration of Y is tripled while the initial concentration of X is decreased to one-ninth its original value, how will the initial rate be affected?

A. It will be decreased to one-third its previous value.

B. It will remain the same.

C. It will increase to 3 times its previous value.

D. It will increase to 9 times its previous value.

7. Elementary reactions require all reactants to collide in a specific way, allowing the reaction to take place in a single step. While these reactions most often involve one or two reactant molecules, they can occasionally involve three. The reaction below is an example of a termolecular elementary chemical reaction. The reaction is allowed to take place and its initial rate is measured.

$$2\ NO + O_2 \rightarrow 2\ NOCl$$

If the concentration of NO is quadrupled, how will the measured initial rate change?

A. It will quadruple.

B. It will increase by a factor of 8.

C. It will increase by a factor of 16.

D. This question cannot be answered without more information.

8. A biochemical process involves the combination of reactants A, B, and C to form a single organic product. If several experimental trials produced the kinetic data below, what must be the order of reactant B?

Trial	[A]	[B]	[C]	Observed initial rate (M/s)
1	0.010 M	0.005 M	0.200 M	6×10^{-2} M/s
2	0.010 M	0.015 M	0.650 M	1.8×10^{-1} M/s
3	0.030 M	0.005 M	0.200 M	1.8×10^{-1} M/s
4	0.060 M	0.005 M	0.400 M	3.6×10^{-1} M/s

A. Zero order
B. First order
C. Second order
D. Third order

Independent Question Explanations

1. C is correct. Since the products of this reaction contain less energy than the reactants, energy must have been released during the reaction; thus, the process must be exergonic. Catalysts do not change ΔG, or the energy change between reactants and products, so the addition of a catalyst would not change the nature of this reaction. However, adding a catalyst would decrease the activation energy, which is denoted here by the label "A."

2. D is correct. The exponents for the reactants included in the rate law sum to 3, so this is a third-order reaction. The units for the rate constant for such a reaction are $M^{-2}s^{-1}$. Even if you did not know this, you can reason it out by plugging in the units for the other components of the rate law, remembering that the unit for concentration is molarity (M), while the units for rate are molarity per second (M/s).

$$rate = k[X][Y]^2$$

$$\frac{M}{s} = k[M][M]^2$$

$$k = \frac{M}{s \cdot M^3} = \frac{1}{s \cdot M^2} = M^{-2}s^{-1}$$

3. D is correct. The transition state of a reaction is found at the peak of the reaction coordinate. The distance between the energy of the reactants and the energy of this state is termed the activation energy. Catalysts lower the activation energy, which is the same as stabilizing the transition state (eliminate choices B and D). Here, the solid palladium catalyst is in a different phase than the gaseous and liquid reactants; for this reason, it is termed a heterogenous catalyst.

4. C is correct. Plotting a second-order reaction on a coordinate system with respect to one reactant (here, R) yields a linear plot when $\frac{1}{[R]}$, the reciprocal of the concentration, is graphed over time. In contrast, graphing concentration ([R]) over time yields a linear plot for zero-order reactions, and graphing the natural log of the concentration (ln R) gives a linear graph for first-order reactions.

5. A is correct. The rate law of an elementary reaction can be determined from looking at the balanced reaction. Only reactants are included in rate laws; products are not, allowing us to eliminate options C and D. (Do not confuse rate laws with equilibrium expressions!) Each reactant listed in a rate law should be raised to the power of its coefficient, which is 1 here for both reactants. The "3" in NO_3 is a subscript, not a coefficient, so that term should not be cubed (eliminate choice B).

6. C is correct. Tripling the concentration of Y, which is third order, will increase the rate by a factor of $3^3 = 27$. However, decreasing the concentration of X, which is first order, to one-ninth its original value will decrease the rate proportionally (that is to say, it will divide it by 9). Combining these two effects leads to a new rate that is $\frac{27}{9} = 3$ times the previous rate.

7. C is correct. Since this reaction is elementary (one-step), we can find out its rate law simply by looking at the balanced chemical reaction and raising each reactant to its coefficient.

$$rate = k[NO]^2[O_2]$$

This reaction is thus second order with regard to NO. Quadrupling a second-order reactant will cause the initial rate to increase by a factor of 4^2, or 16.

8. B is correct. Since we do not know the order of any of the three reactants, we will need to work through this problem in multiple steps. First, look for any cases where the concentrations of two reactants stayed constant while the third changed. This will ensure that any alterations to the rate occurred due to that reactant alone. Between Trials 1 and 3, only [A] changed; specifically, it tripled, and the rate tripled as well. Since reactant A produced a linear change in initial rate, it must be first order. The next step is slightly harder, but now that we know the effect that changes in [A] have, we can look for a set of trials where only [A] and the concentration of one other reactant changed. Consider Trials 3 and 4, where both [A] and [C] doubled. The rate also doubled, which is the change we would expect from a doubling of [A] alone. Since the increase in [C] had no apparent effect, reactant C must be zero order. Since C is zero order, we can ignore that entire column, as changes made to it will not affect the rate. We can finally look at Trials 1 and 2, where [B] tripled and [A] remained constant. This produced a linear tripling in the initial rate, so the reaction must be first order with respect to B.

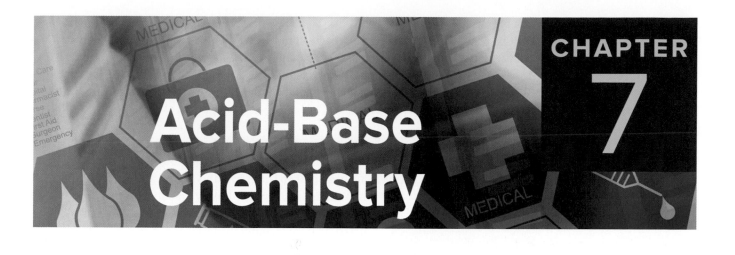

CHAPTER 7

Acid-Base Chemistry

0. Introduction

Congrats on making it halfway through this book! In this chapter, we will discuss one of the most striking examples of overlap between subjects on the MCAT: acid-base chemistry. The principles underlying acidity and basicity connect chemistry to organic chemistry, biochemistry, and even biology, and for this reason, you absolutely *must* understand them to excel on Test Day. If you have read Chapter 2 of your biochemistry book, you may remember the impact of acidic or basic side chains on the charge of an amino acid. If you have reviewed Chapter 5 of the same book, you will recall isoelectric focusing, a procedure that uses these charge differences to separate amino acids or proteins along a pH gradient. And later in this very book, you will read a considerable amount about organic functional groups and their acidic or basic tendencies. If any of these concepts are unclear, we strongly encourage you to read this chapter, then return to those topics with a renewed understanding of the underlying acid-base chemistry.

> > CONNECTIONS < <

Chapters 2 and 5 of Biochemistry and Chapter 10 of Chemistry

Throughout this chapter, keep in mind the fundamental ideas of stability and charge. The stability of a compound and its ionic form(s) has a direct impact on its tendency to act as an acid or a base, and a compound's charge can be altered through protonation and deprotonation. In turn, charge affects other fundamentals, such as solubility in water or organic solvents and the ability to easily diffuse through a cell membrane. Keeping these basic concepts in mind will help you see the interconnections between these topics and predict the likely focus of MCAT questions.

1. Definitions and Nomenclature

First, let's begin with a simple question: what is an acid, and what is a base? This question can actually be answered in different ways depending on the definitions we use. For the MCAT, you should be familiar with three ways of defining acids and bases, although some are broader, more modern, and/or more MCAT-relevant than others.

The earliest of these three systems is the Arrhenius definition of acids and bases. In 1884, Svante Arrhenius proposed that acids and bases dissociate in aqueous solution to form ions, or charged species. In particular, acids dissociate in a manner that increases the concentration of protons (H^+ ions) in solution, while the dissociation of a base increases the concentration of hydroxide (OH^-) ions. This very narrow definition makes Arrhenius acids and bases easy to spot. Arrhenius acids must contain H^+; examples include HBr, H_2CO_3, and H_3PO_4. Bases, then, must contain OH^-, as exemplified by NaOH, KOH, and $Ba(OH)_2$. In modern times, this definition is considered too limiting for general use. You may already be aware of some compounds that break the Arrhenius definition—for example, ammonia (NH_3) is a common base that does not contain hydroxide.

The next set of acid-base definitions addresses this very limitation. It is the Brønsted-Lowry system, developed in 1923. The Brønsted-Lowry definition of an acid is a proton donor, or in other words, a compound that can lose a proton to another compound or to solution. This seems awfully similar to the Arrhenius definition, and in fact it is. Where the Brønsted-Lowry system differs is in its definition of a base. A Brønsted-Lowry base is a proton *acceptor*, or any compound that can gain a bond to H^+. Remember ammonia, our base which violated the Arrhenius definition? Ammonia, or NH_3, can gain a proton to yield ammon*ium*, or NH_4^+. As such, ammonia is a classic Brønsted-Lowry base. Since the Brønsted-Lowry system categorizes some compounds as bases even though they do not contain the hydroxide ion, it is broader than the Arrhenius system.

MCAT STRATEGY > > >

Unless you are told otherwise, assume the MCAT is using the Brønsted-Lowry definition of acids and bases. We will thus focus a great deal on proton donation and acceptance in the rest of this chapter.

Before moving on to the third acid-base classification system, let us outline two major concepts that stem from the Brønsted-Lowry scheme. Recall that a Brønsted-Lowry acid is a proton donor. After such an acid has lost its proton, the resulting species is termed the *conjugate base* of the original acid. For example, consider the Brønsted-Lowry acid hydrofluoric acid (HF). After losing its proton, HF becomes F^-; this fluoride ion is thus the conjugate base of HF. It is a base because it can act as a proton *acceptor* to re-form the original HF molecule, and it is a conjugate because it is closely related to HF. On the other hand, when a Brønsted-Lowry base (or proton acceptor) gains a proton, it becomes its own *conjugate acid*. Returning to our example of NH_3, the gain of one proton produces ammonium, or NH_4^+. Ammonium (NH_4^+) is thus the conjugate acid of ammonia (NH_3). Figure 1 shows another example of conjugates in the context of an organic reaction.

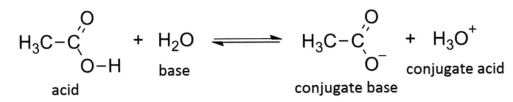

Figure 1. The reaction of acetic acid (the acid) with water (the base) to form acetate (the conjugate base) and H_3O^+ (the conjugate acid).

The broadest scheme for classifying acids and bases is the Lewis definition, which, like the Brønsted-Lowry system, was proposed in 1923. Lewis proposed that acids are electron acceptors, while bases are electron donors (which provides us with a nice first-letter mnemonic: *a*cids are *a*cceptors of electrons). For example, in the reaction shown in Figure 2, the lone pair of electrons on NH_3 attacks the central boron atom in BF_3. Therefore, NH_3 serves as an electron donor (or Lewis base), while BF_3 acts an electron acceptor (or Lewis acid) in this reaction. From this example alone, we can see the key advantage of the Lewis definition. Under either Arrhenius or Brønsted-Lowry, BF_3 would never be considered an acid, simply because it contains no hydrogen ions to donate. However, BF_3 does react with the basic NH_3, so a definition of an acid that excluded BF_3 would be incomplete. The Lewis system addresses this problem by defining acids and bases in terms of electron transfer, which also helps us tie acid-base behavior to the important ideas of oxidation and reduction.

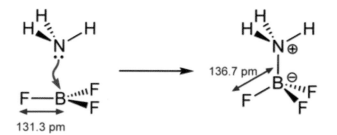

Figure 2. Acid-base reaction between BF_3 (a Lewis acid) and NH_3 (a Lewis base).

Under the Brønsted-Lowry or Lewis definition, some compounds can act as either an acid or a base, depending on the other reactants present. These compounds are characterized as amphoteric. For the sake of MCAT acid-base chemistry, you will usually see this concept in the context of the Brønsted-Lowry definition. Here, amphoteric species are those which can either accept or donate a proton. (As such, they are given the more specific descriptor of "amphiprotic.") Common examples include water, which can either gain a proton to become H_3O^+ or lose one to become OH^-, and amino acids.

Let's wrap up this section with a brief discussion of acid naming. The nomenclature of simple, hydrogen-containing acids follows a few simple guidelines. Acids that lack oxygen are named by combining the prefix *hydro-*, the root of the parent anion, and the suffix *-ic acid*.

Cl^-	Chloride	HCl	Hydrochloric acid
F^-	Fluoride	HF	Hydrofluoric acid

Oxyacids—acids that contain oxygen atoms—use a slightly more complex nomenclature system. (Note that the term "oxyacid" typically refers to inorganic oxygen-containing acids. Organic acids, which contain -COOH, are generally not termed "oxyacids," even though they do contain oxygen. The naming of organic acids will be discussed in Chapter 10 of this book.)

> For oxyanions that contain the suffix *-ate*, the acid uses the suffix *-ic acid*.
> If an oxyanion contains one more oxygen atom that the corresponding "*-ate*" ion, then the acid uses the prefix *per-* and the suffix *-ic acid*.

MCAT STRATEGY > > >

To identify Lewis acids, pay attention to electrons! Lewis acids, or electron acceptors, usually "want" to gain electrons because they are electron-deficient on their own. Some of the most commonly tested Lewis acids—BF_3, BCl_3, $AlCl_3$, and AlF_3—fit this criterion because their incomplete octet results in them having six electrons on the central atom instead of the coveted eight.

> > CONNECTIONS < <

Chapter 2 of Chemistry

MCAT STRATEGY > > >

As we have mentioned before, pay attention to the words used to describe chemistry concepts! Here, we see the prefix "ampho-" or "amphi-," which derives from the Greek term meaning "both" or "on both sides." Do you remember other uses of this prefix in MCAT science? (We'll answer this one for you: the most important example is the term "amphipathic," which describes compounds that contain both polar and nonpolar regions.)

> > If an oxyanion contains one fewer oxygen atom that the corresponding "-*ate*" ion, then the acid uses the suffix -*ous acid*.

> > If an oxyanion contains two fewer oxygen atoms that the corresponding "-*ate*" ion, then the acid uses the prefix *hypo-* and the suffix -*ous acid*.

If you are scratching your head in confusion after reading these bullet points, you're in luck, because we've outlined what is by far the most MCAT-relevant example of this naming convention below: the chlorine-containing oxyacids.

ClO^-	Hypochlorite	$HClO$	Hypochlorous acid
ClO_2^-	Chlorite	$HClO_2$	Chlorous acid
ClO_3^-	Chlorate	$HClO_3$	Chloric acid
ClO_4^-	Perchlorate	$HClO_4$	Perchloric acid

2. Acid and Base Equilibria

In Chapter 4 of this book, we introduced the concept that chemical reactions typically do not go to completion—that is, 100% of reactant molecules are not converted to products. Instead, most reactions reach a final state known as equilibrium, where the rate of conversion of reactants to products is equal to the rate of conversion of products to reactants. Acid-base reactions are no different. As we mentioned above, unless told otherwise, you will generally be dealing with the Brønsted-Lowry definition of acidity and basicity. As such, we will spend this section discussing the equilibria of reactions in which protons are gained and lost. First, we must clarify one key point of confusion: when we say "protons," we may initially think of H^+ cations, but H^+ actually does not exist on its own in aqueous solution. Instead, it associates with a water molecule to produce H_3O^+, the hydronium cation. For the remainder of this chapter, just keep in mind that the terms "hydronium" and "proton," as well as the species H^+ and H_3O^+, are functionally equivalent.

You may recall that a value known as the equilibrium constant (K_{eq}) denotes the relative concentration of products and reactants at equilibrium. K_{eq} is a general term for this constant; for specific reactions, it can take on more specialized names. The first specific type of equilibrium constant we will discuss is K_w, the constant for the autoionization of water (H_2O).

> > CONNECTIONS < <

Chapters 4 and 5 of
Chemistry

If you have never heard of autoionization, don't panic—its name gives away its meaning. "Auto-" means "self," while "ionization" is the process by which ions, or charged species, are formed. Autoionization, then, must refer to the reaction of water molecules with each other to form ions. The reaction in question is shown below.

$$H_2O \ (l) + H_2O \ (l) \leftrightarrow H_3O^+ \ (aq) + OH^- \ (aq)$$

In a solution of pure water, the vast majority of species present are H_2O molecules, but a very small proportion of H_3O^+ and OH^- ions also exist, formed through the autoionization reaction above. A given number of water molecules react to form *equal* numbers of H_3O^+ and OH^- ions, resulting in a neutral solution. If we think back to Chapter 4, we can easily write out the equilibrium expression for this process, shown below. Remember, pure liquids are not included in the expression!

$$K_w = [H_3O^+][OH^-]$$

The value of K_w at standard (room) temperature (25°C, or 298.15 K) is 1.0×10^{-14}. Note that this is only true at standard temperature! Like all equilibrium constants, K_w is temperature-dependent; water ionizes more readily at high temperature, yielding a larger value for K_w. Let's break down exactly what this means, as it is a common point of confusion. To make things simple, we'll begin with the assumption that our temperature is 25°C. In a container of pure water, what must be our H_3O^+ concentration? Well, recall that for every molecule of H_3O^+, exactly one molecule of OH^- must be present. We can thus say that $[H_3O^+] = [OH^-]$ and set both equal to x.

$$K_w = [x][x]$$
$$1.0 \times 10^{-14} = x^2$$
$$x = [H_3O^+] = 1.0 \times 10^{-7} \text{ M}$$

We will later see that this concentration is associated with a pH of 7. Since pure water is neutral, we must also have an OH^- concentration of 1.0×10^{-7}. But what happens when we deviate from standard temperature? Let's move our container of pure water to a colder room, where the ambient temperature is 0°C (273.15 K). Since water tends to ionize to a greater extent in warm temperatures, it must ionize *less* in cold temperatures. The value for K_w at 0°C fits this prediction: 0.114×10^{-14}, or 1.14×10^{-15}. Let's try calculating our H_3O^+ concentration under these new conditions.

> ## MCAT STRATEGY > > >
>
> When finding the square root of a number written in scientific notation, simply *square root the coefficient* and *cut the exponent in half*. Here, the square root of 1.0 is 1.0, and half of −14 is −7.

$$K_w = [x][x]$$
$$1.14 \times 10^{-15} = x^2$$

At this point, we run into a minor calculation obstacle: halving −15 would yield an exponent of −7.5, which breaks the convention of whole-number exponents. A simple way to circumvent this is to rewrite 1.14×10^{-15} as 11.4×10^{-16}, which is equivalent in value but has an even exponent and a larger, easier-to-square-root coefficient. The square root of 11.4 falls somewhere between 3 and 4, so let's just say 3.5, and one-half of −16 is −8.

> ## > > CONNECTIONS < <
>
> Chapter 8 of Verbal & Quantitative Reasoning

$$x = [H3O^+] = 3.5 \times 10^{-8} \text{ M}$$

We can now see that this value is significantly less than the H_3O^+ concentration at 25°C, which was 1.0×10^{-7} M. (Remember, a *larger* negative number corresponds to a *smaller* overall value, and vice versa.) Does this mean that our new, colder water is less acidic than our room-temperature water? No! Since we are still dealing with pure water, our OH^- concentration will also be 3.5×10^{-8} M. Commit this fact to memory: as long as hydronium and hydroxide concentrations are equal, the solution is neutral. Pure water is thus neutral at any temperature, although we will later see that its pH is not necessarily 7.

Let's now widen our discussion beyond water and start to discuss acidic and basic solutions. Like water, acids and bases ionize in solution, and as such, they have their own equilibrium constants. Each acid has its own acid dissociation constant, or K_a, while each base has a base dissociation constant (K_b). The dissociation of a generic acid is shown below. In this process, the acid reacts with water to yield a hydronium ion and the conjugate base of the acid.

$$HA\ (aq) + H_2O\ (l) \leftrightarrow H_3O^+\ (aq) + A^-\ (aq)$$

For example, consider hydrofluoric acid (HF), which dissociates in water as shown below.

$$HF\ (aq) + H_2O\ (l) \leftrightarrow H_3O^+\ (aq) + F^-\ (aq)$$

The equilibrium expression for this reaction is $Ka = \frac{[H_3O^+][F^-]}{[HF]}$. Unlike the K_w expression, the K_a (as well as the K_b) expression contains a denominator, since HF is aqueous and thus must be included. Now, we can easily see that the expression represents a ratio of products (hydronium and conjugate base) to reactants (original acid). A high K_a thus must correspond to an acid that dissociates more readily, while a low K_a corresponds to an acid that does not dissociate to a large degree.

Base dissociation reactions are slightly different, but they follow the same principles. The dissociation of a generic base in water is shown below. Here, B denotes a weak base, which will be discussed in more depth later in this chapter.

$$B\ (aq) + H_2O\ (l) \leftrightarrow BH^+\ (aq) + OH^-\ (aq)$$

The base accepts a proton from a water molecule to yield a hydroxide ion and its conjugate acid. From this reaction, we can write the K_b expression for this same generic weak base.

$$K_b = \frac{[BH^+][OH^-]}{[B]}$$

As in our K_a expression, the constant K_b represents a ratio of products to reactants. The greater the degree of dissociation, the larger the K_b, and vice versa.

3. Acid Strength and the pH Scale

From the previous section, we now know that acids which dissociate to a large extent have high K_a values, while those which dissociate less have low K_as. Acids vary enormously in their level of dissociation. On one end of this spectrum lies a small number of acids that dissociate fully—that is, virtually all of their molecules ionize when placed in water. These acids are termed "strong" acids and have extremely large K_a values, reflecting the fact that their products greatly outnumber reactants at equilibrium. (The strong acid hydrobromic acid, or HBr, has a K_a of about 1.0×10^9.)

In contrast, any acid that does *not* fully dissociate is termed a weak acid. When a weak acid is placed in water, most of its molecules remain intact, with only a few dissociating to form conjugate base and hydronium ions. Since the weak acid equilibrium favors the reactants, its K_a will be small (for example, hydrofluoric acid, which we mentioned earlier, has a K_a of around 7×10^{-4}). Notice something very interesting about this K_a value! Its exponent is negative, while the K_a of our strong acid, HBr, had a positive exponent. This distinction stems from the extreme nature of acids, at least those which you will see on the MCAT. The products of a strong acid dissociation are heavily favored, while a weak acid dissociation significantly favors the reactants. On the MCAT, you are unlikely to see any acid "in the middle," where neither products nor reactants greatly predominate and where the K_a falls close to 1.

When dealing with acid strength, resist the urge to call an acid strong unless you know for certain that it fully dissociates in solution. This is a rare phenomenon, and as such, there are only a handful of strong acids you must memorize for the MCAT. Table 1 lists these strong acids, along with the strong bases that you must know, which we will discuss next.

STRONG ACIDS	STRONG BASES
Hydrochloric acid (HCl)	Lithium hydroxide (LiOH)
Hydrobromic acid (HBr)	Sodium hydroxide (NaOH)
Hydroiodic acid (HI)	Potassium hydroxide (KOH)
Chloric acid ($HClO_3$)	Cesium hydroxide (CsOH)
Perchloric acid ($HClO_4$)	Calcium hydroxide ($CaOH_2$)
Sulfuric acid (H_2SO_4)	Strontium hydroxide ($SrOH_2$)
Nitric acid (HNO_3)	Barium hydroxide ($BaOH_2$)

Table 1. Strong acids and bases to know for the MCAT.

Note that, while the seven strong acids listed above are the only ones you will need to remember for the MCAT, strong bases are not so simple. For general chemistry, just be sure to know the eight listed above (all of which are hydroxides of alkali or alkaline earth metals). In organic chemistry, however, you may encounter others, including NH_2^- (the conjugate base of ammonia, or NH_3), the hydride anion (H^-), and methoxide (CH_3O^-), ethoxide ($CH_3CH_2O^-$), and *tert*-butoxide (($CH_3)_3CO^-$).

Like a strong acid, a strong base fully reacts when placed in water. This produces the base's conjugate acid along with hydroxide ion. Since products greatly outnumber reactants at equilibrium, the K_b of a strong base will be very large, just like the K_a of a strong acid. The fact that strong acids and bases fully dissociate leads us to another fundamental concept: the concentration of a strong acid or base will be equal to the concentration of hydronium or hydroxide ion, respectively, at equilibrium. For example, a 2 M solution of hydrobromic acid (HBr) will produce a 2 M solution of H_3O^+ upon dissociation, while a 0.75 M solution of KOH will produce a final solution with an [OH^-] concentration of 0.75 M.

> ## MCAT STRATEGY > > >
>
> When memorizing lists, it can be helpful to focus not only on the terms that are included, but also on what is *not* included. For example, the common acids hydrofluoric acid (HF), carbonic acid (H_2CO_3), and phosphoric acid (H_3PO_4) are not strong acids. Remembering this can help you avoid traps into which many students have fallen before!

However, acidity and basicity are not always described strictly in terms of exact H_3O^+ and OH^- concentrations. Instead, a system termed the pH scale is commonly used, along with its counterpart, pOH. The pH scale is logarithmic, making it particularly effective at describing a wide range of concentrations using a narrower interval of more relatable numbers. The prefix "p" denotes "negative logarithm," as shown in the equations for pH and pOH, below.

Equation 1. $pH = -\log[H^+]$ (or technically, $-\log[H_3O^+]$)

Equation 2. $pOH = -\log[OH^-]$

If your use of logarithms is a bit rusty, consider reviewing them in your Verbal & Quantitative Reasoning book before moving on, although we will also discuss them here. Let's begin with an example. Say you have an aqueous solution of 1 mol hydrochloric acid in 10 L of water. The molarity of this solution is (1 mol)/(10 L), or 0.1 M HCl.

Since HCl is a strong acid, it fully dissociates to yield 0.1 M H$^+$, which we can plug into our pH equation. (Here's a helpful hint: convert to scientific notation before plugging in a concentration value to find pH.)

$$pH = -\log [H^+] = -\log[0.1 \text{ M}] = -\log [1 \times 10^{-1} \text{ M}]$$

Since the coefficient of 1×10^{-1} is 1, the logarithm of this value is equal to its exponent (-1), meaning that the *negative* logarithm of 1×10^{-1} is $-(-1)$ or 1. This brings us to a helpful rule: when the hydronium/proton concentration written in scientific notation is 1×10^{-x}, the pH is equal to x, or the negative value of the exponent to which 10 is raised. What if the coefficient is something other than 1? If the answer choices are sufficiently far apart, you can use estimation. For example, let's say you are asked to find the value of $-\log (9 \times 10^{-8})$. 9×10^{-8} falls between 1×10^{-8} and 10×10^{-8}, or 1×10^{-7}. Our answer, then, must fall between 8 and 7. Since 9×10^{-8} is much closer to 1×10^{-7} than to 1×10^{-8}, our answer must be closer to 7, perhaps around 7.1. Alternatively, a handy trick exists to help you calculate negative logarithms while avoiding the potential confusion that comes with estimation. To find the negative logarithm of 9×10^{-8} using this trick, take the positive value of the exponent (here, 8). Then, take the coefficient (9) and move its decimal place one position to the left to make it 0.9. Finally, subtract 0.9 from 8 to yield 7.1. This trick (taking the positive value of the exponent and subtracting 0."coefficient") works well enough for the MCAT, although it does not always yield a perfectly accurate answer.

The concepts of pH and pOH are intricately related to K_a, K_b, and K_w, which we discussed in the previous section. Recall the equilibrium expression below for K_w, the autoionization constant of water.

$$K_w = [H_3O^+][OH^-] = 1 \times 10^{-14} \text{ at } 25°C$$

If we take the negative logarithm of both sides, we get the following:

$$-\log(K_w) = -\log ([H_3O^+][OH^-])$$

Terms that are multiplied together within a log expression can be separated into individual logarithms, as shown below:

$$-\log(K_w) = -\log[H_3O^+] + -\log[OH^-]$$

This is a great time to mention that the negative logarithm of *any* value can be described using the prefix "p," just as the negative logarithm of the H$^+$ concentration is described as pH. The negative logarithm of K_w, then, is termed pK_w, and since K_w is equal to 1×10^{-14} at standard temperature, pK_w is equal to 14 under the same conditions.

Equation 3 (general). $pK_w = pH + pOH$

Equation 4 (standard temperature). $14 = pH + pOH$

Equation 4 makes it simple to find pOH if you are given pH, or vice versa. For example, under standard conditions, a solution with a pH of 3 must have a pOH of 11. Be careful, though: some students mistakenly interpret Equation 4 as implying that the pH and pOH scales range from 0 to 14. In reality, values lower than 0 and higher than 14 are possible. Imagine a 10 M solution of HCl, which is synonymous with a 10 M (or 1×10^1 M) concentration of protons. The negative logarithm of 1×10^1 M is actually -1, meaning that the pH of this acidic solution is negative.

Just as pK_w is the negative logarithm of K_w, pK_a and pK_b are the negative logarithms of K_a and K_b. Here, the negative sign has a significant impact. If you recall from the previous section, high values for K_a and K_b denote strong acids and bases, respectively. High values for pK_a corresponds to *weak* acids. Just like pH and pOH, pK_a and pK_b can be negative. In fact, the strong acid H_2SO_4 has a pK_a of -3 for its first proton. In keeping with the fact that weaker acids have higher pK_a values, the pK_a of carbonic acid—a weak acid—is around 6.3, and the pK_a of a so-weak-it's-virtually-neutral generic alkane is approximately 50.

Now that we have introduced pK_a and pK_b and have an understanding of the mathematical relationships in Equations 3 and 4, let us outline some additional relationships you should be aware of.

> **MCAT STRATEGY > > >**
>
> You can remember that small pK_as correspond to stronger acids by relating pK_a to pH, which looks similar. Small pH values correspond to more acidic solutions.

Equation 5. $$K_a \cdot K_b = K_w = 1 \times 10^{-14} \text{ at } 25°C$$

Equation 6. $$pK_a + pK_b = pK_w = 14 \text{ at } 25°C$$

Note that K_a and K_b here refer to an acid and *its own conjugate base*, not an acid and some random other base, and certainly not the exact same species. For example, at standard conditions, the K_a of HCO_3^- and the K_b of CO_3^{2-} must multiply to yield 1×10^{-14}. The larger the K_a of the acid, the smaller the K_b of the corresponding conjugate base, meaning that the stronger an acid, the weaker its conjugate base, and vice versa. This does NOT mean that all weak acids have strong conjugate bases, or that all weak bases have strong conjugate acids! It only means that, if Acid A is stronger than Acid B, the conjugate base of Acid A must be weaker than the conjugate base of Acid B.

> **> > CONNECTIONS < <**
>
> **Chapter 2 of Biochemistry**

Earlier in this section, we calculated the pH of a solution of strong acid, which is fairly simple due to the fact that strong acids and bases fully dissociate. pH calculations become more complex when they involve weak acids or bases. Since weak species dissociate very little, we cannot consider the concentration of the original acid or base to be equal to the concentration of H_3O^+ or OH^- at equilibrium. Instead, we must use the K_a or K_b to predict the extent of dissociation. The good news is that the MCAT does not expect you to memorize K_a or K_b values for random acids or bases. Instead, they will give these values directly when they are needed, or they will give their analogous pK_a or pK_b values.

Let's try this out with an example, using the weak organic acid benzoic acid ($HC_7H_5O_2$). What is the pH of a 0.1 M solution of benzoic acid in distilled water at 25°C ($K_{a \text{ benzoic acid}} = 6.5 \times 10^{-5}$)? To solve, we must first determine the concentration of each species at equilibrium. This is often accomplished using an ICE table, where the initial (I) concentration, change (C) in concentration, and equilibrium (E) concentration of each species is listed.

$$HC_7H_5O_2 \leftrightarrow H_3O^+ + C_7H_5O_2^-$$

	$HC_7H_5O_2$	H_3O^+	$C_7H_5O_2^-$
I	0.1 M	0 M	0 M
C	−x	+x	+x
E	0.1 − x	x	x

As shown above, we set the amount of benzoic acid that dissociates equal to x. For each benzoic acid molecule that dissociates, exactly one H_3O^+ and one $C_7H_5O_2^-$ ion is produced, so we can call each of those concentrations x, as well. You may be wondering what this ICE table accomplished, since our concentrations are in the form of variables rather than numbers. Now that we have equilibrium concentrations, however, *even though they are in terms of x*, we can plug them into the equilibrium expression for the dissociation of benzoic acid.

$$K_a = \frac{[H_3O^+][C_7H_5O_2^-]}{[HC_7H_5O_2]} = \frac{(x)(x)}{0.1\ M - x} = 6.5 \times 10^{-5}$$

The binomial term in the denominator greatly complicates the math required to solve for x, so let's stop and think for a moment. As a weak acid, benzoic acid must only dissociate to a tiny degree. Compared to the original concentration of 0.1 M, then, x will be a very small number, and "0.1 – x" will be virtually equivalent to 0.1 alone. For the sake of the MCAT, you can therefore drop the x term in the denominator, yielding the following:

$$\frac{x^2}{0.1\ M} = 6.5 \times 10^{-5}$$

$$x^2 = (6.5 \times 10^{-5})(1 \times 10^{-1}) = 6.5 \times 10^{-6}$$

$$x = [H_3O^+] \approx 2.5 \times 10^{-3}$$

$$pH = -\log[2.5 \times 10^{-3}] \approx 2.75$$

In reality, the pH of a 0.1 M benzoic acid solution is about 2.60, so our estimated value is close enough to answer any MCAT question. If you have been paying close attention, you may wonder why we neglected to account for the H_3O^+ contributed by the water in this aqueous solution. Pure water contains 1×10^{-7} M of H_3O^+, and the H_3O^+ contributed by our benzoic acid in this example will lower that value even more due to Le Châtelier's principle. When the H_3O^+ contributed by water is very low in comparison to the H_3O^+ from the acid, we can assume that it is negligible. For the sake of the MCAT, you can always ignore the contribution of H_3O^+ or OH^- by water unless the concentration of H_3O^+ or OH^- from the acid or base is extremely low (think less than 10^{-6} M).

> > CONNECTIONS < <

Chapter 4 of Chemistry

4. Buffers

In the body and in the lab, it is sometimes desirable to avoid the large shifts in pH that can result from the addition of acid or base to an existing solution. For example, our blood is kept at a pH of approximately 7.4, with a range of 7.35-7.45 depending on various factors. Deviation from this range can cause extreme sickness, failure of body systems, and even death. Such deviation does not need to be large—a blood pH of 6.7 would almost certainly result in fatal acidosis (acidic plasma), while a pH of 7.9 would constitute fatal alkalosis (alkaline or basic plasma). However, conditions ranging from heavy exercise to irregular respiration can impact the pH of our blood plasma. How do our bodies ensure that this pH remains at a physiologically optimal level?

> > CONNECTIONS < <

Chapter 9 of Biology

The answer to this question lies in the concept of buffers. A buffer is a solution that resists changes in pH upon addition of acid or base. While buffers cannot protect against addition of large amounts of acid/base, they are highly effective at maintaining pH when small to moderate quantities are added. Let's discuss how these solutions work using the example of the bicarbonate buffer system, an important physiological example of how the blood protects against dramatic changes in pH. A buffer must contain either a weak acid and its conjugate base or a weak base and its conjugate acid. In the bicarbonate buffer system, the weak acid is carbonic acid (H_2CO_3), while the weak base is bicarbonate (HCO_3^-).

Imagine that we are trying to replicate the bicarbonate buffer system in the laboratory. We add 5 moles of H_2CO_3 and 5 moles of HCO_3^- to 10 L of water. (These two species will interconvert to some extent in solution, but let's neglect to consider this for the sake of simplicity.) Now, let's add 1 mole of HCl to the solution. This will produce 1 mole of free protons, which will quickly protonate 1 mole of the basic HCO_3^- ions. We are left with 6 moles of H_2CO_3 and 4 moles of HCO_3^-. Since pH is calculated based on free proton/hydronium concentration, and since our protons were "used up" by the bicarbonate ions, our pH will hardly change at all. Compare this to the addition of 1 mole HCl to 10 L distilled water. The resulting solution will have a hydronium concentration of 0.1 M, corresponding to a pH of 1. This is a 6-unit drop from our initial neutral pH of 7, assuming that we were at standard temperature! We can thus see how a buffer solution of weak acid/weak base conjugates protects enormously against pH change. Of course, if we added enough HCl, we could overcome even our bicarbonate buffer solution, at which point we would have reached a value termed the buffer capacity. The higher the molar amounts of conjugate acid and base, the larger the buffer capacity.

The pH of a buffer solution can be calculated using the Henderson-Hasselbalch equation (Equation 7), where HA refers to a generic weak acid and A^- refers to its conjugate weak base. For the fraction part of this equation, we can plug in either moles or concentration for both species, since it is a ratio and both acid and conjugate base are held in the same volume of solution.

Equation 7.
$$pH = pK_a + \log\frac{[A^-]}{[HA]}$$

We can solidify our understanding of this equation through an example. How many moles of sodium acetate (CH_3COONa) must be added to 100 mL of a 0.05 M solution of acetic acid (CH_3COOH) to produce a buffer with a pH of 6.74 ($pK_{a\ acetic\ acid} = 4.74$)?

$$(0.1\ L)(0.05\ M) = 0.005\ mol\ CH_3COOH = 5 \times 10^{-3}\ mol\ CH_3COOH$$

$$pH = pKa + \log\frac{[A-]}{[HA]}$$

$$6.74 = 4.74 + \log\frac{x\ mol\ CH_3COO^-}{5 \times 10^{-3}\ mol\ CH_3COOH}$$

$$6.74 - 4.74 = \log\frac{x}{5 \times 10^{-3}}$$

$$2 = \log\frac{x}{5 \times 10^{-3}}$$

$$100 = \frac{x}{5 \times 10^{-3}}$$

$$x = (1 \times 10^2)(5 \times 10^{-3}) = 5 \times 10^{-1}\ mol = 0.5\ mol\ CH_3COO^-$$

More simply put, since we wanted our final pH to be 2 units higher than the pK_a of acetic acid, and since pH is on a logarithmic scale, we needed to include 100 (or 10^2) times more conjugate base than conjugate acid. This would actually not be a very effective buffer, as buffer efficacy is highest when the concentrations of conjugate species are close to equal. When equal concentrations of acid and conjugate base are present, the "log" term of the H-H equation drops out, and $pH = pK_a$. As such, we can say that a buffer will be most effective at the pH that is equal to the pK_a of its component acid. When choosing an acid-base pair to use as a buffer, then, be certain to choose one where the acid has a pK_a close to the desired pH of the buffered solution.

The above discussion of buffers includes the full scope of content required for the MCAT on this topic. However, MCAT questions can still trip up even those students who understand buffer chemistry. One such point of confusion stems from what we have termed "hidden

MCAT STRATEGY > > >

When asked to calculate the pH of a solution, first ask yourself whether the solution contains a strong acid (or base) alone, a weak acid (or base) alone, or a buffer. Knowing this from the beginning can speed up calculations.

buffer" questions. Envision a situation in which 1 mole of HBr is added to 2 moles of NH_3 to form 1 L of solution. Many MCAT students become stumped here—it doesn't appear to be a buffer solution, because it does not contain a weak acid or base and its own conjugate, but it certainly is not an acid or base by itself. Interestingly, this solution *is* a buffer! When in doubt, think about stoichiometry. 1 mole of HBr will neutralize exactly 1 mole of NH_3, leaving 1 mole of NH_3 remaining. The neutralized ammonia will now exist in the form of 1 mole of NH_4^+. Our final solution, then, has equal concentrations of the weakly basic ammonia and its conjugate, making it an effective buffer.

5. Titrations

Our final section of this chapter deals with titrations, a procedure that you likely have conducted in the lab. In broad terms, a titration is a technique that aims to determine the concentration of a solution of unknown molarity. To accomplish this, a solution of *known* concentration is added until an endpoint is reached. This endpoint usually coincides with a color change, and the amount of known solution required to reach the endpoint can be used to determine the concentration of the unknown reactant. In a titration, the solution of unknown concentration is termed the analyte, while the known-concentration solution is called the titrant. Multiple types of titration exist, the two most MCAT-relevant being acid-base titrations and oxidation-reduction titrations. In this chapter, we will focus on acid-base titrations. Oxidation-reduction reactions will be covered in the next chapter of this book.

The endpoint of an acid-base titration, alternatively termed the equivalence point, occurs when the original acid or base has been fully neutralized by the added base or acid. To flesh out this concept, let's imagine that we are titrating an acid of unknown concentration with 1 M NaOH. As we progressively add drops of base, more and more acid molecules become deprotonated. Eventually, we reach a point where *all* of the original acid molecules have lost their proton, and at this point, the acid has been neutralized. We will later see that on the curves made to depict titrations, equivalence points appear in the center of steeply-sloping regions.

The language we have used so far assumes that the acid in question contains only one acidic proton, as is true for species such as HCl and HCN. Such acids are categorized as monoprotic. However, other acids are diprotic, such as H_2SO_4, and some are even triprotic, like H_3PO_4 (Figure 3). (Note that acids that can lose more than one H^+ ion are often lumped together under the heading of "polyprotic.") For polyprotic acids, a complete titration involves neutralization of multiple protons, so it is important to clarify which proton is being discussed. (Here's another interesting point regarding polyprotic acids: their conjugate bases are amphiprotic, meaning they can either lose or gain a proton. Consider HSO_4^-, for example, or $H_2PO_4^-$.)

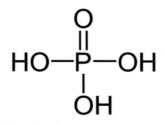

Figure 3. Phosphoric acid, a triprotic acid.

The existence of polyprotic acids complicates the description of acid concentration. Until now, we have described concentration only using molarity (moles acid per liter). However, a solution of 1 M H_2SO_4 actually contains twice the acidic protons as an equal-volume solution of 1 M HCl. This brings us to the concept of normality, a special concentration measurement. Normality can be used for a variety of chemical processes, including redox reactions and precipitations. On the MCAT, however, you will virtually always encounter it in the context of acid-base chemistry. Normality can be calculated using Equation 8, below.

Equation 8.
$$\text{normality} = \frac{\text{moles of equivalents}}{\text{liters solution}}$$

By "equivalents," we mean acidic protons or hydroxide ions. For example, consider our 1 M solution of H_2SO_4, and imagine that it is held in 1 L of solution. This solution contains 1 mole of sulfuric acid molecules, but it contains *two* moles of acidic protons. The normality of the solution is thus 2 moles divided by 1 L, or 2 N. This simple example shows us an alternate way to calculate normality: simply multiply the molarity of the acid solution by the number of acidic protons per molecule.

Let's return to the concept of neutralization. The amount of base (or acid) required to fully neutralize an acid (or base) is given by Equation 9, which relates the normalities and volumes of the two solutions.

Equation 9.
$$N_{acid}V_{acid} = N_{base}V_{base}$$

For monoprotic species, where normality and molarity are equal, this simplifies to the fundamental truth of "moles acid = moles base," while for polyprotic species, it can be described as "moles H^+ = moles OH^-." As we stated earlier, in a titration, complete neutralization occurs at a position termed the equivalence point. Equation 9, then, is *only* valid at the equivalence point, rather than at any random point over the course of the titration. If we know the normality of the titrant, the volume of the analyte solution, and the volume of titrant required to reach the equivalence point, we can plug these values directly in to Equation 9 to easily calculate the normality of unknown analyte. To do this, however, we must be able to tell when the equivalence point has been reached! This is accomplished through the use of an indicator. Indicators are weak acids or weak bases that take on different colors depending on their protonation state. For example, phenolphthalein (Figure 4) is colorless when protonated and pink when deprotonated. Consider the titration of an acid using phenolphthalein as an indicator. The solution is initially colorless, but as drop after drop of base is added, its pH nears and then exceeds the pK_a of the indicator. Progressively more phenolphthalein molecules are deprotonated, turning the solution pink. Once the color change is spotted, the titration is stopped. A general rule of thumb when choosing an indicator is that the pK_a of the indicator should be as close as possible to the predicted pH of the solution at its equivalence point.

> **MCAT STRATEGY > > >**
>
> If Equation 9 looks familiar, it probably is. A very similar equation is used for dilutions, in which water is added to a solution to weaken its concentration. You may have seen this equation as $M_1V_1 = M_2V_2$ or as $C_1V_1 = C_2V_2$. Finding relationships between different equations can help you understand the fundamentals rather than blindly memorizing.

Figure 4. A solution turned pink by phenolphthalein, indicating a basic solution.

We have now talked quite a bit about titrations without introducing the most classically familiar part of this topic: the graphical representations known as titration curves. Before broaching that subject, let's outline our fundamentals, assuming that our analyte is a monoprotic acid. We already know that neutralization of this analyte occurs at a position termed the equivalence point. We also know that at this point, the moles of original acid present are equal to the moles of base added. Titration curves include another important position: the *half*-equivalence point, which marks the position where one-half of the volume of titrant required to reach the equivalence point has been added. One great feature of titration curves is their proportionality—the point *halfway* to the equivalence point, where *one-half* of the titrant required to reach the equivalence point has been added, is also the position where *one-half* of our original acid molecules are deprotonated. At the half-equivalence point, then, half of our acid molecules exist in their original form, while the other half exist in the form of the acid's own conjugate base.

Do you remember the Henderson-Hasselbalch equation from the previous section? Recall that, when the concentration of weak acid and its conjugate base are equal, the logarithm term drops out, and pH = pK_a. While not all titrations occur with weak acids or bases, it still holds true that at the half-equivalence point, the pH of the solution is equal to the pK_a of the acid. This is a very useful way to find pK_a if it is not directly given! Along these lines, a solution undergoing a titration will act most like an effective buffer at its half-equivalence point, which predictably falls in the center of a flat, plateau-like region of the titration curve. Table 2 outlines the differences between the equivalence and half-equivalence points, which you should be sure to master by Test Day. Again, for the sake of simplicity, this table describes the titration of a monoprotic acid.

EQUIVALENCE POINT	HALF-EQUIVALENCE POINT
Represents full neutralization	Represents half-neutralization
Moles acid = moles base added	Moles acid = moles conjugate base
Solution has virtually no buffering ability	Solution acts as a relatively effective buffer
Located in the middle of a steep part of the titration curve	Located in the middle of a plateau on the titration curve

Table 2. Equivalence vs. half-equivalence point.

Let's finally look at some titration curves corresponding to different scenarios. The appearance of these curves can vary based on the identity of the analyte (acid or base) and the strengths of the species involved. For example, imagine that 50 mL of 0.1 M HCl (a strong acid) is titrated with 0.2 M NaOH (a strong base). Initially, the solution will maintain a low pH because the molar amount of H^+ present is significantly greater than the concentration of OH^- added. As more base is added, the curve begins to rise. It then increases steeply and passes the equivalence point when the amount of OH⁻ is equal to (and thus neutralizes) the amount of H⁺ initially present. After this point, the neutralization is technically over, but if we continue to add base, OH⁻ will predominate in solution and the pH will become increasingly basic. The entirety of this titration procedure is depicted in Figure 5.

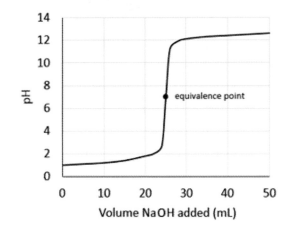

Figure 5. The titration curve for 50 mL 0.1 M HCl titrated with 0.2 M NaOH.

Let's ask ourselves a question: what is the pH of the solution at the equivalence point of this strong acid/strong base titration? To figure this out, simply remember that the equivalence point marks the position at which all of the original HCl has been neutralized by NaOH. The two species present in solution, then, will be H_2O and NaCl. H_2O is neutral, but what about NaCl? Well, Na^+ is a common spectator ion and does not possess acid-base activity, and chloride ion is the conjugate base of HCl, a strong acid. Do you remember our principle, stated earlier in this chapter, that the stronger the acid, the weaker its conjugate base? In fact, *strong* acids like HCl have conjugate bases so weak that they are functionally neutral. (To conceptualize this, recall that HCl fully dissociates into H⁺ and Cl⁻ in solution. This means that the reverse reaction, where Cl⁻ would act as a base and gain a proton, takes place to a negligible extent.) Both H_2O and NaCl, then, are neutral, meaning that the solution will have a pH of 7 at the equivalence point, assuming standard temperature. This is true of all strong acid/strong base titrations. Note what we did here: when estimating the pH of the equivalence point, we focused not on the original acid and base, but rather on the products—water and a salt—produced by the neutralization.

Next, let's examine the titration curve for a weak acid reacted with a strong base (Figure 6). Suppose that 50 mL of 0.1 M acetic acid (CH_3COOH) is titrated with 0.2 M NaOH. Notice that the initial pH is higher for this weak acid than for a strong acid, as is the equivalence point. In fact, the equivalence point for a weak acid/strong base titration is always higher than 7 under standard conditions. To explain this, we again turn to the products present at the *end* of the neutralization: here, H_2O and CH_3COONa, or sodium acetate. Water and sodium are neutral, but the acetate anion is the conjugate base of the weak acid acetic acid. Since acetic acid is weak, acetate is moderately basic, and the solution will be basic overall as a result.

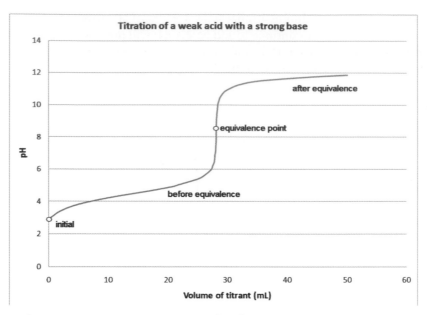

Figure 6. Titration curve for 50 mL 0.1 M CH_3COOH titrated with 0.2 M NaOH.

Notice in Figure 6 that the half-equivalence point (or halfway to the equivalence point along the x-axis) falls between 4.5 and 5. In fact, the pK_a of acetic acid is approximately 4.8. This is a great example of how a titration curve can give us valuable information!

MCAT STRATEGY > > >

We have seen how strong acid/strong base titrations differ from weak acid/strong base titrations in the pH of their equivalence points. However, a common misconception is that they also differ in the *quantity of base required* to reach this point. In reality, it does *not* require more moles of base to titrate a strong acid than a weak one. If this seems confusing, think about stoichiometry. NaOH and the weak acid HF react in a 1:1 ratio, just as NaOH and the strong acid HBr do.

The final type of titration is a strong acid/weak base titration. Predictably, the equivalence point of such a titration has a pH of less than 7 under standard conditions. For example, consider the titration of HNO_3 with NH_3. At the equivalence point, only H_2O and NH_4NO_3 will remain; NH_4^+ is a weak acid, while NO_3^- (the conjugate base of a strong acid) is functionally neutral. As such, the equivalence point will fall at an acidic pH.

Until now, we have discussed the titration of an acid analyte with a basic titrant. We can just as easily conduct the titration of a basic analyte with an acid titrant; the only difference will be the starting point of this titration, which will correspond to a basic pH. The curve will then slope downward instead of upward. Otherwise, the fundamental principles are the same.

What about polyprotic titrations, or those in which more than one proton is neutralized? As we mentioned before, phosphoric acid (H_3PO_4) is a polyprotic acid that can undergo multiple ionization steps. Note that the first proton is lost the most readily and corresponds to the largest K_a value. The second proton is more difficult to lose, as it must be lost from an anion, to which it is electrostatically attracted. The third proton is even harder to lose and has the smallest of the three K_a values.

$$H_3PO_4 \leftrightarrow H_2PO_4^- + H^+ \qquad K_{a1} = 7.5 \times 10^{-3}$$
$$H_2PO_4^- \leftrightarrow HPO_4^{2-} + H^+ \qquad K_{a2} = 6.2 \times 10^{-8}$$
$$HPO_4^{2-} \leftrightarrow PO_4^{3-} + H^+ \qquad K_{a3} = 4.8 \times 10^{-13}$$

Since the dissociation of each proton is associated with a unique K_a, there must also be three relevant pK_a values and thus three half-equivalence points. Since each proton must be fully neutralized, three equivalence points will also be present. This is a helpful general rule: the number of acidic protons is always equal to the number of equivalence points *and* the number of half-equivalence points on the titration curve. The curve for H_3PO_4 is shown in Figure 7.

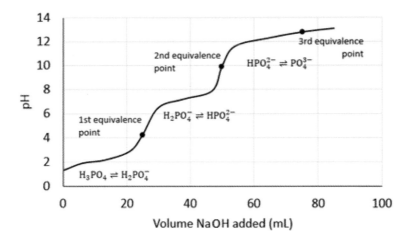

Figure 7. Titration curve for H_3PO_4. Note that the third proton is only very weakly acidic, so the third equivalence point is not in the middle of a steep curve like most equivalence points.

Before the first half-equivalence point is reached, the predominant species in solution is H_3PO_4. At the first half-equivalence point, $[H_3PO_4] = [H_2PO_4^-]$; between this position and the first equivalence point, the $H_2PO_4^-$ concentration exceeds the H_3PO_4 concentration, until the first proton has been entirely neutralized at the first equivalence point. Similarly, the second equivalence point marks the full neutralization of the second proton (leaving only HPO_4^{2-} in solution), and the final equivalence point denotes the full neutralization of the third and final proton, yielding PO_4^{3-}.

The MCAT commonly tests polyprotic titrations in the form of titrations of amino acids. Nonpolar amino acids, like alanine and valine, have only two equivalence points, corresponding to their carboxylic acid and amino termini. Acidic and basic amino acids, such as glutamic acid and lysine, display three equivalence points. As in a typical titration, each *half*-equivalence point corresponds to the pK_a of the relevant group, whether carboxylic acid terminal, amino terminal, or acidic or basic side chain. It is very important to understand the pH ranges at which a given amino acid position will be protonated or deprotonated. Take lysine, for example, held in a solution of pH 1 and titrated with NaOH. Lysine has pK_a values of approximately 2, 9, and 10.5, where 10.5 is the pK_a of its side chain. Initially, lysine will be protonated at every possible position, yielding a net charge of + 2 (0 for the carboxylic acid terminal, + 1 for the amino terminal, and + 1 for the basic side chain). Once its first equivalence point is reached, its -COOH terminal will have been fully deprotonated, giving it a charge of + 1. Its second equivalence point denotes the deprotonation of its amino terminal, yielding a charge of 0, and its final equivalence point represents the deprotonation of its side chain. An important value associated with amino acids is the isoelectric point (pI), which refers to the pH at which the amino acid carries a net charge of 0. What would be the isoelectric point of lysine? As we just stated, lysine is uncharged at its second equivalence point, which falls exactly halfway between its second half-equivalence point (pH = pK_{a2} = 9) and its third half-equivalence point (pH = pK_{a3} = 10.5). The pI of lysine, then, is the average of its two highest pK_a values, or about 9.75.

> > CONNECTIONS < <

Chapter 2 of Biochemistry

6. Must-Knows

> Acid-base definitions:
> — Arrhenius: acid donates H^+, base donates OH^-
> — Brønsted-Lowry: acid donates H^+, base accepts H^+
> • When a B-L acid loses H^+, it becomes its conjugate base
> • When a B-L base gains H^+, it becomes its conjugate acid
> — Lewis: acid accepts electron pair, base donates electron pair
> Acid nomenclature:
> — For acids that do not contain oxygen, use prefix "hydro-" and suffix "-ic acid"
> — For inorganic oxyacids: named as follows, depending on # of oxygen atoms
> • Per____ic acid, ____ic acid, ____ous acid, hypo____ous acid
> Rules for chemical equilibria apply to acid-base reactions!
> K_w = autoionization constant for water
> — $K_w = [H_3O^+][OH^-] = 1 \times 10^{-14}$ at 25°C
> — $[H_3O^+] = [OH^-] = 1 \times 10^{-7}$ at 25°C
> — K_w is temperature-dependent, but $[H_3O^+] = [OH^-]$ in pure water
> K_a = equilibrium constant for acid dissociation; high K_a corresponds to greater dissociation/stronger acid
> — "Strong" acids = acids that fully dissociate in water to produce H_3O^+
> • HI, HBr, HCl, HNO_3, H_2SO_4, $HClO_4$, $HClO_3$
> K_b = equilibrium constant for base dissociation; high K_b corresponds to greater dissociation/stronger base
> — "Strong" bases = bases that fully ionize in water to produce OH^-
> • Hydroxides of alkali and alkali earth metals
> pH = $-\log[H_3O^+]$; pOH = $-\log[OH^-]$
> pK_w = pH + pOH = 14 at 25°C
> $K_a \cdot K_b = K_w = 1 \times 10^{-14}$ at 25°C; $pK_a + pK_b = pK_w = 14$ at 25°C
> Buffers: solutions that resist large changes in pH
> — Include weak acid + its conjugate base (or weak base + its conjugate acid)
> — Follow Henderson-Hasselbalch equation: pH = $pK_a + \log \frac{[A-]}{[HA]}$
> — Physiological example: bicarbonate buffer system (H_2CO_3 and HCO_3^-)
> Polyprotic acids: contain more than one H^+ (example: H_2SO_4)
> Titrations: conc. of unknown solution (analyte) is found using known solution (titrant)
> — Equivalence point = "endpoint" = full neutralization
> • Moles H^+ = moles OH^-; found on steep segment of curve
> • Indicator changes color (ideal pK_a of ind. = pH range of eq. point)
> — Half-equivalence point = half of volume required for full neutralization
> • Moles acid = moles conjugate base; pH = pK_a; found on flat segment of curve (plateau)
> Normality: concentration measurement used for acids, bases
> — normality = $\frac{\text{moles of equivalents}}{\text{liters solution}}$
> $N_{acid}V_{acid} = N_{base}V_{base}$ (equation for vol. required to reach equivalence point)

This page left intentionally blank.

Practice Passage

Homeostasis of the ideal pH level in the human body is vitally important for a number of reasons, among them prevention of tissue degradation due to excessive acidity or basicity, and creation of an internal environment in which catalyzed biochemical reactions can proceed at appropriate rates.

Systems which help to stabilize pH levels include respiratory feedback mechanisms, which decrease the level of CO_2 in blood plasma and thus avoid accumulation of excess carbonic acid. Fundamental physical processes such as diffusion and proton transfer ordinarily limit the rate of hydration, so special strategies are required to attain physiological rates of pH maintenance. Blood buffer systems, catalyzed by carbonic anhydrase ($k_{cat} = 10^6$ s^{-1}), utilize both carbonic acid (pK_a = 3.5) and bicarbonate to maintain ideal pH. Students conducted an experiment by creating a similar buffering system and a titration procedure was applied. The students measured pH as a function of the percent composition of the buffering solution. Their measurements are shown in Figure 1.

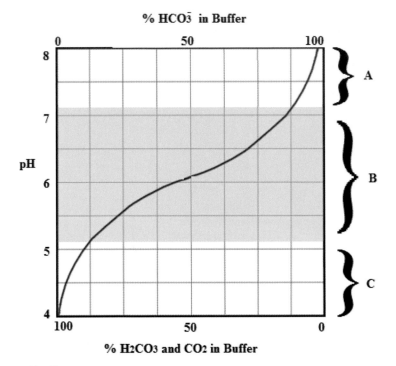

Figure 1 pH as a function of buffer component percentage

The kidneys also play a role in the regulation of blood [H$^+$] concentration. These organs can excrete either H$^+$ or HCO_3^-, depending on which direction the blood must shift to reach a safe plasma pH range. Metabolic alkalosis causes a significant number of the remaining carbonic acid molecules to dissociate.

1. If respiratory function is interrupted at a time when excessive CO_2 is in the blood, then the pH will:
   A. Increase, because increased CO_2 means increased acidity.
   B. Decrease, because excessive CO_2 will cause elevated levels of carbonic acid.
   C. Remain constant, because CO_2 will simply convert itself into H_2CO_3 by combining with a water molecule.
   D. Remain constant, because CO_2 does not have a hydrogen atom and hence cannot affect pH level.

2. A follow up experiment was conducted with a solution where pOH = pH at 25 °C and 1 atm. At this point, the values of $[H^+]$ and $[OH^-]$ will be:
   A. 10^{-7}, because the product of $[H^+]$ and $[OH^-]$ under these environmental conditions must be 10^{-14}.
   B. 10^{-8}, because under these environmental conditions, the sum of pH and pOH must be 16.
   C. 10^{-9}, because K_W will equal both pH and pOH, and $K_W = 10^{-9}$ at 25 °C and 1 atm.
   D. incalculable, because pH and pOH cannot accurately be calculated when they are equal.

3. What best accounts for the rate of pH change shown in Figure 1 as the $[H^+]$ changes from 10^{-7} to 10^{-8}?
   A. Increased HCO_3^- levels resulting in the donation of more $[OH^-]$ ions, causing a basic mixture of H_2O and OH^- to form.
   B. Ionization of water
   C. The fact that titration occurred in the laboratory caused more inefficient functioning of the buffer system compared to how it would have operated in a living specimen.
   D. Exhaustion of carbonic acid levels which could otherwise help to correct increased basicity.

4. Titration of potassium acetate in solution was conducted in a further attempt to determine a superior buffer system. The equation describing the reactions preceding titration appears below:

$$CH_3COOK + H_2O \rightarrow K^+ + CH_3COO^- + H_2O \rightleftharpoons CH_3COOH + OH^-$$

   What best describes what occurs in this process?

   A. An acidic salt is hydrolyzed.
   B. A basic salt is hydrolyzed.
   C. A weak acid is dissolved.
   D. A strong acid is dissolved.

5. The ionization constant of H_2CO_3 is most nearly:
   A. 1
   B. 10^{-2}
   C. 10^{-4}
   D. 0

6. Which of the following is expected to have the lowest pK_b?
   A. R_3N
   B. KOH
   C. RNH_2
   D. NH_4^+

7. What volume and mass of RbOH would be needed for the students to neutralize 50 ml of 0.06 M H_2SO_4 solution if an equimolar basic solution is used?
   A. 50 ml, 300 mg
   B. 50 ml, 600 mg
   C. 100 ml, 300 mg
   D. 100 ml, 600 mg

Practice Passage Explanations

Homeostasis of the ideal pH level in the human body is vitally important for a number of reasons, among them prevention of tissue degradation due to excessive acidity or basicity, and creation of an internal environment in which catalyzed biochemical reactions can proceed at appropriate rates.

Key terms: ideal pH

Systems which help to stabilize pH levels include respiratory feedback mechanisms, which decrease the level of CO_2 in blood plasma and thus avoid accumulation of excess carbonic acid. Fundamental physical processes such as diffusion and proton transfer ordinarily limit the rate of hydration, so special strategies are required to attain physiological rates of pH maintenance. Blood buffer systems, catalyzed by carbonic anhydrase ($k_{cat} = 10^6$ s^{-1}), utilize both carbonic acid ($pK_a = 3.5$) and bicarbonate to maintain ideal pH. Students conducted an experiment by creating a similar buffering system and a titration procedure was applied. The students measured pH as a function of the percent composition of the buffering solution. Their measurements are shown in Figure 1.

Key terms: stabilize pH, respiratory feedback, buffer experiment, carbonic acid; carbonic anhydrase

Cause and effect: respiratory = $\downarrow CO_2 \rightarrow \downarrow H_2CO_3 \rightarrow \uparrow pH$; H_2CO_3/HCO_3^- buffer

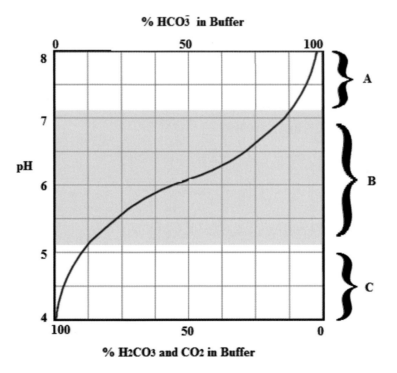

Figure 1. pH as a function of buffer component percentage

Figure 1 shows that the ideal buffering range (when ΔpH is minimal) occurs around 6; ΔpH slowest when solution is ~ 50% HCO_3^-

The kidneys also play a role in the regulation of blood [H$^+$] concentration. These organs can excrete either H$^+$ or HCO_3^-, depending on which direction the blood must shift to reach a safe plasma pH range. Metabolic alkalosis causes a significant number of the remaining carbonic acid molecules to dissociate.

Key terms: regulation, kidneys, metabolic alkalosis

Cause and effect: kidneys secrete H^+ / HCO_3^- to correct ΔpH; alkalosis = ↑pH → ↓H_2CO_3 → ↓H^+ + HCO_3^-

1. B is correct. CO_2 will combine with water, H_2O, to form carbonic acid, H_2CO_3. Increased carbonic acid means a more acidic solution because the acid will donate a proton, H^+, to other molecules in the surrounding environment. More acidic solutions have lower pH levels.

    A: Increased acidity will result in a lower pH, not a higher one.
    C: Although CO_2 will indeed combine with water to form H_2CO_3, this is the chemical formula for carbonic acid, which will make the blood plasma more acidic and lower its pH level.
    D: Substances can react to form acids even though they themselves lack an H atom which can become an H^+ ion. The passage indicates that CO_2 is one of these substances because it can form carbonic acid.

2. A is correct. K_W, the dissociation constant for pure water (H_2O → H^+ + OH^-) is defined as the product of [H^+] and [OH^-]. The K_W for all aqueous solutions at 25°C and 1 atm is 1×10^{-14} (eliminate choice C). We were told that [H^+] = [OH^-], so each can be calculated by taking the square root of K_W; which results in 1×10^{-7}.

    B: At standard temperature 25°C, the sum of pH and pOH must be 14, not 16.
    D: When dealing with pure water under standard conditions, [H^+] = [OH^-] and an equilibrium exists, where a very small number of H_2O water molecules will dissociate into [H^+] and [OH^-] ions and vice versa. The concentration of either ion is never zero nor incalculable.

3. D is correct. The hydrogen concentrations in the question stem indicate we want to focus on the pH changes between pH = 7 and pH = 8. Exhaustion of one of the two components of a buffer system will take away its ability to resist pH changes. In this case, depletion of carbonic acid will prevent the buffer's acid component from releasing hydrogen ions [H^+] that could neutralize excessive basicity, i.e. prevent pH from rising too much. Figure 1 shows that the slope between the pH ranges 7 and 8 takes place when the concentration of carbonic acid (H_2CO_3) is low.

    A: No component of the chemical reaction involved in the specified buffer system involves donation of OH^-.
    B: Ionization of water will occur in every solution, as well as pure water—it does not, by itself, explain the specific ineffectiveness of the buffer system at extreme pH ranges.
    C: Buffer systems comprise fairly simple chemical reactions that do not operate differently *in vitro* than they would *in vivo*.

4. B is correct. Potassium acetate is a basic salt—in other words, its components come from a strong base and a weak acid. In the specific case of potassium acetate, its K^+ component comes from a strong base (KOH, potassium hydroxide) and its CH_3COO^- component comes from a weak acid (CH_3COOH, acetic acid). Hydrolysis of this salt (hydrolysis being defined as separating the components through interaction with water) occurs when the salt is dissolved into K^+ and CH_3COO^-.

    A: An acidic salt would have components which come from a strong acid and a weak base. Here, CH_3COO^- comes from a weak acid and K^+ comes from a strong base.
    C, D: Potassium acetate does not qualify as an acid. After dissolution, neither the K^+ ion nor the CH_3COO^- acetate ion will donate an H^+ ion or accept an OH^- ion. (The reaction equation shows that the CH_3COO^- acetate ion can accept an H^+ ion, which means it is acting as a base, but it will not act as an acid.

5. C is correct. The dissociation constant for an acid is also known as the K_a. We should know that carbonic acid is a weak acid, meaning its conjugate (bicarbonate) will also be a weak base. This would mean that is has a very

low, but non-zero, K_a. We can also use the passage information (pK_a carbonic acid = 3.5) to calculate the exact K_a = 5 × 10^{-4}. Using the shortcut: $p(C \times 10^{-e}) = (e-1).(10-C)$.

6. B is correct. A lower pK_b means the molecule has a higher K_b, which means the question is really asking us to identify the strongest base. Do not waste time evaluating the different amines (general more substituted amines are better bases). We can eliminate the ammonium ion because it is acidic (i.e. it will donate protons), and pick the classic strong base, consisting of a group I/II metal and a hydroxide ion.

7. D is correct. First, we need to calculate how many acid groups we have in solution, then we can determine how many base groups we will need to neutralize them. We are told the basic solution is equimolar to the acidic solution, meaning the concentration of the base = 0.06M. We can use the equivalence point equation, but do not forget to convert the molarity of each species into normality (the moles of acid/base groups per molecule):

$$N_a V_a = N_b V_b \rightarrow V_b = N_a V_a / N_b = (2 \text{ equiv/mol})(0.06 \text{ mol/L})(50 \text{ ml}) / (0.06 \text{ mol/L}) = 100 \text{ ml of } 0.06 \text{ M RbOH}$$

Next, we need to find the mass required, by using the gram equivalent weight of RbOH (102 g/equivalent).

$$m_{base} / g \text{ eq. wt.} \rightarrow N_a V_a \quad m_{base}/102 \text{ g} = (2)(0.06)(50)$$

$$m_{base} = 102(2)(0.06)(50) = 100(2)(0.06)(50) = (2)(6)(50) = 600 \text{ g RbOH}$$

Independent Questions

1. The molecule BF_3 is best described as which of the following?
   A. A Lewis base
   B. A Brønsted-Lowry base
   C. A Lewis acid
   D. A Brønsted-Lowry acid

2. H_2CO_3 is a stronger acid than HCN. From this information alone, we can determine that:
   A. CO_3^{2-} is a weaker base than CN^-.
   B. HCO_3^- has a higher pK_b than CN^-.
   C. CN^- is a strong base.
   D. HCO_3^- has a higher K_b than CN^-.

3. What is the normality of a 0.75 M H_2SO_4 solution?
   A. 0.375 N
   B. 0.75 N
   C. 1.5 N
   D. 2.25 N

4. As temperature increases, the ionization constant for water (K_w) also increases. Which of the following statements is true of a beaker of pure water at 100°C?
   A. Its pOH is lower than 7.
   B. Its pH is equal to 7.
   C. Its pH is no longer equal to its pOH.
   D. It is not considered a neutral solution.

5. The K_a of hydrofluoric acid (HF) is 7.2 x 10^{-4}. The pK_b of fluoride ion (F^-) under standard conditions is closest to which of the following?
   A. 3.28
   B. 9.85
   C. 10.72
   D. 11.28

6. A laboratory technician creates a 10.0 M HI solution. The pH of this solution is expected to be:
   A. −1.
   B. 0.
   C. 1.
   D. 2.

7. Which of the following statements is NOT true regarding the titration of 50 mL of 2.0 M NaOH?
   A. The half-equivalence point can be reached by adding 50 mL of 1.0 M HCl.
   B. To reach the equivalence point, the same number of moles of acid must have been added as moles of base were initially present.
   C. Titrating with HF will produce an equivalence point that is higher than 7.
   D. Titrating with 1.0 M HF would require a larger volume of acid to reach the equivalence point than titrating with 1.0 M HBr.

8. What is the approximate pH of a solution made by adding 0.5 moles of KOH to 1.0 moles of HCN in 1 L of water? (K_a of HCN = 6.2×10^{-10})
   A. 4.75
   B. 8.55
   C. 9.31
   D. 10.42

Independent Question Explanations

1. C is correct. In boron trifluoride (BF_3), the central boron atom has an incomplete octet. As such, it is able to accept an electron pair. Electron acceptors are termed Lewis acids. In contrast, Lewis bases are electron donors, making choice A incorrect. The Brønsted-Lowry definitions of acids and bases revolve around protons, which are not of interest here.

2. B is correct. Since H_2CO_3 is a stronger acid than HCN, the conjugate base of H_2CO_3 must be a *weaker* base than the conjugate base of HCN. To find the conjugate base of each molecule, simply remove a proton. Thus, HCO_3^- must be a weaker base than CN^-. Weaker bases have higher pK_b values, making choice B the correct answer. Regarding choice A, CO_3^{2-} is not the conjugate of H_2CO_3, so we cannot assume this statement to be true. Choice C is also not valid; we cannot deduce that CN^- must be a strong base simply because HCN is a weak acid. Finally, choice D is the reverse of an accurate statement (remember, the trend for K_b is opposite that for pK_b).

3. C is correct. When dealing with acids, normality is defined as the number of moles of protons per liter of solution. Here, normality can be calculated by multiplying the molarity of the solution (0.75 M) by the number of protons per molecule of H_2SO_4 (2). This yields an answer of 1.5 N.

4. A is correct. Remember, pH+ pOH = pK_w. (We often think of this equation as pH+ pOH = 14, but this only holds true under standard conditions of 25°C.) As the temperature increases above 25°C, the value of K_w also increases, which means that pK_w *decreases*. At 100°C, then, pH and pOH will sum to a value lower than 14. However, each molecule of water dissociates into an equal number of hydroxide and hydronium ions, meaning that the pH should still equal the pOH and the solution will still be neutral (eliminate choices C and D). To sum to a value less than 14, then, both the pH and the pOH must be less than 14, making choice A our answer.

5. C is correct. Remember, pK_a (acid) + pK_b (conjugate base) = 14 under standard conditions. Thus, if we convert the K_a of HF to its pK_a, we can easily find the pK_b of F^- by subtracting the pK_a from 14.

$$pK_a = -\log(K_a)$$
$$pK_a = -\log(7.2 \times 10^{-4})$$

Since 7.2×10^{-4} falls between 10^{-4} and 10^{-3}, the pK_a of HF must fall between 3 and 4. 14 − 3 = 11, and 14 − 4 = 10; therefore, our answer for the pK_b of F^- must exist between 10 and 11. The only answer that fits this description is choice C.

6. A is correct. Do not fall for the trap of assuming that pH cannot be negative! pH is defined as the negative logarithm of the H^+ concentration. Hydroiodic acid (HI) is a strong acid, so it will fully dissociate and produce a 10.0 M [H^+] solution.

$$-\log(10.0) = -\log(10^1) = -1$$

7. D is correct. Titrating 50 mL of 2.0 M NaOH would require 100 mL of 1.0 M HF to reach the equivalence point, as that is where the same number of moles of acid have been added as moles of base initially present. Similarly, titrating that same volume of 2.0 M NaOH would also require 100 mL of 1.0 M HBr. It does not matter that HBr is a strong acid, while HF is weak. Thus, choice D is the false statement and the correct answer here. Choice A is true, as 50 mL of 1.0 M HCl will neutralize half of the NaOH molecules present. Choice B is true as well, as it represents the definition of the equivalence point. Finally, titrating a strong base (NaOH) with a weak acid (HF) will yield an equivalence point that is higher than 7, making option C accurate also.

8. C is correct. 0.5 moles of KOH will neutralize exactly 0.5 moles of HCN, leaving us with a solution that contains 0.5 moles of our original HCN and 0.5 moles of its conjugate base, CN^-. According to the Henderson-Hasselbalch equation, a solution that contains equal concentrations of weak acid and its own conjugate base constitutes a buffer with pH = $pK_{a\,(acid)}$. To find the pK_a of HCN from the given K_a, note that $pK_a = -\log(K_a)$. Since 6.2×10^{-10} falls nearly in the middle of 10^{-10} and 10^{-9}, the negative logarithm of this value should fall between 9 and 10. This gives us choice C as the best answer here.

Redox Reactions and Electrochemistry

0. Introduction

In this chapter, we cover two topics that are perennially challenging for MCAT students: oxidation-reduction (redox) reactions and electrochemistry. These topics are closely related, and the essence of both is closely tracking the movement of electrons. There are two basic things that you need to understand about electrons: first, that they are negatively-charged particles that make up the outer layers of atomic structure; and second, that electron exchange is at the heart of all chemical reactions.

That said, a thorough understanding of atomic structure and bonding will help you study redox reactions with optimal effectiveness, so we do recommend that you review the corresponding chapters (Chapters 1 and 2 of this textbook and Chapter 12 of Physics) if you feel at all shaky.

> > CONNECTIONS < <

Chapters 1 and 2 of Chemistry and Chapter 12 of Physics

One of the challenges of studying redox chemistry for the MCAT has to do with the need to thoroughly master definitions that are somewhat counterintuitive and apply them in novel contexts. For this reason, the first section of this chapter will deal with important redox definitions and how to set up and analyze simple redox reactions. We will then proceed to the topic of reduction potentials, which are commonly tested on the MCAT and are often a source of particular confusion. Next, we will explore how galvanic and electrolytic cells work. This corresponds to the core content of redox chemistry and electrochemistry, but there are a few other topical crossovers that can come up on the MCAT, so in the last part of the chapter we will discuss redox titrations and the interconnections between electrochemistry and thermodynamics, which have useful applications in biochemistry.

1. Redox Definitions and Redox Reactions

We'll start this chapter by presenting the single most important fact you need to know for the MCAT: oxidation means *losing* electrons, and reduction means *gaining* electrons. Although you ideally need to know a lot more about redox chemistry to thoroughly prepare for MCAT success, if you were to know only one thing, this would be it. Unfortunately, this is one of those situations where the terminology we use has historical roots that can make it harder to understand what each term refers to. One way to remember which term is which is to focus on the idea that reduction (which sounds like it should have something to do with 'lowering') takes place when the oxidation state of an atom decreases. However, for this to make sense, you need to have a solid understanding of what an oxidation state is. We'll talk more about this shortly.

In the introduction to this chapter, we mentioned that moving electrons around is at the heart of all chemical reactions. A natural follow-up question would be: if this is true (which it is), what makes redox reactions special? The answer to this is that redox reactions are those in which electrons are transferred between atoms such that one atom clearly gains one or more electrons while another atom clearly loses one or more electrons. Stepping back for a minute, we can note that this isn't the case for many reactions. Consider, for instance, the classic example of nucleophilic substitution reactions. These are discussed in more depth in Chapter 11, but for our purposes it suffices to note that the central carbon atom just swaps out one substituent for another. It's still sharing the same quantity of electrons, which means that such a reaction would not count as a redox reaction. More technically, we can summarize this reasoning by saying that a redox reaction is one in which the oxidation states of compounds change.

MCAT STRATEGY > > >

One common mnemonic for oxidation and reduction is *OIL RIG*: oxidation is loss, reduction is gain. Another mnemonic you may have encountered is "*LEO* the lion goes *GER*," where *LEO* stands for "lose electrons – oxidation" and *GER* stands for "gain electrons – reduction." It doesn't matter which mnemonic you use—or even whether you use a mnemonic at all—but you must know this information cold on Test Day.

However, saying that the oxidation states of compounds change in a redox reaction just leads to yet another question: what is an oxidation state? This is worth investing some time in. Although most MCAT students have worked with oxidation states before, there's an unfortunate tendency for many chemistry classes to deliver the message "don't worry about what an oxidation state *is*, just memorize the rules for calculating it!" As always for the MCAT, since you may be asked to apply your knowledge in unfamiliar contexts, it's helpful to understand the *why* of a concept before memorizing rules.

A useful way of thinking about the oxidation state (which is measured using oxidation numbers) is as a method for keeping track of how electrons are shared within a molecule. Since all atoms have slightly different electronegativity values, it will always be the case that in a bond between atoms belonging to different elements, the electrons will be shared unequally. The discrepancy in electron sharing may be complete (in the case of ionic bonds), partial but significant (in the case of polar covalent bonds), or minimal (in the case of nonpolar covalent bonds), but it will always be present. Oxidation states are essentially a model of electron distribution where we simplify things by assigning the electron to the more electronegative atom in a bond.

Since oxidation states are a model of electron distribution, and electrons are charged, it is not surprising that the rules for determining oxidation states have some overlap with the charge of a molecule. While each atom within a molecule has its own oxidation state, the rules for how those oxidation states are summed together generally correspond to the charge of the molecule. The overall rules—for individual atoms and for molecules as a whole—are summarized below:

> Pure elements have an oxidation state of zero. This applies even if they are found in diatomic molecules, such as O_2 or F_2.
> The oxidation state of monoatomic ions is equal to their charge. Thus, the Fe^{2+} ion has an oxidation state of + 2, and the chloride anion (Cl^-) has an oxidation state of −1.
> The sum of the oxidation states of the components of molecules and polyatomic ions is equal to their charge (that is, zero for neutral molecules and some integer value for polyatomic ions).

Given these rules, we can see that assigning oxidation states for pure elements and monoatomic ions is trivial. The same principle (overall oxidation state = overall charge) applies to polyatomic ions and molecules too, but here it gets more complicated, because individual atoms within these structures have different oxidation states that mathematically cancel each other out. This means that we need some rules for assigning oxidation states to individual atoms within a compound. These are summarized below, in order of priority:

> The oxidation state of F is –1, because it is the most electronegative element.
  – Other halogens will usually have an oxidation state of –1, unless they are bonded to a more electronegative halogen, N, or O. In that case, their oxidation state may be + 1, + 3, + 4 (for Br), + 5, or even + 7. (This scenario is not common on the MCAT, but you should be aware of the possibility. For example, the oxidation state of chlorine in $HClO_4$ is + 7.)
> The oxidation state of H is + 1, except when it is bonded to a more electropositive element, in which case it will be –1. The examples you are most likely to encounter of this on the MCAT are the reducing agents NaH, $NaBH_4$, and $LiAlH_4$.
> The oxidation state of O is usually –2, with some important exceptions, such as peroxides, in which it is –1.

The oxidation state of alkali metals (the first column in the periodic table) is always + 1 (at least in scenarios that you will see on the MCAT), and that of alkaline earth metals (the second column in the periodic table) is always +2.

Once you apply these rules, you can use simple algebra to figure out the oxidation state of the other atoms in a compound. Let's take the example of carbon in a carboxylic acid functional group (R–C–**COOH**). This species is neutral, so the overall oxidation states have to sum up to zero. The C–C bond doesn't affect the oxidation state of the –COOH carbon, so we don't have to worry about it. We have one hydrogen, which has an oxidation state of +1, and two oxygens, with oxidation states of –2, and these sum to a preliminary oxidation state of –3: +1 from the H+ (–4) from the two oxygens. In order for the overall oxidation state to sum to 0, the oxidation state of the carbon has to be +3. Returning to our original idea that the oxidation state should indicate how the electrons are distributed in a compound, this makes sense. Carbon has four valence electrons, and in this configuration, one valence electron is shared equally with another carbon and three are being siphoned off by electronegative oxygen molecules. As we will discuss in greater depth in further chapters on organic chemistry, the carbon in carboxylic acid functional groups has a significant partial positive charge, so the formal mechanics of oxidation state calculations actually map pretty well onto our intuitions about what's going on with this functional group.

Next, let's see what happens if we deal with the same question, but in a carboxylate ion (R–C–**COO⁻**). The difference between this and the previous structure we analyzed is that the –OH oxygen is deprotonated, leaving a negative charge in place. In this case, the oxidation states of the compound need to sum up to –1. As in the previous example, we ignore the C–C bond. The oxidation state of oxygen is –2 according to our rules, so the two oxygens add up to –4. There's no H in this case, so we can proceed straight to the step of balancing out the oxidation state using the carbon. The carbon must have an oxidation state of + 3 for the overall compound to have an oxidation state of –1. Notably, this is the same exact value we calculated in the previous example! This may seem surprising at first, but it's actually pretty logical, and it corresponds to the physical intuition that deprotonating an oxygen shouldn't do anything to how the valence electrons of the carbon are distributed.

Let's work through one other example containing carbon that illustrates a few useful points. What about the carbon in a molecule of methane (CH_4)? We can analyze this molecule fairly quickly. The overall oxidation state is zero, and the H atoms all have oxidation states of + 1, resulting in a total of + 4. The only way to balance this out is for C to have an oxidation state of –4. This is correct, but it may seem counterintuitive. The issue here is that C, with an electronegativity value of 2.5, is slightly more electronegative than H, with an electronegativity value of 2.1. Therefore, the electrons can be thought of as being *slightly* more on the C side of the bond. The key point here is that this tendency is *very* slight. The negative oxidation state of C in this compound does not meaningfully correspond to a partial negative charge, unlike the example of the carboxylic acid group, in which the positive oxidation state of C did correspond to a partial positive charge. A final point to note here is that C—like all elements not accounted for in our rules above—can have various oxidation states depending on the compound.

As a final set of examples, let's look at a few ionic compounds, which are the most common type of compounds usually encountered in electrochemistry. Let's start with a super-simple example: calcium oxide (CaO). The oxidation states will sum to zero, and our rules tell us that the oxidation state of O is −2 and that of Ca (an alkaline earth metal) is +2, so the problem is solved. The only thing to note here is that this is a situation where you can think of the oxidation states as representing the charges on the two components of the ionic compound, since ionic bonds are defined by complete electron transfer. Now let's look at a slightly more complicated example: Fe_2O_3. As always,

MCAT STRATEGY > > >

Chemistry textbooks often focus on ionic compounds when discussing redox chemistry, for good reason—common applications such as batteries most commonly involve ionic compounds. However, the MCAT also tests redox chemistry of organic compounds, under the rubrics of organic chemistry and biochemistry. Therefore, it really pays off for the MCAT to pay close attention to how the basic definitions of redox chemistry apply *both* to organic and inorganic compounds.

for an uncharged molecule, the oxidation states of its constituents must add up to zero, and the three oxygen molecules each have an oxidation state of −2, resulting in a total of −6. The two Fe atoms must balance this out, so each of them must have an oxidation state of $(+6/2) =$ +3. Thus, the substance Fe_2O_3 is known as iron(III) oxide, which distinguishes it from compounds such as iron(II) oxide (FeO), where iron has a +2 oxidation state. Next, let's consider an ionic compound in which one of the components is a polyatomic ion, such as the oxidizing agent $KMnO_4$. The oxidation states of the four oxygen molecules add up to −8, which has to be balanced out by K and Mn. According to our rules, K must have a +1 oxidation state in an ionic compound, so the oxidation state of Mn is +7.

Now that we've covered the definition of oxidation states and how you can calculate them, we can move on to redox reactions. As mentioned above, these are reactions in which the oxidation state of a reactant changes. In order to solidify what this definition means, it might be helpful to look at some examples of redox and non-redox reactions.

> Non-redox reactions. Many interesting things may be happening, but the oxidation states don't change, because the overall distribution of electrons remains the same.
  – *Acid-base chemistry.* The oxidation state does not change in common proton transfer reactions (see the example we worked above comparing –COOH and –COO⁻ carbons) or in classic neutralization reactions (e.g., HCl + NaOH → NaCl + H_2O).
  – *Precipitation reactions.* An example would be KCl(*aq*) + $AgNO_3$(*aq*) → AgCl(*s*) + KNO_3(*aq*). The ions are being rearranged, and some bind tightly with each other to fall out of solution, but no real electron transfer is happening and the oxidation states of the ions do not change.
  – *Many substitution reactions.* Consider a classic example of nucleophilic substitution chemistry, in which OH⁻ + CH_3Br → CH_3OH+ Br⁻. On both sides of the reaction, the oxidation state of O is −2, that of Br is −1, that of H is +1, and that of C is −2.
  – *Many double displacement reactions.* In double displacement reactions, ions switch places. The participating ions can have different charges (i.e., oxidation states), but this is accounted for via stoichiometry, not via oxidation state changes. In fact, acid-base neutralization reactions and precipitation reactions are just specialized examples of this more general category.
> Redox reactions. In addition to 'classic' redox reactions, which are mostly single replacement reactions, a surprising amount of biologically relevant reactions are redox reactions. Some important examples of redox reactions include:
  – *'Classic' redox (single displacement reactions).* In these reactions, a free element displaces one element of an ionic compound, liberating it as another free element. An example would be Cu + 2 $AgNO_3$ → $Cu(NO_3)_2$ +

2 Ag. Copper starts with an oxidation state of 0 and is then oxidized to a + 2 oxidation state. Silver starts with an oxidation state of + 1 and is reduced to an oxidation state of + 0.

— *Combustion.* Combustion is often neglected as a type of redox reaction, but it is indeed an important example! Consider the combustion of methane: $CH_4 + 2 O_2 \rightarrow CO_2 + 2 H_2O$. The oxidation state of the carbon in methane is −4, but it becomes +4 in carbon dioxide. Thus, as we see, carbon is very intensely oxidized in this reaction. Correspondingly, oxygen is reduced; the oxidation state of O_2 is zero, because it is a free element, while the oxidation state of oxygen in both water and carbon dioxide is −2.

— *Combination reactions.* In combination reactions, free elements combine to form a molecule. A classic example is the formation of ammonia from hydrogen and nitrogen gas: $3 H_2 + N_2 \rightarrow 2 NH_3$. By definition, the oxidation state of free elements is zero, so such reactions are automatically redox.

— *Many metabolic reactions.* Glycolysis as a whole is actually a net redox reaction. Glucose ($C_6H_{12}O_6$) is oxidized to two molecules of pyruvate ($C_3H_3O_3^-$)—note the conversion of multiple C–O single bonds to C=O double bonds—and the electron carrier NAD^+ is reduced to NADH. Moreover, redox reactions appear in both the citric acid cycle and the electron transport chain, as well as in non-carbohydrate metabolism, such as the beta-oxidation of fatty acids. As we discuss in the Biochemistry textbook, redox reactions and electron transfer are fundamental to the basic logic of metabolism.

> > **CONNECTIONS** < <

Chapters 1, 7, and 8 of Biochemistry

Now that we've identified what a redox reaction is, we need to discuss how to balance redox reactions. To do this, it's useful to split up redox reactions into half-reactions, focusing on the net ionic products. Consider, for instance, the reaction $2 AgNO_3 + Zn \rightarrow 2 Ag + Zn(NO_3)_2$. Nothing is happening to the nitrate ion in term of redox chemistry, so we can neglect it and write two half-reactions: (1) a reduction half-reaction for silver ($Ag^+ \rightarrow Ag$) and (2) an oxidation half-reaction for zinc ($Zn \rightarrow Zn^{2+}$). Using half-reactions to describe redox reactions is very common, and we'll be seeing more of it throughout the rest of this chapter.

Next, let's review how to balance redox reactions. The basic idea is the same as balancing reactions in general—we manipulate the reaction in various ways to properly reflect conservation of mass and charge—but it can be useful to approach redox reactions systematically. Let's illustrate this with an example: how do we balance the reaction $MnO_4^- + H_2C_2O_4 \rightarrow Mn^{2+} + CO_2$ in acidic conditions?

1. Split into half-reactions: (1) $MnO_4^- \rightarrow Mn^{2+}$ and (2) $H_2C_2O_4 \rightarrow CO_2$. At this point, although it's technically not necessary for the balancing process, we may want to step back and double-check which side is reduction and which side is oxidation. In this reaction, the oxidation state of Mn will change from +7 to +2, and that of C will change from +3 to +4. Therefore, Mn is being reduced and C is being oxidized.

2. Balance the (non-O and non-H) atoms. In the first atom-balancing step, focus on non-oxygen and non-hydrogen atoms and make sure that they balance on each side of the half-reaction. In our half-reactions, there's obviously some oxygen missing in $MnO_4^- \rightarrow Mn^{2+}$, but we're going to deal with that later. We do have an unbalanced carbon in $H_2C_2O_4 \rightarrow CO_2$, so we have to adjust this to $H_2C_2O_4 \rightarrow 2 CO_2$.

3. Balance the oxygens. The way to balance oxygens in acidic solution is to add H_2O. Our half-reaction with C has balanced oxygens (four on each side), but we need to add oxygens to the Mn half-reaction. Doing so, we get $MnO_4^- \rightarrow Mn^{2+} + 4 H_2O$.

4. Balance the hydrogens. Since we're doing this in an acidic environment, we can add H^+ as needed. This results in (1) $8 H^+ + MnO_4^- \rightarrow Mn^{2+} + 4 H_2O$ and $H_2C_2O_4 \rightarrow 2 CO_2 + 2 H^+$.

5. Add electrons to balance the charge. Charge must be conserved, so we have to add electrons to ensure that charge is balanced. (Remember, electrons are negative!) In $8 H^+ + MnO_4^- \rightarrow Mn^{2+} + 4 H_2O$, we see a + 7 charge

on the reactant side and a + 2 charge on the product side, so we need to add 5 electrons to the reactant side to balance this out. Likewise, in $H_2C_2O_4 \rightarrow 2\,CO_2 + 2\,H^+$, we have a 0 charge on the reactant side and a +2 charge on the product side, so we need to add 2 electrons to the product side to balance it out. This results in (1) $5\,e^- + 8\,H^+ + MnO_4^- \rightarrow Mn^{2+} + 4\,H_2O$ and (2) $H_2C_2O_4 \rightarrow 2\,CO_2 + 2\,H^+ + 2\,e^-$.

6. <u>Multiply so that both half-reactions have the same number of electrons</u>. We need to multiply the Mn half-reaction by 2 and the C half-reaction by 5 to do so, resulting in:

$$10\,e^- + 16\,H^+ + 2\,MnO_4^- \rightarrow 2\,Mn^{2+} + 8\,H_2O$$

$$5\,H_2C_2O_4 \rightarrow 10\,CO_2 + 10\,H^+ + 10\,e^-$$

7. <u>Add and cancel like terms</u>. If the same item is present on both sides of the reaction, we can add and cancel them, resulting in our final equation:

$$6\,H^+ + 2\,MnO_4^- + 5\,H_2C_2O_4 \rightarrow 2\,Mn^{2+} + 8\,H_2O + 10\,CO_2$$

The procedure above was specific for acidic conditions. In basic conditions, the same logic applies, except that we need to use OH^- to balance out the oxygen molecules and H_2O to balance out the hydrogen molecules.

MCAT STRATEGY > > >

Balancing redox reactions is absolutely testable content for the MCAT, so you should be aware of the process, but you should also remember that process of elimination is a useful technique for multiple-choice questions. If you're ever faced with an equation-balancing question (redox or non-redox), a first step might be to skim the answer choices and eliminate anything that makes an obvious error, like failing to conserve atoms or charge.

There's one final point of terminology that we need to cover before moving on: oxidizing agents and reducing agents. An oxidizing agent is a compound that you can add to a reaction mixture to cause another substance to be oxidized, and a reducing agent is a compound that you can add to a reaction mixture to cause another substance to be reduced. This means that oxidizing agents are themselves reduced, and reducing agents are themselves oxidized.

A useful application of oxidizing and reducing agents is to be able to predict the outcome of a reaction on the MCAT. Oxidizing agents generally contain oxygen or another electronegative element. Common examples you may see in MCAT organic chemistry include CrO_3, $Na_2Cr_2O_7$, and pyridinium chlorochromate (PCC). Reducing agents, in contrast, tend to be hydrogen delivery machines, with common examples including $NaBH_4$ and $LiAlH_4$.

2. Reduction Potentials

In section 1, we discussed redox reactions at length, but did not address one very important question: given a mix of ions that could participate in redox reactions, how do we predict which will be reduced and which will be oxidized? It turns out that some species 'like' to be reduced more than others. We can measure this using a parameter called the standard reduction potential, and use that to predict which way a redox reaction will run under spontaneous conditions.

Reduction potentials ($E°$) are measured in volts and are defined relative to the standard hydrogen electrode ($2\,H^+$ $(aq) + 2\,e^- \rightarrow H_2(g)$), which is defined as being 0 V. Greater (that is, more positive) reduction potentials indicate that a substance 'wants' to be reduced more, while smaller (that is, more negative) reduction potentials indicate that a substance 'wants' to be reduced less, and would 'prefer' oxidation if possible. An important point to note here is that the reduction potential doesn't tell you much by itself. At most, it gives you a general sense of how a substance might behave. Thus, if we see that the E° for $Cl_2(g) + 2\,e^- \rightarrow 2\,Cl^-\,(aq)$ is + 1.36 V, the most we can say is "wow, I guess chlorine likes being reduced!" On one hand, that's nice, but on the other hand, it's not really all that useful. Reduction potentials start being useful when we *compare* them.

Table 1 below presents some selected reduction potentials that we can use as examples. You are *not* expected to memorize any reduction potentials for the MCAT (besides knowing that the standard hydrogen electrode is defined as 0 V); if this content is explicitly and quantitatively tested, they will give you a table.

MCAT STRATEGY > > >

This may be a useful place to go back to review the definition of voltage (electric potential). Must like gravitational potential (*h*), voltage is defined as the difference in electric potential between two points. The fact that reduction potentials are basically comparative is actually a reflection of the nature of electric potential itself.

REDUCTION HALF-REACTION	E° (V)
$F_2(g) + 2\,e^- \rightarrow 2\,F^-(aq)$	+ 2.87
$O_2(g) + 4\,H^+(aq) + 4\,e^- \rightarrow 2\,H_2O(l)$	+ 1.23
$Cu^{2+}(aq) + 2\,e^- \rightarrow Cu(s)$	+ 0.34
$S(s) + 2\,H^+(aq) + 2\,e^- \rightarrow H_2S(g)$	+ 0.14
$2\,H^+(aq) + 2\,e^- \rightarrow H_2(g)$	0.00
$Zn^{2+}(aq) + 2\,e^- \rightarrow Zn(s)$	−0.76
$Li^+(aq) + e^- \rightarrow Li(s)$	−3.04

Table 1. Selected reduction potentials (for aqueous solution).

Although you don't need to memorize any numerical values for reduction potentials, the concept is key for the MCAT, so it's worth taking a few of these values and relating them to qualitative things that we know about chemistry. First, let's note the top two reduction potentials in our table, which are for the reduction of F_2 to F^- and the reduction of O_2 to $2\,H_2O$. Upon some reflection, it shouldn't surprise us that these reduction potentials are high. Fluorine is a good leaving group, which means that F^- is pretty comfortable hanging out in water, so it shouldn't surprise us that this is a favorable half-reaction. With regard to oxygen, this reaction is what happens in the last step of the electron transport chain; since the reduction of elemental oxygen to water is extremely common and fundamental to all forms of aerobic life, it shouldn't stun us that it has a relatively high reduction potential. On the other end of the scale, let's think about $Li^+ \rightarrow Li(s)$. In general, lithium is not a substance to mess around with, but lithium ion (Li^+) is relatively stable—it's present in ocean water, for instance. In contrast, elemental lithium is an immediately explosive, unstable compound. Therefore, it's not too surprising that the standard reduction potential for lithium is very low (negative), meaning that Li^+ *really* doesn't want to get that electron back and turn into $Li(s)$. This aspect of lithium's behavior is connected to its valence electron configuration. However, you don't want to try to derive E° values from the periodic table. Seeing how selected E° values correspond to other facts that you have seen is helpful for solidifying the concept, but for practical purposes, the MCAT will always give you numbers for E°.

Now, let's imagine that we have a reaction mixture containing two of the species from Table 1, with our possibilities being (1) $S(s) \rightarrow H_2S(g)$, with an E° of + 0.14 V, and (2) $Cu^{2+}(aq) \rightarrow Cu(s)$, with an E° of + 0.34 V. What will happen? In a redox reaction, we need one reduction half-reaction and one oxidation half-reaction. The higher E^0 value of the Cu reduction half-reaction means that it will happen as written and will be paired with the oxidation of S, which means that we have to write the S reaction in the opposite direction ($H_2S(g) \rightarrow S(s)$). Thus, our overall (unbalanced) reaction will be $Cu^{2+}(aq) + H_2S(g) \rightarrow Cu(s) + S(s)$.

The next step might seem to be balancing this reaction, but it actually turns out that we don't need to worry about that as long as we're focusing on reduction potentials, because reduction potentials are not affected by stoichiometric constants. This point is often confusing to students, so it's worth making sure you understand why this is the case. A common misconception is to think of voltage as being something you "get" from a reaction, in which case it would seem tempting to think that doubling your reactants and products would double your voltage. However, that is *not true!* The simplest way to remember this is to think of reduction potential as being a measure of how much something wants to be reduced, which will not change regardless of whether you start with one mole or two moles of it. The fuller explanation for this relates to the definition of voltage as electric potential difference. In the physics textbook, we systematically build analogies between electric forces and gravitation. In this context, the best comparison to voltage would be height, which is a measure of gravitational potential that does not change regardless of whether an object has a mass of 10 g or 10 kg.

A follow-up question to this discussion might be: why *reduction* potentials, not *oxidation* potentials? In fact, we can talk about oxidation potentials, and the oxidation potential of an oxidation half-reaction can be found simply by flipping the sign on the reduction potential of the reduction half-reaction. Thus, if $S(s) \rightarrow H_2S(g)$ has a reduction potential of + 0.14 V, its oxidation counterpart $H_2S(g) \rightarrow S(s)$ will have an oxidation potential of −0.14 V. The reason why the reduction potential, not the oxidation potential, is defined as the standard potential of the cell is simply because it's easier to pick one measure to use as a standard. As we will see in the next section, in some cases it can be helpful to think about oxidation potentials, but we need to be really careful about sign usage when we do so.

3. Galvanic and Electrolytic Cells

If we carry out redox reactions in a contained space that is set up appropriately, we can either generate chemical energy from spontaneous reactions or apply electrical energy to make a non-spontaneous reaction happen. All electrochemical cells must have two electrodes, which are where the redox half-reactions happen. The electrode where oxidation happens is known as the anode, while the electrode where reduction happens is known as the cathode. Therefore, a surplus of electrons is generated at the anode (because electrons are lost during oxidation), and they travel to the cathode.

MCAT STRATEGY >>>

The mnemonic *AN OX* (anode = oxidation) and *RED CAT* (reduction = cathode) is often used to remember which electrode is which.

In a galvanic cell (also known as a voltaic cell), a spontaneous redox reaction is used to generate a positive potential difference that can drive current. The total standard potential generated by a cell, E_{cell}, can be calculated from the standard reduction potentials of the half-reactions. The simplest way of defining E_{cell} is presented below:

Equation 1. $E_{cell} = E°_{cathode} - E°_{anode}$

>> CONNECTIONS <<

Chapters 6 and 7 of Physics

Since this is an important calculation that is frequently tested on the MCAT, let's work through how to approach it systematically. A common problem-solving set-up is for you to be given a table of standard reduction potentials and then be asked to calculate the potential of the galvanic cell that would be set up using two specific half-reactions. Here's how to tackle that problem:

> Identify which half-reaction has the higher reduction potential. That will be your cathode, because it 'wants' to be reduced more (remember that we're limiting ourselves to *spontaneous* reactions here). The other half-reaction will be your anode.
> Plug those values into the equation $E_{cell} = E°_{cathode} - E°_{anode}$.
> Understand that the actual half-reaction that happens at the anode will be the *reverse* of the one shown in the table of reduction potentials, because oxidation happens at the anode.

> **MCAT STRATEGY > > >**
>
> Studying electrochemistry is a great opportunity for you to review your knowledge of the physics of electricity, and vice versa. These concepts are usually presented in different places, and are frequently tested separately, but much of the underlying conceptual content in terms of what electrical potential *means* is actually shared.

As we mentioned before, the oxidation potential of an oxidation half-reaction has a magnitude equal to that of the reduction half-reaction, but with the sign flipped. This means that you could also define E_{cell} as the reduction potential of the cathode *plus* the oxidation potential of the anode. This is worth briefly mentioning because you may have seen it before and because it's technically possible for a question to be framed this way on the MCAT, but don't agonize over it. The point here is that these are two mathematical formulations of *the same exact idea*, so you should pick the method that is the simplest and stick to it. Framing these problems in terms of two standard reduction potentials (E°) is more common on the MCAT, so we recommend thinking about it that way—as reflected in Equation 1—whenever possible.

However, as is often the case in chemistry and biochemistry, there may be a difference between the standard values of a parameter (which assume standard conditions) and the values of a parameter in non-standard (that is, real-world) conditions. The Nernst equation helps us account for how the electrical potential of a cell is affected by conditions including temperature and the concentration of reactants. You may encounter the Nernst equation in two different forms. The first is the more theoretically general one:

Equation 2A.
$$E'_{cell} = E°_{cell} - \frac{RT}{zF} \ln Q$$

In this equation, E'_{cell} refers to the actual cell potential under a given set of conditions, $E°_{cell}$ is the standard cell potential, R is the ideal gas constant, T is temperature (in Kelvin), z is the number of moles of electrons transferred, F is the Faraday constant (a measure of charge per mole of electrons, defined as 96,485 C/mol), and Q is the reaction quotient (i.e., the concentration of products divided by the concentration of reactants, with each product or reactant raised to the power of its stoichiometric coefficient). In physiology, a simplified version of this equation that uses base-10 logs, assumes physiological temperature, and pre-calculates all of the constants is used to calculate cellular potential:

Equation 2B.
$$E'_{cell} = E°_{cell} - \frac{0.05916}{z} \log_{10} Q$$

Understanding the basic definition of a galvanic cell and how the cell potential can be predicted is often all that you need to succeed on MCAT questions about this topic, but it is nonetheless useful to invest some time into understanding the physical setup of galvanic cells. The most common example you will see is known as a Daniell cell. This type of cell was developed in 1836 by a scientist named John Frederic Daniell, and it is commonly used for classroom demonstrations and theoretical discussions because it clearly illustrates the principles of a galvanic cell. That said, although the battery of—for instance—your remote control can be thought of as a galvanic battery in general terms, don't make the mistake of thinking that batteries used in modern electrical and industrial applications are just scaled-down Daniell cells. The crucial point, though, is that for the MCAT, the Daniell cell is the prototype of a galvanic cell.

In a Daniell cell, the half-reactions are carried out in two physically separated half-cells. The electrodes are connected by a conductive wire, and the half-cells are additionally connected by a salt bridge—typically containing a salt such as KNO_3 or KCl that will not interfere with the intended redox reaction—that prevents a strong charge gradient from building up and hindering the progress of the reaction. A Daniel cell for a redox reaction involving zinc and copper is shown below in Figure 1.

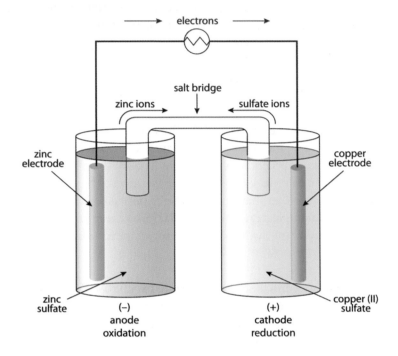

Figure 1. A Daniell cell.

The full redox reaction taking place here is $Zn(s) + Cu^{2+}(aq) \rightarrow Zn^{2+}(aq) + Cu(s)$. We can predict this from the fact that the reduction potential for $Zn^{2+}(aq) \rightarrow Zn(s)$ is -0.76 V and that of $Cu^{2+}(aq) \rightarrow Cu(s)$ is $+0.34$ V. Therefore, zinc will be the anode and copper will be the cathode, and the total E_{cell} will be 0.34 V $- (-0.76$ V$) = +1.10$ V. The sulfate ions in solution are not especially important from the point of view of redox reactions on the MCAT. However, it is worth noting what happens to the electrodes over the course of the reaction. The zinc electrode will shrink, because $Zn(s)$ atoms are being pulled off of it to undergo oxidation, while the copper electrode will grow, because $Cu^{2+}(aq)$ ions are being reduced to $Cu(s)$. This accumulation onto the cathode is known as plating. (Back to the sulfate ions— these are spectator ions present for the purpose of migrating across the salt bridge and preventing the buildup of a charge gradient, which would slow the reaction. Can you predict which direction these ions must move? Since electrons are traveling along the wire from anode to cathode, the sulfate ions must travel the opposite direction— from cathode to anode—to prevent the anode from becoming excessively positive.)

A common shorthand is used for these cells, in which the anode and the anode solution are specified on the left-hand side of a pair of double bars (‖) and the cathode solution and cathode are specified on the right-hand side. For this cell, assuming 1 M concentrations of the solutions, we could represent it as $Zn(s) \mid Zn^{2+}(aq)$ (1 M) ‖ $Cu^{2+}(aq)$ (1 M) $\mid Cu(s)$. You may see this notation on Test Day, but as always, since the MCAT is a standardized test, you will not have to use it independently yourself. The most important thing is recognizing that the anode is on the left and the cathode is on the right—if you notice that, you can save some time and effort.

By convention, the anode of a galvanic cell is considered to have a negative charge because it is the source of electrons, while the cathode is considered to have a positive charge because it is where electrons are taken out of solution via a reduction reaction.

In the Daniell cell, the two half-reactions are physically separated, but it is possible to create a galvanic cell in which the two half-reactions take place in the same chamber. Such cells are known as concentration cells, and they must satisfy two conditions: first, there needs to be a concentration difference between two regions of the cell; and second, the electrodes need to be made out of the same material. The reduction half-reaction will then take place at one electrode and the oxidation half-reaction will take place at another electrode. The concentration difference of the species participating in the redox reactions means that there will be an electric potential difference measured in volts, and current will flow as a result until the concentrations are equalized.

Concentration cells have a few interesting applications. One that you may have come across in chemistry labs is a pH sensor. The idea here is that one end of the pH sensor is an electrode at which a redox reaction takes place with the H^+ ions in solution, while the other end is a reference sensor with a known concentration. The potential difference (in volts) that is set up in this concentration cell is a way to measure the concentration of H^+ ions, and therefore pH. Biological membranes are another common example of this. The concentrations of various ions (predominantly Na^+, K^+, and Cl^-) on each side of the cell membrane are tightly regulated, and the difference in those concentrations sets up a potential difference, known as the resting membrane potential (usually about −70 mV for neurons).

In an electrolytic cell, the idea is to *apply* energy to the system rather than to *obtain* energy from the system. This means that the redox reaction will be carried out in the nonspontaneous direction. To take the example that we used in Figure 1, instead of $Zn(s) + Cu^{2+}(aq) \rightarrow Zn^{2+}(aq) + Cu(s)$ (the spontaneous reaction shown in that figure), we'll reverse it, to get $Zn^{2+}(aq) + Cu(s) \rightarrow Zn(s) + Cu^{2+}(aq)$.

The name 'electrolytic' reflects the fact that these cells are often used to break down compounds into their constituent parts through the application of electrical energy. A classic example of this is the breakdown of water into hydrogen and oxygen gas. Another application is known as electroplating; in this process, a non-spontaneous reduction reaction of a metal ion in solution is driven via electrical current, resulting in the deposition of solid metal onto the electrode.

Let's take a look at the electrolysis of water. Our overall reaction in this process will be $2 H_2O(l) \rightarrow 2 H_2(g) + O_2(g)$. Our first step in tackling this reaction conceptually is to work through the oxidation states of all of the constituents to understand what is being reduced and what is being oxidized. In H_2O, the hydrogen atoms each have an oxidation state of +1, while the oxidation state of H_2 is zero by definition. Since the oxidation state of hydrogen is going from +1 to 0, it is being reduced. In intuitive terms, you can think of this as hydrogen 'getting back' the electrons that it shared with oxygen in water. In contrast, the oxidation state of oxygen in water is −2, while that of O_2 is zero by definition. Since its oxidation state is increasing, oxygen is being oxidized. Intuitively, you can think about this as oxygen having to give up the electrons that it got from hydrogen, at which point it has to form a double bond with itself in order to maintain a full valence shell.

MCAT STRATEGY > > >

As you're studying redox chemistry, get in the habit of always calculating the oxidation states for the atoms in examples or practice problems. If you can turn oxidation state calculations into a reflex, you will easily be able to double-check which species is being reduced and which is being oxidized, potentially avoiding errors on Test Day. Additionally, you'll find that building this skill will help you understand electrochemistry better in general.

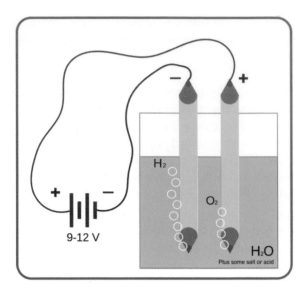

Figure 2. Electrolysis of water.

There's nothing special about the makeup of the electrodes in a cell for the electrolysis of water; usually, they are just composed of a metal that is conductive but will not engage in unwanted side reactions, such as stainless steel. However, once current is applied, each half-reaction will take place at a different electrode. The electrode where hydrogen is produced is the cathode, because by definition, reduction occurs at the cathode, while the electrode where oxygen is produced is the anode, because oxidation always takes place at the anode.

As you can see in Figure 2 in an electrolytic cell, the cathode (where reduction is carried out) is marked with a negative charge, while the anode (where oxidation is carried out) is marked with a positive charge. This is the opposite of the charge convention used in galvanic cells, and reflects the fact that the anode is linked to the positive side of the battery, and therefore attracts negatively-charged anions, while the cathode is linked to the negative side. The charge convention used for an electrolytic cell is the same as that used for electrophoretic biochemical procedures like SDS-PAGE and isoelectric focusing. For these techniques, remember: the cathode is negative, while the anode is positive!

> ## MCAT STRATEGY > > >
>
> Remember that the *charge* conventions change between galvanic/voltaic and electrolytic cells, *not* the definitions of anode and cathode in terms of oxidation and reduction. Those definitions, and their corresponding mnemonic (AN OX and RED CAT), are universally applicable.

If we are using an electrolytic cell to carry out electroplating, it turns out that we can predict the amount of metal that will be deposited. In such a set-up, the mechanism of electroplating is the reduction of metal ions in solution. Schematically, we can represent this as $M^{n+} + n\,e^- \rightarrow M(s)$, where M is a metal and n represents the oxidation state of the metal ion. Don't overcomplicate this: it's just a more general formulation of the fact that adding (for example) two electrons to a Fe^{2+} ion will result in elemental iron, Fe(s). In an electrolytic cell, we're forcing this to happen by providing current, which in turn is made up of moving electrons. Therefore, we can relate the amount of metal formed to the amount and duration of current that is provided to the cell.

This topic is frequently challenging for MCAT students, so let's walk through the logic of how the formula for calculating this works, rather than just presenting it. Given the above reasoning, the first thing we have to do is to come up with an estimate of how many electrons have been introduced to the electrolytic cell via current. First, remember that the unit for charge is the coulomb (C) and that current is charge per unit time. If we're given a current in amperes (1 A = $1\frac{C}{s}$), then we can multiply current by time to cancel out the denominator and get a value in coulombs. This is a step in the right direction, but again, coulombs are a unit of charge, and we need to figure out the number of electrons.

To convert between units of charge and moles of electrons, we need to use the Faraday constant (F). The Faraday constant is actually just a simple dimensional conversion process. By definition, 6.02×10^{23} electrons are in a mole, and each electron has a charge of 1.6×10^{-19} C. Therefore, to get a measure of charge per mole, we can derive the Faraday constant as follows:

Equation 3.
$$F = \frac{1.6 \times 10^{-19}C}{e-} \times \frac{6.02 \times 10^{23}e^-}{1\ mole} = 96,485\ \frac{C}{mol\ e^-}$$

With this definition, we can take our value for the total charge supplied to the cell and divide it by the Faraday constant to get moles of electrons. The final thing we have to account for is n, or the number of electrons necessary to reduce the metal ion to its elemental state. We can incorporate n into the denominator. This gives us the following equation for electroplating:

Equation 4A.
$$moles\ of\ metal = \frac{I \times t}{nF}$$

In this equation, I is current, t is time, n is the number of electrons needed to reduce the metal ion to its elemental state, and F is the Faraday constant. This equation can be difficult to remember, so it may be useful to review how the units fit together, as shown in Equation 4B, which presents a step-by-step simplification of the right-hand side of the units in Equation 4A.

Equation 4B.
$$mol = \frac{(\frac{C}{s}) \times s}{\frac{C}{mol}}$$
$$mol = \frac{C}{\frac{C}{mol}}$$
$$mol = C \times \frac{mol}{C}$$

$$mol = mol$$

If you're ever asked to carry out one of these calculations on the MCAT, which is a real possibility, you can simplify the Faraday constant to 100,000 C/mol (or, in scientific notation, 1×10^5 C/mol). One final point to note regarding the Faraday constant is that the same logic can be applied to electrolytic processes involving the production of gas (as in our example of the hydrolysis of water). You would go about solving the problem in the exact same way; the only difference is whether the products are deposited or released as gas.

> **MCAT STRATEGY > > >**
>
> Whenever you're faced with a strange-looking or unfamiliar equation, it is a good idea to write out the units and see how they fit together, as in Equation 4B. This will help you develop an understanding of what the equation actually *means*, so that it can be more readily incorporated into your equation toolkit on Test Day.

So far, we've been treating galvanic/voltaic cells and electrolytic cells as two completely separate devices, but in reality, they can be combined. In fact, this is what happens in the rechargeable batteries that we use every day! For the MCAT, you should be aware of a few main types of rechargeable batteries, although you certainly don't need to delve into the engineering intricacies that allow them to reliably power tiny devices. The basic principle of a rechargeable battery is the design of a physical setup that can both discharge spontaneously (acting as a galvanic cell that produces current) and be recharged (acting as an electrolytic cell).

The first type of rechargeable battery to be developed, and one that is still used in a range of applications including car batteries and cell phone towers, is known as a lead storage battery or a lead-acid battery. Lead-acid batteries have a relatively low energy density, which means that a heavier battery is needed for a given amount of output than other battery designs. In its charged state, a lead storage battery has a lead oxide electrode and a lead electrode, separated by an area that contains concentrated H_2SO_4, as shown in Figure 3.

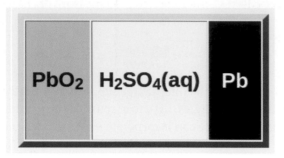

Figure 3. Charged form of lead-acid battery.

Two redox half-reactions take place. The oxidation half-reaction takes place at the Pb electrode, and can be summarized as $Pb(s) + HSO_4^-\ (aq) \rightarrow PbSO_4(s) + H^+\ (aq) + 2e^-$. As always, let's practice our fundamentals by verifying that this is indeed oxidation. $Pb(s)$ has an oxidation state of 0, while the Pb in $PbSO_4(aq)$ has an oxidation state of +2. The oxidation state of lead increased, and we can see that electrons are produced as a product of this reaction; both of these pieces of information confirm that this is the oxidation half-reaction. The reduction half-reaction is $PbO_2(s) + HSO_4^- + 3H^+\ (aq) + 2e^- \rightarrow PbSO_4(s) + 2\ H_2O(l)$. In this half-reaction, the oxidation state of Pb goes from +4 in PbO_2 to +2 in $PbSO_4(s)$. There are two important things to note about this cell: (1) $PbSO_4(s)$ is the product of *both* half-reactions, and (2) $PbSO_4(s)$ is *solid*, because it is very poorly soluble in water. This means that when the spontaneous galvanic cell reactions proceed to completion, we're left with a coating of $PbSO_4(s)$ and some dilute leftover H_2SO_4, as shown in Figure 4.

Figure 4. Discharged form of lead-acid battery.

Once the lead-acid battery is discharged, current can be applied to it to recharge it, reversing the reactions that we described above.

Nickel-cadmium batteries are another example of rechargeable batteries. These batteries were once commonly used for personal electronic devices, but have since largely been supplanted by other, more environmentally friendly battery designs. Nonetheless, you are expected to be aware of the basics of nickel-cadmium batteries for the MCAT. As the name suggests, they have one cathode containing nickel (more precisely, nickel oxide-hydroxide [NiO(OH)]) and one cathode containing cadmium. When discharging, the oxidation half-reaction is $Cd + 2\ OH^- \rightarrow Cd(OH)_2 + 2\ e^-$, and the reduction half-reaction is $2\ NiO(OH) + 2\ H_2O + 2\ e^- \rightarrow 2\ Ni(OH)_2 + 2\ OH^-$. As with lead-acid batteries, during recharging, the reactions in nickel-cadmium batteries are reversed.

As spontaneous reactions are discharging, the resulting electric potential difference (corresponding to the cell potential of the battery, as discussed in the beginning of this section) can be utilized to drive current through a conductive wire. This is the setup for direct circuits, which are discussed in Chapter 7 of the Physics textbook. The potential difference that drives current is sometimes known as the electromotive force, or emf. Therefore, we can measure the 'strength' of a battery in voltage and/or emf. A common everyday example is the 9-volt battery, which is commonly used in applications like powering smoke and carbon monoxide detectors. It's important to avoid confusion here: the emf is *not actually a force*. This is misleading terminology left over from earlier eras of research, and reflects the intuitive idea that voltage 'drives' current through a conductor.

4. Titrations

Just as we can use titrations to monitor the progress of acid-base reactions, we can use them to monitor oxidation-reduction reactions. In fact, we can apply a similar principle of colorimetric indicators. The key to colorimetric redox titrations is to find an indicator that changes color between its oxidized and reduced form. One example is Mn. The polyatomic MnO_4^- ion, in which Mn has an oxidation state of +7, is purple in aqueous solution, whereas Mn^{2+} is colorless. MnO_4^- is also a strong oxidizing agent, so it is likely to participate in redox reactions with other species in solution.

With this in mind, let's consider a situation in which we have an unknown concentration of Sn^{2+} in aqueous solution. It turns out that MnO_4^- will readily oxidize Sn^{2+} to Sn^{4+}, in the following redox reaction: $16\ H^+ + 2\ MnO_4^- + 5\ Sn^{2+} \rightarrow 2\ Mn^{2+} + 5\ Sn^{4+} + 8\ H_2O$. As we start this titration, we add purple-colored MnO_4^- dropwise. As the MnO_4^- drops make contact with the solution of Sn^{2+}, they will immediately oxidize Sn^{2+}, and the solution will remain clear. As soon as some purple color from the MnO_4^- remains in the reaction mixture, we have reached the equivalence point, because that means that there is no more Sn^{2+} for the MnO_4^- to react with.

In the same way that we did for acid-base concentrations, if we know the concentration of the MnO_4^- solution and how much we had to add to get to the equivalence point, as well as the volume of the Sn^{2+} solution, we can calculate the concentration of Sn^{2+}. The equations we use are the same:

MCAT STRATEGY > > >

Focus on the principle of how the lead-acid battery works, not primarily on memorizing the constituent parts. The MCAT is highly unlikely to ask you exactly which strong acid is generally used in these batteries (for example); instead, you should understand the mechanism and be able to answer questions about it if given diagrams like Figures 3 and 4.

> > CONNECTIONS < <

Chapter 7 of Physics

> > CONNECTIONS < <

Chapter 7 of Chemistry

MCAT STRATEGY > > >

If you have any uncertainty about the mechanism of *how* titration works to determine the concentration of an analyte in solution, review the information about acid-base titrations presented in Chapter 7. In the context of the MCAT, redox titrations should be thought of as an extension of the principle of acid-base titrations to a new context where we're focusing on electron flow rather than protonation/deprotonation, so make sure your acid/base fundamentals are solid.

Equation 5A. $$M_1V_1 = M_2V_2$$

Equation 5B. $$N_1V_1 = N_2V_2$$

Equation 5A gives you the formula in terms of molarity, while Equation 5B gives you the equation in terms of normality. In acid-base chemistry, normality relates to the number of protons (or hydroxide ions) that appear in solution when one mole of substance is dissolved. In redox chemistry, normality relates to the number of electrons that are either given up or absorbed by one mole of a species in the corresponding redox reaction. In our example, this is 5 for Mn (because its oxidation state goes from +7 to +2) and 2 for Sn (because its oxidation state goes from +2 to +4). Normality can be calculated by multiplying each of these values by the molarity of the associated solution.

Let's see how this plays out quantitatively. Imagine that we had 200 mL of Sn^{2+} and that it took 40 mL of 0.20 M MnO_4^- to reach the equivalence point. We could use Equation 5B and plug in values as follows:

$$N_1V_1 = N_2V_2$$

$$(5)(0.20 \text{ M } MnO_4^-)(40 \text{ mL}) = 2(x \text{ M } Sn^{2+})(200 \text{ mL})$$

$$\frac{5(0.20 \text{ M } MnO_4^-)(40 \text{ mL})}{(2)(200 \text{ mL})} = x \text{ M } Sn^{2+}$$

$$0.10 \text{ M} = x \text{ M } Sn^{2+}$$

MCAT STRATEGY > > >

As with acid-base titrations, for redox titrations you don't need to be intimately familiar with every possible configuration, but you do need to understand the principle clearly. A useful exercise for yourself would be to explain verbally to a study partner what the similarities and differences are between acid-base titration problems and redox titration problems.

Redox titrations have many applications. One well-known example in biochemistry is the use of Benedict's reagent to test for reducing sugars, which after heating reduce Cu^{2+} to Cu^+, causing a color change. You may have also experimented with iodometric titrations in chemistry labs, which take advantage of the fact that the iodide ion readily participates in redox reactions and that iodine combined with starch results in a vivid dark blue color.

In potentiometric titrations, the potential difference in volts is measured between a reference electrode that is insensitive to the properties of the solution and a detector electrode that is immersed in the analyte (that is, the solution being analyzed). pH sensors also work using a slightly adapted version of this principle.

5. Connections with Thermodynamics

Throughout this chapter, we've been talking about spontaneous versus non-spontaneous reactions in galvanic/voltaic and electrolytic cells. As a general rule of thumb, whenever you hear the word "spontaneous," you should immediately think of thermodynamics, because whether or not a reaction is spontaneous is directly connected to whether or not it is exergonic. More specifically, reactions with a $\Delta G < 0$ are spontaneous, whereas those with a $\Delta G > 0$ are non-spontaneous.

The $\Delta G°$ of a redox reaction turns out to be directly connected with the $E°_{cell}$ value, as given in the following equation:

Equation 6A. $$\Delta G° = -nFE°_{cell}$$

In this equation, $\Delta G°$ is the standard Gibbs free energy change of a reaction, and $E°_{cell}$ is the standard cell reduction potential. The additional variables n and F refer to the moles of electrons exchanged in the reaction and Faraday's constant, respectively. As we did with Equation 4, for determining the number of moles of metal deposited in an electrolytic cell, it's useful to do a units check with this equation to see how these pieces fit together. Before we do so, note that $\Delta G°$ will have to be expressed in joules, not kilojoules, and that a coulomb (C) is definable as a joule divided by a volt (from $J = C \times V$; this is not the most common definition of a joule that you will see, but this relationship is useful when defining a volt).

Equation 6B.

$$\Delta G° = -nFE°_{cell}$$

$$J = mol \left(\frac{C}{mol}\right) V$$

$$J = CV$$

$$J = \left(\frac{J}{V}\right)V$$

$$J = J$$

Things get even more interesting when we remember that spontaneity is associated with the equilibrium constant; that is, whether products predominate over reactants at equilibrium or not. The equation for the equilibrium constant, K_{eq}, is given below for reference. It is defined with regard to the generalized reaction $aA + bB \rightarrow cC + dD$.

Equation 7.

$$K_{eq} = \frac{[C]^c[D]^d}{[A]^a[B]^B}$$

For more details about equilibrium and thermodynamics, see chapter 4; the crucial point from our perspective in this chapter is just that if there are more products than reactants at equilibrium, the reaction is spontaneous and $K_{eq} > 1$, while if there are more reactants than products at equilibrium, the reaction as a whole is non-spontaneous and $K_{eq} < 1$. The relationship between $\Delta G°$ and K_{eq} can be defined as follows:

> **> > CONNECTIONS < <**
>
> **Chapter 4 of Chemistry**

Equation 8.

$$\Delta G° = -RT\ln K_{eq}$$

Combining Equation 6A and Equation 8, we get an expression linking $E°_{cell}$ to K_{eq}:

Equation 9.

$$nFE°_{cell} = RT\ln K_{eq}$$

It is possible that you would be asked to perform a calculation with this equation, although it would almost certainly be set up in a way that would minimize the likelihood that you would have to do by-hand calculations involving the natural logarithm (ln). However, it is essential that you master the conceptual relationships among the parameters of ΔG, $E°_{cell}$, and K_{eq} and how they relate to spontaneity, as shown below in Table 2:

	SPONTANEOUS	NON-SPONTANEOUS
ΔG	Negative (<0)	Positive (>0)
$E°_{cell}$	Positive (>0)	Negative (<0)
K_{eq}	Greater than 1 (>1)	Less than 1 (<0)

Table 2. Spontaneity and ΔG, $E°_{cell}$, and K_{eq}.

MCAT STRATEGY > > >

You should know Table 2 by heart on Test Day, both because these relationships can be (and are) tested directly and because a qualitative understanding of these phenomena allows you to do a reality check if you're given a calculation-based problem, because you can double-check that your numerical outcome corresponds with the behavior of the reaction or cell that you would predict.

6. Must-Knows

> Oxidation = losing electrons, reduction = gaining electrons.
  – Mnemonics: *OIL RIG* (oxidation is loss, reduction is gain) and *LEO* the lion goes *GER* (lose electrons = oxidation, gain electrons = reduction)
  – **Know the definitions of oxidation and reduction**. If you know nothing else, know this.
> Oxidation state: basis for defining oxidation-reduction (redox) reactions:
  – Pure elements: oxidation state of 0, ions: overall oxidation state = charge.
  – Oxidation state rules for atoms within compounds:
    • F: –1, most other halogens usually –1 as well, unless bonded to a more electronegative atom
    • H: +1, unless bonded to a more electropositive element (e.g., NaH)
    • O: –2, except –1 in peroxides
    • Alkali metals (column I): +1, alkaline earth metals (column II): +2
    • Other compounds: calculated as needed to reach overall oxidation state.
> Reduction potentials: for a given reduction half-reaction, E° (in V) measures how much a compound 'wants' to be reduced. More positive = reduction is more likely.
> Galvanic/voltaic cells: a spontaneous redox reaction is carried out, creating a potential difference that can be used to drive current.
  – $E_{cell} = E°_{cathode} - E°_{anode}$
  – Cathode will be half-reaction with the higher (more positive) reduction potential.
  – Equations that reflect how actual potential is affected by non-standard conditions:
    • $E'_{cell} = E°_{cell} - \frac{RT}{zF} lnQ$
    • $E'_{cell} = E°_{cell} - \frac{0.05916}{z} \log_{10}Q$
> Concentration cells: electrodes made of same material; at beginning, concentration difference drives electric potential difference; as battery discharges, concentration equalizes.
> Electrolytic cells: current is supplied to drive non-spontaneous redox reaction.
  – Electroplating given a current *I* for a time *t*: *moles of metal* $= \frac{I \times t}{nF}$
  – F = Faraday constant (96,485 C/mol) measures how much charge is carried by a mole of electrons.
> Rechargeable batteries combine galvanic/voltaic and electrolytic functionality; examples include lead-acid and nickel-cadmium batteries. Voltage of a battery, which drives current, is sometimes called electromotive force (emf), but this is not actually a force.

> Redox titrations: indicators that change color between oxidized and reduced forms, or potentiometric titrations that measure changes in potential difference. Same basic principle as acid-base titrations, but measure electron transfer instead of (de)protonation.

> Thermodynamics:
  - $\Delta G° = -nFE°_{cell}$
  - $nFE°_{cell} = RT\ln K_{eq}$ because $\Delta G° = -RT\ln K_{eq}$
  - Spontaneous: $\Delta G < 0$, $E°_{cell} > 0$, $K_{eq} > 1$
  - Non-spontaneous: $\Delta G > 0$, $E°_{cell} < 0$, $K_{eq} < 1$

Practice Passage

Falls often cause severe health consequences with possible injuries, including bone fractures or intraperitoneal and intracranial bleedings. This danger necessitates means of detecting a fall and immediately sending an alarm. Experiments with the triboelectric effect revealed the relationship between movement and the accumulation of electric charge. Researchers have developed a stretchable conductive nylon fabric for patients to wear that is also used as the electrodes of a triboelectric generator (TEG) and an interconnection between battery cells. The electrical energy harvested from the TEG through human body motions continuously runs a 3-axis accelerometer that records human body motions. Upon the unexpected fall occurring, software discriminates the fall signal and an emergency alert is immediately sent.

Early experiments analyzing the relationship between electricity and the body revealed that human muscle tissue not only responds mechanically to electrical stimulation, but is also a conductor of charge. Further experiments demonstrated that this phenomenon was not limited to human tissue. For instance, soaking a paper towel in an electrolytic solution allowed for conduction of electricity when placed in contact with metals.

Scientists eventually were able to rank various metals to create the first electrochemical series (Table 1), and associated electromotive forces, based on the idea that various electrodes have a potential to cause charges to move in a conducting material. Equations 1 and 2 were developed to predict the potentials and energy changes associated with electrochemical cells:

$$E_{cell} = E° - (RT/nF) \ln Q \qquad \textbf{Equation 1}$$

$$\Delta G° = -nFE_{cell} \qquad \textbf{Equation 2}$$

where R = 8.3 J•K^{-1}•mol^{-1}, T is the absolute temperature, n is the moles of electrons in the balanced reaction and F is Faraday's constant.

Table 1. Select Standard Reduction Potentials

Reduction Half-Reaction	E° (V)
F_2 (g) + 2 e$^-$ ⟶ 2 F$^-$ (aq)	+ 2.87
MnO_4^- (aq) + 8 H$^+$ (aq) + 5 e$^-$ ⟶ Mn^{2+} (aq) + 4 H$_2$O (l)	+ 1.51
$Cr_2O_7^{2-}$ (aq) + 14 H$^+$ (aq) + 6 e$^-$ ⟶ 2 Cr^{3+} (aq) + 7 H$_2$O (l)	+ 1.33
O_2 (g) + 4 H$^+$ (aq) + 4 e$^-$ ⟶ 2 H$_2$O (l)	+ 1.23
Ag^{+1} (aq) + e$^-$ ⟶ Ag (s)	+ 0.80
O_2 (g) + 2 H$_2$O (l) + 4 e$^-$ ⟶ 4 OH$^-$ (aq)	+ 0.40
Cu^{2+} (aq) + 2 e$^-$ ⟶ Cu (s)	+ 0.34
2 H^{2+} (aq) + 2 e$^-$ ⟶ H$_2$ (g)	0.00
Ni^{2+} (aq) + 2 e$^-$ ⟶ Ni (s)	- 0.28
Cd^{2+} (aq) + 2 e$^-$ ⟶ Cd (s)	- 0.40
Zn^{2+} (aq) + 2 e$^-$ ⟶ Zn (s)	- 0.76
2 H$_2$O (l) + 2 e$^-$ ⟶ H$_2$ (g) + 2 OH$^-$ (aq)	- 0.83
Li^{+1} (aq) + e$^-$ ⟶ Li (s)	- 3.05

(Note: F = 96,485 C/mol e$^-$ and at 25° C, [RT/nF] ln Q = (0.06/n)(log Q)

Adapted from Jung, S., Hong, et al. (2015). Wearable Fall Detector using Integrated Sensors and Energy Devices. Scientific Reports, 5, 17081 under CCBY 4.0

1. An electrochemical cell is built around on the following redox reaction at 25 °C:

$$Cu^{2+} (aq) + Zn (s) \rightarrow Zn^{2+} (aq) + Cu (s)$$

what is the cell potential when $[Cu^{2+}] / [Zn^{2+}] = 10^8$?

   A. -0.18 V
   B. 1.10 V
   C. 1.34 V
   D. 1.57 V

2. According to Table 1, which species is the best oxidizing agent?
   A. $MnO_4^- (aq)$
   B. $Cr_2O_7^{2-} (aq)$
   C. Zn (s)
   D. Li (s)

3. Which of the following is NOT equivalent to electrical potential?
   A. $A \cdot \Omega$
   B. W/A
   C. J/C
   D. $kg \cdot m/s^2$

4. Which of the following would be true regarding a cell comprised of a fluorine cathode and a nickel anode?

   I. The reaction is nonspontaneous and $\Delta G > 0$.
   II. Electrons flow through the circuit from the anode to the cathode.
   III. The anode is negatively charged.
   IV. The cell is galvanic.

   A. I and IV only
   B. II and III only
   C. I, III and IV only
   D. II, III and IV only

5. What is the oxidation state of a chromium atom in $Cr_2O_7^{2-}$?
   A. Cr^{2+}
   B. Cr^{3+}
   C. Cr^{6+}
   D. Cr^{12+}

6. Which of the following species is least likely to occur at the anode of an electrolytic cell?
   A. Phosphoenolpyruvate → pyruvate
   B. NADP → NADPH
   C. Propanol → propanal
   D. $Fe^{1+} \rightarrow Fe^{2+}$

7. Which of the following reactions will provide the lowest current through the accelerometer circuit discussed in the passage?
   A. Reaction 1, $K_{eq} = 3.47 \times 10^{-4}$
   B. Reaction 2, $K_{eq} = 1$
   C. Reaction 3, $K_{eq} = 9.11 \times 10^3$
   D. Reaction 4, $K_{eq} = 6.82 \times 10^8$

Practice Passage Explanations

Falls often cause severe health consequences with possible injuries, including bone fractures or intraperitoneal and intracranial bleedings. This danger necessitates means of detecting a fall and immediately sending an alarm. Experiments with the triboelectric effect revealed the relationship between movement and the accumulation of electric charge. Researchers have developed a stretchable conductive nylon fabric for patients to wear that is also used as the electrodes of a triboelectric generator (TEG) and an interconnection between battery cells. The electrical energy harvested from the TEG through human body motions continuously runs a 3-axis accelerometer that records human body motions. Upon the unexpected fall occurring, software discriminates the fall signal and an emergency alert is immediately sent.

Key terms: triboelectric effect, conductive nylon, accelerometer, TEG

Cause and effect: movement → charge buildup/storage → powers electronic fall monitor

Early experiments analyzing the relationship between electricity and the body revealed that human muscle tissue not only responds mechanically to electrical stimulation, but is also a conductor of charge. Further experiments demonstrated that this phenomenon was not limited to human tissue. For instance, soaking a paper towel in an electrolytic solution allowed for conduction of electricity when placed in contact with metals.

Key terms: muscle, electrical conduction, electrolytic solution

Cause and effect: electricity → muscle movement; conduction occurs in tissue and electrolytic solutions

Scientists eventually were able to rank various metals to create the first electrochemical series (Table 1), and associated electromotive forces, based on the idea that various electrodes have a potential to cause charges to move in a conducting material. Equations 1 and 2 were developed to predict the potentials and energy changes associated with electrochemical cells:

$$E_{cell} = E° - (RT/nF) \ln Q \qquad \textbf{Equation 1}$$

$$\Delta G° = -nFE_{cell} \qquad \textbf{Equation 2}$$

where $R = 8.3 \text{ J} \cdot \text{K}^{-1} \cdot \text{mol}^{-1}$, T is the absolute temperature, n is the moles of electrons in the balanced reaction and F is Faraday's constant.

Key terms: electrochemical cells, electromotive forces

Cause and effect: varied metal redox abilities → different currents; E of a cell varies from its standard E, directly proportional to the concentration of products

Table 1. Select Standard Reduction Potentials

Reduction Half-Reaction	E° (V)
F_2 (g) + 2 e$^-$ $\longrightarrow$ 2 F$^-$ (aq)	+ 2.87
MnO_4^- (aq) + 8 H$^+$ (aq) + 5 e$^-$ $\longrightarrow$ Mn^{2+} (aq) + 4H$_2$O (l)	+ 1.51
$Cr_2O_7^{2-}$ (aq) + 14 H$^+$ (aq) + 6 e$^-$ $\longrightarrow$ 2 Cr^{3+} (aq) + 7 H$_2$O (l)	+ 1.33
O_2 (g) + 4 H$^+$(aq) + 4 e$^-$ $\longrightarrow$ 2 H$_2$O (l)	+ 1.23
Ag^{+1} (aq) + e$^-$ $\longrightarrow$ Ag (s)	+ 0.80
O_2 (g) + 2 H$_2$O (l) + 4 e$^-$ $\longrightarrow$ 4 OH$^-$ (aq)	+ 0.40
Cu^{2+} (aq) + 2 e$^-$ $\longrightarrow$ Cu (s)	+ 0.34
2 H^{2+} (aq) + 2 e$^-$ $\longrightarrow$ H$_2$ (g)	0.00
Ni^{2+} (aq) + 2 e$^-$ $\longrightarrow$ Ni (s)	- 0.28
Cd^{2+} (aq) + 2 e$^-$ $\longrightarrow$ Cd (s)	- 0.40
Zn^{2+} (aq) + 2 e$^-$ $\longrightarrow$ Zn (s)	- 0.76
2 H$_2$O (l) + 2 e$^-$ $\longrightarrow$ H$_2$ (g) + 2 OH$^-$ (aq)	- 0.83
Li^{+1} (aq) + e$^-$ $\longrightarrow$ Li (s)	- 3.05

Table 1 shows reduction potentials (E°), which we can use to calculate cell emf, where $E_{cell} = E°_{cathode} - E°_{anode}$; larger E° indicate the species would prefer to be at the cathode (Red Cat An Ox)

(Note: F = 96,485 C/mol e$^-$ and at 25° C, [RT/nF] ln Q = (0.06/n)(log Q))

Adapted from Jung, S., Hong, et al. (2015). Wearable Fall Detector using Integrated Sensors and Energy Devices. Scientific Reports, 5, 17081 under CCBY 4.0

1. C is correct. We can use Equation 1 to answer this question. Note that the constants in Equation 1 are given in the caption, but we are also given a note at the bottom of the passage where the combination of the constants is given and the natural logarithm is converted to the log base 10 form, giving a new form of the equation, E = E° - (0.06/n) log Q. The value of the E° is the sum of the reduction potential of Cu^{2+} and the oxidation potential of Zn, E° = 0.34 + 0.76 = 1.10 V. From the question, we can see that n = 2 and Q = [products]/[reactants] = [Zn^{2+}]/[Cu^{2+}] = 1/10^8 = 10^{-8}. Substituting this information into the equation and using 0.06 as 6.0×10^{-2} gives:

$$E = (1.10) - [(6 \times 10^{-2})/2] \log (10^{-8})$$
$$E = 1.10 - (3 \times 10^{-2})(-8)$$
$$E = 1.10 + (2.4 \times 10^{-1})$$
$$E = 1.34 \text{ V}$$

2. A is correct. An oxidizing agent is a reactant that gets reduced. Both permanganate and dichromate are reactants of a reduction half-reaction, and therefore are potential oxidizing agents. We next need to turn our attention to the voltages and since the more positive the voltage, the more spontaneous the reaction (per ΔG = -nFE), permanganate is the best oxidizing agent and choice A is the correct answer. Since both zinc and lithium metal are the products of the reduction half reactions in Table 1, they would most likely to be reducing agents, and choices C and D can be eliminated.

3. D is correct. Electrical potential, also known as voltage or electromotive force, is the potential energy per unit charge, so there must be some unit associated with the charge in the answer, which is missing in choice D.

A, B, C: According to Ohm's law, V = IR, where I is the current in amperes (and R is resistance in ohms (Ω), therefore choice A can be eliminated. Electrical power in watts (W) is P = VI, so V = P/I, and choice B can be eliminated. Since a Watt is power, or Joules per second, W = J/s, and an ampere is the coulombs of charge per second, substituting these units into the units of choice B, gives W/A = (J/s)/(C/s) = J/C, choice C. Note the units for the constants in the Nernst equation from the passage also give this set of units.

4. D is correct. According to Table 1, building the cell described by the question gets us E_{cell} = 2.87 – (-0.76) = +3.6 V. When E_{cell} > 0, this is a galvanic (voltage-producing) cell (IV is true, eliminate A, B). The relationship between cell potential and Gibbs free energy change is, $\Delta G = -nFE_{cell}$. Thus, a positive E_{cell} gets us a negative ΔG (I is false).

   II: Electrons always flow from the anode to the cathode in any electrochemical cell.

   III: In galvanic cells, the anode is negative and the cathode is positive. To remember which electrode is positive and which is negative, the mnemonic is the word "gain" = "Galvanic Anode Is Negative".

5. C is correct. The total charge of the polyatomic ion (-2) must equal the sum of the oxidation numbers of the atoms in the formula. The total oxide is given an oxidation number of -2 and we can call the value of the oxidation number of chromium x, giving the formula, which rearranges and gives:

$$-2 = 2x + 7(-2)$$
$$-2 = 2x - 14$$
$$12 = 2x$$
$$6 = x$$

6. B is correct. Recall that for all cells, reduction occurs at the cathode and oxidation occurs at the anode. This means we would least expect a reducing reaction to occur at the anode. The only reaction scheme shown is the conversion of NADP to NADPH. All the other reactions listed are oxidation reactions.

7. B is correct. The questions wants us to find the lowest current moving through the fall monitor electronics. This means we need to relate K_{eq} to E_{cell}. For the exam we should recognize the relationship between $\Delta G°$, K_{eq}, and E_{cell}. We should know that $\Delta G° = -RT \ln K_{eq}$. Combined with the passage information $\Delta G° = -nFE_{cell}$ (you should know this equation by test day), we get:

$$-RT \ln K_{eq} = -nFE_{cell} \rightarrow RT \ln K_{eq} = nFE_{cell} \rightarrow E_{cell} = (RT \ln K_{eq}) / nF.$$

Thus, we can see that the smaller the K_{eq}, the smaller the E_{cell}. If K_{eq} = 1, then $\ln K_{eq} = 0$, and there is no voltage supplied to the device and thus, no current.

A: K_{eq} < 0 would mean that the cell is non-spontaneous, and would actually draw voltage from the TEG, this would result in some current moving through the device.
C, D: These reactions would provide positive voltage to the circuit, resulting in current moving through it.

Independent Questions

1. What is the oxidation state of chlorine in the molecule $HClO_2$?
   A. −1
   B. +1
   C. +3
   D. +5

2. Which of the species below is expected to be the LEAST effective choice for an oxidizing agent?
   A. H_2O_2
   B. F^-
   C. H_2
   D. CrO_3

3. Consider the standard reduction potentials shown below.

Half-reaction	°E (V)
Cu^{2+} (aq) + 2 e⁻ → Cu (s)	+0.34 V
Pb^{2+} (aq) + 2 e⁻ → Pb (s)	−0.13 V
Mg^{2+} (aq) + 2 e⁻ → Mg (s)	−2.37 V

   Of the following, which is expected to serve as the most effective reducing agent?

   A. Cu^{2+}
   B. Pb (s)
   C. Mg^{2+}
   D. Mg (s)

4. Midway through an electrochemical reaction, the E_{cell} is measured at +0.20 V. The reaction takes place at 0°C. Which of the following statements must be true in this case?
   A. $\Delta G°$ for the reaction is negative.
   B. $\Delta G°$ for the reaction is positive.
   C. K_{eq} for the reaction is negative.
   D. This question cannot be answered without more information.

5. Isoelectric focusing, a technique used to separate proteins and amino acids by their charge, utilizes an apparatus that functions like an electrolytic cell. All of the following describe differences between an isoelectric focusing (IEF) apparatus and a galvanic cell EXCEPT:

   A. reduction happens at the cathode in the galvanic cell, while it occurs at the anode in the IEF apparatus.
   B. the anode of the galvanic cell is negative, while the anode of the IEF apparatus is positive.
   C. the IEF apparatus has to be powered by an outside source, while the galvanic cell does not.
   D. the galvanic cell has an E_{cell} that is greater than 0, while the IEF apparatus does not.

6. Consider the standard potentials shown below.

   Ag (s) → Ag^+ (aq) + e⁻   −0.80 V

   Au (s) → Au^{2+} (aq) + 2 e⁻   −1.50 V

   When a voltaic cell is constructed using gold, gold cation, silver, and silver cation, what occurs at the anode?

   A. Solid silver is oxidized.
   B. Solid gold is oxidized.
   C. Silver cations are oxidized.
   D. A voltaic cell cannot be constructed using half-cells with the standard potentials given above.

7. In a galvanic cell, which of the following accurately describes the function of the salt bridge?
   A. It allows negative ions to move toward the cathode.
   B. It allows positive ions to move toward the cathode.
   C. It allows electrons to move toward the cathode.
   D. A salt bridge is typically not included in a galvanic cell.

8. An opportunistic jeweler is attempting to use electroplating to coat extra copper jewelry with gold, in an effort to sell it to his customers for a high price. If he operates an electrolytic cell at a 10 A current for 6 minutes, how many grams of gold will be plated? Note that Faraday's constant is approximately 10^5 C/mol e⁻ and any gold cation is in the form of Au^{3+}.
   A. 0.24 g
   B. 1.2 g
   C. 2.4 g
   D. 7.2 g

Independent Question Explanations

1. C is correct. Hydrogen has an oxidation state of + 1, except in metal hydrides; since this is not a metal hydride, the oxidation state of H will be +1. When not in a peroxide, oxygen has an oxidation state of –2. This gives us a total of (+1) + 2(–2) = –3. Since the overall $HClO_2$ molecule is uncharged, the oxidation state of Cl must be +3 to allow the oxidation states to sum to zero.

2. B is correct. An oxidizing agent is a molecule, ion, or element that oxidizes another species by becoming *reduced* itself. Since this is a LEAST question, we need to choose the option that is least likely to become reduced. Although we are not given reduction or oxidation potentials, we should be able to realize that F⁻ is entirely incapable of being reduced, since it cannot have an oxidation state that is less than –1. Thus, F⁻ is the worst choice for an oxidizing agent of those listed. The remaining options can serve as oxidizing agents; the oxygen in H_2O_2 can become reduced from its –1 oxidation state to –2, and H_2 can act as an oxidizing agent when it reacts with solid metal to form a hydride. (For example, consider the reaction H_2 + 2 Li → 2 LiH. H_2 becomes reduced from an oxidation state of 0 to one of –1, acting as an oxidizing agent in the process.) Finally, CrO_3 is a common oxidizing agent that you may have encountered in organic chemistry.

3. D is correct. Reducing agents are species that reduce *other* molecules or ions. In other words, reducing agents *themselves* effectively become oxidized. The reactions given are reduction reactions, so we must reverse them to find the corresponding oxidation potentials:

Cu (s) → Cu^{2+} (aq) + 2 e⁻	−0.34 V
Pb (s) → Pb^{2+} (aq) + 2 e⁻	+ 0.13 V
Mg (s) → Mg^{2+} (aq) + 2 e⁻	+ 2.37 V

   The species most likely to become oxidized will have the most positive oxidation potential. This species is Mg (s), making choice D our answer. Note that Mg^{2+} and Cu^{2+} are likely to become reduced, not oxidized, allowing us to quickly eliminate options A and C.

4. D is correct. According to the equation $\Delta G° = -nFE°_{cell}$, a positive $E°_{cell}$ should correspond to a negative $\Delta G°$. However, the question stem did not give us $E°_{cell}$, or the standard-state cell potential, which requires a temperature of 25°C, a pressure of 1 atm, and concentrations of 1 M. The temperature in the question stem is 0°C, which is not standard conditions. It is possible to find $E°_{cell}$ using a non-standard E_{cell} value, but that would require using the following equation:

$$E_{cell} = E°_{cell} - \frac{RT}{nF} \ln Q$$

We have no way of finding the Q value for this reaction, so we cannot know anything sufficiently conclusive about $E°_{cell}$ to allow us to answer this question. Thus, choice D is correct. Regarding choice C, note that K_{eq} is a ratio of product to reactant concentrations and can never be negative.

5. A is correct. In essence, this question is asking us to find the statement that does NOT accurately characterize a difference between a galvanic and an electrolytic cell. (Again, note that the IEF apparatus is functionally an electrolytic cell.) Choice A is the answer to this NOT question because reduction occurs at the cathode and oxidation at the anode regardless of the type of cell. The remaining statements are true. The anode of a galvanic cell is negative, while the anode of an electrolytic cell is positive. Electrolytic cells only function when powered, while galvanic cells are spontaneous and do not require an outside power/ voltage source. Finally, galvanic cells have E_{cell} values that are greater than 0, while electrolytic cells have negative E_{cell} values.

6. A is correct. Note that the question stem gives oxidation potentials. A voltaic cell is synonymous with a galvanic cell, meaning that it will be spontaneous and must have a positive overall $E°_{cell}$. For this to occur, we must reverse the half-reaction with the more negative potential. We are left with the following:

Ag (s) → Ag⁺ (aq) + e⁻	−0.80 V
Au^{2+} (aq) + 2 e⁻ → Au (s)	+ 1.50 V

   In other words, silver must be oxidized and gold must be reduced if we want our overall standard cell potential to be positive (specifically, it will be + 0.70). It is solid silver that is oxidized, which eliminates choice C, and we are left with option A.

7. B is correct. In a galvanic cell, electrons move toward the cathode, but they do so through the wire connecting the two half-cells, not through the salt bridge (eliminate choice C). This movement of negative charge from anode to cathode causes the cathode to become relatively negative, which repels electrons. This effect would quickly stop the cell from functioning, so a salt bridge is typically incorporated. This bridge allows ions not otherwise involved in the reaction to move to balance out the negative charge. Positive ions moving toward the cathode would do exactly this. Note that negative ions could also be used, but they would need to move toward the anode, not the cathode.

8. C is correct. First, note that current (amps, or A) is equivalent to coulombs divided by seconds. We can thus find total coulombs (charge) by multiplying current by time in seconds:

$$10 \, \frac{C}{s} \times 360 \, s = 3600 \, C$$

Next, we can divide by Faraday's constant to convert coulombs to moles of electrons:

$$3600 \, C \times \frac{1 \text{ mol electrons}}{10^5 \, C} = \frac{3.6 \times 10^3}{1 \times 10^5} = 3.6 \times 10^{-2} \text{ mol electrons}$$

Don't be hasty here; moles of electrons does not necessarily equal moles of metal plated. In fact, note that it requires three electrons to reduce Au^{3+} to solid Au. The moles of solid gold plated is thus:

$$3.6 \times 10^{-2} \text{ mol electrons} \times \frac{1 \text{ mol Au}}{3 \text{ mol e}^-} = 1.2 \times 10^{-2} \text{ mol Au}$$

Finally, we must multiply this value by the molar mass of Au to find the grams of gold plated. The molar mass of Au is approximately 197 g/mol, which we can round to 200 g/mol, or 2×10^2 g/mol in scientific notation.

$$1.2 \times 10^{-2} \text{ mol Au} \times \frac{2 \times 10^2 \text{ g Au}}{\text{mol}} = 2.4 \text{ g Au}$$

This page left intentionally blank.

CHAPTER 9

Organic Chemistry Basics

0. Introduction

In this chapter, we move from general chemistry to organic chemistry, which is the study of the carbon-containing compounds that make up the basis of all life. Carbon's ability to form chains of single, double, and triple bonds with itself is what provides it with the flexibility to become the chemical scaffold of life.

On a more practical level, organic chemistry coursework is often a memorable experience for many premeds, and not necessarily for good reasons. Not only is the subject challenging in its own right, but organic chemistry courses are often used to 'weed out' aspiring premeds. However, organic chemistry is not an especially large component of the science content tested on the MCAT. On average, it will make up approximately 15% of the content tested in the Chemical and Physical Foundations and 5% of the content tested in the Biological and Biochemical Foundations section, corresponding therefore to 10% of the content in the 'core' science sections and 5% of the exam overall, including CARS and Psychological/Social/Biological Foundations.

Students commonly are tempted towards one of two extreme courses of action with regard to organic chemistry: either to transfer all of the anxiety from their college coursework onto MCAT organic chemistry, allowing it to become a primary focus of energy, attention, and concern, or to neglect it because of the misconception that it's no longer important for the new (post-2015) MCAT. Your task with organic chemistry is to steer away from both extremes. On one hand, it is important to understand that it *is* tested on the 2015 MCAT, to a non-trivial extent: ~10% of the 'core' science content is no joke. On the other hand, it's important to focus on organic chemistry within the larger content of MCAT science. For the most part, the MCAT is interested in ensuring that you have a solid understanding of the basic principles of organic chemistry, with a special focus on factors that help predict biologically/pharmacologically relevant properties of compounds. This translates into the following core areas that we will explore in this chapter and in the remaining chapters of this textbook:

> Nomenclature: We have to be able to know what chemicals we're talking about.
> Structure and Behavior: How does the structure of organic molecules contribute to their behavior? This general topic includes properties like resonance stabilization, as well as functional groups and their basic properties.
> Key Reactions: How do organic molecules interact with each other? This topic is tested in less breadth and depth than it is in most college-level organic chemistry courses, but it is nonetheless important.

> > Lab Techniques: How do we tell which molecule is which (and/or determine their structures) and separate them from each other? This is a seriously non-obvious problem and one that is of considerable practical importance in the lab.

In the present chapter, we'll discuss nomenclature and structure, with a special focus on stereochemistry. The next chapter (Chapter 10) will provide a comprehensive overview of the functional groups that you need to know for the MCAT, including the key reactions that they participate in. Chapter 11 is a deep dive into some of the reaction mechanisms that you should be familiar with for the MCAT, and Chapter 12 will deal with some key lab techniques.

As you're studying organic chemistry for the MCAT, keep the following three principles in mind. They will help you hone your studying to get the most out of the time that you invest into it for Test Day.

1. Don't neglect the simple stuff. Another way to frame this is to embrace seemingly 'dumb' questions and keep pushing until they're resolved. The MCAT can and does ask straightforward questions about topics like stereochemistry that are often covered in the early segments of organic chemistry coursework, and simple topics are the foundation for more complex material. Don't rush through the basics! Whenever you read through something and get that feeling (which everyone has had at times) that an explanation *should* make sense to you but doesn't quite connect, that's your signal to slow down and invest some more time into figuring out what's going on.

2. Visualize things in space. If you have an old molecular model kit from your previous coursework, now is the time to dust it off—and if you don't, you might think about investing in one. Another possibility is to be active with drawing out structures and reactions on paper, or even to use gestures and/or objects at hand in your study space to illustrate them.

3. Follow the charge! This advice applies to biochemistry as well as organic chemistry. Charge-based interactions are at the heart of both the chemical and physical properties of molecules and reaction mechanisms. This manifests in two main ways: intermolecular forces, which contribute to general chemical and physical properties, and the localization of electrons, which helps account for reaction mechanisms by explaining which atoms in a molecule do what, and also contributes to an understanding of the stability/instability of various molecules depending on whether they can delocalize charges.

With all of the above in mind, let's get started!

1. Nomenclature and Structure

Tens—if not hundreds—of millions of possible organic compounds exist, so it is fundamental for practical purposes for us to develop a system of unambiguously describing the structure of organic compounds. IUPAC nomenclature is the way to do this. In this section, we will first describe how IUPAC nomenclature applies to hydrocarbons— the simplest examples of organic molecules, made up only of carbon and hydrogen atoms—and then extend those principles to more complicated molecules.

Alkanes are the simplest of hydrocarbons, and have only single bonds between carbons, as well as enough bonds between carbon and hydrogen to ensure that the octet rule is respected (practically speaking, this means that carbon makes a total of four bonds). Generally, a carbon skeleton is used to depict organic compounds, in what is known as bond-line notation. In this system, carbon atoms are nodes between which bonds are drawn. Hydrogens are not indicated explicitly at all, but you can assume that carbon atoms are bound to the number of hydrogen atoms necessary to ensure that each carbon atom makes four bonds. Other atoms are indicated explicitly. Figure 1 illustrates this for some simple compounds.

Figure 1. Examples of bond-line notation.

Alkanes are named in the following steps:

1. Identify and name the longest chain of carbons.

1	CH_4	Methane	6	$CH_3(CH_2)_4CH_3$	Hexane
2	CH_3CH_3	Ethane	7	$CH_3(CH_2)_5CH_3$	Heptane
3	$CH_3CH_2CH_3$	Propane	8	$CH_3(CH_2)_6CH_3$	Octane
4	$CH_3(CH_2)_2CH_3$	Butane	9	$CH_3(CH_2)_7CH_3$	Nonane
5	$CH_3(CH_2)_3CH_3$	Pentane	10	$CH_3(CH_2)_8CH_3$	Decane

2. Label each carbon so that the substituents have the lowest possible numbers.

3. Identify and assign a number to each substituent. The general rule for naming alkane substituents is to use –yl as the suffix. Di-, tri-, and tetra- are used when two, three, and four of the same substituents are present, respectively.

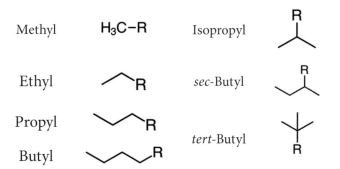

4. Name the compound by placing the substituents in alphabetical order before the name of the parent molecule. Prefixes such as di-, tri-, *sec*-, *tert*-, etc., should be ignored for alphabetical ordering.

Let's work through an example of a relatively complicated alkane, as shown below in Figure 2A.

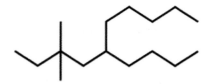

Figure 2A. A relatively complicated alkane.

Our first task is to identify the longest carbon chain. This sounds trivial, but be careful—it can be easy to jump to a decision based on familiar shapes without properly accounting for the actual number of carbons. In this case, it might be tempting to see this molecule as being a modification of the straight-chain alkane that runs across the bottom of the image, but it turns out that this is not the case. The correct identification of the longest carbon chain is shown below in Figure 2B.

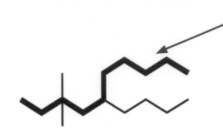

Identify the longest
carbon chain: this
will be some kind of
a decane!

Figure 2B. Identifying the longest carbon chain.

The next step is to identify and name the substituents, taking care to number the carbons such that the substituents have the smallest possible numbers. This is shown in Figure 2C.

Two methyl groups
at carbon 3

A butyl group at
carbon 5

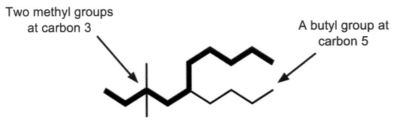

5-butyl-3,3-dimethyldecane

Figure 2C. Identifying the substituents.

We then arrange the substituents in alphabetical order, resulting in 5-butyl-3,3-dimethyldecane.

Our next task is to scale this system up to handle more complicated molecules. The key concept for these purposes is a functional group. A functional group is a specific group of atoms/bonds within a molecule that is responsible for a characteristic set of behaviors. There is a set of functional groups that you need to be familiar with for the MCAT, and their properties and key reactions are presented in more detail in Chapter 10. In this section, we will present functional groups very briefly, with an eye towards seeing how they are reflected in nomenclature.

To make this discussion simpler, let's take a closer look at the name of our sample molecule, 5-butyl-3,3-dimethyldecane. Alkanes can be considered a functional group, and we can note that the suffix *–yl* is used for prefixed alkane substituents, while the suffix *–ane* is placed at the end of a molecule to denote that it overall belongs to the class of alkanes. In fact, every bit of this nomenclature tells us some information about the molecule. This is shown in Figure 3, which uses color-coding and presents the 'question' that every piece of the name of this molecule 'answers'.

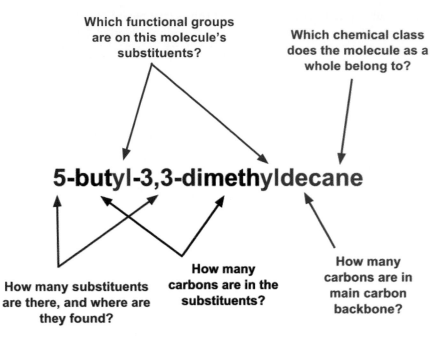

Figure 3. Information shown by nomenclature.

With this in mind, we're ready to deal with other structures. Let's start simple, with two common functional groups: hydroxyl groups (–OH), which form compounds known as alcohols, and amine groups (–NR₃, where R is a H or a C atom), which form compounds known as amines. Figure 4 shows some simple alcohols and amines, some with additional alkyl substituents.

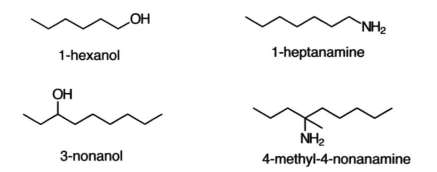

Figure 4. Alcohols and amines.

For the most part, we can name the compounds in Figure 4 in the same way that we named alkanes. The only difference is that we need to specify where the non-alkane functional group is. Although by convention, if you only say 'hexanol,' it is assumed that you mean 1-hexanol, in IUPAC nomenclature, we do technically need to distinguish among 1-hexanol, 2-hexanol, and 3-hexanol.

What if we have *both* an amine group and a hydroxyl group on a molecule? We need to have some way of determining which functional group takes priority and is assigned the coveted slot at the very end of the compound's name. This is simply done by convention. In the case of amines and alcohols, by convention, the hydroxyl group takes priority. This means that the molecules shown in Figure 5, which have both –OH and –NH₂ groups, are technically considered to be substituted hexanols. Note that this is true regardless of where the –OH and –NH₂ groups are located in the molecule; the molecule on the right, 6-amino-3-methyl-2-hexanol, is still considered a hexanol even though it might "look" like an amine at first glance. The key here is to be systematic, not to react based on gut-level impressions.

4-amino-3-methyl-1-hexanol   6-amino-3-methyl-2-hexanol

Figure 5. Two compounds with –OH and –NH₂ groups.

This principle applies to functional groups in general. IUPAC has defined a hierarchy of priority for functional groups, as shown below in Table 1. The basic organizing principle is that more oxidized carbons have higher priority. Oxidation and reduction as applied to organic compounds are discussed in more detail in Chapter 10, but the basic idea is that the more bonds carbon has to oxygen or to another carbon molecule (i.e., double-bonded alkenes are oxidized in comparison to single-bonded alkanes), the more oxidized it is. Therefore, the hierarchy in Table 1 can be roughly summarized as follows: carboxylic acids > carboxylic acid derivatives > other carbonyl-containing compounds > sulfur-containing functional groups > nitrogen-containing functional groups > hydrocarbons.

GROUP	PREFIX	SUFFIX	STRUCTURE	PRIORITY
Carboxylic acid	carboxy-	-oic acid	R—C(=O)—OH	High
Ester	oxycarbonyl-	-oate	R—C(=O)—OR'	
Acid chloride	halocarbonyl	-oyl halide	R—C(=O)—Cl	
Amide	carbamoyl-	-amide -carboxamide	R—C(=O)—N(R')R''	
Aldehyde	oxo-, formyl-	-al -carbaldehyde	R—C(=O)—H	
Ketone	oxo-	-one	R—C(=O)—R'	
Alcohol	hydroxy-	-ol	R—O—H	
Thiol	mercapto-	-thiol	R—S—H	
Amine	amino-	-amine	R—N(R')R''	
Alkene	alkenyl-	-ene	$R-C \equiv C-R'$	
Alkyne	alkynyl-	-yne	$R_1R_2C = CR_3R_4$	
Alkane	alkyl-	-ane	$R(CH_2)_n$	Low

Table 1. Functional groups by priority.

Thus, the workflow for naming a compound with multiple functional groups is as follows: (1) follow the first general steps of IUPAC nomenclature (i.e., find the longest carbon chain and identify possible substituents), (2) identify which functional group is highest-priority, (3) name the molecule such that it ends with the *suffix* of the highest-priority substituent, and then (4) name the substituents using their *prefixes*.

You may have noticed that some of the prefixes in Table 1 are in light gray. This is because they are unlikely to come up on the MCAT. It's not *impossible* that you could run into a compound containing a carboxylic acid functional group on one end and a carboxylic acid derivative functional group on the other end, but it's not especially likely, and if you do, understanding the general principles of nomenclature will probably suffice for handling such a situation.

MCAT STRATEGY > > >

IUPAC nomenclature is fair game on the MCAT, but remember that this isn't organic chemistry class, where your professor might give you some ridiculously complicated molecule, ask you to name it, and then deduct points because you put the comma in the wrong place or because you misspelled *mercapto-*. In fact, many MCAT questions will test nomenclature indirectly by making an understanding of nomenclature a prerequisite to tackling the question correctly. However, if you put in the effort to understand the principles of nomenclature and apply them carefully on Test Day, if you do run into a question that tests it directly, it should be more or less a free point.

In addition to the functional groups listed in Table 1, there are a few functional groups that are lower-priority than alkanes, meaning that they are essentially just treated as alkane substituents. Probably the most common example of this that you will encounter are haloalkanes (also known as alkyl halides)—that is, alkanes that have one or more halogen substituents. An example would be 2-bromopentane. Another example are ethers, which have an oxygen connected to two alkyl groups (C–O–C). A simple ether with a methane and an ethane group attached would be referred to as methoxyethane (i.e., the simpler substituent is attached as an 'alkoxy-' prefix).

Turning away from nomenclature, there are some aspects of the structure of organic molecules that you need to thoroughly master for the MCAT—most importantly, resonance and electron delocalization.

Resonance was introduced in Chapter 2 as what happens when it is possible to draw more than one reasonable Lewis structure for a given molecule. While that approach can be useful in some contexts, it's more accurate to think of resonance as reflecting the delocalization of electrons. Figure 6 below shows resonance structures for carboxylate anions and peptide bonds, two of the most common—and both simple and biologically relevant—examples of resonance. Carboxylate anions are the deprotonated form of carboxylic acids (–COOH), which, as we will see in Chapter 10, are one of the most important functional groups for the MCAT, and peptide bonds are the bonds formed between amino acids that form the backbone of proteins.

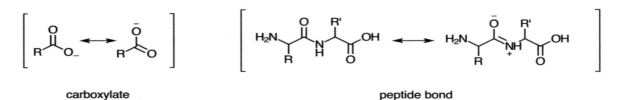

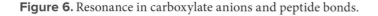

Figure 6. Resonance in carboxylate anions and peptide bonds.

You may have heard it said that the 'true' structure of a molecule can be thought of as a blend of its resonance structures, but the more accurate statement is actually that resonance structures are attempts to represent the underlying form of the molecule, in which the electrons are delocalized. Electron delocalization can significantly affect the chemical properties of a compound. For example, the resonance in the carboxylate anion provides a way of stabilizing the negative charge, which means that the anion is relatively stable compared to other ions containing an $-O^-$ anionic group. This in turn, as we will see, means that carboxylic acids are relatively acidic. Likewise, the resonance of peptide bonds contributes to their stability.

A special case of resonance is known as conjugation, which occurs when three or more adjacent p-orbitals are aligned with each other, forming not just a π bond, but a π *system*. Electrons can delocalize throughout that π system. While the above definition is theoretically more correct—and has the advantage of being able to account for radicals, carbocations, and p orbitals that contain lone pairs of electrons—for the purposes of the MCAT, you should associate conjugation with structures containing alternating single and double bonds in carbon chains. Figure 7 shows you an example of such a molecule (retinal).

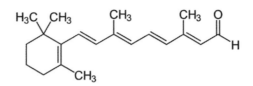

Figure 7. Molecule with a conjugated system (retinal).

An important characteristic of compounds with conjugated systems is that they absorb ultraviolet (UV) light, and can therefore be well visualized using UV spectroscopy.

Aromatic compounds are conjugated cyclic molecules with a planar structure that also satisfy an additional criterion known as Hückel's rule: having $4n + 2$ π-electrons, where n is an integer. The most important and well-known example of an aromatic compound is benzene. However, many other biologically relevant aromatic rings contain non-carbon molecules, for which reason they are known as heterocyclic rings. These include pyridine (present in the vitamin niacin), pyrimidine and purine (present in nucleic acids), imidazole (present in many important drugs), and pyrrole (which is a component of the porphyrins contained in heme). Interestingly, nothing in the technical definition of aromaticity requires carbon. An aromatic compound known as borazine contains a ring made up of alternating boron and nitrogen atoms. Its chemical properties are strikingly similar to those of benzene; practically speaking, this is largely just an interesting point of trivia not directly relevant to the MCAT, but it does underscore the point that aromaticity is not limited to benzene and its derivatives.

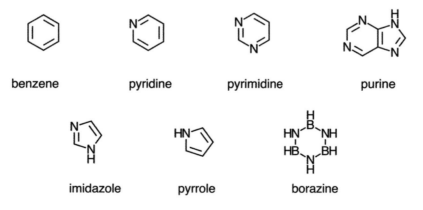

Figure 8. Aromatic compounds.

It's also important to understand that resonance—and its subcategories, conjugation and aromaticity—are not just empty formalism, but instead are necessary to explain a wide range of very real chemical phenomena. One of the simplest, but most striking, examples of the chemical effects of resonance has to do with bond length. Let's consider the benzene ring. The standard depiction of benzene makes it look like benzene has alternating C–C and C=C bonds. Well, we know that C–C bonds have a length of 154 pm, while C=C bonds have a length of 133 pm. It turns out that the length of the carbon-to-carbon bonds in the benzene ring is actually 139 pm, which is intermediate between these two values. This is a direct confirmation of the fact that distinct resonance structures are just a way of capturing the "real" structure of a molecule.

Another classic example is the heat of hydrogenation of benzene compared to cyclohexene. The hydrogenation of cyclohexene (i.e., converting cyclohexene to cyclohexane) is an exothermic process that releases 120 kJ/mol of energy. If benzene was essentially just a cyclohexatriene (that is, if the commonly used structural representation of benzene containing alternating single and double bonds was empirically correct), we would predict that the hydrogenation of benzene would release $3 \times 120 = 360$ kJ/mol of energy. In reality, the hydrogenation of benzene releases only 208 kJ/mol. The difference, 152 kJ/mol, reflects the resonance stabilization of benzene. It's worth pausing to ensure that you understand *why* this is the case. The idea is that the hydrogenation of benzene releases less energy because benzene was in a state of lower internal energy to begin with due to resonance/aromaticity.

In Chapters 10 and 11, we will see other instances of how resonance and aromaticity affect chemical properties—most notably, acid-base chemistry—and reaction mechanisms. In both cases, the underlying idea is that resonance allows molecules to stabilize charge configurations that wouldn't otherwise be stable. In the case of acid-base chemistry, resonance generally allows compounds to be more acidic than would otherwise be expected by stabilizing the negative charge on the deprotonated conjugate base form of an acid. For instance, alcohols (with a –OH group) are generally only very weakly acidic, but phenols, in which the –OH group is attached to a benzene ring, are meaningfully acidic for organic compounds (although still technically weak acids). Alternatively, resonance can stabilize the additional positive charge that occurs in a carbocation, with implications for various reaction mechanisms, as we will see in Chapter 11.

2. Isomers and Stereochemistry

In this section, we'll discuss molecules that share the same molecular formula but differ in their structure. Such molecules are known as isomers, and the general topic of how molecules are arranged in space in different ways is known as stereochemistry. Stereochemistry is an essential topic for the MCAT, and is one of the highest-yield domains in organic chemistry. The reason for this is that stereochemistry is one of the two basic principles—along with charge interactions—for explaining why molecules behave the way they do. However, stereochemistry can be an intimidating concept for many MCAT students, for two main reasons. First, in organic chemistry courses in college, stereochemistry is often quickly covered at the beginning of the course, before many students develop the study skills necessary to succeed at organic chemistry and/or a sense of how stereochemistry fits into the bigger picture. Second, there's no way around the fact that stereochemistry *does* involve a large number of similar-sounding terms that must be mastered. Both of these problems have the same solution: slow down and review the terminology carefully, taking care to understand how each term is exemplified by various molecules and how each term fits into the bigger picture of stereochemistry.

The first high-level category of isomers refers to the different ways that atoms can be connected with each other given a single molecular formula. Such isomers are known as structural isomers or constitutional isomers. A simple example is provided by C_5H_{12}, which, as shown in Figure 9, can correspond to structures including pentane, isopentane (also known as 2-methylbutane) or neopentane (also known as 2,2-dimethylpropane). As suggested by the IUPAC nomenclature of these compounds, they are completely different structures.

pentane   isopentane   neopentane

Figure 9. Structural isomers of pentane.

This point is further underscored if we look at a more complex example: what if we add an oxygen to the mix, and explore the structural isomers of $C_5H_{12}O$? The first examples that come to mind might be 1-pentanol, 2-pentanol, and 3-pentanol, but as shown in Figure 10, there is actually a surprisingly wide range of structures that we could draw, not all of which are alcohols.

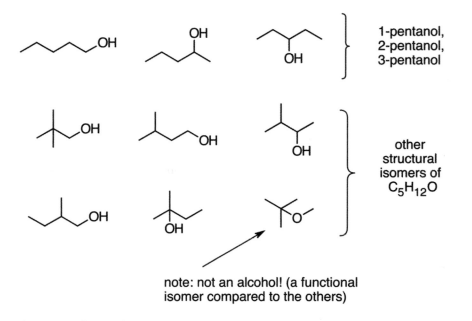

Figure 10. Structural isomers of $C_5H_{12}O$

There are a couple important lessons to learn from the example of the structural isomers of $C_5H_{12}O$. First, there is no way to directly predict the number or configuration of structural isomers by looking at the molecular formula. You have to draw them out and be creative—not all structural isomers are obvious! Second, structural isomers may have fundamentally different chemical properties. This is exemplified by the ether that is contained in Figure 10 along with all the alcohols. Ethers have very different chemical and physical properties than alcohols. Structural isomers with different functional groups are known as functional isomers. Figure 11 shows further examples of potentially surprising pairs of structural isomers that will help reinforce these lessons.

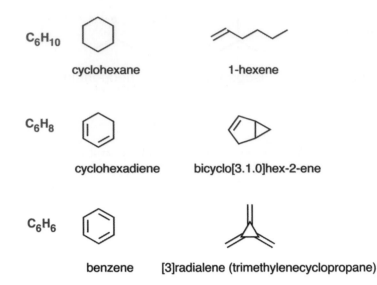

Figure 11. Surprising pairs of structural isomers.

A final subcategory of structural isomers that you should be familiar with are tautomers. This term refers to structural isomers that interconvert with each other and exist in equilibrium. The most commonly encountered is keto-enol isomerism, which is illustrated in Figure 12. At room temperature, the keto form is favored, but the enol form contributes significantly to some reaction mechanisms, and the deprotonated intermediate (known as an enolate ion) is also important for some reactions, as discussed further in Chapters 10 and 11.

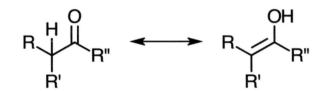

Figure 12. Keto-enol tautomerism.

Although keto-enol tautomerism is by far the most important example of tautomerism for the MCAT, it is not the only one. As shown in Figure 13, tautomerization also takes place between enamines and imines (the second most important example), lactams and lactims, and amides and imidic acids. It is important to understand that tautomers and resonance structures are not the same thing. As we discussed above, resonance is a phenomenon in which electrons are delocalized, and we use resonance structures as a somewhat crude way of representing a *single* underlying, delocalized structure of the molecule. In contrast, tautomers are two *different* structures that interconvert via the breaking and re-formation of bonds (see Chapter 11 for more details).

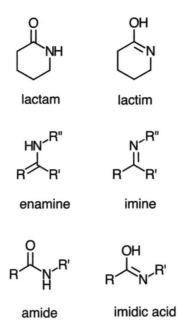

Figure 13. Other examples of tautomerism.

Next, we move on to the second highest-level category of isomers: stereoisomers. This is a broad category that describes how molecules with a single pattern of connectivity among its constituent atoms can have different spatial configurations. In other words, stereoisomers are subsets of a single structural isomer. The terminology surrounding stereoisomerism can be even more confusing than the terminology dealing with structural isomerism, so as a first step, let's clarify the contexts in which we have to worry about stereochemistry:

1. <u>Arrangements of single bonds</u>. Single bonds can rotate without being broken, and some of the resulting configurations—known as conformational isomers—are more favorable than others.

2. <u>Orientation across a double bond</u>. A substituent can be located on one side or another of a double bond, and the terms *cis* and *trans*, as well as the *E/Z* system, are used to describe this phenomenon.

3. <u>Orientation at a chiral center</u>. Briefly, a chiral center is formed by a carbon that has four different substituents, and multiple systems exist for describing such orientations, most notably the *R/S* system and the *d/l* (+/−) system.

Let's start with rotation around a single bond, which generates conformational isomers. One common example of a conformational isomer involves the orientation of butane, which is usually visualized using Newman projections. Newman projections are a way of visualizing organic compounds in which a carbon-carbon bond extends directly into the page, with the front carbon represented by a central dot and the back carbon represented by a circle. The carbon substituents are represented spatially by three lines radiating from each carbon in either staggered or eclipsed (overlapping) conformations.

Some of these conformations are more stable and predominate in solution. Conformations with eclipsed, bulky substituents experience torsional strain and are higher in potential energy, which makes them much more unstable than staggered conformations that maximize the separation between bulky substituents.

The two flavors of staggered conformations are known as 'anti' and 'gauche'. The anti conformation is the most stable because the bulky substituents are maximally separated at an angle of 180°. In the gauche conformation, the substituents are staggered, with a separation of 60° between bulky substituents. Eclipsed conformations contain overlapping substituents, and totally eclipsed conformations with bulky substituents that directly overlap are even more unstable. Figure 14 illustrates the structures and potential energies of butane conformational isomers.

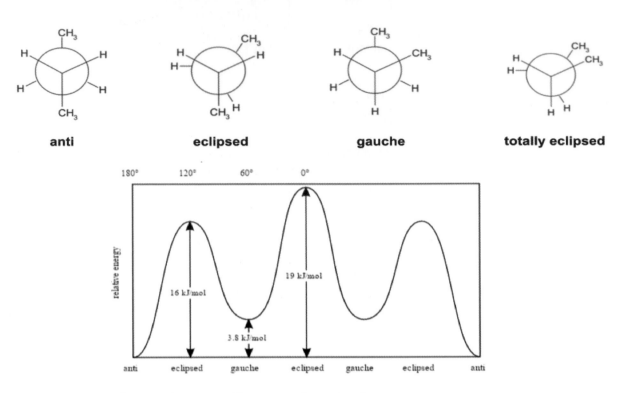

Figure 14. Structures and potential energies of butane conformational isomers.

Another type of conformational isomerism arises in cycloalkanes due to angle strain, torsional strain, and steric strain. Angle strain occurs when the angle between single-bonded carbon atoms deviates from 109.5°, and—as discussed above for butane—torsional strain is created by eclipsing substituents on neighboring atoms. Steric stain is caused by substituents (even hydrogen substituents!) getting in each other's way. In order to resolve these forms of strain, cyclohexane alternates between chair, twist-boat, and boat conformations. The chair conformation is the most stable, and is preferred by cyclohexane.

Figure 15. Conformational isomers of cyclohexane.

The substituents of cyclohexane can either be in an axial orientation (sticking up or down from the ring) or in an equatorial orientation (extending in the approximate plane of the ring). Each carbon in a cyclohexane ring has one axial and one equatorial substituent, as shown for the hydrogens in cyclohexane in Figure 16.

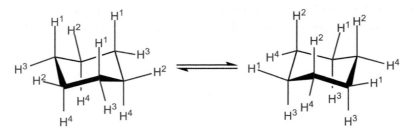

Figure 16. Axial and equatorial positions in cyclohexane.

Figure 16 also illustrates an important point, which is that at equilibrium, two different chair conformers interconvert, which allows a given substituent to alternate between equatorial and axial positions. For cyclohexane derivatives that have bulkier substituents—most often illustrated with alkyl substituents—this interconversion allows steric strain to be minimized. The basic principle is that bulkier substituents 'want' to be positioned equatorially, so the conformation that allows that to be the case will predominate at equilibrium.

A final point to note about cyclohexane ring conformers is that each carbon has a substituent that points down and a substituent that points up. This is obvious for the axial substituents, but somewhat less so for the equatorial substituents. However, if you look carefully, you can see that the equatorial substituents also point slightly up or down (by about 19.5°, as a consequence of the tetrahedral geometry of sp^3-hybridized carbons). If a cyclohexane ring has two substituents that both point up or down, it is referred to as *cis*, while if the two substituents point in different directions, the configuration is referred to as *trans*.

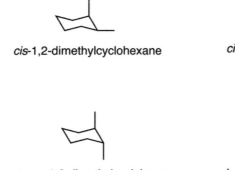

cis-1,2-dimethylcyclohexane

cis-1,3-dimethylcyclohexane

trans-1,2-dimethylcyclohexane

trans-1,3-dimethylcyclohexane

Figure 17. *Cis* and *trans* substituted cyclohexanes.

The *cis* and *trans* substituted cyclohexanes are stable. A *cis* isomer cannot be converted to a *trans* isomer without breaking and reforming a bond. However, the chair conformations of each of these isomers *can* interconvert in order to optimize steric hindrance. This is shown in Figure 18.

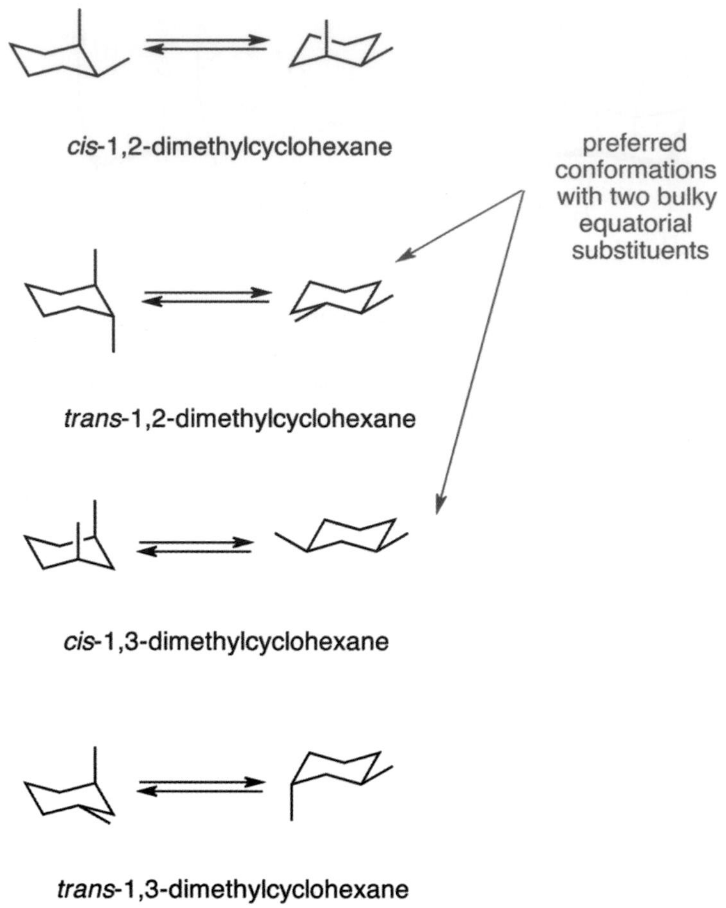

cis-1,2-dimethylcyclohexane

preferred
conformations
with two bulky
equatorial
substituents

trans-1,2-dimethylcyclohexane

cis-1,3-dimethylcyclohexane

trans-1,3-dimethylcyclohexane

Figure 18. Interconversion of disubstituted cyclohexanes.

As can be seen in Figure 18, if you have a choice between a conformation with two equivalent axial substituents and two equivalent equatorial substituents, the equatorial arrangement will be preferred. In contrast, if one methyl substituent is axial and one is equatorial, it doesn't really matter which is which. If you're dealing with a situation where one substituent is bulkier than the other (for example, if you have one methyl group and one *tert*-butyl group), the conformation with the bulkier substituent in an equatorial position will be preferred.

The next broad category of stereochemistry we need to cover deals with the spatial orientation of atoms around a double bond, which is also known as geometric isomerism. While C–C bonds can rotate freely, that is not true for C=C bonds, which have a fixed planar shape. Keeping in mind that each carbon generally forms a total of four bonds, this means that a carbon that forms a double bond will have two other substituents, one on each side of the double bond. There are two systems used for the stereochemistry of double bonds: *cis-trans* isomerism and the E-Z classification scheme.

Cis-trans refers to the positioning of two identical substituents across a double bond. When both substituents are on the same side of the double bond—either above or below—a *cis* double bond is formed. When two identical substituents are diagonal from one another across a double bond, a *trans* double bond is formed. This is shown in Figure 19.

Figure 19. *Cis* and *trans* isomers of 1,2-dichloroethene.

Although this usage does not technically correspond to the definition we gave of *cis-trans* isomers—specifying that both substituents must be identical—the terms *cis* and *trans* are frequently used to describe the orientation of bonds in fatty acid chains. Figure 20 compares *cis* and *trans* unsaturated (i.e., double-bond-containing) fatty acids. Unsaturated fatty acids produced in nature almost always have the *cis* orientation, preventing them from evenly stacking. In contrast, *trans* fats are produced in industrial processes, stack easily, and have been shown to have negative effects on human health.

> > CONNECTIONS < <

Chapter 9 of Biochemistry

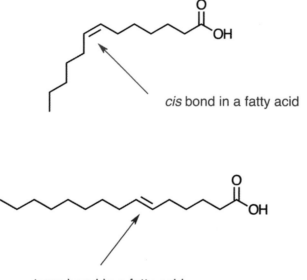

Figure 20. *Cis* and *trans* fatty acids.

A more generic system for classifying geometric isomers is the E-Z classification scheme. The distinction from *cis-trans* isomerism is that E-Z isomerism specifies the orientation of the two highest-priority substituents, which are not necessarily identical to one another. In this system, the two highest priority substituents are on the same side in (Z)-isomers and on the opposite side in (E)-isomers. According to the Cahn-Ingold-Prelog priority rules, the priority of substituent groups is determined by the atomic weights of the atoms attached to the central atom, with heavier atoms taking higher priority. If two bonded atoms are identical, the atomic weights of the atoms attached to each of those atoms are compared, and so forth. Multiple bonds are higher priority than single bonds when their atomic weights are the same.

A common point of confusion is that all *cis* isomers are (Z)-isomers and all *trans* isomers are (E)-isomers. Let's put that misconception to rest. Examine 2-bromo-2-butene in Figure 21. Notice that the two methyl groups on either side of the double bond would make this molecule a *trans* isomer. However, bromide is higher priority than a methyl group, so technically the higher priority substituents are on the same side of the double bond, making it a (Z)-isomer.

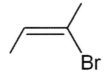

Figure 21. Structure of (Z)-2-bromo-2-butene.

Last but not least, we need to explore the spatial orientation of substituents at chiral centers (also known as stereocenters), which are atoms that are connected to four unique groups within a molecule. For example, the central carbon in the structure shown in Figure 22 is a stereocenter because it is attached to four unique substituents. Bold lines represent atoms projecting out of the page, and dashed lines represent atoms projecting into the page. This molecule is therefore considered chiral, because it is not superimposable upon its own mirror image.

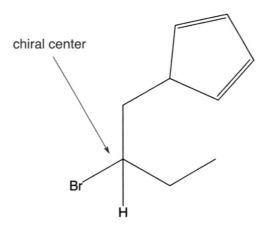

Figure 22. A simple chiral molecule.

A helpful visual analogy is to consider handedness: your right and left hands are mirror images but will not match up when superimposed, or laid over one another. This principle is exemplified in Figure 23, which illustrates how the chirality of amino acids—which have a central chiral carbon—is analogous to the chirality of one's hands. Molecules that are non-superimposable mirror images of each other are known as enantiomers. In contrast, achiral molecules possess a plane of symmetry and are superimposable.

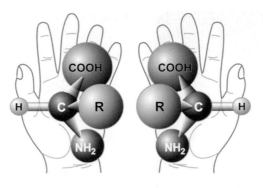

Figure 23. Amino acid chirality.

The number of stereoisomers that are possible for a given structure is equal to 2^n, where n is the number of stereocenters. Consider the structure of testosterone shown below. It has six chiral centers, so the maximum number of stereoisomers for testosterone is equal to $2^6 = 64$.

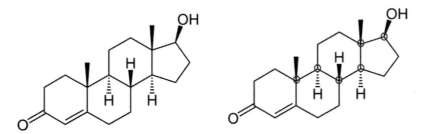

Figure 24. Chiral centers in testosterone.

Note in Figure 24 that each chiral center has a substituent denoted with a bold line or a dashed line. This is a common feature of how chiral centers are represented, and as such can be a valuable shortcut if you encounter a question on Test Day asking you to identify how many stereocenters a given molecule has (which is a very real possibility). However, you should be careful to double-check that there are indeed four *distinct* substituents at every site. As shown in Figure 25, it is possible both for bold/dashed lines to be used to denote substituents of a non-chiral carbon and for a chiral carbon not to have bold/dashed lines for its substituents.

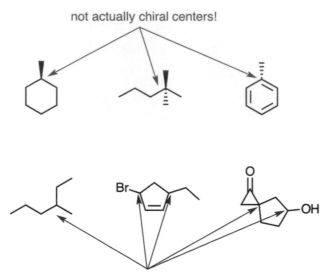

Figure 25. Misleading non-chiral and chiral compounds.

Another potential trap you need to be aware of is posed by so-called meso compounds. Meso compounds are molecules that have multiple stereocenters (usually two, in most examples you'll see on the MCAT) but are not chiral, because they have a plane of symmetry running through the molecule that divides it into two superimposable mirror images. If you identify a compound that has two stereocenters and an internal plane of symmetry, it is highly likely to be a meso compound if the substituents at both stereocenters are pointed the same way (into or out of the page). Some meso and non-meso compounds are shown in Figure 25.

An interesting manifestation of chemical 'handedness' (chirality) is that solutions of chiral compounds rotate planes of polarized light at angles unique to each compound. This is defined as the specific rotation [α] of the molecule. Compounds that produce clockwise (+) rotation of plane-polarized light are dextrorotatory (*d*), and compounds that produce counterclockwise (–) rotation are levorotatory (*l*). The specific rotation of a chiral compound in solution can be calculated according to the equation:

Equation 1.
$$[\alpha] = \frac{\alpha}{c\ell}$$

In Equation 1, α is the observed rotation, c is the concentration in g/mL, and ℓ is the length of the polarimeter tube in decimeters (dm).

A mixture with an equal 50:50 composition of two enantiomers of a given compound is known as a racemic mixture, and such mixtures do not rotate plane-polarized light at all, because the optical activity of each enantiomer cancels out that of the other. This observation has two consequences: first, if one enantiomer has a specific rotation of [+ α], its opposite enantiomer will have a rotation of [−α]; and second, we can work backwards from the observed rotation of a mixture—if we know [α] to calculate the distribution of enantiomers in a solution. The formula we can use for this is given below:

Equation 2.
$$\text{enantiomeric excess (\%)} = \frac{[\alpha]_{observed}}{[\alpha]_{pure}} \times 100$$

Equation 2 gives us a quantity known as enantiomeric excess, which specifically refers to the difference in percentage points between two enantiomers in a sample. Let's work through a simple example. If we know that the optical activity ([α]$_{pure}$) of the (*d*) enantiomer of a compound is + 20°, and we observe a rotation ([α]$_{observed}$) of + 10°, plugging those numbers into Equation 2 will quickly yield 50%. This does *not* mean that the (*d*) enantiomer comprises 50%

of the sample; after all, that would be a racemic mixture, with an optical activity of 0°. Instead, it means that the percentage of the (*d*) enantiomer must exceed that of the (*l*) enantiomer by 50 percentage points, which means that the (*d*) enantiomer actually makes up 75% of the solution, while the (*l*) enantiomer makes up 25%.

As suggested in the above discussion, optical activity is one way to refer to the different enantiomers of a compound. This was done historically, and is still done in some contexts, but it has limitations as a form of chemical nomenclature, because it tells you nothing about the structure of a compound. That is, there is no way to look at the structure of a chiral compound and predict which way it will rotate light, and the problem gets even worse when we have to account for molecules with multiple chiral centers (remember our example of testosterone with 64 possible stereoisomers!). As a result, chemists developed a system of absolute configuration (known as the *R/S* system) that utilizes the Cahn-Ingold-Prelog priority rules discussed above for *E/Z* isomerism. To determine whether a given stereocenter has an *R* or *S* notation, use the following steps:

1. Assign priorities to each substituent. Recall that atoms with greater atomic weights receive higher priority.

2. If the lowest priority substituent is in the back, move on to step 3. If not, draw the lowest priority so that it is in the back.

3. Determine whether the order of substituents from highest to lowest priority runs in the clockwise (*R*) or counterclockwise (*S*) direction.

4. If the orientation of the lowest priority group was changed in step 2, then the true absolute configuration will be the opposite of that found in step 3.

Let's see how this works in practice with an example. What is the absolute configuration of the two stereocenters in 2,3-butanediol?

Let's handle this step by step:

1. 2,3-Butanediol has two stereocenters. First, we will assign priorities to each substituent.

2. Next, we will place the lowest priority substituent in the back at each stereocenter.

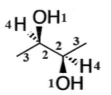

3. Then, we will draw a circle from the highest to lowest front-facing substituents to determine the absolute configuration.

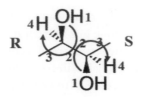

4. The orientation of the lowest priority substituent at position 3 had been changed, so the absolute configuration at that position must also be changed back (R→S). The name of this compound is (2*R*,3*S*)-2,3-butanediol.

When dealing with molecules that have multiple chiral centers, a distinction is made between enantiomers and diastereomers. As we have discussed, enantiomers are non-superimposable mirror images of each other, and for this to be true in a compound with multiple stereocenters, *all* the stereocenters must be oppositely oriented. In contrast, diastereomers are compounds that do not satisfy the strict criteria through which enantiomers are defined. This means that pairs of compounds with multiple stereocenters in which some have the same orientation are diastereomers, as are—technically speaking—pairs that include meso compounds and examples of *E/Z* isomerism. Figure 26 provides a simple illustration of how this works for compounds with two chiral centers.

for a compound with two stereocenters:

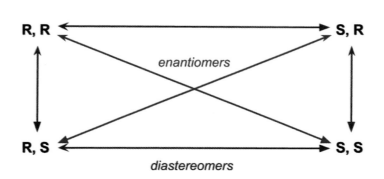

Figure 26. Enantiomers versus diastereomers.

Now that we've reviewed the various types of isomers that you may encounter for MCAT organic chemistry, it is useful to step back and look at the bigger picture. Figure 27 presents a flow-chart of the various types of isomerism.

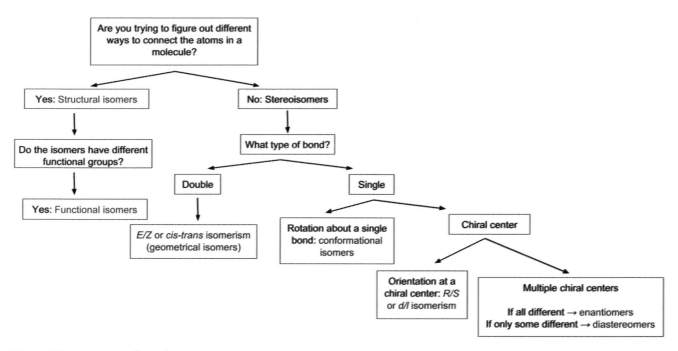

Figure 27. Isomerism flow chart.

3. Must-Knows

> IUPAC nomenclature for alkanes: (1) identify and name longest carbon chain (1C = methane, 2C = ethane, 3C = propane, 4C = butane, 5C = pentane, etc.); (2) label carbons such that substituents have lowest possible #'s; (3) identify all substituents (methyl, ethyl, etc.); (4) place substituents in alphabetical order.

> Other functional groups have a suffix (when they are the highest-priority group) and a prefix (when there is a second, higher-priority group) present. –COOH (-oic acid) is highest priority, followed by carboxylic acid derivatives, aldehydes/ketones (suffix: -al/-one, prefix: oxo), alcohols (suffix: -ol, prefix: hydroxy-), amines (suffix: -amine, prefix: amino-), thiols (suffix: -thiol, prefix: mercapto), and hydrocarbons.

> Resonance: when >1 Lewis structure accounts for electrons; multiple structures indicate electron delocalization in the main structure.

> Aromatic compounds: conjugated cyclic molecules w/ planar structure + satisfy Hückel's rule: having $4n + 2$ pi-electrons, where n is an integer. Common example = benzene.

> Cahn-Ingold-Prelog rules for assigning priority to substituents: (1) look at atoms directly connected to the stereocenter; heavier atoms have higher priority; (2) if two atoms are the same, move one atom further down the substituents and re-rank by substituents; (3) continue until tie is broken; multiple bonds are higher-priority than single bonds.
>
> — E/Z system for double bonds: E if higher-priority substituents are on opposite sides of double bond, Z if higher-priority substituents are on the same side.
>
> — R/S system for chiral centers: orient molecule such that lowest-priority substituent faces into the page and connect substituents from high to low priority; if doing so traces a clockwise pattern, molecule is R; if counterclockwise, S.

> Chirality: non-superimposable mirror images (enantiomers); C must have 4 different substituents; if >1 chiral center, enantiomers have opposite orientation at all chiral centers, while diastereomers only differ at some. For n chiral centers, 2^n stereoisomers.

Practice Passage

The International Union of Pure and Applied Chemistry (IUPAC) code has long been used to name organic molecules. With the exponential increase of biochemistry research and results near the turn of the 21st century, a new system was devised to specify nucleic acids. This code has contributed to representations of recognition sequences; codon degeneracy; phylogenetics; and polymorphic nucleic acids. The code can be extended to represent 2- and even 3-nucleotide sequences.

Table 1. Nucleotide Identification Code

Symbol	Mnemonic	Translation
A		A (adenine)
C		C (cytosine)
G		G (guanine)
T		T (thymine)
U		U (uracil)
R	puRine	A or G (purines)
Y	pYrimidine	C or T/U (pyrimidines)
M	aMino group	A or C
K	Keto group	G or T/U
S	Strong interaction	C or G
W	Weak interaction	A or T/U
H	not G	A, C or T/U
B	not A	C, G or T/U
V	not T/U	A, C or G
D	not C	A, G or T/U
N	aNy	A, C, G or T/U

Research has associated high-fat intakes with a high incidence of age-related macular degeneration due to oxidation. Lutein and zeaxanthin (L, Z) isomers (Figure 1) may counteract reactive oxygen species produced by oxidative stress. A study was conducted to determine the possible effects of L/Z administration on the lipid profile and protein genes associated with oxidative stress in the obesity induced by a high-fat diet (HFD) in rats.

Lutein

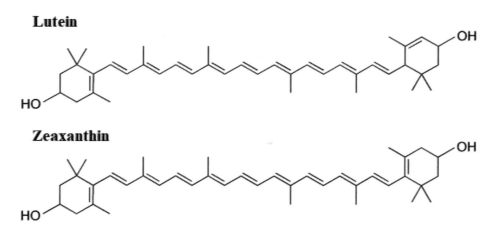

Zeaxanthin

Figure 1. Anti-oxidative drug structures

Lutein and zeaxanthin are the two main xanthophylls, which are an oxygenated form of carotenoids. They have the basic C40 isoprenoid structure similar to the other carotenoids and have an ionone ring at each terminal end which contains hydroxyl groups attached to the 3 and 3' positions. These molecules cannot be synthesized in humans due to the absence of the relevant carotenoid synthesis enzyme. Therefore, dietary intake of carotenoids at an adequate level is important to health. These carotenoids are contained in the retina, especially at the fovea, in much higher concentrations compared to the other tissues.

Following the feeding with HFD, increased levels of glucose, insulin, cholesterol, triglyceride, and free fatty acids (FFA) appeared in the serum of rats. When compared with the control group, there was no significant difference in the release of glucose, insulin, cholesterol, triglyceride and FFA in the L/Z treatment group ($P = 0.12$) after 1 week. Nevertheless, L/Z supplementation for 8 weeks was accompanied by reduction of glucose, insulin, cholesterol, triglyceride and FFA compared to control ($P = 0.009$).

Adapted from Tuzcu, M., et al. (2017). Lutein and zeaxanthin isomers modulates lipid metabolism and the inflammatory state of retina in obesity-induced high-fat diet rodent model. BMC Ophthalmology, 17, 129 under CCBY 4.0

1. What is a correct name for the molecule below?

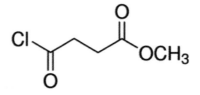

   A. Methyl 4-chloro-4-oxybutanone
   B. Ethyl succinyl chloride
   C. Ethyl vinyl chloride
   D. Methyl 4-chloro-4-oxobutanoate

2. According to the passage, which symbol could be used to represent the nucleotide below?

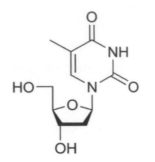

A. A
B. U
C. B
D. R

3. Efavirenz is a commonly prescribed antiretroviral medication used to treat and prevent HIV/AIDS.

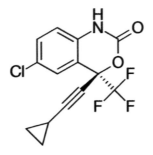

All of the following functional groups are found on efavirenz EXCEPT:

A. aldehyde.
B. phenyl.
C. urethane.
D. alkyne.

4. The high-fat diet fed to the rats also contained two common dietary monosaccharides, glucose and galactose.

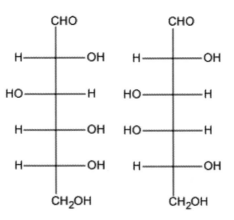

These nutrients represent what types of isomer?

A. Enantiomers
B. Diastereomers
C. Cis/trans isomers
D. Structural isomers

5. The ionone rings on L and Z are connected by a conjugated system that is stabilized by the interaction of which of the following electron sources?
   I. Pi-bonds
   II. Carbenium ions
   III. Lone pairs
   IV. Radicals

A. I only
B. I and II only
C. II and III only
D. II, III, and IV only

6. The equilibrium of the carbohydrate anomers shown below is an example of:

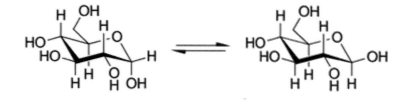

A. Resonance
B. Epimerization
C. Constitutional isomerism
D. Conformational isomerism

7. What is the absolute configuration of the ionone ring below?

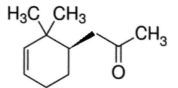

A. E
B. Z
C. S
D. R

Practice Passage Explanations

The International Union of Pure and Applied Chemistry (IUPAC) code has long been used to name organic molecules. With the exponential increase of biochemistry research and results near the turn of the 21st century, a new system was devised to specify nucleic acids. This code has contributed to representations of recognition sequences; codon degeneracy; phylogenetics; and polymorphic nucleic acids. The code can be extended to represent 2- and even 3-nucleotide sequences.

Key terms: IUPAC, nucleic acids

Cause and effect: IUPAC devised new code for nucleotides

Table 1. Nucleotide Identification Code

Symbol	Mnemonic	Translation
A		A (adenine)
C		C (cytosine)
G		G (guanine)
T		T (thymine)
U		U (uracil)
R	puRine	A or G (purines)
Y	pYrimidine	C or T/U (pyrimidines)
M	aMino group	A or C
K	Keto group	G or T/U
S	Strong interaction	C or G
W	Weak interaction	A or T/U
H	not G	A, C or T/U
B	not A	C, G or T/U
V	not T/U	A, C or G
D	not C	A, G or T/U
N	aNy	A, C, G or T/U

Research has associated high-fat intakes with a high incidence of age-related macular degeneration due to oxidation. Lutein and zeaxanthin (L, Z) isomers (Figure 1) may counteract reactive oxygen species produced by oxidative stress. A study was conducted to determine the possible effects of L/Z administration on lipid profile and protein genes associated with oxidative stress in the obesity induced by a high-fat diet (HFD) in rats.

Key terms: high-fat intakes, reactive oxygen species, L/Z drugs

Cause and effect: high-fat → oxidation → tissue damage; L/Z tx → change in oxidative stress?

Lutein

Zeaxanthin

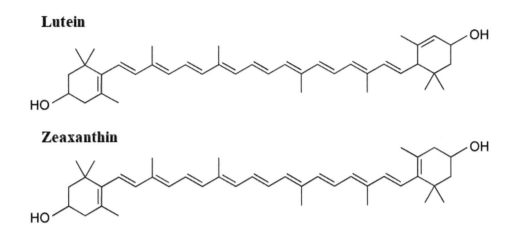

Figure 1. Anti-oxidative drug structures

Lutein and zeaxanthin are the two main xanthophylls which are an oxygenated form of carotenoids. They have the basic C40 isoprenoid structure similar to the other carotenoids and have an ionone ring at each terminal end which contains hydroxyl groups attached to the 3 and 3' positions. These molecules cannot be synthesized in humans due to the absence of the relevant carotenoid synthesis enzyme. Therefore, dietary intake of carotenoids at an adequate level is important to health. These carotenoids are contained in the retina, especially at the fovea, in much higher concentrations compared to the other tissues.

Key terms: lutein, zeaxanthin, isoprenoid, ionone

Cause and effect: L/Z = anti-oxidative molecules; L/Z precursors found more in eye (less oxidation)

Following the feeding with HFD, increased levels of the glucose, insulin, cholesterol, triglyceride, and free fatty acids (FFA) appeared in the serum of rats. When compared with the control group, there was no significant difference in the release of glucose, insulin, cholesterol, triglyceride and FFA in the L/Z treatment group ($P = 0.12$) after 1 week. Nevertheless, L/Z supplementation for 8 weeks was accompanied by reduction of glucose, insulin, cholesterol, triglyceride and FFA compared to control ($P = 0.009$).

Key terms: HFD, control group, L/Z treatment

Cause and effect: HFD → increased oxidative signals; L/Z reduces signals at 8 weeks

Adapted from Tuzcu, M., et al. (2017). Lutein and zeaxanthin isomers modulates lipid metabolism and the inflammatory state of retina in obesity-induced high-fat diet rodent model. BMC Ophthalmology, 17, 129 under CCBY 4.0

1. D is correct. Following IUPAC rules, we need to identify the highest priority functional group first. Here we have a carbonyl C attached to an –OR group, indicating this molecule is an ester (-oate). Starting with the ester carbon, the Cl atom and 2nd carbonyl group are both on carbon 4.

   B: While the molecule does contain a succinyl group (below), the proper name would be methyl succinyl chloride, as there is a methyl group on the ester.

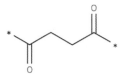

   C: The group contained in the molecule is a succinyl group, not a vinyl group (shown below).

   R

   A: The suffix –one indicates a ketone, which is not the highest priority group shown.

2. C is correct. The nucleotide shown is thymine. While we do not necessarily have to memorize the exact structures of the nucleotide bases, at the very least we should be able to distinguish purines (2-ring structure, A, G) from the pyrimidines (1-ring structure, C, T, U). Thus, we can eliminate A and R. According to Table 1, B identifies any nucleotide that is not A.

3. A is correct. The drug contains a phenyl group (2, benzene as a substituent), a urethane (1, an organic compound with both ester and amide groups with the formula NR_2COOR), and an alkyne (3, two C atoms triple bonded to each other). An aldehyde (RCOH) is not on efavirenz. While the test makers do NOT necessarily expect us to know what a carbamate/urethane is, they DO expect us to recognize the other groups, and recognize that an aldehyde is absent.

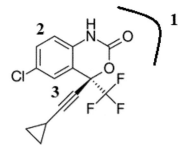

4. B is correct. Glucose and galactose are an example of epimers, a special sub-category of diastereomers in which 2 sugars differ at exactly 1 of their stereocenters (here it is carbon 4).

    A: Enantiomers are a pair of molecules with the same formula, same atomic connections, but are non-superimposable mirror images of each other, like our hands (e.g. they have opposite configurations at all their chiral centers).
    C: Cis/trans isomers are molecules which share the same formula, the same connections, but differ in the orientation around a π bond (e.g. cis- and trans- but-2-ene).
    D: Structural isomers are molecules which share the same molecular formula, but contain entirely different functional groups (e.g. butane and 2-methyl propane).

5. A is correct. The hydrocarbon chains between the terminal rings on L/Z are conjugated. A conjugated system is a system of connected p-orbitals with delocalized electrons in molecules with alternating single and π bonds. This helps to lower the overall energy of the molecule and increase stability. The electrons that can contribute to the delocalization may come from: a carbon (or other atom) with an empty p orbital (a carbocation like carbenium, CH_3^+); a carbon with a half-filled p orbital (radicals); a carbon with a lone pair (carbanion); any atom with a lone pair (N, O, etc.) Only π bonds are on L/Z.

6. B is correct. The figure shows the 2 sugars α- and β-D-glucopyranose undergoing mutarotation. Mutarotation is the change in specific rotation of a chiral compound (usually a carbohydrate) due to epimerization. The sugars ring opens up, and rearranges the orientation at the anomeric carbon.

    A: Resonance involves the rearranging of valence electrons from one atom to another. That is not happening during mutarotation.
    C: Constitutional isomers, also known as structural isomers, will have completely different functional groups.
    D: Conformational isomers are molecules which have the same molecular formula, the same connections, yet are comprised of bonds that are freely rotatable (e.g. σ bonds) so substituents will rotate around these bonds and assume multiple conformations of the same molecule, depending on the electron clouds of their substituents (e.g. eclipsed versus staggered butane, as seen in Newman projections).

7. D is correct. Examining the chiral center on the ionone ring, we must first identify and prioritize the 4 substituents attached to this carbon.

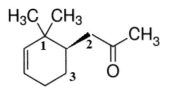

    We can see that as we progress from high to low priority (1 → 2 → 3), we are moving in the clockwise direction, indicating the R designation. Finally, check to see where the lowest priority substituent is. Here it is the undrawn H atom, behind the ring. Since the 4th priority substituent is facing away from us, we can keep our absolute configuration as R.

    A, B: E and Z are isomer designations used for poly-substituted alkenes, not chiral centers.

Independent Questions

1. The structure of GABA, a neurotransmitter, is shown below:

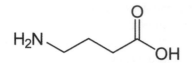

What is the IUPAC name for GABA?

A. 4-amino-1-carboxypropane
B. 3-aminopropanoic acid
C. 4-aminobutanoic acid
D. *gamma*-aminobutyric acid

2. A chemist is conducting a reaction involving the use of aluminum chloride, a strong Lewis acid. To minimize side reactions and maximize yield, the chemist should use which solvent(s)?
A. Aqueous methanol
B. Hexane and heptane
C. Aqueous acetic acid
D. Liquid ammonia

3. The shortest carbon-carbon bond is present in which of the following molecules?
A. Benzene
B. Ethyne
C. 2-methylpropan-2-ol
D. Propene

4. Which of the following is the most nucleophilic?
A. Potassium benzoate
B. Potassium cyanide
C. Sodium *tert*-butoxide
D. Pyridine (C_5H_5N)

5. The carbon-carbon single bond in ethane measures approximately 1.5 Å, and the carbon-carbon double bond in ethene measures approximately 1.3 Å. Which of the following accurately describes the carbon-carbon bonds in benzene?
A. They have bond lengths that are greater than 1.5 Å.
B. They have bond lengths that are less than 1.3 Å.
C. They have bond lengths between 1.3 Å and 1.5 Å.
D. At any given instant, half of the bonds are approximately 1.3 Å long and half are 1.5 Å long.

6. The acidity of a given proton in a molecule decreases as the strength of the covalent bond connecting that hydrogen to the rest of the molecule increases. Which of the following ethanol derivatives has the most acidic proton?
A. 2,2-dimethylpropan-1-ol
B. 2,2,2-tribromoethanol
C. 2,2,2-trichloroethanol
D. 2,2,2-trifluoroethanol

7. Suppose a chemistry student sketches the structure of propa-1,2-diene. The student depicts the entire molecule lying in a single plane. This depiction is:
A. accurate, because double bonds are rigid and do not freely rotate.
B. accurate, because a conjugated π system requires parallel π orbitals.
C. inaccurate, because two π orbitals derived from the same carbon atom cannot be parallel.
D. inaccurate, because the sp^2 hybridized carbon atoms have trigonal pyramidal geometry.

8. Which of the following are constitutional isomers?
A. *n*-pentane and neopentane (2,2-dimethylpropane)
B. Cyclohexane and benzene
C. Levothyroxine and dextrothyroxine
D. Ethanol and isopropanol (C_3H_8O)

NUMBER OF CARBONS	STRAIGHT-CHAIN ISOMER			BRANCHED ISOMER		
	Name (formula)	Structure	Boiling point	Name (formula)	Structure	Boiling point
1	Methane (CH_4)	H–C–H (with H above and below)	−161°C	None		
2	Ethane (C_2H_6)	H_3C-CH_3	−89°C			
3	Propane (C_2H_8)	(structure)	−42°C			
4	Butane (C_4H_{10})	(structure)	−1°C	2-Methylpropane (C_4H_{10})	(structure)	−12°C
5	Pentane (C_5H_{12})	(structure)	36°C	2,2-Dimethylpropane (C_5H_{12})	(structure)	9°C
6	Hexane (C_6H_{14})	(structure)	68°C	2,3-Dimethylbutane (C_6H_{14})	(structure)	58°C

Table 2. Boiling points of alkanes according to molecular weight and branchedness.

Hydrocarbons have no acid-base chemistry to speak of. They are very stable and not particularly reactive molecules, and show no meaningful tendency to become protonated or deprotonated. For example, the pK_a of pentane is approximately 45, which means that in an entire mole of pentane, comprising 6.02×10^{23} molecules (an almost unfathomably large number, corresponding to roughly 81 *trillion* times the current population of earth), you could expect to find literally about 20 protons at a given time. This means that spontaneous dissociation of pentane into H+ and its conjugate base is extraordinarily rare. (You may remember from organic chemistry class that terminal alkynes, although still extremely weak acids, can be deprotonated by strong bases in reactions used to make new carbon-carbon bonds, but this is not tested on the MCAT).

Haloalkanes, or alkyl halides, are alkanes with halogen substituents (F, Cl, Br, or I). They can be made from alkanes through a free-radical mechanism, from alkenes through hydrohalogenation, or from alcohols through substitution with hydrogen halides, as shown in Figure 1.

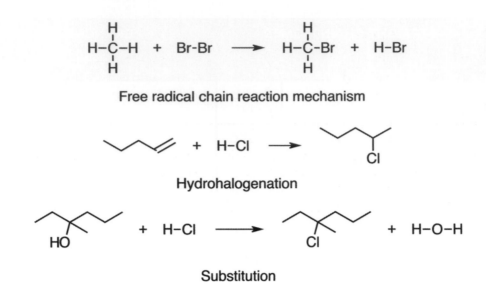

Free radical chain reaction mechanism

Hydrohalogenation

Substitution

Figure 1. Formation of haloalkanes.

Haloalkanes are mostly of note for the MCAT because they are quite reactive and readily undergo substitution and elimination reactions because halogens are generally excellent leaving groups. Since halogens are highly electronegative, the carbon attached to the halogen substituent becomes electron-deficient, making it an electrophile. Figure 3 shows examples of substitution and elimination reactions in which haloalkanes are used to generate alcohols and alkenes, respectively. The mechanisms of these reactions are discussed in more detail in Chapter 11.

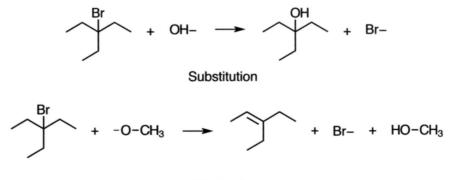

Substitution

Elimination

Figure 2. Substitution and elimination reactions of haloalkanes.

Alkenes are largely important for MCAT organic chemistry for two main reasons that have little to nothing to do with their reactivity. First, alkenes and alkene derivatives are the prototypical examples used to illustrate E/Z (cis/trans) isomerism, as discussed in Chapter 9. Second, molecules with alternating C=C double bonds form conjugated systems of bonds, which involve connected p-orbitals with delocalized electrons. Conjugated systems are often visualized well in ultraviolet (UV) spectroscopy, as discussed in greater detail in Chapter 12.

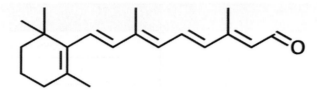

Figure 3. Molecule with a conjugated system (retinal).

Similarly to alkanes, alkenes are involved in some reactions that are relevant for the MCAT not primarily because of their products—the current MCAT does not actually test any alkene-specific reactions—but because they provide a simple case of useful principles that can be applied to other, more complicated reactions. In particular, alkenes provide a useful example illustrating how to think about reduction and oxidation in organic chemistry. For example, alkenes can be reduced in a process known as hydrogenation, in which an alkene reacts with H_2 in the presence of a catalyst (usually Ni, Pd, or Pt) to form an alkane. Alkenes can also be oxidized in a variety of ways. One example is the reaction of alkenes with cold, dilute $KMnO_4$ to form a 1,2-diol. These reactions are shown in Figure 4.

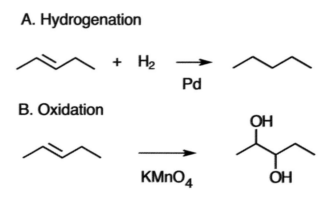

Figure 4. (A) Hydrogenation of an alkene. (B) Oxidation of an alkene with cold, dilute $KMnO_4$.

The results of these reactions are not particularly important for the MCAT. The more important question is why the reaction in Figure 4A is reduction, while the reaction in Figure 4B is oxidation. In Figure 4A, each carbon breaks a C–C bond and forms a C–H bond, meaning its oxidation state decreases (reduction). In Figure 4B, a C–C bond is broken and a C–O bond is formed, meaning that the oxidation state of carbon increases (oxidation). Working through oxidation state changes for each reaction can be time-consuming, so it may be helpful to learn the following equivalent definitions for reduction and oxidation in the context of organic chemistry.

REDUCTION	OXIDATION
Gain of an electron	Loss of an electron
Decreased oxidation state	Increased oxidation state
Formation of a C–H bond (e.g., alkene → alkane)	Loss of a C–H bond (e.g., alkane → alkene)
Loss of a C–O or C–N bond (or any bond between carbon and an electronegative atom)	Gain of a C–O or C–N bond (or any bond between carbon and an electronegative atom)

Table 2. Reduction and oxidation in organic chemistry.

2. Alcohols

Alcohols have the functional group –OH, also known as a hydroxyl group. In IUPAC nomenclature, alcohols are denoted using the suffix –ol, while hydroxyl substituents in molecules with other, higher-priority functional groups are named using the prefix hydroxy-. In common nomenclature, the alcohol group can be denoted using an –yl suffix, followed by "alcohol," such that "ethyl alcohol" is the common name for ethanol.

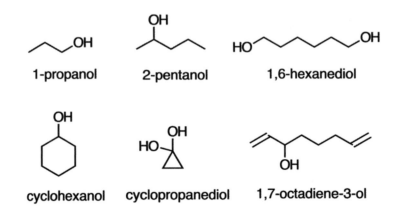

Figure 5. Examples of alcohols.

Throughout this chapter, we will want to pay attention to a special set of alcohols, in which a hydroxyl group is added to an aromatic benzene ring. These compounds are known as phenols, and have special nomenclature, as well as distinct chemical and physical properties due to the ability of resonance to stabilize the conjugate base forms of these molecules (known as phenoxides). The terms *ortho* (*o*), *meta* (*m*), and *para* (*p*) are used to describe the orientation of two substituents on a benzene ring with regard to each other. Let's consider examples of phenols with an additional substituent. If the additional substituent is adjacent to the phenol, then the molecule is described as *ortho* (*o*). If the additional substituent and the phenol are separated by a single carbon, the molecule can be described as *meta* (*m*), while *para* (*p*) is used to describe substituents on the opposite sides of the benzene ring, separated by two carbons. Examples of this are given in Figure 6.

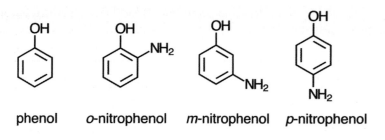

Figure 6. Examples of phenols.

Alcohols have high melting and boiling points because they readily undergo hydrogen bonding. This effect increases with additional hydroxyl groups, as shown in Table 3.

STRUCTURE	NUMBER OF HYDROXYL GROUPS	BOILING POINT
Pentane	0	36.1°C
2-Pentanol	1	119.3°C
1,5-Pentanediol	2	242°C
1,3,5-Pentanetriol	3	320.2°C

Table 3. Melting points of alcohols.

In general, alcohols are weakly acidic, and their conjugate bases (alkoxides) are weak bases. Alcohols tend to have pK_a values in the range of 15-17, making them weaker acids than water (pK_a = 14). However, phenols are notably more acidic due to resonance stabilization of the conjugate base; for example, phenol itself has a pK_a of approximately 10, which makes it a weak acid, but one that is strong enough to be relevant for acid-base chemistry. The acidity of alcohols (and phenols) can be increased by adding electron-withdrawing substituents that help stabilize the negative charge on the conjugate base, or decreased by adding electron-donating substituents. This is technically true of all acids and bases, but alcohols are an especially good example because of the very wide range of pK_a values that can be generated this way. For example, 2,4-dinitrophenol (which contains two electron-withdrawing groups) has a pK_a of 4.11. This pK_a value is still weakly acidic, technically speaking, but is more than low enough for 2,4-dinitrophenol to be meaningfully acidic in biological contexts. For comparison, the pK_a values of the side chains of aspartic acid and glutamic acid are 3.9 and 4.07, respectively, and that of acetic acid is 4.76.

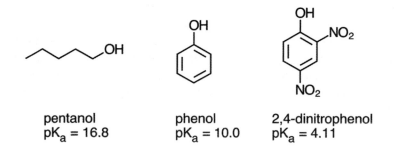

pentanol
pK_a = 16.8

phenol
pK_a = 10.0

2,4-dinitrophenol
pK_a = 4.11

Figure 7. Alcohols with various pK_a values.

To summarize, there are two basic things to understand about the physical and chemical properties of alcohols: (1) hydrogen bonding, (2) weak but modifiable acidity.

The largest set of MCAT-relevant reactions involving alcohols is oxidation. In this context, oxidation means the conversion of a hydroxyl group bound to a carbon to a carbonyl group (C=O, corresponding to either an aldehyde or ketone depending on its location within the molecule) or a carboxylic acid (COOH). Oxidation of an alcohol can be thought of as proceeding in two steps: first, oxidation to a carbonyl group, and then further oxidation to a carboxylic acid. The outcome of the oxidation of alcohols depends on whether the alcohol is primary or secondary and on the oxidizing agent that is used.

MCAT STRATEGY >>>

If you see a primary alcohol oxidized to an aldehyde (terminal C=O) on the MCAT, the oxidizing agent must have been PCC.

Pyridium chlorochromate (PCC) is a weak oxidizing agent that turns C–OH groups into carbonyl (C=O) groups. When applied to a primary alcohol, this results in an aldehyde, whereas a ketone results when a secondary alcohol is treated with PCC.

Stronger oxidizing agents, such as $NaCr_2O_7$, $K_2Cr_2O_7$, and CrO_3, oxidize primary alcohols to carboxylic acids. When applied to secondary alcohols, they result in ketones, because the oxidation process can go no further in that location.

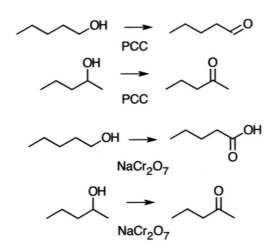

Figure 8. Oxidation of alcohols.

The oxidation of certain phenols is biologically relevant, although the actual chemistry is not meaningfully different than how other alcohols are oxidized. The molecule *p*-benzenediol is additionally known as hydroquinone, and when it is oxidized, it becomes quinone (2,5-cyclohexadiene-1,4-dione). Note that quinone itself is *not* an aromatic molecule, although it undergoes resonance stabilization when acting as an electrophile and it is entirely possible for derivatives of quinone to contain aromatic rings. Derivatives of quinone are known as quinones, and form a class of biologically important molecules that generally serve as electron acceptors.

An especially important example of a biologically important quinone is ubiquinone, also known as coenzyme Q. Ubiquinone is an electron carrier involved in complexes I, II, and III of the electron transport chain. Its amphipathic structure (polar head and long alkyl tail) allows it to be both lipid-soluble and a functional electron carrier. When carrying one electron, one of its carbonyl (C=O) groups is reduced to an alcohol, resulting in a molecule known as ubisemiquinone, and when carrying two electrons—as is commonly the case—both carbonyl (C=O) groups are reduced, and the molecule is known as ubiquinol. Similar reactions underpin the function of other biological electron carriers, such as NAD^+/NADH and FAD/FADH/$FADH_2$.

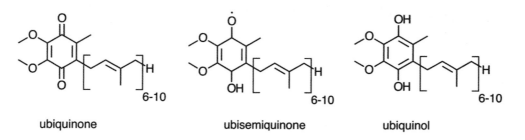

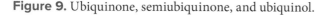

ubiquinone ubisemiquinone ubiquinol

Figure 9. Ubiquinone, semiubiquinone, and ubiquinol.

Alcohols are generally fairly reactive molecules, and in organic synthesis processes it may become necessary to "protect" an alcohol group to ensure that another functional group on a molecule undergoes a reaction without involving the alcohol group. Consider the example shown in Figure 10, where we have a molecule with an alkene group and a hydroxyl group, and we want to use HCl to carry out hydrohalogenation of the alkene group. How do we prevent HCl from engaging in a substitution reaction to replace the –OH group with –Cl, potentially resulting in a complex mixture of products?

The answer to this dilemma is to protect the –OH group by reversibly treating it with another compound that makes the –OH group non-reactive. Once the desired reaction is completed, the protecting group can be removed. Many types of protecting groups have been developed, but there are three major classes that you should be aware of for the MCAT: silyl ethers, mesylates, and tosylates. Silyl ethers involve a Si–O bond that can be broken with fluoride after the desired reaction is completed. Mesylates and tosylates are formed by reacting the alcohol with methylsulfonyl chloride and toluenesulfonyl chloride, respectively. Mesylates and tosylates are also good leaving groups, so the effect of treating alcohols with methylsulfonyl chloride or toluenesulfonyl chloride may be either to protect them or to facilitate a substitution reaction in which the hydroxyl group is replaced by something else. The specific outcome depends on details of the reaction setup that are beyond the scope of the MCAT.

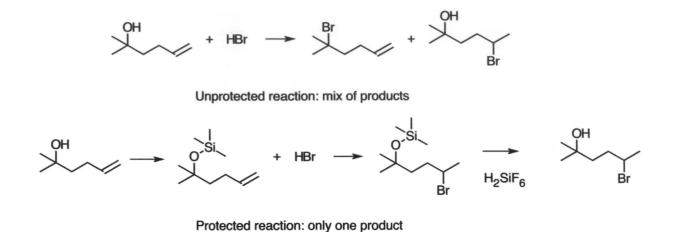

Unprotected reaction: mix of products

Protected reaction: only one product

Figure 10. Unprotected and protected hydrohalogenation reactions.

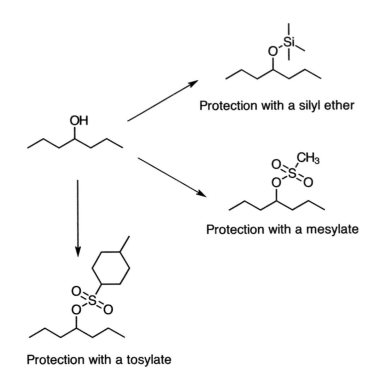

Protection with a silyl ether

Protection with a mesylate

Protection with a tosylate

Figure 11. Alcohols protected with silyl ethers, mesylates, and tosylates.

In addition to being protected, alcohols can also be used to protect other functional groups. Consider the compound in Figure 12. Imagine that we want to reduce the carboxylic acid functional group (–COOH) to an alcohol using LiAlH$_4$, while not affecting the carbonyl group (C=O). The challenge here is that LiAlH$_4$ is capable of reducing both groups. Treatment of the carbonyl carbon with two equivalents of an alcohol (often accomplished by using a single equivalent of a diol) results in the formation of an acetal group, which is not affected by LiAlH$_4$ and can easily be removed under acidic conditions after the carboxylic acid functional group is reduced.

Desired reaction:

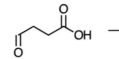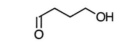

Unprotected:

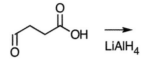

LiAlH$_4$

Both functional
groups reduced

Protected using a diol to form an acetal:

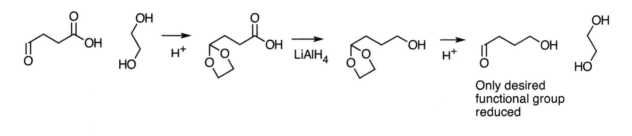

LiAlH$_4$

H$^+$

Only desired
functional group
reduced

Figure 12. Protection using acetals.

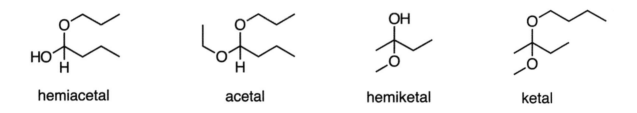

hemiacetal   acetal   hemiketal   ketal

Figure 13. Acetals, hemiacetals, ketals, and hemiketals.

As shown in Figure 13, the central C atom in acetals is connected to one H, one R group (R$_1$, corresponding to the rest of the molecule's structure), and two OR groups (OR$_2$ and OR$_3$, where R$_2$ and R$_3$ are structures that start with another C). Hemiacetals are an intermediate step in the formation of acetals and include one –OH group in place of one of the two OR groups found in acetals. Ketals and hemiketals are the corresponding structures for ketones. In laboratory conditions, hemiacetals are often very unstable and quickly proceed to acetals. However, cyclic hemiacetals and hemiketals are common in sugar chemistry, corresponding to the cyclic forms of glucose and fructose, correspondingly.

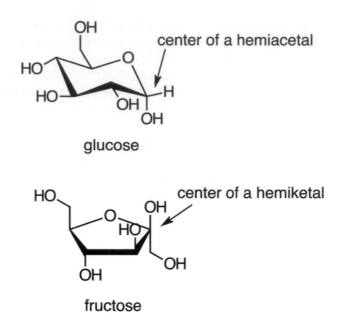

center of a hemiacetal

glucose

center of a hemiketal

fructose

Figure 14. Cyclic forms of glucose and fructose as hemiacetals and hemiketals.

> > CONNECTIONS < <

Chapter 6 of Biochemistry

3. Aldehydes and Ketones

Aldehydes and ketones are defined by the presence of a carbonyl (C=O) group; in aldehydes, the carbonyl group is terminal (at the end of the molecule), while in ketones, it occurs within the molecule proper. Aldehydes end in the suffix –al, and ketones end in the suffix –one. If an aldehyde is attached to a ring, the suffix –carbaldehyde may be used instead. The prefix –oxo is used if another, higher-priority functional group is present, although –keto may be used in some biological contexts. For some ketones, the traditional name is still generally used; the most common example of this is acetone, the simplest ketone.

hexanal

3-oxobutanoic acid
(common name:
acetoacetic acid)

2-hexanone

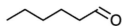

cyclopentanecarbaldehyde

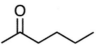

cyclooctanone

Figure 15. Nomenclature and structures of aldehydes and ketones.

The physical and chemical properties of aldehydes and ketones are determined by the carbonyl group. The carbonyl group contains a strong dipole, meaning that aldehydes and ketones experience dipole-dipole interactions. This raises their melting and boiling points compared to alkanes, but these interactions are not as strong as the hydrogen bonding that is characteristic of alcohols. Therefore, the melting/boiling points of aldehydes and ketones are between those of alkanes and alcohols. For example, the boiling point of pentanal is 102°C, which is much higher than that of pentane (31.6°C), but also markedly lower than that of 1-pentanol (137°C).

In terms of acidity and basicity, the action for aldehydes and ketones takes place with the α-hydrogen—that is, hydrogens attached to carbons adjacent to the carbonyl carbon. (Recall that the α-carbon is adjacent to a functional group, the β-carbon is one carbon removed from a functional group, and so on for γ and δ if needed). At first this may seem puzzling, because hydrogens on alkyl chains are not generally acidic. What makes the α-hydrogen on aldehydes and ketones special? The answer is resonance stabilization. Removal of the α-hydrogen generates a negative charge on the carbon, resulting in a carbanion. However, in aldehydes and ketones, resonance can stabilize this negative charge by shifting it onto the carbonyl oxygen in some of the major resonance contributors to the deprotonated molecule. This structure is known as an enolate, because these major resonance contributors can be thought of as having a double C=C bond and a deprotonated hydroxyl group (with the negative charge on the oxygen).

Figure 16. Resonance stabilization of an enolate.

These α-hydrogens are still only weakly acidic; their pK$_a$ values tend to be in the range of 17-19, which is still less acidic than water. The α-hydrogens of ketones tend to be less acidic than those of aldehydes due to the electron-donating effects of the additional alkyl substituent in ketones. However, these hydrogens are just acidic enough to be removed by an extremely strong base (such as NaH), which is the initial step in many reactions involving carbanions. Additionally, in β-dicarbonyl compounds (that is, compounds with two carbonyl groups separated by a carbon), the pK$_a$ value of the α-hydrogen between the two carbonyl groups can be as low as 9, which is reasonably acidic for a weak organic acid and certainly acidic enough to be protonated by a regular strong base, such as NaOH. The reason for this is that the presence of two adjacent carbonyl groups increases the extent of resonance stabilization, and the electron-withdrawing effects of the carbonyl oxygen also help to stabilize the additional negative charge.

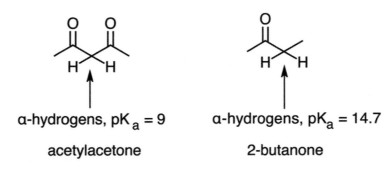

Figure 17. Structures and pK$_a$ values of selected α-hydrogens (acetylacetone and 2-butanone).

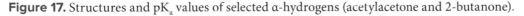

MCAT STRATEGY > > >

Trends in the acidity of α-hydrogens are useful because they illustrate two general trends that you can apply when reasoning about molecules you've never seen before. First, electron-donating groups, such as alkyl substituents, stabilize positive charges (e.g., carbocations) but destabilize negative charges (e.g., carbanions). Second, resonance plays a role in delocalizing and stabilizing charges, and the more contributing resonance structures present, the greater the effect can be expected to be.

Aldehydes and ketones are involved in a broad range of reactions that you are expected to be familiar with on Test Day. A special feature of aldehydes and ketones is that they can act as nucleophiles and electrophiles, depending on the reaction. This statement may seem surprising at first, but it contains nothing paradoxical. Because the α-hydrogens of aldehydes and ketones are acidic, reactions can take place in two locations: the carbonyl carbon, which has a δ+ charge due to the adjacent oxygen and therefore acts as an electrophile, and the α-carbon of a carbanion, which has a negative charge and therefore acts as a nucleophile. These mechanisms are explained in more detail in Chapter 11; however, it is worth noting that in reactions involving the carbonyl carbon, aldehydes tend to be somewhat more reactive than ketones due to the steric hindrance imposed by the additional R group in ketones compared to the –H in aldehydes.

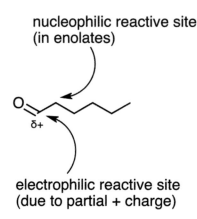

nucleophilic reactive site
(in enolates)

δ+

electrophilic reactive site
(due to partial + charge)

Figure 18. Nucleophilic and electrophilic sites in aldehydes and ketones.

Aldehydes and ketones can be thought of as occupying an intermediate place on the spectrum of oxidation and reduction between alcohols (most reduced) and carboxylic acids (most oxidized). Aldehydes can be further oxidized to carboxylic acids by any oxidizing agent stronger than PCC, with common examples including $Na_2Cr_2O_7$, $K_2Cr_2O_7$, CrO_3, $KMnO_4$, Ag_2O, and H_2O_2. Ketones cannot be further oxidized because it would be impossible to do so without breaking a C–C bond. Aldehydes and ketones can be reduced to alcohols both by $NaBH_4$, a milder reducing agent, and $LiAlH_4$, a stronger reducing agent.

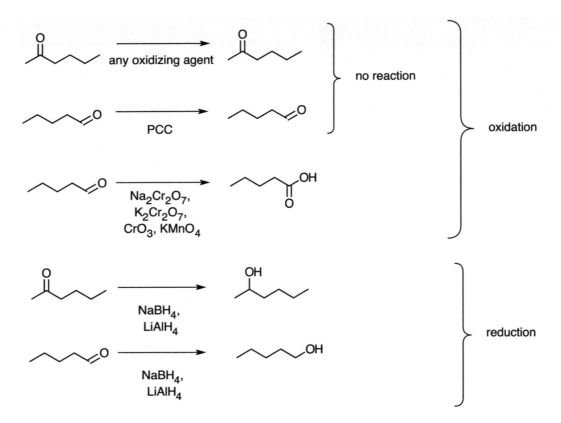

Figure 19. Oxidation and reduction of aldehydes and ketones.

Aldehydes and ketones undergo several reactions in which a nucleophile attacks the carbonyl carbon and either adds a substituent or replaces the carbonyl oxygen. These reactions are summarized below in Table 4 and illustrated in Figure 20.

NUCLEOPHILE	WHAT HAPPENS?	PRODUCT	NOTES
Water (H_2O)	H_2O adds to the carbonyl C.	Geminal diol (two —OH groups on the carbonyl C)	This process is referred to as hydration.
Alcohol (ROH)	ROH adds to the carbonyl C; in second round of addition the original carbonyl O is protonated and leaves.	Hemiacetal/hemiketal (one equivalent of ROH), acetal/ketal (two equivalents of ROH)	In laboratory conditions, reaction usually goes to completion and acetals/ketals are formed.
Hydride reagents ($NaBH_4$, $LiAlH_4$)	Hydrogen is added to the carbonyl group	Alcohol	This is how aldehydes and ketones are reduced.
Amine (NH_3, etc.)	The nitrogen from the amine "replaces" the carbonyl oxygen; a C = N double bond is formed.	Imine	Imines undergo tautomerization and form an equilibrium with enamines, as discussed in section 5.
Hydrogen cyanide (HCN)	The carbon in the deprotonated CN^- (cyanide) ion adds to the carbonyl carbon.	Cyanohydrin (former carbonyl carbon now has an —OH group and a —C≡N group)	

Table 4. Nucleophilic addition reactions to the carbonyl carbon.

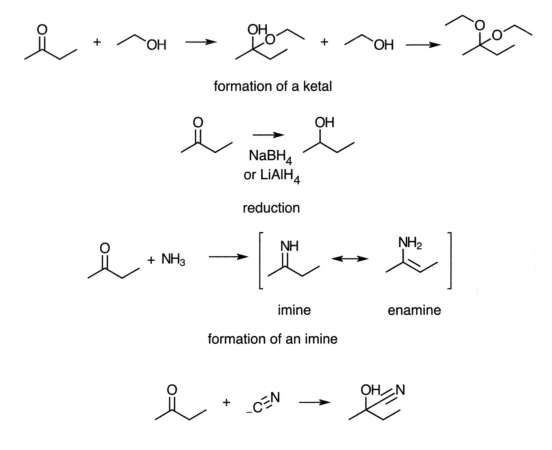

Figure 20. Nucleophilic addition reactions to the carbonyl carbon.

Aldehydes and ketones also undergo a set of important reactions involving the α-carbon. Before exploring these reactions, it is necessary to cover some prerequisites. The acidity of the α-hydrogens enables ketones to undergo keto-enol tautomerization; that is, an equilibrium process in which ketones convert between keto forms (the standard structural representation of a ketone) and enol forms, which have a C=C double bond (hence the "en" part of the name, like "alkene") and a –OH group attached to the carbonyl carbon (like an alcohol, hence the "ol" part of "enol"). In most cases, the keto tautomer is predominant under standard conditions, with the notable exceptions of phenols, in which the enol form is stabilized by the aromatic ring. This process means that any aldehyde or ketone with a chiral α-carbon will be converted into a racemic mixture due to the interconversion between the aldehyde and ketone forms. This process is known as α-racemization.

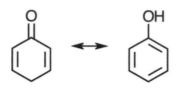

Figure 21. Keto-enol tautomerization.

Keto-enol tautomerization is a relatively higher-yield topic within this subject area, because it involves a relatively limited amount of knowledge that can either be tested directly, resulting in straightforward discrete or pseudodiscrete questions, or applied to solve passage-based questions.

So far, we have not discussed where the double bond is formed in an enol isomer or an enolate (it is often more useful to discuss this process in terms of enolates, which can be thought of as both the deprotonated version of an enol and the major resonance contributor to the carbanion generated by removing the α-hydrogen). For symmetric compounds like acetone, this is irrelevant—although we could imagine drawing the double bond on either the left or the right side of the oxygen, that would not correspond to any actual chemical difference. However, for asymmetric ketones, this does correspond to a real difference between two enolate compounds.

It turns out that different enolates are favored in different reaction conditions, with corresponding implications for the eventual products of the reaction. A distinction is made between kinetically favored and thermodynamically favored enolates. By definition, the kinetically favored enolate is formed more quickly but is less stable over the long term. In kinetically favored enolates, the double bond tends to involve the less substituted carbon because less steric hindrance is present. Therefore, kinetic control tends to exist in reactions that are rapid and irreversible, are conducted at low temperatures, and use strong and sterically hindered bases to deprotonate the α-hydrogen (because those bases will tend to favor the less sterically hindered α-carbon). In contrast, thermodynamically favored enolates form less quickly, but are more stable over the long term. Thermodynamic control generally leads to the double bond being present between the carbonyl carbon and the more substituted α-carbon, and is favored with the opposite set of conditions: high temperatures, weaker and less sterically hindered bases, and slower and more reversible reaction conditions that allow the formation of the product that is ultimately more stable.

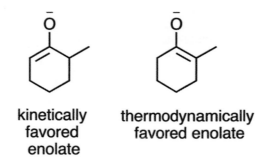

kinetically
favored
enolate

thermodynamically
favored enolate

Figure 22. Kinetic versus thermodynamic control.

Aldehydes and ketones can react with each other in an important reaction known as aldol condensation. The basic mechanism involves the nucleophilic enolate ion of one aldehyde/ketone attacking the electrophilic carbonyl carbon of the other. The molecules join together, and the immediate result is an aldol—that is, a molecule that combines the features of an aldehyde (or ketone) and an alcohol—and is technically known as a β-hydroxyaldehyde or β-hydroxyketone. This simply refers to the fact that there is a single carbon separating the carbonyl and hydroxyl functional groups.

That accounts for the "aldol" part of "aldol condensation," but what about the "condensation" part? Condensation refers to the next step in the reaction, in which the –OH is removed through an elimination reaction catalyzed by a strong base, resulting in a compound known as an α,β-unsaturated aldehyde or ketone (where "unsaturated" refers to the presence of a double bond, similarly to the terminology used to discuss fatty acids, and "α,β" specifies the location of the double bond relative to the carbonyl group), or as a conjugated enone (where "conjugated" describes the alternating double bonds present in the molecule and "enone" describes the alk*ene* and ket*one* functionalities of the molecule).

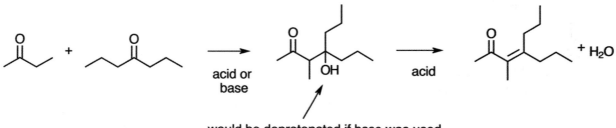

acid or
base

would be deprotonated if base was used

acid

+ H_2O

Figure 23. Aldol condensation.

The aldol condensation process is reversible, and the reverse reaction is known as the retro-aldol reaction. It has the effect of breaking the bonds between the α and β-carbons of an aldehyde or ketone. In laboratory conditions, it is favored by high temperatures and basic conditions, and in physiological conditions can be catalyzed. It actually takes place in the fourth step of glycolysis, in which fructose-1,6-bisphosphate is cleaved by fructose-bisphosphate aldolase to form glyceraldehyde-3-phosphate and dihydroxyacetone phosphate, which are both ultimately converted to pyruvate in later steps of the pathway.

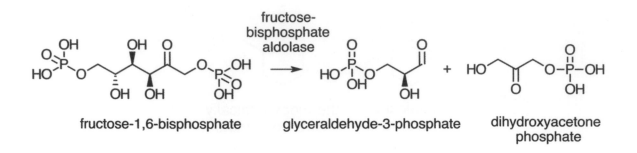

Figure 24. Retro-aldol reaction in glycolysis.

4. Carboxylic Acids and Derivatives

Along with aldehydes and ketones, carboxylic acids and their derivatives are among the most important functional groups for the MCAT. They are especially relevant for the biochemistry of amino acids and proteins, two perennial high-yield biochemistry topics.

> **MCAT STRATEGY > > >**
>
> The key to working through aldol condensation/retro-aldol problems on Test Day is to stay calm and work through the geometry of the molecules carefully. Remember the basics, use your scratch paper, and don't panic!

> **> > CONNECTIONS < <**
>
> Chapter 2 of Biochemistry

The nomenclature of carboxylic acids and their derivatives is important to master, because doing so can allow you to answer relatively straightforward questions simply and effectively: Test Day is not the time to get confused about the difference between an amide and an amine, or an ester and an ether!

Carboxylic acids are characterized by a –COOH functional group, while in carboxylic acid derivatives, the –OH is replaced by something else; that is, all carboxylic acid derivatives essentially have a carbonyl group plus *something*, although that something can vary. The carboxylic acid derivatives you must know for the MCAT are amides, esters, and anhydrides.

Carboxylic acids are characterized by the suffix "-oic acid" in IUPAC nomenclature. Many carboxylic acids fall under the biochemical category of fatty acids, and many such carboxylic acids have common names ending in –ic acid; for example, pentanoic acid is also known as valeric acid. The most frequently encountered example of this is likely acetic acid (ethanoic acid), although you should also be prepared to encounter formic acid (methanoic acid) and proprionic acid (propanoic acid). Carboxylic acids have the highest priority of all functional groups in the IUPAC nomenclature system, although the prefix "carboxy-" can be used if needed. Cyclic carboxylic acids are named using the name of the cyclic compound followed by "-carboxylic acid," such as "cyclohexanecarboxylic acid." However, many cyclic carboxylic acids are commonly referred to using common names that you do not have to be aware of for the MCAT. Carboxylic acids with two –COOH groups are referred to with the suffix "-dioic acid."

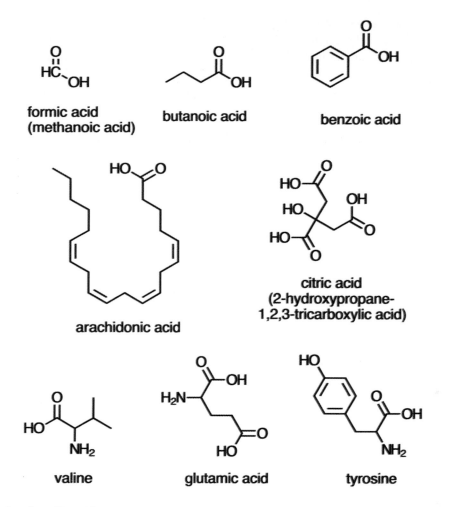

Figure 25. Selected carboxylic acids.

Similarly to alcohols, the physical properties of carboxylic acids are fundamentally defined by their ability to hydrogen-bond. The intermolecular interactions present within carboxylic acids are even stronger than those that take place among alcohols, due to the strong molecular dipole in the carbonyl carbon that is bound to two electronegative oxygen atoms. For instance, the boiling point of 1-pentanol is 137°C, while that of pentanoic acid is 186°C.

Carboxylic acids are quite acidic for organic weak acids, with typical pK_a values in the range of 4-5, with lower values possible in the presence of other structural factors that stabilize the carboxylate ion corresponding to an acid's conjugate base. Additionally, similarly to aldehydes and ketones, the α-hydrogens on the carbon chain can be acidic in certain structures known as β-dicarboxylic acids—that is, molecules with two carboxylic acid functional groups separated by a single carbon. In such molecules, resonance can stabilize the negative charge generated by removing this proton to the point that it is weakly acidic, with pKa values on the order of 9 to 14.

A special case of acid-base chemistry involving carboxylic acids is known as saponification (Latin *sapo* means "soap," so this literally means something like "soapification"). Under basic conditions (e.g., when mixed with NaOH or KOH), carboxylic acids are deprotonated and their conjugate bases form salts, according to the following template: $RCOOH + Na^+ + OH^- \rightarrow RCOO^-Na^+ + H_2O$. The acid-base chemistry of this process is basically straightforward; saponification is mostly of note for historical interest and because its wide range of applications opens the door for it to be introduced as a way of testing organic chemistry and general chemistry principles in a passage on Test Day.

Amides are carboxylic acid derivatives with an amine ($-NH_2$, $-NHR$, or NR_1R_2) attached to the carbonyl carbon instead of the $-OH$ group. Instead of the suffix "-oic acid," they have the suffix "-amide," and substituents attaching to the nitrogen of the amide group are named with *N*. A completely different name exists for cyclic amides; such molecules are known as lactams. Classes of lactams are named using Greek letters to refer to which non-carbonyl carbon binds to the nitrogen atom to form a cyclic structure: lactams where the β-carbon plays this role are known as β-lactams, with other classes of lactams including γ-lactams and δ-lactams. One of the major reasons that the MCAT expects you to be aware of lactams is the fact that β-lactams form a very large class of broad-spectrum antibiotics, including penicillin and its derivatives as well as many other medically important drugs.

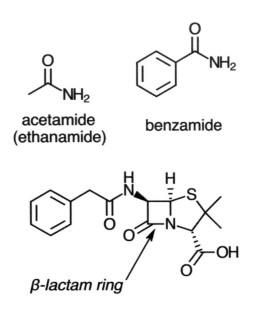

acetamide
(ethanamide)

benzamide

β-lactam ring

penicillin

Figure 26. Selected amides.

The physical properties and acid-base chemistry of amides are strongly dependent on whether the nitrogen atom in the amide has alkyl substituents. In particular, the more hydrogens present on this atom, the greater the degree to which amides can participate in hydrogen bonding. Nonetheless, the intermolecular forces present in amides tend to be weaker than those in carboxylic acid. Thus, pentanamide has a boiling point of approximately 101°C, which is markedly lower than the corresponding values for pentanol (137°C) or pentanoic acid (186°C). If the molecular weight is held constant, the presence of alkyl substituents will tend to reduce the melting/boiling points by reducing the ability of the amide to undergo hydrogen bonding.

Amides are extremely weak bases, to the point that for the purposes of the MCAT you can consider them as essentially not involved in acid-base chemistry. The reason for this is the adjacent carbonyl group and its oxygen, which has two consequences: first, the electronegativity of the oxygen attracts the lone pair of electrons on the amide nitrogen; and second, the lone pair of electrons on the nitrogen is involved in a resonance system with the carbonyl group, delocalizing the electrons. The latter fact about amides is relevant for some of the structural properties of peptide bonds.

> > CONNECTIONS < <

Chapter 2 of Biochemistry

In esters, the $-OH$ group is replaced by an $-OR$ group. The nomenclature of esters is a bit tricky because esters contain two alkyl groups that must be included and differentiated in the nomenclature. The suffix

"-oate" is applied to the main alkyl chain that contains the carbonyl group, and the esterifying group is named as a prefix ending in "-yl." Be sure to practice with this until it becomes familiar, because this is a relatively rare opportunity for the MCAT to ask about nomenclature in a tricky way. Like amides, special nomenclature exists for cyclic esters. Cyclic esters are known as lactones. Similarly to lactams, lactones are named as β-lactones, γ-lactones, and δ-lactones depending on which carbon from the main alkyl chain bonds with the oxygen to form the ester.

> **MCAT STRATEGY > > >**
>
> Keep lactams and lactones straight by remembering that lact*ams* are *amides*, while lact*ones* have oxygen like ket*ones*. Additionally, make sure you don't confuse esters with ethers!

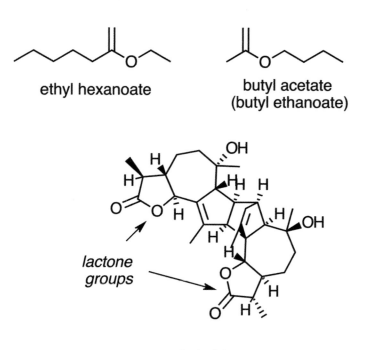

ethyl hexanoate

butyl acetate
(butyl ethanoate)

lactone groups

absinthin

Figure 27. Selected esters.

The physical and chemical properties of esters are generally unremarkable. Their melting and boiling points are relatively low due to their inability to engage in hydrogen bonding; for instance, the boiling point of methyl butanoate is 102°C, which is close to that of pentamide and much less than those of pentanol and pentanoic acid. Esters do not engage in acid-base chemistry to any appreciable extent. However, esters are quite relevant for biochemistry, because triglycerides—which, along with their derivatives, form a major class of lipids—are esters formed between fatty acids and glycerol.

Acid anhydrides are formed by the condensation of two carboxylic acids; that is, the substituent that replaces the –OH of one carboxylic acid is actually another carboxylic acid. Symmetric anhydrides are named by replacing the word "acid" with "anhydride," and asymmetric anhydrides are named by listing the names of the acid chains in alphabetical order with the suffix "-oic," such as butanoic ethanoic anhydride. Cyclic anhydrides do exist, but no special nomenclature exists for them except for a tendency to use common names instead of IUPAC nomenclature, such as phthalic acid (corresponding to the IUPAC name of 2-benzofuran-1,3-dione).

> **> > CONNECTIONS < <**
>
> Chapter 9 of Biochemistry

A strong reducing agent is needed to reduce carboxylic acids to alcohols. For the purposes of the MCAT, this means LiAlH$_4$, *not* NaBH$_4$. It is difficult to reduce carboxylic acids to aldehydes, because this essentially means stopping halfway through the process; NaBH$_4$ is too weak to do any reduction at all, and LiAlH$_4$ is so strong that the reaction will proceed all the way to alcohol formation. A reducing agent known as diisobutylaluminium hydride (DIBAL or DIBALH) can do this, however, but only if care is taken with the stoichiometry to include only one unit of DIBAL for each unit of carboxylic acid.

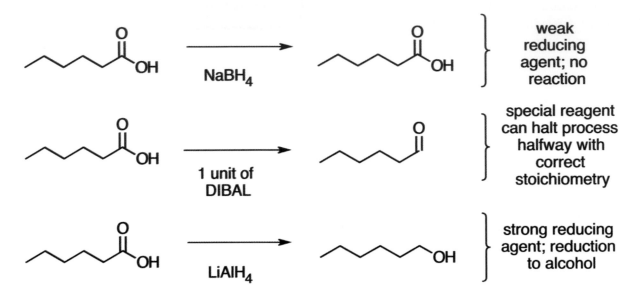

Figure 28. Reduction of carboxylic acids.

Carboxylic acids with another carbonyl group separated by a single carbon (that is, 1,3-dicarboxylic acids and β-ketoacids) can also lose a –COOH group in a process known as decarboxylation, in which the –COOH group is lost as CO_2. This process is favored by high temperatures and can also be significantly upregulated by enzymatic activity. It is a fundamentally important type of reaction in many biochemical pathways, perhaps most notably because it occurs in the conversion of pyruvate to acetyl-CoA and at two points in the Krebs cycle, corresponding to changes in the number of carbons in the substrate. It is also important from a pharmacological perspective; the non-psychoactive compound Δ9-tetrahydrocannabinolic acid found in cannabis undergoes decarboxylation when heated to form the derivative Δ9-tetrahydrocannabinol, which is responsible for the psychoactive effects of cannabis. This is why raw cannabis leaves are non-psychoactive.

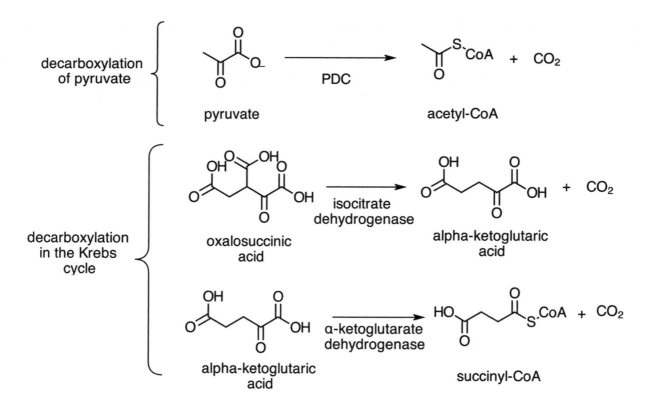

Figure 29. Decarboxylation of pyruvate and Krebs cycle intermediates.

Carboxylic acids undergo many reactions involving nucleophilic substitution at the carbonyl carbon. Unlike aldehydes and ketones, carboxylic acids have an excellent leaving group (–OH), so essentially an appropriate nucleophile can replace the –OH group. This is how the major carboxylic acid derivatives are formed: amides are formed when ammonia or an amine acts as the nucleophile, esters are formed when an alcohol acts as a nucleophile (in a process known as Fischer esterification), and acid anhydrides are formed when a carboxylic acid acts as the nucleophile. These are considered condensation reactions, because in each of these reactions, two larger molecules are joined together with the loss of water. This mechanism is discussed at greater length in Chapter 11, but the schematic results are presented below in Figure 30.

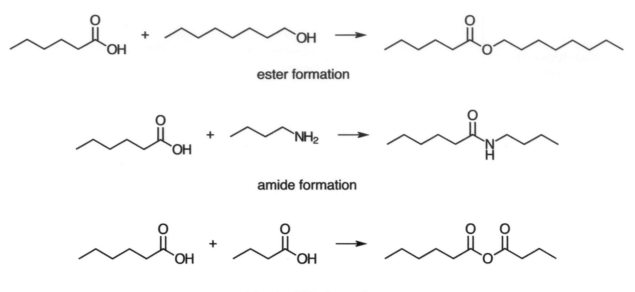

Figure 30. Formation of major carboxylic acid derivatives.

A final reaction involving carboxylic acids to be aware of is Hell-Volhard-Zelinsky halogenation, in which carboxylic acids are halogenated at the α-carbon due to the slight acidity of the α-hydrogen, as discussed above. Using bromination as an example, this reaction occurs by the addition of a catalytic amount of PBr_3 followed by Br_2. First, an acyl halide is formed, in which a –Br substituent replaces the –OH. At this point, keto-enol tautomerism generates an enol form, and the Br_2 can react with the alkene bond of the enol to brominate the α-carbon. The first bromine (the one that replaced the –OH group of the carboxylic acid) is then spontaneously lost.

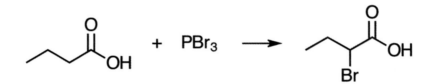

Figure 31. Hell-Volhard-Zelinsky halogenation.

Since carboxylic acid derivatives are closely interrelated molecules, it is not surprising that they can be interconverted among each other. This process follows a scale of reactivity; more reactive carboxylic acid derivatives can be converted to less reactive carboxylic derivatives through nucleophilic substitution, but not vice versa. To "climb" the reactivity scale would be to convert a carboxylic acid derivative back to a carboxylic acid and then generate a new carboxylic acid derivative according to the processes described above. This flow chart is illustrated in Figure 32.

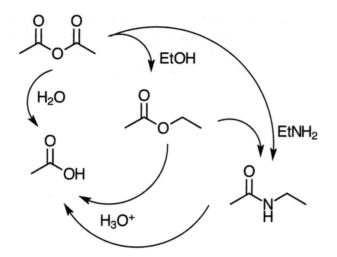

Figure 32. Interconversion of carboxylic acid derivatives.

The relative reactivity of carboxylic acid derivatives can be thought of in terms of how electrophilic the carbonyl carbon is, which in turn reflects the partial positive charge created by adjacent or nearby electron-withdrawing groups. Anhydrides have three nearby electronegative oxygens, while esters have two, and amides have a less strongly electronegative nitrogen atom in place of an oxygen. This consideration affects the general reactivity of these classes of molecules, but when considering the reactivity patterns of a *specific* reaction, it is important to consider steric hindrance as well; steric hindrance will cause carboxylic acid derivatives (and molecules in general) to be less likely to undergo nucleophilic attack.

There are also some special reactions involving carboxylic acid derivatives that you should be aware of for the MCAT. One of these is transesterification, which occurs when an ester is reacted with an alcohol distinct from the original alcohol that makes up the ester (the esterifying group). The result is that these alcohol molecules replace each other, resulting in a different alcohol and a different ester. For example, if ethyl hexanoate reacted with propanol, transesterification would result in propyl hexanoate and ethanol.

Figure 33. Transesterification.

Another reaction to be aware of is the hydrolysis of amides to the parent carboxylic acid and an amine. Hydrolysis is a very common reaction type, and this reaction is not especially remarkable from a strictly mechanistic point of view. However, it is important to be familiar with for two main reasons. First, it is the only interconversion reaction that amides undergo, since amides are the least reactive of carboxylic acid derivatives. Second, and most notably, the hydrolysis of amides is the mechanism involved in breaking peptide bonds in amino acid sequences. Enzymes (peptidases) exist that can catalyze this process with considerable specificity.

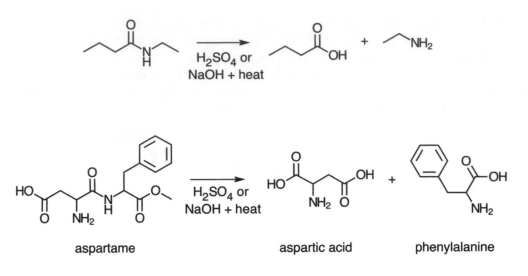

Figure 34. Hydrolysis of an amide.

When attempting to predict the outcome of a reaction involving carboxylic acid derivatives, you should keep the following principles in mind:

1. Relative reactivity. As discussed above, anhydrides > esters > amides. Simple nucleophilic substitution can move you down that scale, but not up.

2. Steric hindrance. Molecules with greater steric hindrance are less likely to undergo nucleophilic substitution reactions.

3. Electronic effects. Electron-withdrawing groups, such as oxygen, tend to make the carbonyl carbon more reactive. Resonance can stabilize negative charges, increasing (for example) the acidity of carboxylic acids both at the –OH group and at the α-hydrogen.

4. Strain. In cyclic molecules, ring strain increases reactivity. An example of this is provided by β-lactam antibiotics; as shown in Figure 26, β-lactam molecules have a strained 4-member ring, which is an important reactive site both for how they interact with penicillin-binding proteins to inhibit peptidoglycan sequence and for how they are cleaved by β-lactamase enzymes that provide bacteria with resistance to these drugs.

5. Amines, Imines, and Enamines

Amines, imines, and enamines are nitrogen-containing compounds. Amines are actually not included on the list of key functional groups that you are expected to know as part of the organic chemistry content of the MCAT, but they are nonetheless important for two reasons. First, they occur as precursors of several structures that you are responsible for, such as amides. Second, they are very important in biochemistry, because a knowledge of the properties of amines is essential for understanding the structure and function of amino acids.

Amines are derivatives of ammonia (NH_3), in which one or more of the hydrogens are replaced by a *single bond* to an organic substituent. They are named with the suffix "-amine" or the prefix "amino-" if a higher-priority functional group is present. Amines undergo hydrogen bonding unless all three hydrogen atoms are replaced by organic substituents, and they therefore generally have moderately high melting and boiling points. For instance, the boiling point of pentylamine is approximately 94-110°C, which is in the range of that of pentanal (102°C), much higher than that of pentane (31.6°C), but also much lower than that of 1-pentanol (137°C).

Amines are weak bases, as they contain a lone pair of electrons. However, alkyl amines, in which the organic substituents are alkyl groups, are distinguished from aryl amines, which have an aromatic substituent. This is similar to the distinction between alcohols and phenols. Aromatic amines, such as aniline (shown in Figure 35) are less basic than typical alkyl amines. The reason for this is that the lone pair of electrons is delocalized throughout the resonance structure of the aromatic ring; essentially, the aromatic rings provides support for that lone pair, such that the nitrogen doesn't "want" to use it to pick up an extra hydrogen in an acid-base reaction.

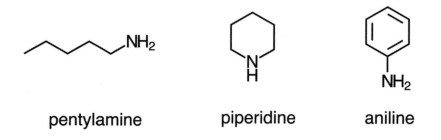

Figure 35. Amines (including aniline).

Amines are defined by single bonds between nitrogen and carbon. In contrast, imines are characterized by a C = N double bond. You should think of them as being analogous to carbonyl groups; like oxygen, nitrogen has at least one available lone pair in many organic contexts and is more electronegative than carbon. As discussed in section 3, imines are formed from carbonyl groups. The analogy with oxygen-containing compounds can be extended; just as enols have a C=C bond and a C–O bond, enamines (named using the same principle: en for alk*ene* plus *amine*) have a C=C bond and a C–N bond. Moreover, imines and enamines are tautomers that interconvert in a process very similar to keto-enol tautomerism. Imines in which an organic R group replaces the remaining hydrogen are known as Schiff bases; this term may be familiar from your organic chemistry coursework, but the chemistry of Schiff bases is beyond the scope of the MCAT.

As discussed in section 4, amides are carboxylic acid derivatives with an amine group instead of a hydroxyl group.

A very common and entirely preventable source of error regarding nitrogen-containing functional groups on the MCAT is becoming confused about which structures are referred to by the similar-sounding terms "amine," "amide," "imine," and "enamine." Be sure to review Figure 36 below until they are familiar.

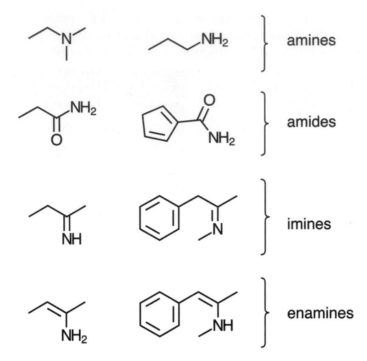

Figure 36. Nitrogen-containing compounds.

6. Sulfur-Containing Groups

> > CONNECTIONS < <

Chapters 2 and 12 of
Biochemistry

MCAT STRATEGY > > >

When you see "thio-," think of sulfur! Usually this will point you in the direction of the correct structure, as long as you replace oxygen with sulfur.

Sulfur-containing functional groups are not a major area tested by the MCAT, but you should be aware of them in general terms. There are three sulfur-containing groups you should know as structures similar to major oxygen-containing functional groups: thiols (-RSH, analogous to alcohols), sulfides or thioethers (R-S-R', analogous to ethers), and thioesters (R-CO-S-R', analogous to esters). Thioesters are highly reactive and play a notable role in several biochemical pathways, most notably in the form of acetyl-CoA. Additionally, you should be aware of disulfides (R-S-S-R'; this is analogous to a peroxide [R-O-O-R'], but peroxides are not critical for the MCAT). Disulfides are an important structure because disulfide bonds between cysteine amino acid residues are a crucial aspect of the tertiary structure of proteins.

7. Must-Knows

> Nomenclature and major chemical/physical properties:

NAME	NOMENCLATURE	STRUCTURE	RELEVANT INTERMOLECULAR FORCES	MELTING/ BOILING POINT	ACID-BASE PROPERTIES
Alkanes	-ane	C_nH_{2n+2}	London dispersion forces	Low	Negligible
Alkenes	-ene -en-	C_nH_{2n}	London dispersion forces	Low	
Alcohol	-ol hydroxy-	RC–OH	Dipole-dipole, H-bonding	High	Weak acids (phenols stronger)
Aldehyde	-al oxo-	RC(=O)H	Dipole-dipole	Medium	Negligible
Ketone	-one oxo-, keto-	R(C=O)R'			
Carboxylic acid	-oic acid	R(C=O)H	Dipole-dipole, H-bonding	High	Less weak acids
Amide	-amide	$R(C=O)NH_2$, R(C=O)NHR', R(C=O)NR'R''	Dipole-dipole, H-bonding (maybe)	Medium	Very weak bases
Ester	X-yl Y-ate (X = esterifying group)	R(C=O)OR'	Dipole-dipole	Medium	Negligible
Acid anhydride	X-oic Y-oic anhydride	R(C=O)O(C=O)R'	Dipole-dipole	Medium	Negligible
Amine	-amine amino-	$R-NH_2$, R–NHR', R–NR'R''	Dipole-dipole, H-bonding (maybe)	Medium	Weak bases
Imine	-imine	R = NH, R = NR'			
Enamine	enamine	$RC = NH_2$, C = NHR', C = NR'R''			

> Major reactions:
> - Reduction/oxidation on scale OH > C=O > COOH
>   - Mild oxidizing agent: PCC; strong oxidizing agents: $NaCr_2O_7$, $K_2Cr_2O_7$, and CrO_3; mild reducing agent: $NaBH_4$, strong reducing agent: $LiAlH_4$
> - Keto-enol tautomerism
> - Acetal/hemiacetal formation
> - Aldol condensation and retro-aldol reaction
> - Formation of carboxylic acid derivatives
> - Transesterification
> General principles:
> - Factors affecting acidity, most notably resonance
> - Factors affecting reactivity: electron-withdrawing groups, resonance, steric effects, strain

Practice Passage

In 1952, Urey and Miller conducted an experiment to simulate the conditions thought to be present when early life emerged on earth. They used water, methane, ammonia, and hydrogen gas, sealed in glass flasks, connected by tubes, forming a closed loop. The water was heated and a voltage-triggered spark was applied to simulate the energy input from natural lightning. Condensation was allowed to trickle back into the original flask and over time, the solution became darkly colored. Spectroscopic analysis of the final samples indicated the presence of amino acids, enamines, and monosaccharides. In addition, a number of polycyclic aromatic compounds were formed.

Evidence suggests that this primitive atmosphere contained significant levels of CO_2, N_2, H_2S, and SO_2. Further experiments using these gases, combined with the reagents used in the original Urey-Miller experiment, have produced additional biomolecules. In order to generate aromatic amino acids under primitive earth conditions it is necessary to use hydrogen-poor mixtures. Most of the natural amino acids, and components of nucleotides, have been produced in variants of the Urey-Miller experiment. Known reactions between the components of these modified Urey-Miller experiments can produce reactive intermediates (Reactions 1-4).

Reaction 1. $\qquad$ $CO_2 + CH_4 \rightarrow 2\ CH_2O$

Reaction 2. $\qquad$ $CH_4 + H_2O \rightarrow CO + 3\ H_2$

Reaction 3. $\qquad$ $CO + NH_3 \rightarrow HCN + H_2O$

Reaction 4. $\qquad$ $CH_4 + NH_3 \rightarrow HCN + 3\ H_2$

Formaldehyde, ammonia, and HCN can then react to form amino acids, such as the formation of glycine shown in Reactions 5-7. Reaction 8 shows the production of ribose, a carbohydrate which can be enzymatically modified and used as a nucleic acid precursor.

Reaction 5. $\qquad$ $CH_2O + NH_3 \rightarrow CH_2NH + H_2O$

Reaction 6. $\qquad$ $CH_2NH + HCN \rightarrow NH_2CH_2CN$

Reaction 7. $\qquad$ $NH_2CH_2CN + 2\ H_2O \rightarrow NH_3 + NH_2CH_2CO_2H$

Reaction 8. $\qquad$ $5\ CH_2O \rightarrow C_5H_{10}O_5$

These experiments showed that in primitive atmospheric conditions, a solution could be produced that would be conducive to the formation of even increasingly complex biomolecules, such as fatty acids, isoprenoids, cholesterol, and others, eventually allowing the formation of carbon-based life.

1. Which of the following atmospheric components was purposely excluded from the original Urey-Miller experiment?
   A. N_2, due to the relative stability of its sp hybridized orbitals.
   B. O_2, due to the potential for a highly exothermic response.
   C. Ar, due to its highly oxidative nature.
   D. CO_2, due to its behavior as an acidic oxide.

2. Which of the following amino acids formed by the experiments described in the passage could NOT have been produced as a racemic mixture?
   A. G
   B. Q
   C. W
   D. N

3. The formaldehyde and ammonia reactions discussed form what type of organic compound?
   A. An amide
   B. An imide
   C. An imine
   D. An enamide

4. Which of the following correctly shows the backbone which links the nucleotides acids produced by modified Urey-Miller experiments?

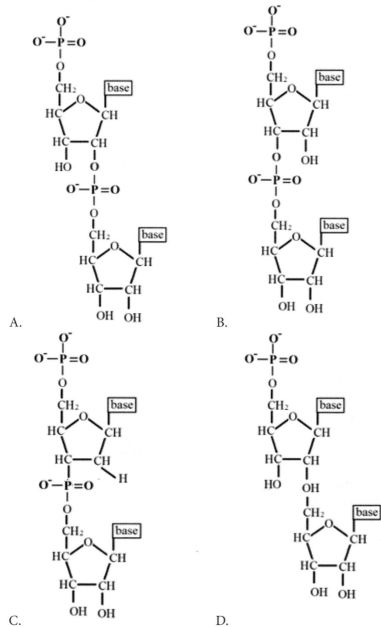

A.

B.

C.

D.

5. Which of the following are most likely to be found in the nucleotides formed in the modified Urey-Miller experiments?

  I.   Purine
  II. Pyrimidine
  III. Phosphate

  A. I only
  B. I and II only
  C. II and III only
  D. I, II, and III

6. According to the passage, which of the following was least likely to be found during spectroscopic analysis of the samples tested?

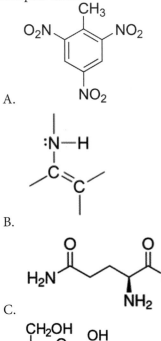

A.

B.

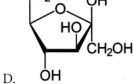

C.

D.

7. The phosphorylated form of the product of Reaction 8 can be generated in the human body by:
  A. glycolysis.
  B. the pentose phosphate pathway.
  C. the electron transport chain.
  D. gluconeogenesis.

Practice Passage Explanations

In 1952, Urey and Miller conducted an experiment to simulate the conditions thought to be present when early life emerged on earth. They used water, methane, ammonia, and hydrogen gas, sealed in glass flasks, connected by tubes, forming a closed loop. The water was heated and a voltage-triggered spark was applied to simulate the energy input from natural lightning. Condensation was allowed to trickle back into the original flask and over time, the solution became darkly colored. Spectroscopic analysis of the final samples indicated the presence of amino acids, enamines, and monosaccharides. In addition, a number of polycyclic aromatic compounds were formed.

Key terms: experiment, early life conditions, AA, monosaccharides, aromatic compounds

Cause and effect: simple C, H, O, N compounds combined in solution and supplied E → biologically important molecules

Evidence suggests that this primitive atmosphere contained significant levels of CO_2, N_2, H_2S, and SO_2. Further experiments using these gases, combined with the reagents used in the original Urey-Miller experiment, have produced additional biomolecules. In order to generate aromatic amino acids under primitive earth conditions it is necessary to use hydrogen-poor mixtures. Most of the natural amino acids, and components of nucleotides, have been produced in variants of the Urey-Miller experiment. Known reactions between the components of these modified Urey-Miller experiments can produce reactive intermediates (Reactions 1-4).

Key terms: primitive atmosphere, aromatic AA, modified U-M experiments

Cause and effect: adding more reagents to the U-M procedure yields more complex biomolecules such as AA, purines, pyrimidines, ribose sugars

Reaction 1. $\qquad CO_2 + CH_4 \rightarrow 2\ CH_2O$

Reaction 2. $\qquad CH_4 + H_2O \rightarrow CO + 3\ H_2$

Reaction 3. $\qquad CO + NH_3 \rightarrow HCN + H_2O$

Reaction 4. $\qquad CH_4 + NH_3 \rightarrow HCN + 3\ H_2$

Reactions 1-4 are a series of unrelated reactions, none of which produce the biomolecules discussed in the passage, save detailed analysis for later

Formaldehyde, ammonia, and HCN can then react to form amino acids, such as the formation of glycine shown in Reactions 5-7. Reaction 8 shows the production of ribose, a carbohydrate which can be enzymatically modified and used as a nucleic acid precursor.

Key terms: glycine, ribose

Cause and effect: the products from Reactions 1-4 can be combined to form the biomolecules glycine and ribose

Reaction 5. $\qquad CH_2O + NH_3 \rightarrow CH_2NH + H_2O$

Reaction 6. $\qquad CH_2NH + HCN \rightarrow NH_2CH_2CN$

Reaction 7. $NH_2CH_2CN + 2\,H_2O \rightarrow NH_3 + NH_2CH_2CO_2H$

Reaction 8. $5\,CH_2O \rightarrow C_5H_{10}O_5$

Reactions 5-7 are better known as Strecker synthesis; Reaction 8 produces ribose, which can be phosphorylated (Ribose-5-PO₄) and used in nucleic acid synthesis

These experiments showed that in primitive atmospheric conditions, a solution could be produced that would be conducive to the formation of even increasingly complex biomolecules, such as fatty acids, isoprenoids, cholesterol, and others, eventually allowing the formation of carbon-based life.

Key terms: increasingly complex biomolecules

1. B is correct. The goal of the experiment was to create biomolecules, which generally contain C, N, H and O. Oxygen was excluded from the original Urey-Miller experiment for a couple of reasons. Oxygen is produced as a result of photosynthesis, so it is unlikely to have been a part of the early earth atmosphere. Since this is not something we would be expected to know for the exam, there must be a 2nd reason. This is that the passage tells us that a voltage-induced spark was used to supply energy to the reaction. Molecular oxygen is highly combustible, and if combined with a spark, could have produced an explosion.

   A, D: While these statements are accurate with regards to the molecules (CO_2 as an acidic oxide reacts with water to form carbonic acid), they would not explain why the experimenters would not want to include these species in the experiment.
   C: Argon, as a noble gas, is not highly reactive. There is no indication it was necessary to achieve the desired results: H-, C-, N-, and O-containing compounds relevant to life.

2. A is correct. As stated in the passage, the chiral amino acids produced by the Urey-Miller experiment were racemic mixtures. However, glycine does not have a chiral carbon atom and therefore does not have optically active isomers.

   B, C, D: Glutamine, tryptophan, and asparagine all have chiral carbons that could potentially create a racemic mixture of enantiomers.

3. C is correct. Aldehyde + ammonia is a direct reference to Reaction 5. The product of Reaction 5 is $H_2C = NH$, an imine.

   A: An amide is an organic functional group in which the hydroxyl of an organic acid is replaced by a -NR₂ to give (R'CO)NR₂.
   B: An imide is where there are two carbonyl carbons attached to the same nitrogen, (R'CO)₂NR.
   D: An enamide is an amide and alkene in one. A carbonyl carbon attached to a nitrogen, which is attached to an alkene carbon.

4. B is correct. The backbone of nucleic acids is the phosphodiester link. This bond is formed between the 3' carbon atom of one (de)oxyribose molecule and the 5' carbon atom of another (de)oxyribose.

5. B is correct. As stated in the passage, purines, pyrimidines, and carbohydrates, including ribose, were all produced by the modified Urey-Miller experiments and are components of nucleotide and nucleic acids.

    III: Phosphorus was not a component of these experiments (but is a component of nucleic acids). Therefore it was not possible for phosphate to be found in the final products.

6. A is correct. According to the first paragraph, analysis revealed the presence of amino acids (choice C), enamines (choice B), and monosaccharides (choice D). While it does also mention they found polycyclic aromatic compounds, choice A is aromatic but not polycyclic.

7. B is correct. The product of reaction 8 is ribose. This 5-carbon sugar can be produced in a phosphorylated form, known as ribose-5-phosphate, along with NADPH, via the pentose phosphate pathway when the body is in need of additional lipids, cholesterol, or nucleic acids.

Independent Questions

1. Of the following, the most acidic proton is found on:
   A. the carbonyl carbon of a ketone.
   B. the alpha carbon of an amide.
   C. the central alpha carbon of an acid anhydride.
   D. the central alpha carbon of a β-carbonyl compound.

2. In solution, two carboxylic acid groups can dimerize via hydrogen bonding. Consider acetic acid, which is soluble in most organic solvents. Acetic acid dimerization would be most favorable in which of the following solvents?
   A. Water
   B. Methanol
   C. Hexane
   D. Dichloromethane

3. Which of the choices below includes two functional groups or forms that can tautomerize with each other?
   I.   Ketones and enols
   II. Ketones and carboxylic acids
   III. Imines and enamines
   IV. Amides and enamines

   A. I and III only
   B. I and IV only
   C. I, III, and IV only
   D. I, II, III, and IV

4. Triglycerides, a major constituent of total fat content in the human body, are composed of three fatty acid molecules linked to a single glycerol molecule. Which of the following functional groups is present in all triglyceride molecules?
   A. Amide
   B. Ether
   C. Ester
   D. Aldehyde

5. Carboxylate groups are known to coordinate metal ions in enzyme active sites. Coordination of Mg^{2+} by aspartate residues is a particularly common interaction in biological systems. Examination of such a complex by X-ray crystallography would most likely reveal:
   A. the Mg^{2+} ion resides closer to the negatively charged oxygen atom in the carboxylate.
   B. the Mg^{2+} ion resides closer to the neutral oxygen atom in the carboxylate.
   C. the Mg^{2+} ion resides equidistant from the two oxygen atoms in the carboxylate.
   D. the Mg^{2+} ion complexes with the protonated oxygen atom only.

6. Of the following, which must contain a carbon-nitrogen double bond?
   A. An imine
   B. An enamine
   C. A lactam
   D. An amine

7. Sodium borohydride ($NaBH_4$) is a relatively mild reducing agent that is routinely employed in the conversion of carbonyls to alcohols. $NaBH_4$ readily reduces most ketones, but it will not reduce carboxylic acids. Which of the following is most likely true regarding the reactivity of $NaBH_4$?
   A. $NaBH_4$ will reduce aldehydes, because they are less electrophilic than ketones.
   B. $NaBH_4$ will not reduce aldehydes, because they are less electrophilic than ketones.
   C. $NaBH_4$ will reduce esters, because they are less electrophilic than ketones.
   D. $NaBH_4$ will not reduce esters, because they are less electrophilic than ketones.

8. Ester hydrolysis under acidic conditions yields a carboxylic acid and an alcohol. Analogous hydrolysis of a thioester yields:
   A. a carboxylic acid and an amine.
   B. a carboxylic acid and a thiol.
   C. a thiocarboxylic acid and an alcohol.
   D. an alcohol and a thiol.

Independent Question Explanations

1. D is correct. An alpha carbon, or the carbon adjacent to a C=O functionality, is typically more acidic than other groups consisting of C-H bonds. This is true due to resonance stabilization. Only choice D describes a position that is alpha to *two* carbonyl groups, making it even more acidic than the other choices. (Regarding choice A, the carbonyl carbon of a ketone is not actually attached to any hydrogen atoms.)

2. C is correct. Polar moieties are more likely to associate with one another when they reside in a nonpolar environment. In this way, unfavorable interactions between polar and nonpolar groups can be avoided. In contrast, when polar moieties are dissolved in polar solvents, no such unfavorable interactions occur; the polar groups are thus less likely to associate with each other (dimerize) and more likely to associate with solvent molecules. Therefore, polar acetic acid molecules are most likely to dimerize to the greatest extent when dissolved in hexane, the most nonpolar of the choices listed.

3. A is correct. Ketones and enols (which are marked by an alcohol attached to one end of a double bond) are a classic example of forms that can interconvert via tautomerization. Imines and enamines can also do this; note the similarity of the word "enol" with "enamine"! Carboxylic acids do not tautomerize to become ketones, and amides do not tautomerize to become enamines.

4. C is correct. Esters are carboxylic acid derivatives in which the hydroxyl group is replaced by an alkoxy group. Glycerol has three free alcohol groups, which react with the carboxylic acid groups present in the free fatty acids. The resulting esterification reaction is accompanied by the loss of a stoichiometric amount of water.

5. C is correct. Deprotonated carboxylic acid groups carry an overall negative charge that is distributed between the two oxygen atoms by resonance. The two major resonance structures contribute equally to the overall character of the moiety, and neither oxygen atom is significantly more negative than the other. Consequently, a coordinated ion will experience equal attractive electrostatic forces from each atom.

6. A is correct. Imines are functional groups that are characterized by C=N bonds. Enamines, in contrast, contain a C=C alkene bond and a C-N bond (or, in other words, an alkene with one of its carbons attached to an amine functionality). Amines do not necessarily contain any double bonds at all. Finally, lactams are cyclic amides, meaning that they contain a C=O bond but are not marked by a C = N bond.

7. D is correct. Aldehydes are generally more electrophilic than ketones because hydrogen atoms do not inductively donate electron density to the same extent as carbon atoms. This leaves the carbonyl carbon atom of most aldehyde groups more electron-deficient than the analogous carbon atom in most ketones (eliminate choices A and B). Esters tend to be less electrophilic than ketones because the replacement of a carbon atom with an oxygen atom permits electron donation to the carbonyl carbon atom by resonance. Reducing agents (electron donors) such as $NaBH_4$ will more readily react with electrophilic sites such as ketones and aldehydes, while displaying less reactivity towards esters and carboxylic acids.

8. B is correct. Hydrolysis of a thioester proceeds in the same manner as ester hydrolysis. Since sulfur atoms are relatively large and can effectively distribute negative charge, the thiol group readily leaves the thioester and is replaced by a hydroxyl group. The result is a carboxylic acid and a free thiol.

This page left intentionally blank.

Organic Reaction Mechanisms

CHAPTER 11

0. Introduction

In this chapter, we'll take a closer look at *how* organic reactions happen. Reaction mechanisms can be an intimidating topic, but your goal for the MCAT should be to focus on the essential principles. Unlike in organic chemistry courses, where you're presented with a sometimes-bewildering variety of reaction mechanisms that you must know, for the MCAT, the best strategy is to focus on a relatively small core of key reaction types, and then extend that knowledge to less common reactions that are still fair game.

There are two basic parameters that govern reaction mechanisms: (1) sterics (that is, whether the reactants can physically interact with each other in the way needed to push the reaction forward) and (2) charge-based interactions. On a very simple level, the attractive forces between positive and negative charges drive reactions forward, but the picture gets more complicated because we need to account for factors that stabilize or destabilize charge in certain structures.

Reactions happen when a bond is formed between an electrophile and a nucleophile. Electrophiles are species that 'want' more electrons. Often, electrophiles are positively charged or partially positively charged. In contrast, nucleophiles are species that have an excess of electrons, and therefore 'want' to use those electrons to form a bond with an electrophile. Nucleophiles are defined by the presence of at least one free pair of valence electrons.

In common practice, the formation of an organic bond is indicated by drawing arrows in so-called 'electron-pushing' notation. This means that the arrows focus on the movement of electrons, which can correspond either to breaking a bond or making a bond, depending on the context. This can be a little bit confusing, but it's essential that you become familiar with this type of notation, because it is possible that you'll encounter it on Test Day. For this reason, read the text describing each figure carefully, because throughout this chapter, we'll explain what's happening in each step of the mechanism both through a figure and through a verbal description.

The first topic we'll cover in this chapter is S_N1, S_N2, and elimination chemistry, which is the single most important topic for you to master in the domain of organic chemistry mechanisms for the MCAT. We'll then proceed to cover some important examples of nucleophilic addition and substitution, followed by a review of some other representative mechanisms, and concluding with a presentation of the mechanisms involved in enolate chemistry.

In order to get the most out of this chapter, be sure to study each mechanism carefully, with a focus on understanding which atom acts as a nucleophile and which as an electrophile in each reaction. It is possible that on Test Day, you will see a reaction *mechanism* that you have studied in the context of *molecules* that you haven't seen before, so your real task in this chapter is to push beyond studying reactions as input-output pairings of functional groups (as presented in Chapter 10) towards understanding the principles of reactivity that can be applied in seemingly novel contexts.

1. S$_N$1, S$_N$2, and elimination

Nucleophilic substitution is probably the single most-tested reaction mechanism on the MCAT, so let's step back and think about what that term implies. The term 'nucleophilic' tells us that the reaction mechanism will involve a nucleophile (that is, an electron-rich atom) attacking an electrophile. 'Substitution' means that the attacking nucleophile replaces a substituent on the target molecule, which is known as the leaving group. For nucleophilic substitution reactions, you ultimately want to identify three things:

1. <u>What is the nucleophile? What makes it nucleophilic?</u> In other words, you want to find the compound with one or more free lone pairs of electrons that will be shared with the target molecule.

2. <u>What is the electrophile? What creates an electrophilic region on the target molecule?</u> In this step, your goal is to pinpoint where the electrons on the attacking nucleophile will go. This generally means finding an area of positive or partial positive charge on the target molecule.

3. <u>What is the leaving group?</u> Nucleophilic *substitution* (as compared to nucleophilic addition, which we will discuss more below) is characterized by a substituent being 'kicked out' or 'leaving.' You'll want to identify which substituent that is likely to be, although context may make it obvious. In general, a good leaving group will be a species that with the one extra pair of electrons it gets when a single bond is broken, 'pushing it out,' will be stable in aqueous solution. You may also need to think about possible steps that make the leaving group better. As we will see, protonation is a frequent option.

Figure 1 shows the general scheme of a nucleophilic substitution reaction, where *Nu* indicates the nucleophile, *El* the electrophile, *LG* the leaving group, and *R* indicates whatever other substituents the electrophile may have.

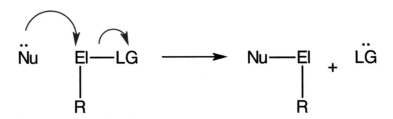

Figure 1. General nucleophilic substitution reaction.

The general scheme in Figure 1 is fairly simple, but we have to account for some complications in real-world reaction scenarios. First, let's note that Figure 1 contains two steps: (1) the nucleophilic attack and (2) the transfer of electrons to the leaving group as the bond between it and the electrophile is broken. It actually turns out that these steps can occur in either order, which is at the heart of the difference between the S$_N$1 and S$_N$2 mechanisms we will discuss below. Additionally, as mentioned above, some reaction mechanisms include steps—most commonly, protonation—that make the leaving group more likely to leave.

For the MCAT, you will have to distinguish between two types of nucleophilic substitution mechanisms: S$_N$1 and S$_N$2. The 'S' stands for 'substitution' and the subscript 'N' stands for 'nucleophilic,' while the numbers '1' and '2' describe the rate laws associated with the reaction. In S$_N$1 reactions, the rate law depends only on the concentration of the substrate, while in S$_N$2 reactions, the rate law depends on the concentrations of both the substrate and the nucleophile. Both the S$_N$1 and S$_N$2 mechanisms are generally illustrated with alkyl halides, although S$_N$2 mechanisms in particular can occur with other substrates.

Let's first look at the S$_N$1 mechanism. The key idea with the S$_N$1 mechanism is that the leaving group leaves *first*, generating a carbocation (that is, a positively charged, electron-deficient carbon). This step is slow, because even a good leaving group will be relatively stable in its default state, and because carbocations are inherently unstable, highly reactive species. Therefore, if we're just sitting around waiting for a carbocation to form, we'll have to wait for a while—but when it does form, it reacts quickly. The next step is nucleophilic attack, followed by deprotonation of the nucleophile once it is attached to the target molecule. The S$_N$1 mechanism is shown in Figure 2.

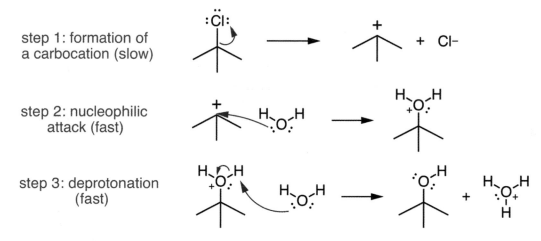

step 1: formation of a carbocation (slow)

step 2: nucleophilic attack (fast)

step 3: deprotonation (fast)

Figure 2. S$_N$1 mechanism.

There are a few things we should note about the S$_N$1 mechanism. First, the fact that step 1 (formation of a carbocation) is slow, while the other steps are fast, means that the carbocation formation step is the rate-limiting step of the reaction. This is why the rate law of an S$_N$1 reaction depends only on the concentration of the substrate. Another consequence of this fact is that anything that promotes the stability of the carbocation will increase the rate of the reaction. As mentioned above, carbocations are generally unstable, highly reactive species, so anything that increases the stability of the carbocation will increase the rate of an S$_N$1 reaction. Carbocation stability is enhanced by the degree to which the carbon is substituted. Tertiary carbocations (carbocations on a carbon with three other non-hydrogen substituents, as in Figure 1) are more stable than secondary carbocations, which are more stable than primary carbocations, which are more stable than methyl carbocations. As a rule of thumb, a carbocation must be on a tertiary or secondary carbon for the reaction to proceed to any significant extent. A third important consequence of the fact that this reaction proceeds through an extremely active carbocation intermediate is that the nucleophile doesn't have to be especially strong for the reaction to go forward. To summarize, *S$_N$1 reactions are all about the carbocation!*

A final point to note about S$_N$1 reactions is that the mechanism is not stereochemically sensitive. An S$_N$1 reaction can certainly take place at a carbon that has four different substituents and is therefore a chiral center, but as soon as the carbocation is formed, the chirality is lost. Therefore, when an enantiomerically pure substrate undergoes an S$_N$1 reaction, the product will exhibit racemization (the outcome may not be a perfect 50:50 racemic mixture, because nothing in chemistry is that simple, but the chiral orientation will certainly not be preserved).

In S$_N$2 reactions, in contrast, the nucleophilic attack pushes the reaction forward. The carbon that is attacked is a relatively weak electrophile, with a partial positive charge due to the inductive electron withdrawing effect of the halide. The nucleophile attacks the electrophilic carbon on the opposite side of the halide substituent in what is known as a backside attack. The reason for this is that the electron-rich nucleophile is going to 'try' to approach at an angle maximally distant from the electron-rich halide leaving group. This leads to the formation of a complex transition state in which a new bond is being formed between the nucleophile and electrophile while a bond is being broken between the electrophile and the leaving group. As the leaving group leaves, the stereochemical orientation of the target molecule is inverted. A common analogy is how an umbrella can be turned inside out by the wind. Figure 3 shows the S_N2 mechanism.

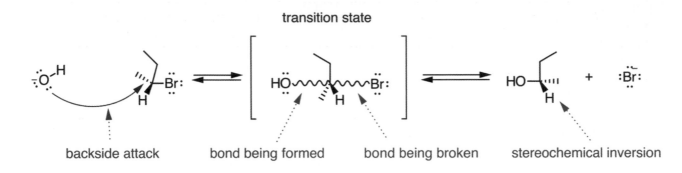

Figure 3. S_N2 mechanism.

Our next question might be, which circumstances favor S_N2 reactions? Because S_N2 reactions are initiated by nucleophilic attack, if we want S_N2 chemistry to happen, the name of the game is manipulating the reaction conditions to make nucleophilic attack more likely. One prerequisite for this is having a strong nucleophile. Note the contrast between Figure 2 (S_N1) and Figure 3 (S_N2) in this regard: for an S_N1 reaction, H_2O, which is only a moderately decent nucleophile, is sufficient, whereas for the S_N2 reaction we use OH⁻, which is a much more aggressive nucleophile. However, it's not enough just for the nucleophile to be strong. It also has to be likely to encounter the electrophilic carbon. This is where steric considerations come in. First, we want to make sure that the nucleophile is both strong and *small*; a big bulky base like *tert*-butoxide will not work effectively here. Second, we need to think about the sterics of the reaction substrate. The less substituted the electrophilic carbon is, the easier it will be for the nucleophile to come into contact with the electrophile. Therefore, S_N2 reactions are favorable at methyl carbons and primary carbons, but less so at secondary carbons, and will essentially not happen at any meaningful rate at tertiary carbons. (Note that the example shown in Figure 3 is not very favorable, because it takes place at a secondary carbon! This choice was made to illustrate the stereochemical inversion more clearly.)

In addition to the points we've made so far comparing S_N1 and S_N2 mechanisms, the solvent can also be a factor favoring one reaction mechanism over another. The relevant distinction is between polar protic and polar aprotic solvents; nonpolar solvents are not generally useful for these reactions. Polar protic solvents are those with a hydrogen atom attached to a polar molecule, most typically involving an O–H or N–H bond. Typical examples include water, methanol, and ethanol. Polar aprotic solvents contain a permanent dipole due to a polar bond (typically C=O), but do not contain a polar bond with hydrogen. Acetone is a typical example, as is dimethyl sulfoxide (DMSO). As is suggested by the definition of polar protic versus aprotic solvents, the difference in their properties has to do with the presence or absence of hydrogen bonding. Polar protic solvents engage in hydrogen bonding, which stabilizes carbocations by providing adjacent regions with partial negative charges and weakens nucleophiles via interactions between nucleophilic electron pairs and the partially positive region of hydrogen bonds. This favors S_N1 chemistry over S_N2 chemistry, because for S_N1 chemistry the critical step is carbocation formation and the nucleophile doesn't have to be particularly strong.

With all of this in mind, we can summarize the characteristic features of S_N1 or S_N2 mechanisms. On Test Day, you may have to predict which reaction mechanism will take place in a given situation, but you may also be told that a given mechanism is S_N1 or S_N2 and need to use that information to predict something about the reaction. Either way, you should be very familiar with the key features of these mechanisms presented in Table 1.

	S_N1	S_N2
'Key' to the mechanism	Carbocation stability	Steric hindrance
Rate law	Unimolecular (substrate concentration only)	Biomolecular (substrate and nucleus concentrations)
Number of steps	2	1
Substituents on carbon	3° > 2° > 1° > 0° (methyl)	0° (methyl) > 1° > 2° > 3°
Strength of nucleophile	Doesn't really matter	Strong (and non-bulky)
Solvent	Polar protic	Polar aprotic
Stereochemistry	Not preserved (racemization)	Inverted (backside attack)

Table 1. S_N1 and S_N2 mechanisms.

In a reaction environment with a nucleophile present, alkyl halides can also undergo a type of reaction in which the halide is kicked out, but the nucleophile doesn't actually add itself as a substituent; instead, a double C=C bond is formed. This type of reaction is known as elimination, and just as there are S_N1 and S_N2 mechanisms, there are E1 and E2 mechanisms.

Most organic chemistry courses emphasize the E1 and E2 mechanisms to the same extent that they do S_N1 and S_N2 reactions. This is *not* the case for the MCAT. S_N1 and S_N2 mechanisms are essential content, while elimination chemistry plays more of a role of background information that it's helpful to be familiar with but is very unlikely to be directly tested. For this reason, we will only briefly review the two elimination mechanisms.

The E1 mechanism is similar to the S_N1 mechanism in that it has a unimolecular rate law and is driven by carbocation formation. The difference is that instead of attacking the carbocation once it is formed, the nucleophile pulls off a proton from an adjacent carbon, which allows a double bond to be created on the target molecule. This is illustrated below in Figure 4.

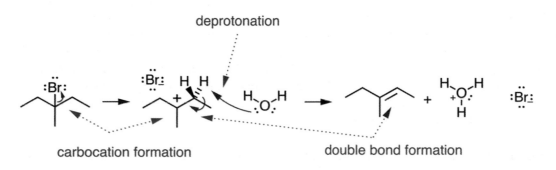

Figure 4. E1 mechanism.

The E2 mechanism is also similar to its S$_N$2 counterpart in that it has a bimolecular rate law and is driven by nucleophilic attack. The difference is that in an E2 reaction, a strong base attacks a proton adjacent to the carbon with a halide substituent. Once that proton is removed, a double C=C bond is formed, which causes the leaving group to be kicked off.

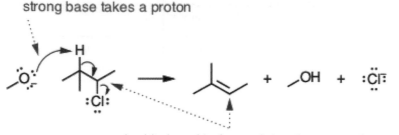

strong base takes a proton

double bond is formed, leaving group leaves

Figure 5. E2 mechanism.

It can be possible for elimination chemistry to occur at the same time as S$_N$1 or S$_N$2 chemistry, and coping with this difficulty can be a real challenge for synthetic chemists. However, the details of this go beyond the scope of the MCAT. Instead, focus on being able to predict whether a mechanism will be S$_N$1 or S$_N$2, and know that elimination chemistry is another theoretical possibility that involves double bond formation.

2. Nucleophilic Substitution and Addition: Examples

Nucleophilic substitution—and its cousin, nucleophilic addition—are the mechanisms through which many biologically relevant reactions take place. In particular, they are common at carbonyl carbons, because the carbonyl oxygen has a partial negative charge and the carbonyl carbon has a partial positive charge. This is also the case for the carbons in carboxylic acid functional groups, but even more so, because of the additional –OH group. This means that the carbonyl carbon can act as an electrophile that is subject to nucleophilic attack.

A prototypical example of nucleophilic substitution at a carboxylic acid group is provided by a process known as Fischer esterification. Fischer esterification is an acid-catalyzed, highly practical technique for turning a carboxylic acid into an ester—that is, replacing the –OH group of the carboxylic acid with the –OR functional group characteristic of an ester. To do this, a carboxylic acid is mixed with an alcohol under acidic conditions. The mechanism of Fischer esterification is shown below in Figure 6.

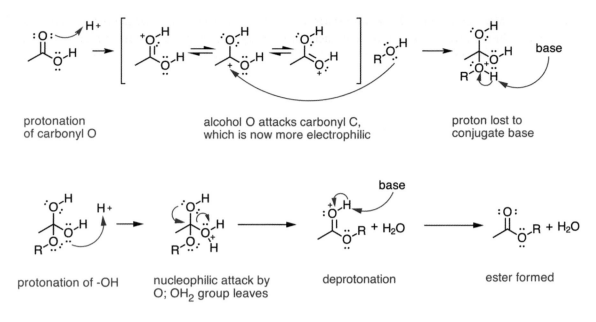

protonation
of carbonyl O

alcohol O attacks carbonyl C,
which is now more electrophilic

proton lost to
conjugate base

protonation of -OH

nucleophilic attack by
O; OH$_2$ group leaves

deprotonation

ester formed

Figure 6. Fischer esterification.

The first step in Fischer esterification is protonation of the carbonyl oxygen. This is a typical first step in nucleophilic reactions involving carbonyl groups, because it adds a positive charge that helps to make the carbonyl carbon even more electrophilic. The resonance structures shown in Figure 6 after protonation make explicit the fact that the positive charge is to some extent shared by the carbon. At this point, now that the carbonyl C is more electrophilic, the oxygen in the alcohol can now attack it. After this step, we now have a complex four-membered structure known as a tetrahedral intermediate. Our goal is now to kick out the –OH group. In order to do that, we need to do some proton shuffling, which is facilitated by the acidic environment. A proton is eventually added to the –OH, making it a good leaving group. Then the oxygen that was originally the carbonyl oxygen executes a nucleophilic attack. This step forms a double bond, regenerating the carbonyl group, and kicks off the –OH$_2$ leaving group. The only remaining step is some additional proton shuffling to regenerate the ester.

Let's step back and review the key steps. As outlined in section 1, there are three keys for understanding nucleophilic substitution reactions: (1) find the nucleophile (in this case, the oxygen in an alcohol), (2) find the electrophile (the carbonyl C, with protonation to activate it), and (3) identify the leaving group (–OH, protonated to H$_2$O). Protonation is important conceptually, because as shown in this mechanism, it can help activate the electrophile and prepare the leaving group, but you don't need to worry about protonation for the MCAT as much as you might have when drawing mechanisms by hand for organic chemistry coursework.

> **MCAT STRATEGY > > >**
>
> Fischer esterification is a classic example of how nucleophilic substitution works for carboxylic acids and their derivatives. Study this mechanism thoroughly, and you will be prepared for any variations you might encounter on Test Day.

Fischer esterification can be reversed through hydrolysis, which is the general term for a reaction in which a compound breaks down through the addition of water. The mechanism for the hydrolysis of an ester is essentially the same as ester formation, with the only difference being that water attacks and the –OR group is the leaving group. Hydrolysis is tremendously important physiologically, because it is the main mechanism through which biological polymers, like proteins, are degraded. However, the specific mechanism of hydrolysis of biomolecules can vary. It is often the case that such reactions are technically favorable, but would be very slow without a catalyst, and the enzymes that catalyze these reactions can be very specific and involve individualized mechanisms and intermediate stabilizing steps. For the MCAT, you should be aware of the general idea of hydrolysis as a form of nucleophilic substitution, and you don't need to worry about the specific details of individual proteases (to take one example of a relevant enzyme class).

Another important nucleophilic substitution reaction, imine formation, takes place at a carbonyl carbon (C=O) (not a carboxylic acid group!). The basic point of this reaction is to replace the carbonyl carbon (C=O) with a nitrogen, creating the C = N double bond that defines an imine. (You may also hear the term 'Schiff base,' which refers to an imine that has an additional carbon substituent [C=N–R]). The imine formation mechanism is shown in Figure 7.

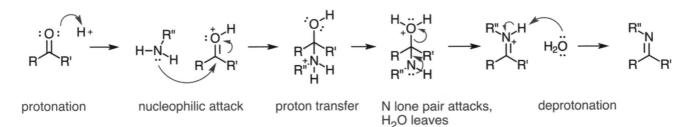

protonation   nucleophilic attack   proton transfer   N lone pair attacks,   deprotonation
                                                                           H₂O leaves

Figure 7. Imine formation.

The first steps of imine formation follow a pattern that is hopefully becoming familiar by now. The carbonyl oxygen is protonated, which activates the carbonyl carbon as an electrophile. This is followed by nucleophilic attack of the nitrogen atom in the reactant amine, which joins with the carbonyl carbon to form a tetrahedral intermediate. The nitrogen is initially positively charged, but acid-base interactions with the medium mediate proton transfer to the oxygen. Once that proton transfer happens, the nitrogen atom regains a nucleophilic lone pair of electrons. This lone pair then attacks the carbon, kicking off the oxygen as part of an H₂O leaving group. The nitrogen now has a double bond with the carbon, but a positive charge, which is then removed in a final deprotonation step, which results in the imine.

To summarize imine formation using the rubric we used above, (1) the nucleophile is an amine; (2) the electrophile is a carbonyl carbon post-protonation; and (3) the leaving group is –OH₂, derived from the carbonyl oxygen. The notable thing about the imine formation mechanism is that the nitrogen atom executes not one, but two nucleophilic attacks, which is enabled by how proton transfer processes allow the nitrogen lone pair to be regenerated.

A similar, but distinct, mechanism is known as nucleophilic addition. As the name implies, nucleophilic addition is similar to nucleophilic substitution, but without the leaving group. In a classic example, an alcohol can attack an aldehyde or a ketone (both characterized by a C=O) bond and add to it. The resulting structure has a central— potentially chiral—carbon with an –OR group (derived from the alcohol) and an –OH group (derived from the original C=O bond). If an aldehyde undergoes this reaction, the resulting structure is known as a hemiacetal, whereas a ketone that undergoes this reaction results in a hemiketal.

Figure 8 shows the mechanism of hemiacetal formation, comparing acidic and basic conditions. The mechanism shown in Figure 8 also works for hemiketal formation if the initial molecule is a ketone, rather than an aldehyde, as in Figure 8. However, the difference between acid- and base-catalysis is worth exploring in some detail. If you've thoroughly studied Fischer esterification, acid-catalyzed hemiacetal formation will be very familiar. The oxygen is protonated to make the carbonyl carbon more electrophilic, the alcohol then executes a nucleophilic attack, and the result, after deprotonation, is a tetrahedral structure.

acid-catalyzed hemiacetal formation

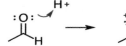

protonation to make carbonyl
carbon more electrophilic

nucleophilic attack by EtOH

deprotonation

base-catalyzed hemiacetal formation

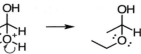

strong base deprotonates EtOH,
making it more nucleophilic

nucleophilic attack by EtO⁻

base gives up H to reprotonate
what was originally the carbonyl O

Figure 8. Hemiacetal formation.

Base-catalyzed hemiacetal formation, in contrast, follows a different logic. Whereas acid catalysis focuses on making the electrophile stronger via protonation, base catalysis works by making the nucleophile more intensely nucleophilic via deprotonation. The alcohol is deprotonated to form an alkoxide, which is a very strong nucleophile capable of directly attacking the carbonyl carbon. Once this happens, the hemiacetal is formed, and the only remaining step is reprotonation to generate the hemiacetal.

This mechanism is especially noteworthy in the biochemistry context because it is what takes place in sugars when they convert from linear forms to cyclic forms, which are predominant in aqueous solution in the body.

> > **CONNECTIONS** < <

Chapter 6 of Biochemistry

Interestingly, it turns out that you have to be very careful about stoichiometry to generate hemiacetals and hemiketals in laboratory conditions. If there is an excess of alcohol, the reaction can keep going, resulting in acetals and ketals, which have two –OR groups instead of one –OR and one –OH group, as seen in hemiacetals and hemiketals. These structures are shown in Figure 9.

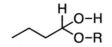

hemiacetal

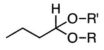

acetal

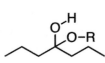

hemiketal

ketal

Figure 9. Hemiacetals, hemiketals, acetals, and ketals.

The connection with biochemistry continues here. When a glycosidic bond is formed between two monosaccharides (isolated sugar molecules) to form a disaccharide, a hemiacetal or hemiketal is converted into an acetal or ketal. This is shown and labeled in the diagram of sucrose, a disaccharide formed from glucose and fructose, Figure 10.

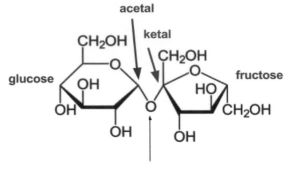

Figure 10. Glycosidic bond.

To summarize, there are three major takeaways of the hemiacetal/hemiketal reaction mechanism:

1. It is an excellent example of acid catalysis (protonation makes the electrophile stronger) versus base catalysis (deprotonation makes the nucleophile stronger). Study this aspect of the mechanism carefully, because these two types of logic can be applied to other reactions as well.

2. It is a useful example of how nucleophilic addition can take place instead of substitution, and also illustrates how stoichiometry can be necessary to obtain the desired reaction outcome.

3. It illustrates how organic chemistry reactions can have close parallels in biological contexts that are not necessarily immediately obvious, because it can be challenging sometimes to visualize functional groups in cyclic conformations with very large –R groups.

3. Keto-enol tautomerism

Tautomerism is a phenomenon in which a molecule has two structures that interconvert at equilibrium. The most common example is keto-enol tautomerism, although tautomerism is also found between enamines and imines (the second most important example), lactams and lactims, and amides and imidic acids. As noted before in Chapter 9, when tautomerism was introduced, tautomerism is not the same thing as resonance. In resonance, electrons are delocalized in the underlying structure of the molecule, and we use resonance structures as a relatively crude way of representing this fact. In contrast, tautomers are two *different* structures that interconvert via the breaking and re-formation of bonds.

Keto-enol tautomerism describes the interconversion between ketone and enol forms. An enol is a functional group with a C=C double bond (hence the *en–* part of the name) and an –OH group (hence the *–ol* part of enol). The interconversion between these two forms is generated by proton transfer that can be accomplished in either acidic or basic conditions. The two mechanisms of keto-enol tautomerism are shown below in Figure 11.

acid-catalyzed keto-enol tautomerism

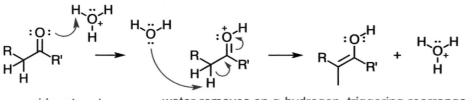

acid protonates
the carbonyl O

water removes an α-hydrogen, triggering rearrangement

base-catalyzed keto-enol tautomerism

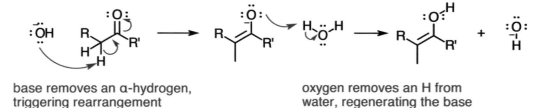

base removes an α-hydrogen,
triggering rearrangement

oxygen removes an H from
water, regenerating the base

Figure 11. Mechanisms of keto-enol tautomerism.

This mechanism provides another opportunity to compare the logic of acid catalysis with that of base catalysis. In acid catalysis, as usual, the first step is to protonate the carbonyl oxygen, after which the conjugate base of the acid (in this case, water) removes an α-hydrogen (that is, a hydrogen located on a carbon *next* to the carbonyl carbon), which triggers rearrangement into the enol form. In contrast, in the base-catalyzed mechanism, a base removes the α-hydrogen in the first step, which triggers the formation of a C=C double bond and the conversion of the C=O double bond to a C–O single bond. The negatively-charged oxygen then picks up a proton from the conjugate acid of the base catalyst, regenerating the base and resulting in the enol form.

In aqueous solution, the keto form generally predominates over the enol form. However, the enol form can predominate in some circumstances. Most importantly, if the enol form is resonance-stabilized, it will be preferred to a non-stabilized keto form. Additionally, hydrogen bonding can stabilize the enol form. To some extent, this means that the solvent can affect the keto-enol equilibrium, but another classic example is provided by 1,3-diketones. Both resonance stabilization and internal hydrogen bonding stabilization of the enol forms are shown below in Figure 12.

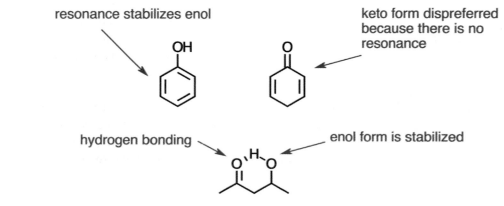

resonance stabilizes enol

keto form dispreferred
because there is no
resonance

hydrogen bonding

enol form is stabilized

Figure 12. Enol stabilization.

An important point about the keto-enol mechanism—in both its acid-catalyzed and base-catalyzed forms—is its dependence on α-hydrogens. If there is no α-hydrogen, tautomerization cannot take place. This means that if you're faced with a compound that might undergo keto-enol tautomerization on Test Day, be sure to double-check that there is at least one hydrogen on the adjacent alpha carbon(s). Figure 13 shows some examples of compounds that *cannot* undergo keto-enol tautomerism for this reason.

4. Enolate chemistry and aldol condensation

Above, in Figure 11, we saw that base-catalyzed keto-enol tautomerism involves an intermediate with a negative charge. This structure is known as an enolate. Enolates are discussed in greater detail in Chapter 10, but the short version of why enolates are remarkable is that resonance allows that negative charge to be distributed onto the α-carbon to some extent, allowing it to act as a nucleophile.

Figure 13. Resonance stabilization of an enolate.

This property of enolates is exhibited in base-catalyzed aldol condensation. This is actually a two-step reaction between two molecules of an aldehyde (or ketone). The basic idea of an aldol condensation reaction is that the two aldehyde/ketone molecules combine via nucleophilic attack to form a product known as an aldol. The name 'aldol' refers to the fact that the product has one aldehyde (or ketone) functionality and one alcohol functional group. Once the aldol is formed, it can undergo spontaneous reduction, in which the alcohol group is kicked out and a C=C double bond is formed, creating an α,β-unsaturated ketone or aldehyde.

step 1: aldol formation

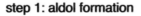
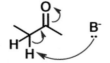
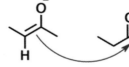
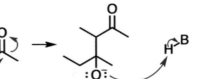
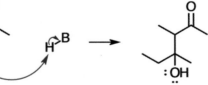

base deprotonation forms an enolate   enolate attacks another aldehyde/ketone molecule   reprotonation to form aldol product

step 2: dehydration

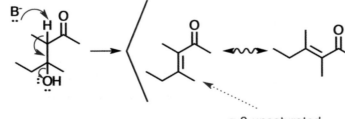

spontaneous base-catalyzed reduction   α,β-unsaturated ketone   same α,β-unsaturated ketone after rotation about a single bond: watch out for this possibility on the MCAT!

Figure 14. Base-catalyzed aldol formation.

As shown in Figure 14, in the first step of base-catalyzed aldol formation, a base removes an α-hydrogen, forming an enolate. This is the same first step that we saw in Figure 11 for base-catalyzed keto-enol tautomerization. The difference is that in this mechanism, the enolate attacks another molecule of the aldehyde/ketone, forming a new C–C single bond. Simple reprotonation forms the aldol product. In order to make sense of aldol condensation for the MCAT, you should focus on identifying how it is similar to and different from other reaction mechanisms you've seen. In terms of similarities, you may note that the actual mechanism itself is virtually identical to the nucleophilic addition mechanism we saw for hemiacetal and hemiketal formation: a nucleophile attacks, is added, and then we have to do some protonation/deprotonation to get the final product. Important differences include the nature of the nucleophile, and in particular, the fact that the enolate ion is a structure that allows carbon to act as a nucleophile because of the resonance-distributed negative charge on the ion. Another remarkable fact about aldol condensation is that it is the only mechanism the MCAT expects you to know about in any detail through which new carbon-carbon bonds are formed.

However, we're not done once the aldol is formed. As we can see in Figure 14, the second step is spontaneous reduction/dehydration. In this step, the base removes another α-hydrogen (further confirming the importance of these specially located hydrogens), which triggers the formation of a double C=C bond, at which point the –OH leaves. This generates a structure known as an α,β-unsaturated ketone/aldehyde. The terms 'saturated' and 'unsaturated' are used more often in biochemistry, but just to review, 'saturated' means a compound in which all the carbon-carbon bonds are single—that is, a compound that is 'saturated' with as many hydrogens as possible. (Recall how bond-line notation omits implicit hydrogens.)

The aldol condensation reaction can be catalyzed by an acid as well, although this mechanism is less important for the MCAT because it doesn't involve an enolate ion. In the acid-catalyzed mechanism, an enol molecule attacks with an activated (that is, protonated) ketone/aldehyde molecule to form the condensation product. The dehydration step to an α,β-unsaturated compound can also occur via acid catalysis.

Although the aldol condensation reaction builds on mechanisms that should be familiar from simpler nucleophilic addition reactions, students often find it challenging. One reason for this is that the final product—especially after the dehydration step—is visually very much unlike the reactants. In general, the MCAT doesn't test you on retrosynthetic analysis (that is, problems that you may have encountered in organic chemistry classes where you have to look at a molecule and figure out what synthetic steps you'd need to take to make it from various simple starting materials), but aldol condensation is a slight exception. It's worth remembering that if you see an α,β-unsaturated carbonyl, aldol condensation is a possibility. Moreover, it can be important to remember that the possibility of rotation around single bonds means that the orientation of aldol products might not correspond to how you imagine the reaction happening in your head, or even how you would draw it out. This possibility is demonstrated at the end of the pathway in Figure 14.

Aldol condensation is an equilibrium process, and as such it can be reversed. The reverse reaction is known as the retro-aldol reaction. An important example of this is found in glycolysis, in which the six-carbon compound fructose-1,6-bisphosphate is cleaved to form the three-carbon compounds dihydroxyacetone phosphate and glyceraldehyde phosphate. Figure 15 shows this mechanism.

> ## MCAT STRATEGY > > >
>
> One way to cope with the potential difficulty of visualizing the outcomes of aldol condensation reactions is to implement simple safety checks like being sure to count carbons and account for the location and orientation of double bonds or other important structural features of a molecule. If nothing else, this will help you rule out answer choices that *cannot* be correct.

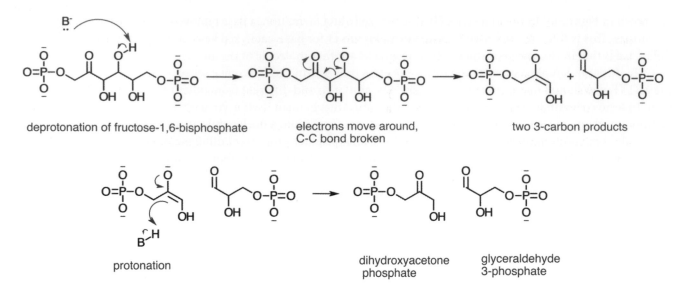

Figure 15. Cleavage of fructose-1,6-bisphosphate.

It is unlikely that you will be directly tested on this mechanism, but you should know what retro-aldol reactions are in general terms, and it is useful to walk through this reaction as an example of how the skills we built up by first analyzing simple nucleophilic substitution reactions can be applied to systematically understand reaction mechanisms that might initially seem intimidating or unfamiliar.

The first step of this reaction is deprotonation of fructose-1,6-bisphosphate by a base. The surplus electrons on the deprotonated oxygen then attack the carbon, forming a C=O double bond. This causes the C–C bond to be broken, and in a process of electron transfers, a C=C bond and a C–O⁻ are formed. This is followed by a protonation step that converts the C=C bond to a C–C bond and allows the C=O bond to be reformed, generating dihydroxyacetone phosphate. In physiological conditions, this reaction is catalyzed by an enzyme known as fructose-1,6-bisphosphate aldolase.

5. Must-Knows

> Basic idea for reaction mechanisms: an electrophile and a nucleophile form a bond.
> - Electrophile: an atom that 'needs' electrons (usually has positive or partial positive charge)
> - Nucleophile: an atom that 'needs' to share its excess electrons (usually has negative or partial negative charge)
> S_N1: nucleophilic substitution with a first-order rate law (depends on substrate concentration only). Carbocation forms, then nucleophile attacks. Favorable factors: highly substituted carbons, polar protic solvent. Stereochemistry not preserved.
> S_N2: nucleophilic substitution with a second-order rate law (depends on substrate *and* nucleophile concentration). Nucleophile performs 'backside attack' and kicks out leaving group, inverting the stereochemistry. Favorable factors: methyl/primary carbons, strong and non-bulky nucleophile, polar aprotic solvent.
> Carboxylic acid: C has strong partial positive charge, is a good electrophile. Nucleophilic substitution is common, as in Fischer esterification and imine formation.
> - Nucleophile attacks carboxylic acid C, then a leaving group is kicked off.

> Nucleophilic addition at carbonyl C (C=O): hemiacetals (–R, –H, –OH, –OR') formed from aldehydes, hemiketals (–R, –R', –OH, –OR'') from ketones. Reaction can repeat with excess alcohol to form acetals and ketals (another –OR group instead of –OH).
  — Nucleophile attacks carbonyl C but no leaving group.
> Keto-enol tautomerism: can be catalyzed by acid or base, α-hydrogen removal is critical in both (first step in base-catalyzed mechanism, second step in acid catalysis)
> Enolate chemistry: resonance-stabilized negative charge on α-carbon allows carbon to be a nucleophile.
  — Aldol condensation: nucleophilic α-carbon attacks electrophilic carbonyl C to form a new C–C bond.

Practice Passage

Industrial saponification most commonly results from the base hydrolysis of triglycerides to form glycerol and the corresponding sodium salts of fatty acids. The production of soap can also be accomplished on a small scale by individuals, in which fat is heated and mixed with an appropriate amount of aqueous lye (NaOH) or potash (KOH). Soap makers often will quote a "saponification number", which represents the mass of potash required to completely hydrolyze 1 g of a fat with a given average molar mass.

After combining the fat with the aqueous base solution, the resulting heterogeneous mixture is stirred to form an emulsion in which the reaction takes place at the interface between the aqueous phase and the liquefied fat. Reaction rate is dependent upon the temperature and the interface surface area. The reaction is exothermic, so once the mixture begins to thicken, the external heat source is removed and the reaction is allowed to continue until the mixture "traces" when stirred. At this point, a scented molecule may be added. For bar soaps, the warm thick mixture is finally poured into molds and allowed to finish reacting and to cool for several hours. Electrostatic interactions help facilitate strong attachments between soap molecules. Thus, while solid soap is made with lye, potash is used to make liquid soaps.

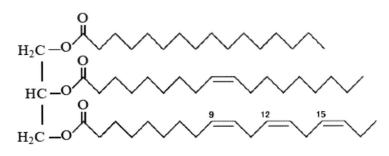

Figure 1. Unsaturated triglyceride

Highly saturated fats, like animal fats, tend to form amorphous solids at room temperature, while highly unsaturated fats that contain a high degree of unsaturation, as in vegetable oils, tend to be liquids at room temperature. Figure 1 shows a triglyceride ($C_{55}H_{98}O_6$; MW = 854 g/mol) in which one of the esters is saturated, one is monounsaturated and a third is polyunsaturated. The chemical composition of fats is not uniform and thus, Figure 1 may not necessarily represent a naturally occurring fatty acid.

1. What is the saponification number for the molecule shown in Figure 1?
    A. 46 mg
    B. 66 mg
    C. 140 mg
    D. 197 mg

2. How many chiral atoms are present in the structure of the fat shown in Figure 1?
    A. 0
    B. 1
    C. 4
    D. 6

3. If a soap maker wanted to make a hard bar of soap, which of the following fatty acids would be most desirable to be the major component of the fat?
   A. Hexadecanoic acid
   B. (9Z)-Octadec-9-enoic acid
   C. (9E)-Octadec-9-enoic acid
   D. (9Z, 12Z, 15Z)-9,12,15-Octadecatrienoic acid

4. In the base catalyzed hydrolysis of fat, what is the most likely first step in the mechanism of the reaction?
   A. Protonation of an oxygen lone-pair of a carbonyl group
   B. Electrophilic attack of sodium ion on the oxygen lone-pair of a carbonyl group
   C. Nucleophilic attack on a carbonyl carbon by water
   D. Nucleophilic attack on a carbonyl carbon by hydroxide

5. If the polyunsaturated ester chain in figure 1 were subject to molecular chlorination, what would be the resulting product?

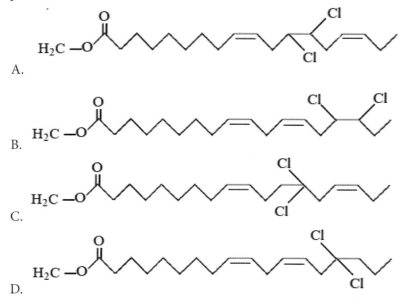

A.

B.

C.

D.

6. The acid-catalyzed conversion of hemiketals to ketals is an example of:
   A. S_N1 by an alcohol nucleophile.
   B. S_N2 by an alcohol nucleophile.
   C. nucleophilic addition of an alcohol.
   D. electrophilic elimination of water.

7. Which of the following reactions will NOT yield a fatty acid?

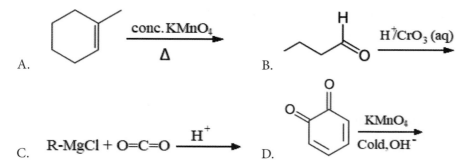

A.

B.

C. R-MgCl + O=C=O $\xrightarrow{H^+}$

D.

Practice Passage Explanations

Industrial saponification most commonly results from the base hydrolysis of triglycerides to form glycerol and the corresponding sodium salts of fatty acids. The production of soap can also be accomplished on a small scale by individuals, in which fat is heated and mixed with an appropriate amount of aqueous lye (NaOH) or potash (KOH). Soap makers often will quote a "saponification number", which represents the mass of potash required to completely hydrolyze 1 g of a fat with a given average molar mass.

Key terms: saponification, base hydrolysis, saponification #, potash, lye

Cause and effect: saponification = soap-making = triglyceride + H_2O → ROH+ Na salts; sapon # ~ level of hydrolysis needed for fat

After combining the fat with the aqueous base solution, the resulting heterogeneous mixture is stirred to form an emulsion in which the reaction takes place at the interface between the aqueous phase and the liquefied fat. Reaction rate is dependent upon the temperature and the interface surface area. The reaction is exothermic, so once the mixture begins to thicken, the external heat source is removed and the reaction is allowed to continue until the mixture "traces" when stirred. At this point, a scented molecule may be added. For bar soaps, the warm thick mixture is finally poured into molds and allowed to finish reacting and to cool for several hours. Electrostatic interactions help facilitate strong attachments between soap molecules. Thus, while solid soap is made with lye, potash is used to make liquid soaps.

Key terms: T-dependent, interface, exothermic, bar soap, liquid soap, traces

Cause and effect: K^+ is larger than Na^+ which reduces the electrostatic interactions between cations and COO⁻ group, thus lowering the melting point of the soap

Contrast: NaOH → solid soap; KOH → liquid soap

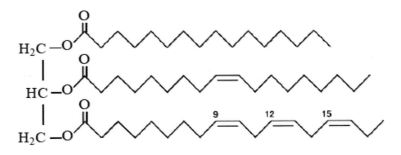

Figure 1. Unsaturated triglyceride

Figure 1 reveals the different level of π-bonds that come with unsaturation; these sp^2 carbons will introduce kinks to the chains, preventing efficient staking and packing

Highly saturated fats, like animal fats, tend to form amorphous solids at room temperature, while highly unsaturated fats that contain a high degree of unsaturation, as in vegetable oils, tend to be liquids at room temperature. Figure 1 shows a triglyceride ($C_{55}H_{98}O_6$; MW = 854 g/mol) in which one of the esters is saturated, one is monounsaturated and a third is polyunsaturated. The chemical composition of fats is not uniform and thus, Figure 1 may not necessarily represent a naturally occurring fatty acid.

Key terms: saturated fats, unsaturated fats, chemical composition

Cause and effect: π-bonds = unsaturation → kinks in structure → less rigid structure → s to l phase shift

1. D is correct. As stated in the passage, the saponification number represents the mass of KOH required to completely hydrolyze 1 g of a specific fat. The molar mass of the fat depicted is 854 g/mol and the stoichiometry of the reaction is 3 moles of KOH for every one mole of fat. The dimensional analysis is:

$$1 \text{ g fat} \times (1 \text{ mol/850 g}) \times (3 \text{ KOH / 1 fat}) \times 56 \text{ g/mol KOH} \times (10^3 \text{ mg/1 g}) \sim 200 \text{ mg}$$

   A, B, C: If we approximate 854 ~ 1000, then the number of mg of KOH needed per gram of fat is 3(56) ~ 168 mg, we can easily eliminate choices A and C. Remembering that the molar mass of the fat was approximated, the answer should be greater than 168. We could get C if we used the molar mass of NaOH (40 g/mol) rather than the molar mass of KOH. We would get choice B if we used a 1:1 molar ratio, rather than a 3:1 molar ratio.

2. B is correct. The only chiral carbon (a C bonded to 4 different substituents) in the fat structure shown in Figure 1 is the central carbon of the glycerol.

3. A is correct. As stated in the passage, fats containing saturated fatty acids tend to be higher melting and solids at room temperature, whereas fats containing unsaturated fatty acids tend to be lower melting and liquids at room temperature. These properties are related to the ability of the alkyl group to rotate around carbon-carbon bonds. Hexadecanoic acid is a saturated fatty acid, which is denoted by the -anoic acid. Choice B, C, and D all represent unsaturated fatty acids as denoted by the -enoic acid and should be eliminated.

4. D is correct. The concentration of hydrogen ions in the aqueous solution will be very low, since the solution is basic. Therefore, it is extremely unlikely that a carbonyl oxygen lone-pair would be protonated, as it might under acid-catalyzed conditions. Choice D is the commonly accepted first step in the base-catalyzed hydrolysis of esters.

   A, B, C: Sodium is an exceptionally poor electrophile and is unlikely to act as a Lewis acid. While water could act as a nucleophile and attack a carbonyl carbon (choice C), water is not nearly as good a nucleophile as hydroxide.

5. A is correct. Addition of a molecular halogen (Br or Cl) results in the anti-addition of 2 Cl atoms across the π – bond with a cyclic intermediate being formed. When the first Cl^- atom attacks the π-bond, it leaves behind one of its electrons with the other Cl that it was bonded to in Cl_2. That other Cl is now a chloride anion and is attracted to the slight positive charge on the carbon atoms. It is blocked from nucleophilic attack on one side of the carbon chain by the first Cl atom and can only attack from the opposite side. As it attacks and forms a bond with one of the carbons, the bond between the first Cl atom and the other carbon atoms breaks, leaving each carbon atom with a single Cl substituent.

6. C is correct. The conversion of ketones to hemiketals, and the subsequent conversion of hemiketals to ketals is identical to the conversion of aldehyde → hemiacetal → acetal. The reaction is essentially just a 1,2-addition of an alcohol to a ketone.

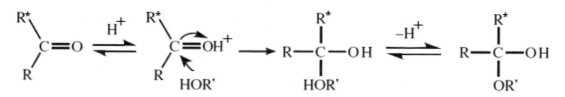

The carbonyl π-bond breaks, and we are left with a tetrahedral compound. As with all [1,2]-additions to carbonyls with nucleophiles, the reaction is faster in the presence of an acid due to is ability to increase the electrophilic character of the target carbon. If we do this process once, we get the hemiketal. If we do it again, the hemiketal converts to a ketal. The overall steps of each reaction are protonation, 1,2-addition, proton transfer, 1,2-elimination, 1,2-addition, and a final deprotonation.

7. D is correct. A fatty acid is equivalent to a carboxylic acid. Thus we need to find the one reaction that will NOT yield a carboxylic acid. Hydroxylation of alkenes results in syn addition of hydroxyl groups across the π bond, not formation of a carboxylic acid.

A, B, C: Strong oxidative cleavage of alkenes, Jones reagent (i.e. an oxidizing agent) treatment of an aldehyde, and carboxylation of a Grignard reagent followed by acidification will all result in the formation of carboxylic acids.

Independent Questions

1. In the transition state depicted below, let X be a generic nucleophile and Y be a generic leaving group. Assume the reaction takes place at a chiral center.

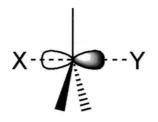

   This transition state most accurately depicts:

   A. a nucleophilic substitution reaction, with inversion of stereochemistry.
   B. a nucleophilic substitution reaction, with retention of stereochemistry.
   C. an electrophilic addition reaction, with a single, unique product.
   D. an electrophilic addition reaction, with multiple, isomeric products.

2. Esterification of the C-terminus of the tripeptide AFS could be accomplished with which of the following reagents?
   A. Concentrated aqueous sodium hydroxide
   B. Acetic anhydride with catalytic pyridine (a non-nucleophilic base)
   C. Excess ethanol with catalytic sulfuric acid
   D. Hydrogen gas with a platinum catalyst

3. Which of the following substituted benzene derivatives is most nucleophilic at its 2, 4, and 6 positions?
   A. Nitrobenzene
   B. Iodobenzene
   C. Benzoic acid
   D. Benzenesulfonic acid

4. When heated in aqueous solution, pyruvic acid will undergo decomposition, yielding all of the following EXCEPT:
   A. carbon dioxide.
   B. an aldehyde.
   C. a primary alcohol.
   D. an increase in entropy from reactants to products.

5. The structure of ascorbic acid is shown below.

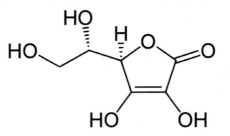

   Suppose a chemist wishes to chemically modify only the secondary alcohol groups in ascorbic acid. Protection of the primary alcohol could be most effectively achieved by treating ascorbic acid with:

   A. sodium hydroxide.
   B. 4-toluenesulfonyl chloride.
   C. chloromethane.
   D. sodium borohydride.

6. Penicillin contains a four-atom ring structure that is vital for its antimicrobial function. This ring contains an amide bond and is known as:
   A. an epoxide.
   B. a lactide.
   C. a lactone.
   D. a lactam.

7. How many units of acetyl-CoA are produced by the complete beta-oxidation of lauric acid ($C_{12}H_{24}O_2$)?
   A. 13
   B. 12
   C. 7
   D. 6

8. Lactose is a disaccharide consisting of a single molecule of α-D-glucose bonded to a molecule of β-D-galactose, a glucose isomer. The glycoside bond bridges the first carbon of galactose and the fourth carbon of glucose. What is the IUPAC name for lactose?
   A. β-D-galactopyranosyl-(1→4)-D-glucose
   B. β-D-glucopyranosyl-(1→4)-D-galactose
   C. α-D-galactopyranosyl-(1→4)-D-glucose
   D. α-D-glucopyranosyl-(1→4)-D-galactose

Independent Question Explanations

1. A is correct. Electrophilic addition reactions occur across double bonds, which do not appear in the given diagram (choices C and D are wrong). The given transition state, in which a leaving group is ejected from the opposite side of an approaching nucleophile, is consistent with an S_N2 reaction. S_N2 reactions produce inversion of stereochemistry at the sp^3 chemical center.

2. C is correct. Here, we are attempting to turn the carboxylic acid group at the C-terminus of the tripeptide into an ester. Concentrated NaOH will not accomplish this (eliminate choice A). Acetic anhydride would be useful for acetylation of a free hydroxyl group, but it will not effectively esterify a carboxylic acid (eliminate option B). Finally, hydrogen gas with a Pt catalyst is used for reducing alkynes and alkenes into alkanes, not for esterification (eliminate choice D). In the presence of catalytic acid, ethanol can act as a nucleophile and displace hydroxide from the carboxylic acid group to form the peptide ethyl ester.

3. B is correct. Due to their substituents, nitrobenzene, benzoic acid, and benzenesulfonic acid have resonance contributors with positively charged ortho/para positions. This renders the ortho/para positions electron-deficient, rather than nucleophilic (eliminate options A, C, and D). On the other hand, substituents with available lone pairs, such as halogens, are able to contribute electron density into the benzene ring and permit resonance structures with negatively charged carbon atoms at the ortho/para positions.

4. C is correct. The pyrolytic decomposition reaction described is a decarboxylation. Alpha-ketoacids, such as pyruvic acid, undergo decarboxylation to produce carbon dioxide and the corresponding aldehyde. The liberation of a gaseous product suggests an increase in entropy. A primary alcohol does not form, making C the correct answer.

5. B is correct. 4-toluenesulfonyl chloride (tosyl chloride) may be used to tosylate free hydroxyl groups. Due to its significant steric bulk and the nucleophilic substitution mechanism by which it adds, tosyl chloride will react selectively with primary alcohols. Although chloromethane possesses an electrophilic site, its smaller size increases the likelihood that it will indiscriminately methylate all free hydroxyl groups. Sodium hydroxide, a strong base, mainly functions to deprotonate acidic positions, and sodium borohydride is a reducing agent.

6. D is correct. Cyclic amides are known as lactams. β-lactam antibiotics, which include penicillin, contain a four-atom lactam ring. Some bacteria express an enzyme, β-lactamase, which cleaves this ring structure and renders the bacterium resistant to penicillin.

7. D is correct. Since lauric acid contains 12 carbon atoms, its digestion produces 6 units of acetyl-CoA. Remember, the acetyl group in acetyl-CoA contains two carbons.

8. A is correct. Since the linkage is formed between the first carbon of galactose and the fourth carbon of glucose, it will be a 1→4 type linkage, and galactose will appear before glucose in the IUPAC name (eliminate choices B and D). Since its anomeric carbon is part of the glycosidic bond, galactose cannot interconvert between the α and β anomers. Therefore, it must remain in the β conformation, and the glycosidic bond is named accordingly.

Spectroscopy and Separations

0. Introduction

Congratulations on reaching the final chapter of this book! You have now learned the principles of MCAT general chemistry, as well as the basics of organic chemistry and the organic reactions with which you should be familiar. This leads us to a new question: once a chemist has performed a reaction procedure, how can he or she be certain that the correct product was formed? And how can this desired product be separated from reactants or side products present in the same flask?

These two questions can be answered using knowledge of separation and analytic techniques. Do not confuse the two! Separation techniques aim to separate a mixture into its pure components or, when this is not possible, to convert the original mixture into multiple mixtures that are each largely composed of a single component. The main separation techniques that will be discussed in this chapter are distillation, extraction, and chromatography. In contrast, analytic techniques aim to identify a compound or determine its properties. In summary: if one component of a mixture is being isolated for later use, a separation technique is being used. If a compound is sent through an apparatus and analyzed, and if no further use is planned, we must be using an analytic technique. In fact, many organic chemistry analytic techniques destroy the compound under analysis. In this chapter, the analytic techniques that you will learn about are spectroscopy (infrared, nuclear magnetic resonance, and ultraviolet-visible) and mass spectrometry.

1. Infrared Spectroscopy and Nuclear Magnetic Resonance

Let's begin with our analytic techniques, which, for the sake of this chapter, are largely spectroscopy methods. For the MCAT, we recommend that you be very comfortable with spectroscopy, or the analysis of organic compounds exposed to electromagnetic (EM) radiation. What exactly *is* electromagnetic radiation? Simply put, it is light, but visible light forms but a small portion of the electromagnetic spectrum (Figure 1).

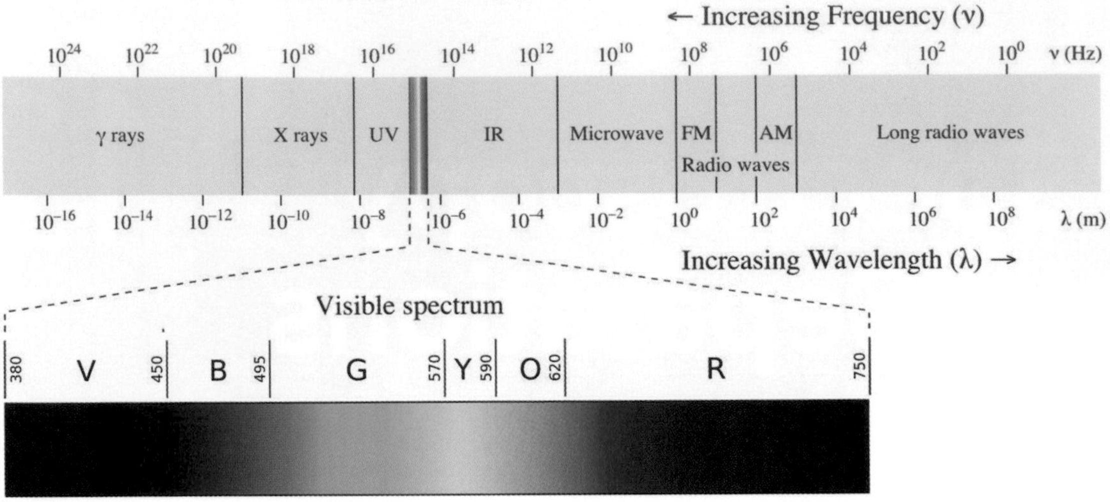

Figure 1. The electromagnetic spectrum.

> > CONNECTIONS < <

Chapter 9 of Physics

MCAT STRATEGY > > >

The terms used to describe concepts can give away a great deal about their meanings. For example, "infra-" means "below," so "infrared" means "a frequency below that of red light." Conversely, "ultra" means "above," so "ultraviolet" light has a frequency higher than that of violet light.

This chapter will touch upon only two forms of electromagnetic radiation: infrared radiation (IR) and ultraviolet radiation (UV). Infrared radiation is a form of electromagnetic radiation with a frequency just below that of visible light. Infrared (IR) spectroscopy is a technique that uses infrared light to vibrate covalent bonds in molecules and measure the vibrations to collect information about functional groups.

Put simply, the bonds that appear on an IR spectrum must have a dipole moment, such as the polar O–H bond in water. In contrast, the Br–Br bond in Br_2 does not have a dipole and thus does not appear on an IR spectrum. The same is true for the N-N bond in N_2, and so on.

An example of an IR spectrum is shown in Figure 2. The y-axis displays percent transmittance (the proportion of IR light transmitted through the sample), which is the reciprocal of absorbance. Regions that have absorbed light will appear as valleys, not peaks, along the graph. The x-axis displays the frequency of light in a unit or measurement known as wavenumbers (cm^{-1}), with frequency increasing from right to left along the x-axis.

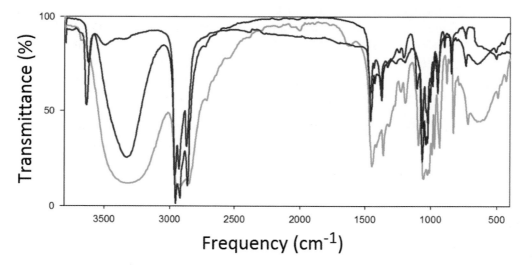

Figure 2. A sample IR spectrum showing multiple compounds, each corresponding to a separate line.

Specific bonds are associated with characteristic absorption frequencies on an IR spectrum. Memorizing these frequencies might very well get you some quick, easy points on the MCAT! Most of these peaks to know appear within the 1500-4000 cm^{-1} range. While it may initially appear that the region below 1500 cm^{-1} contains a large number of notable peaks, this area, termed the fingerprint region, is specific to each compound. Since each molecule has a distinct fingerprint region, this range is generally not very useful when identifying functional groups on an unknown molecule.

The IR frequencies of the most common covalent bonds are listed in Table 1. Among these frequencies, the most commonly tested are the carbonyl (C=O) functional group, which appears as a sharp peak near 1700 cm^{-1}, and the hydroxyl (–OH) functional group, which is marked by a broad peak in the range of 3100–3500 cm^{-1}. By "sharp," we mean that the peak is narrow or pointy; it slopes dramatically downward and back up. On the other hand, a broad peak is wider and takes up a larger area of the IR spectrum.

> > **CONNECTIONS** < <

Chapter 10 of Chemistry

Bond	Wavenumber (cm^{-1})	Shape (if applicable)
C=N	1550-1650	–
C=C	1600-1680	–
C=O	1650-1780	Sharp
C≡C	2100-2260	–
C≡N	2220-2260	–
O-H	3200-3600	Broad
N-H	3300-3500	–

Table 1. IR spectrum frequencies of select bonds.

Unlike IR, which identifies the *bonds* in a molecule, nuclear magnetic resonance (NMR) spectroscopy aims to characterize a molecule's *atoms*. Specifically, this technique places a sample in a magnetic field. If the sample has a nuclear spin due to an odd number of protons or neutrons, then it will be affected by the magnetic field. The atomic nuclei will align *with* the field (a lower-energy state) or *against* the field (a higher-energy state). The frequency of transition between these states, or resonance, is measured by NMR. The major form of NMR that you should understand for the MCAT is ^1H (proton) NMR. To be comprehensive, we will also briefly discuss ^{13}C (carbon) NMR, although it is far less likely to appear on the MCAT exam.

MCAT STRATEGY > > >

Remember from Chapter 1 that ^1H is an isotope of hydrogen, while ^{13}C is an isotope of carbon. While ^1H is by far the most common hydrogen isotope, ^{13}C is actually somewhat rare, as ^{12}C predominates in nature.

Before delving into these methods, we must discuss the general appearance of an NMR spectrum. Resonance frequencies are chemical shifts ranging from zero on the far right to positive values on the far left. A shift of zero is arbitrarily assigned to the peak corresponding to tetramethylsilane (TMS) as a reference point. Figure 3 depicts a sample NMR spectrum. Peaks that are shifted to the right are said to be located upfield, and peaks that are shifted to the left are said to be located downfield.

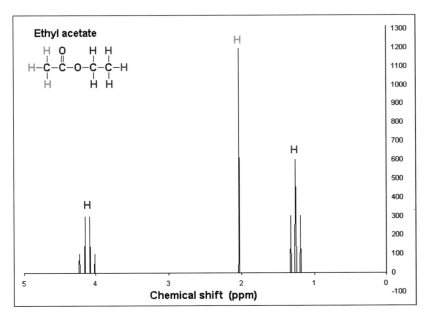

Figure 3. The ^1H NMR spectrum of ethyl acetate.

Let's begin with ^1H NMR, as it is the more confusing and higher-yield of the two methods. In proton NMR, each hydrogen atom (or set of equivalent hydrogen atoms) produces a single peak on the spectrum. Equivalent hydrogen atoms are protons that exist in the same magnetic environment. For example, consider ethyl acetate ($CH_3COOCH_2CH_3$). The three H atoms on the CH_3 group adjacent to the carbonyl carbon rotate freely around the C–C bond and are essentially identical. Because these protons do not differ in any measurable way, they will correspond to only one peak on the spectrum, but the area under that peak will be *three times greater* than the area under a peak that corresponds to a single hydrogen atom. In other words, the peak area (or integration) directly correlates to the number of protons represented by that peak.

Peaks on a proton NMR spectrum can range from 0–12 ppm. Location depends on the extent of shielding or deshielding experienced by ^1H nuclei. Returning to Figure 3, let us consider the blue hydrogen atoms on ethyl acetate located on the terminal carbon of the ethyl group. These hydrogen atoms are surrounded by a relatively large amount of electron density, so they are considered to be shielded, or blocked, from experiencing the full extent of the magnetic field. As a result of shielding, the peak associated with these protons will shift upfield closer to 0 ppm.

In contrast, let's examine the two protons marked in red, which are attached to the non-terminal carbon of the ethyl group. This carbon atom is adjacent to an oxygen atom, which is very electronegative and will lure electrons away that would otherwise surround the H atoms. These deshielded protons now experience the magnetic field to a greater degree, and their peak will be shifted downfield (to the left). In general, the closer a set of protons is to an electron-withdrawing group, the more deshielded they will be, and the farther left their peak will be found. Table 2 lists the chemical shifts associated with common functional groups on a ^{1}H NMR spectrum.

Functional group	Shift (ppm)
$-CH_3$	0.9
$-CH_2OH$	1.0-5.5
$-C\equiv CH$	2.0-3.0
$-CH = CH-$	4.5-6.0
Ar (aromatic ring)$-H$	6.0-8.4
$-CHO$	9.5
$-COOH$	10.5-12.0

Table 2. ^{1}H NMR chemical shifts.

Finally, the generally most confusing aspect of NMR is splitting. Until this point, we've explained ^{1}H NMR signals in a simplified way, implying that each signal is one clearly defined peak. In reality, each signal is affected by protons on atoms adjacent to the carbon to which the proton is attached. To predict splitting patterns, follow the n + 1 rule, which states that any peak will be split into a number of smaller peaks equal to the number of adjacent hydrogen atoms plus one. If a hydrogen atom is positioned on a terminal carbon adjacent to a carbon bound to one additional hydrogen atom, for example, the peak that represents the first hydrogen atom will be split into a doublet (1 adjacent hydrogen atom + 1 = 2). You can remember this rule by recognizing that a proton next to *zero* hydrogen atoms cannot yield a "zero-let." Instead, having no adjacent protons yields a singlet, as 0 + 1 = 1.

To elaborate upon this point, re-examine Figure 3. Here, the peak corresponding to the red hydrogen atoms is split into four smaller peaks (a quartet). We observe this because the red hydrogen atoms are positioned on a carbon adjacent to a carbon containing *three* neighboring protons, in blue (3 + 1 = 4). Now consider the peak marked in green. These methyl protons represented by this peak are adjacent to the carbonyl carbon, which is not bound to any hydrogen atoms. As a result, the green peak is a singlet (0 + 1 = 1). Finally, the peak marked in blue is a triplet because it represents three protons that are *adjacent* to a carbon with two protons (2 + 1 = 3).

Let's try an example. How many peaks will appear on an ^{1}H NMR spectrum of ethanol? And how will each peak be split? First, we need to note that ethanol (CH_3CH_2OH) has three sets of equivalent protons. Thus, the ^{1}H NMR spectrum for ethanol should include three peaks. The hydroxyl hydrogen is adjacent to a carbon bound to two protons, so it will be split into a triplet. The two protons on carbon 1 have four neighboring protons *in total* (three from $-CH_3$ and one from $-OH$), so their peak will be a quintet. Finally, the three protons on carbon 2 will correspond to a triplet due to the two neighboring hydrogens.

Let's wrap up with a brief discussion of ^{13}C NMR spectroscopy, which is far less likely to appear on the MCAT (but we always err on the side of safety). Since this form of NMR is tested less frequently than ^1H NMR, you must only be familiar with a few key pieces of information. Most carbon on Earth exists in the form of ^{12}C, but ^{13}C is used because only nuclei with an odd number of protons have nuclear spin.

If you were to encounter ^{13}C NMR on the MCAT, it would most likely appear in the form of a spin-decoupled spectrum in which all peaks exist as singlets. Be careful, though—just as equivalent protons corresponded to a single peak in ^1H NMR, equivalent *carbon* atoms appear as a single peak in ^{13}C NMR. Symmetrical compounds may have multiple sets of equivalent carbons that are mirror images of each other. The scale of a ^{13}C NMR spectrum is also larger than that of a ^1H spectrum, ranging from 0–200 ppm. As in ^1H NMR, the signals of deshielded carbon atoms are shifted downfield, and vice versa.

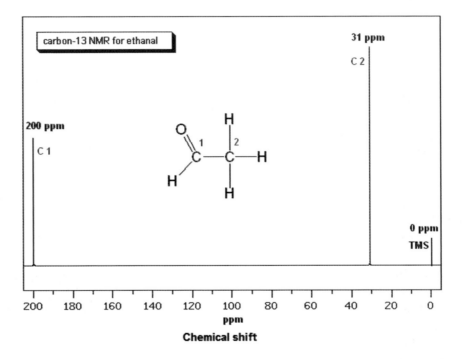

Figure 4. The ^{13}C NMR spectrum of ethanal.

2. Ultraviolet-Visible Spectroscopy and Mass Spectrometry

IR and NMR spectroscopy are the highest-yield MCAT analytic techniques, but we would be remiss if we neglected to mention a few others. To begin, ultraviolet-visible (UV-Vis) spectroscopy is a technique that analyzes the absorbance of visible or ultraviolet light by organic compounds. UV light is slightly higher in frequency than visible light, which is why UV rays from the sun can be damaging to biological molecules. Since frequency and wavelength are inversely proporational, UV light also possesses a *shorter* wavelength than visible light, with a range of 10 nanometers (nm) to 400 nm. (Recall from physics that the wavelength of visible light spans from 400 to 700 nm!)

> **MCAT STRATEGY > > >**
>
> Direct and inverse relationships are often important to understand for the MCAT. Whenever you come across one, be certain to make a mental or written note. Here, that may be as simple as "wavelength decreases as frequency increases."

On a UV-Vis spectrum, the absorbance, or the proportion of light absorbed by the sample, is plotted against the wavelength of this light. Conjugated compounds with alternating single and double bonds tend to readily absorb UV-Vis light due to the delocalization of π electrons. Beta-carotene, a biologically relevant example of such a compound, is shown in Figure 5.

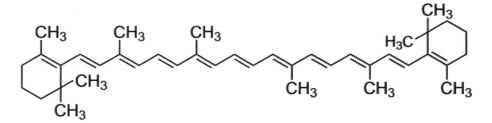

Figure 5. Beta-carotene, a conjugated compound.

Lastly, let us wrap up our discussion of spectroscopic techniques with mass spectrometry, an incredibly useful method for identifying unknown organic compounds. In this technique, a sample is injected into a mass spectrometer, which exposes the molecules to a beam of electrons. These high-energy electrons cause the sample molecules to ionize, or become charged. Removal of one electron from the parent molecule creates the M^+ cation, which has the same molecular weight as the uncharged parent molecule. Sample molecules also fragment into a variety of smaller charged species.

MCAT STRATEGY > > >

On the current MCAT, UV-Vis spectroscopy often appears in the context of identifying aromatic amino acids. Since these amino acid residues have conjugated side chains, they give a distinctive reading on a UV-Vis spectrum. Aromatic amino acids include phenylalanine, tyrosine, and tryptophan.

> > CONNECTIONS < <

Chapter 2 of Biochemistry

The mass and charge of the fragments are measured and plotted on a mass spectrum (Figure 6). The x-axis shows the mass-to-charge ratio (m/z) of the fragments, and the y-axis displays their relative abundance. The peak with the highest m/z value is usually the M^+ peak, which lets us know the molecular weight of the unknown molecule. The peak corresponding to the most abundant fragment is the base peak. The locations of these peaks give researchers information about the size and functional groups of a compound, though in-depth analysis of mass spectra is outside of the scope of the MCAT.

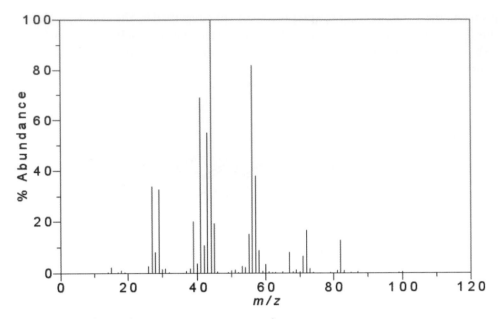

Figure 6. The mass spectrum of an unknown organic compound.

3. Separations: Distillation

With your newfound knowledge of spectroscopy, you may now be able to identify some compounds based on their IR or NMR readings alone (and you certainly have sufficient information to ace MCAT questions)! However, this information would be next to useless if you were first presented with a mixture of organic compounds—your desired product along with side products, leftover reactants, and other contaminants. How can you isolate the single product that you actually wish to analyze? The answer lies in separation techniques.

To decide which technique is best for a given situation, first consider the phases of the compounds involved. For example, is the desired product a solid immersed in liquid? Is it a solid with solid impurities? Or is it a liquid in solution with other liquids? If the answer to this last question is "yes," you may be able to utilize distillation. Most distillation procedures aim to separate one liquid from another by utilizing the difference between the two liquids' boiling points. A distillation apparatus is shown in Figure 7.

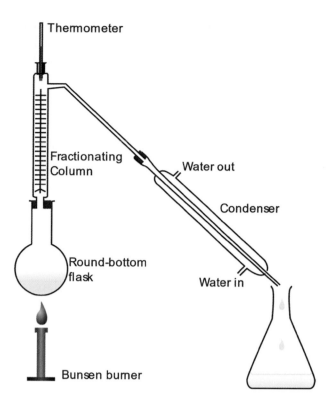

Figure 7. A distillation setup.

Let's take a deeper dive into this figure. Imagine that you are separating two liquids, Liquid A and Liquid B. Liquid A has a boiling point of 80°C, while Liquid B has a boiling point of 125°C. Both liquids are initially held in the same round-bottom flask, which is termed the distilling flask. To begin the procedure, the flask is positioned above a heat source, typically a Bunsen burner. The top of the flask is connected to a column, which leads to a downward-sloping glass condenser. The condenser is held within a glass casing through which cold water is pumped. As the round-bottom flask is heated, the liquid with the lower boiling point (here, Liquid A) will begin to vaporize, and its vapor will travel up the column. Some vapor will pass into the condenser; the adjacent cold water will then cause the vapor to condense into liquid. Since the condenser slopes downward, the liquid will travel down, directly into an empty flask that is positioned below its opening. This vessel is aptly called the receiving flask. Over time, more of Liquid A will pass into the receiving flask, while the majority of Liquid B will remain in the liquid phase in the distilling flask.

> > CONNECTIONS < <

Chapter 5 of Chemistry

But how can we be certain that 100% of Liquid A will vaporize, re-condense, and enter the receiving flask before any of Liquid B begins to vaporize? After all, some liquid molecules are constantly escaping into the vapor phase, even at temperatures below the liquid's boiling point. The answer to this question is simple: we cannot. In fact, distillation is by nature an imperfect technique; we may end up with 90% Liquid A and 10% Liquid B in the receiving flask, which is still fairly impure. To obtain as close to a pure component as possible, repeated distillations are usually necessary.

If you are paying close attention, you'll notice that we have not directly discussed one component of Figure 7: the "fractionating" column. While all distillation procedures include some form of vertical glass structure that connects the round-bottom distilling flask to the condenser, not all procedures include a so-called fractionating column. This brings us to the distinction between simple and fractional distillation. Simple distillation is used when the liquids in question have very dissimilar boiling points; for the sake of the MCAT, they should be at least 25°C apart. (In other words, their vapor pressures are very far apart at a given temperature.) A simple distillation procedure does not include a fractionating column. Instead, the receiving flask is connected very close to the opening of the condenser, resulting in an apparatus that is shorter in height. Since the boiling points are so different, the compound with the lower boiling point will vaporize, rise the short distance, and enter the condenser before the vast majority of the higher-BP compound.

> ## MCAT STRATEGY > > >
>
> When it comes to lab techniques, slower is virtually always better! Fractional distillation takes a great deal of time, but it results in mixtures that are more pure than those formed by simple distillation. Extend this reasoning to other laboratory procedures; it is generally worthwhile to proceed slowly.

Fractional distillation, in contrast, is utilized when the compounds to be separated have boiling points separated by less than 25°C. In such cases, simple distillation is not sufficient; both compounds would vaporize and travel the short distance to the condenser, at least to some extent, and the contents of the receiving flask would thus contain significant proportions of both liquids. To prevent this, a long glass fractionating column—often filled with beads and insulated with foil—is placed between the distilling flask and the top of the condenser. Consider, for example, a distillation procedure involving acetone (BP = 56°C) and methanol (BP = 65°C). The distilling flask is heated, and a significant amount of acetone—along with some methanol—enters the vapor phase and rises through the column. Since the fractionating column is long and filled with packing materials that form available condensation sites, the compound with the higher boiling point (methanol) will tend to condense within the column and fall back down to the distilling flask. On the other hand, at least some of the lower-BP acetone molecules will make it to the top of the column and enter the condenser. While this procedure takes longer than a simple distillation, it provides for better separation between the two liquids. (In fact, the longer the fractionating column, the better the separation.)

> ## MCAT STRATEGY > > >
>
> From Chapter 5 of this book, you should recall that vapor pressure and boiling point of a compound are inversely proportional. In other words, a high vapor pressure at a given temperature corresponds to a relatively low boiling point.

The third and final MCAT-relevant distillation technique is vacuum distillation. To understand this method, you absolutely must recall the definition of boiling point: boiling occurs at the temperature at which the vapor pressure of the liquid in question (P_{vap}) is equal to the atmospheric pressure of the surroundings (P_{atm}). Imagine that you are trying to separate two liquids with boiling points greater than 400°C. If their boiling points are very different, we might predict that simple distillation would be effective, while if they are similar, we may need to use fractional distillation. Regardless, however, it is not feasible to use a Bunsen burner to heat a liquid to a temperature of 400°C or more. When we cannot raise the temperature (which increases the vapor pressure), we must instead *decrease* the atmospheric pressure to meet the vapor pressure. This can be accomplished by attaching a vacuum to the distillation apparatus. Lowering the ambient pressure of the surroundings results in a decreased boiling point for all compounds involved, allowing us to then conduct a typical distillation procedure.

4. Separations: Extractions

From the information presented in this chapter so far, we now know that liquids with different boiling points may be separated using distillation. However, many liquid mixtures do not fit this criterion. Instead, the two (or more) liquid components may differ from each other with regard to *other* physical or chemical characteristics. Once such trait is solubility in aqueous or organic media. On the MCAT, compounds with disparate solubility characteristics are most often separated using liquid-liquid extraction. To conduct an extraction, one must utilize a device known as a separatory funnel (Figure 8). The funnel is hung vertically, with an opening at the top through which solutions may be poured and a stopcock at the bottom that can be opened to let liquid out.

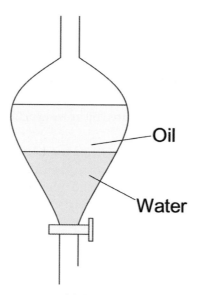

Figure 8. A separatory funnel containing two immiscible liquids: oil (lower density) and water (higher density).

Several variants of extraction procedures exist, but for the sake of the MCAT, you must simply understand those liquid-liquid extractions that take advantage of acid-base characteristics. Let's walk through an example. Imagine that you just finished an organic chemistry lab, and you now have a flask that contains acetic acid (CH_3COOH, a carboxylic acid) and aniline ($C_6H_5NH_2$, an amine) in the same solution, with a diethyl ether solvent. Diethyl ether ($CH_3CH_2OCH_2CH_3$) is relatively nonpolar. To separate the acetic acid from the aniline using extraction, you must first add an aqueous solvent, most often simply water; extractions require two immiscible liquid layers, and nonpolar organic solvents are not miscible with water. You first transfer your organic mixture to a separatory funnel, then add water, and this aqueous solvent settles in its own layer below the organic solution.

You now have a separatory funnel that contains an aqueous layer below an ether-based organic layer. However, how has this brought us any closer to separating acetic acid from aniline? Both are somewhat soluble in ether, so significant proportions of both compounds remain in the organic solvent. If we are to separate the two, we must move one compound into the aqueous layer and pour it off. We can accomplish this by taking advantage of the compounds' acid-base properties. On the

> **MCAT STRATEGY > > >**
>
> As you will learn in physics, a key fact about fluids is that less dense liquids or objects tend to float, while more dense objects or liquids sink. Diethyl ether has a density of approximately 713 kg/m³, while water has a density of 1000 kg/m³. (You do not need to memorize the density of diethyl ether, but be certain to know that of water.)

MCAT, one key concept is that charged compounds are highly polar, much more so than their uncharged states. If we can make one of the two compounds charged, then, most of its molecules will move into the aqueous layer.

At this point, we have a choice. Acetic acid is an acidic molecule, while aniline is basic. While it does not particularly matter, let's opt to move the acetic acid into the aqueous layer. To do so, we can add strong base (for example, NaOH) and shake the funnel. This will deprotonate the acetic acid, forming its conjugate base, CH_3COO^-. The negatively-charged compound is now far more soluble in the polar aqueous layer than the organic ether layer, so it will move to the aqueous layer of the funnel. Now, we can open the stopcock to release the aqueous layer into a beaker waiting below the separatory apparatus. Like distillation, extraction usually must be conducted multiple times to ensure that the product mixtures are as pure as possible.

Although our imaginary procedure is now complete, let us continue the same example to ensure that this technique is understood. What if we had chosen to move the aniline to the aqueous layer rather than the acetic acid?

> > **CONNECTIONS** < <

Chapter 7 of Chemistry

Predictably, just as we added strong base to deprotonate the acetic acid and move it to the aqueous layer, we can add strong *acid* to protonate the basic aniline molecules. As charged species (albeit positively rather than negatively charged), they will then transition to the aqueous layer, which can be poured off as we explained above.

"This is all well and good," you may say, "as long as we have only two molecules (acetic acid and aniline) in solution. Acetic acid is acidic, while aniline is basic, and this allows for easy separation. But could extraction be effective even if we needed to separate two acids?" Absolutely! Consider an imaginary solution of benzoic acid and phenol, again dissolved in a diethyl ether solvent. Moving this mixture to a separatory funnel and adding water will yield the two immiscible layers that we now expect to form. Both benzoic acid and phenol are somewhat acidic, with benzoic acid (a carboxylic acid) being significantly *more* acidic than phenol (an aromatic alcohol). To ensure that one of the compounds exits the organic phase, simply add weak base. The weak base will be sufficiently basic to deprotonate the stronger benzoic acid, but it will leave the weakly acidic phenol molecules untouched. Benzoic acid, being deprotonated and thus negatively charged, will now move into the aqueous layer, where it can be poured from the funnel. Phenol, the weaker and thus less reactive acid, will largely remain in the original ether layer.

5. Separations: Chromatography

Our next separation technique is chromatography, which is actually a broad category that contains several different methods. Chromatography is often used to separate amino acids and proteins, and as such, it is described in great detail in your biochemistry book. In this chapter, then, we will simply touch up on chromatography techniques with a focus on their relation to chemistry. Throughout this discussion, note the common features of these methods. In particular, chromatography involves two phases: a mobile phase, or moving fluid, and a stationary phase, or solid that does not move. A sample is passed through the apparatus, and its components travel at different rates depending on their affinities for the mobile and stationary phases. For each type of chromatography that is discussed, be certain to ask yourself what constitutes the mobile phase and what makes up the stationary phase.

> > **CONNECTIONS** < <

Chapter 5 of Biochemistry

Arguably the most often-discussed organic chemistry chromatography method is thin-layer chromatography, or TLC. The stationary phase in a TLC procedure is a glass or plastic plate coated in adsorbent, most commonly polar silica gel (SiO_2). A chemical sample is dabbed onto the plate, which is then placed in a beaker containing a nonpolar solvent, such as hexane. Capillary action draws the solvent up the plate, and it brings the components of the sample with it. Since the mobile phase is nonpolar, similarly nonpolar components are attracted to it and travel farther down the plate; in contrast, polar components have a higher affinity for the polar plate and thus do not travel as far. Figure 9 depicts a typical TLC plate after thin-layer chromatography of a mixture. Note that the plate must undergo subsequent visualization treatment if the compounds involved are colorless; otherwise, their corresponding spots would not be visible. Such treatment typically involves exposure to ultraviolet (UV) light or iodine.

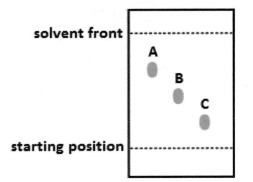

Figure 9. A TLC plate after chromatography. Assuming a nonpolar solvent and a polar plate, compound A must be the most nonpolar, followed by B, then C.

Thin-layer chromatography allows us to make rough measurements of the relative polarities of compounds. The main such measurement is termed the retention factor, or R_f. R_f is equal to the distance traveled by a compound down the plate from its starting position divided by the distance traveled by the solvent (often called the "solvent front"). For example, imagine that a TLC plate is 10 centimeters (cm) long. If the solvent traveled 8 cm while Compound C traveled 2 cm, the R_f of Compound C is (2 cm)/(8 cm) = 0.25. Assuming that the solvent is nonpolar, a higher R_f denotes a more nonpolar compound, since traveling a large distance implies that the compound has a marked affinity for the nonpolar mobile phase.

Although thin-layer chromatography is an effective way to compare the polarities of compounds or detect impurities within a sample, it does not allow us to isolate any separated components for later use. To do this, we can instead utilize column chromatography, in which the stationary phase is a solid adsorbent packed within a vertical column and the mobile phase is a liquid solvent. Again, the many forms of column chromatography are described in detail in Chapter 5 of our biochemistry book, since these techniques are most often tested in relation to protein analysis. For the sake of completeness, however, we will briefly mention them here. First, size-exclusion chromatography is used to separate the components of a mixture by physical size. Its stationary phase consists of pore-studded gel beads; smaller molecules become trapped in the pores and elute through the column slowly, while large molecules pass through rapidly. Two additional forms of chromatography, both grouped under the heading of ion-exchange chromatography, center around electrostatic interactions. Cation-exchange chromatography is utilized to trap *positively-charged* molecules within the column, and as such, it includes a *negatively-charged* stationary phase. On the other hand, anion-exchange chromatography uses a positively-charged stationary-phase rosin to trap negative molecules, or anions, within the column. Finally, the most specific form of column chromatography is affinity chromatography, in which ligands designed to bind to a compound of interest are attached to the beads that make up the column's stationary phase.

> **MCAT STRATEGY > > >**
>
> We have described the most common form of TLC, in which the stationary phase (plate) is polar and the mobile phase is nonpolar. However, be certain to understand that the opposite scenario is possible. If a passage mentions a nonpolar stationary phase, then, you can assume that the mobile phase of the TLC procedure is polar.

The final variations on chromatography that we will discuss in this chapter are gas-liquid chromatography (also known as gas chromatography, or GC) and high-performance liquid chromatography (HPLC). Do you recall the very beginning of this chapter, where we urged you to focus on the phases of matter involved in each separatory technique? Gas-liquid chromatography is the only separatory technique in this chapter to include a gaseous mobile phase, often consisting of helium or nitrogen. The sample to be analyzed is also vaporized into a gaseous state, then passed through an apparatus consisting of a column coated in a thin layer of polymer or liquid. (The polymer or liquid constitutes the stationary phase.) The time taken for the sample to move through the apparatus is measured and used as an estimate of its affinities for the gaseous mobile and liquid/polymer stationary phases. A longer elution time implies a higher affinity for the stationary phase, and vice versa. One final note on gas chromatography: for this method to work properly, the sample must be one which we can force into the gas phase fairly easily. A liquid that does not vaporize below 700°C, for example, would therefore be a poor choice of sample.

MCAT STRATEGY > > >

As always, when reading MCAT content, ask yourself "Why?" Here, we might ask why helium or nitrogen are chosen for the carrier gases that make up the GC mobile phase. The answer relates to the inert nature of these gases, which prevents them from reacting with the sample in unwanted side processes.

Finally, high-performance or high-pressure liquid chromatography (HPLC) involves passing a liquid mobile phase through an adsorbent-packed column, just like many forms of chromatography that we discussed earlier. The distinction, however, is that HPLC takes place under high pressure, allowing the resolution of the sample's components to occur more rapidly. Note that "regular" HPLC shares the characteristics of TLC, in that its stationary phase is polar while its mobile phase is nonpolar. Watch out, however; an alternative technique termed reverse-phase HPLC (RP-HPLC) also exists, and it includes a *nonpolar* stationary phase and a *polar* mobile phase.

6. Other Separation Techniques

We have almost finished our discussion of the separation techniques used in MCAT organic chemistry. Only two methods remain, neither of which fit perfectly within a larger category. The first of these techniques is recrystallization. Until now, we have placed our focus on the separations of liquid and gaseous samples. Often, however, an organic procedure will leave us with a solid product. This solid is likely to contain solid impurities. To purify the compound, we must remove them—but how? The answer lies in a foundational aspect of the solid structures formed by chemical compounds. When a typical solid precipitates out of solution, it forms a specific, ordered crystalline structure. If a solid can be made to precipitate multiple times, it will gradually increase in purity, as every crystallization will exclude additional impurities from the structure.

The procedure of a simple recrystallization is as follows. The desired solid product is placed in a liquid solvent and heated, causing it to dissolve. Upon full dissolution, the solvent-product mixture is cooled, and the solid once again forms as a precipitate. This process is facilitated by the scratching of the side of the flask, which provides rough "seed" regions for crystals to begin to form. The recrystallization process may be repeated multiple times, with the solid becoming progressively higher in purity.

One key decision to make when planning a recrystallization procedure is the identity of the solvent to use. An ideal recrystallization solvent is one in which our desired product is highly soluble at high temperatures (if this were not the case, it wouldn't dissolve at all)! At the same time, however, our product should be relatively *in*soluble in this solvent under low-temperature conditions, or it will never precipitate back out of solution when the mixture is cooled.

> > CONNECTIONS < <

Chapter 5 of Chemistry

Once we are satisfied with our solid product, we may need to isolate it from the liquid solvent in which it is held. This brings us to our final separation technique: filtration. This simple process is used to separate a solid product from unwanted fluids. To conduct a filtration process, set up a filter (often a single piece of filter paper) through which liquid, but not solid, can pass. Pour the liquid-solid mixture over this filter, and the desired solid will remain on the surface of the paper while the liquid will pass through to a flask below to be discarded.

7. Must-Knows

> Analytic techniques: identify features of a molecule or the molecule's identity
  – Often render the sample unusable in the future
  – Examples: IR, NMR, UV-Vis, mass spec
> Separation techniques: convert a mixture into multiple separate, pure samples (to the extent to which this is possible)
  – Samples can then be analyzed or otherwise used later
  – Examples: distillation, extraction, chromatography, recrystallization, filtration
> Infrared (IR) spectroscopy
  – Uses radiation w/a frequency lower than that of visible light to vibrate bonds
  – C=O $\rightarrow$ 1700 cm^{-1}, sharp; O-H $\rightarrow$ 3200-3600 cm^{-1}, broad
> Nuclear magnetic resonance (NMR) spectroscopy
  – Left side of spectrum = "downfield" = deshielded = close to e-withdrawing groups
  – Right side of spectrum = "upfield" = shielded = far from e-withdrawing groups
  – Area under peak corresponds to # of equivalent hydrogens
  – Splitting (singlet, doublet . . .) is determined by # of hydrogens on adjacent atom
> Ultraviolet-visible (UV-Vis) spectroscopy
  – Useful to discern presence of conjugated/aromatic species
> Mass spectrometry
  – Helps determine molecular weight (m/z peak), other features of sample
> Distillation: separates liquids based on boiling point
  – For BPs > 25° apart, use simple distillation
  – For BPs < 25° apart, use fractional distillation
  – For very high BPs, use vacuum distillation to lower atmospheric P $\rightarrow$ lower BPs
> Extraction: separates liquids based on solubility/acid-base properties
  – Requires immiscible aqueous and organic layers in a separatory funnel
  – To send an acid into the aqueous layer, add base (deprotonate it)
  – To send a base into the aqueous layer, add acid (protonate it)
> Chromatography involves a mobile phase and a stationary phase with different properties.
  – TLC: stationary phase is polar (usually silica) while mobile phase is a nonpolar solvent
    • R_f = (distance traveled by compound) / (distance traveled by solvent)
  – Size-exclusion, cation-exchange, anion-exchange, and affinity chromatography are all forms of column chromatography.
  – Gas chromatography (GC) vaporizes sample and passes through a column, then measures retention time.
  – HPLC = rapid method of column chromatography; polar stationary phase and nonpolar mobile phase for regular process, nonpolar stationary phase and polar mobile phase for reverse process (RP-HPLC)
> Other separation techniques: recrystallization, filtration

Practice Passage Explanations

During the last decade, an emerging hallmark has been added to the classical hallmarks of cancer. Lipid synthesis and lipid metabolism ratios inside tumor cells have been identified as potentially crucial factors for further tumor progression. For example, isoprenoid compounds released by human breast cancer tissue are able to suppress cytotoxic T cell responses, suggesting that isoprenoids can directly modulate the anti-tumor immunosuppressive effect.

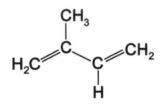

Figure 1. Isoprene unit

The biosynthesis of isoprenoid compounds begins when the α-carbon of an acetyl CoA is deprotonated to form an enolate. What follows is the Claisen condensation between two acetyl CoA molecules (Figure 2). However, when the body burns fat for energy, a related mechanism is responsible for breaking down long-chain fatty acids, one acetyl group at a time.

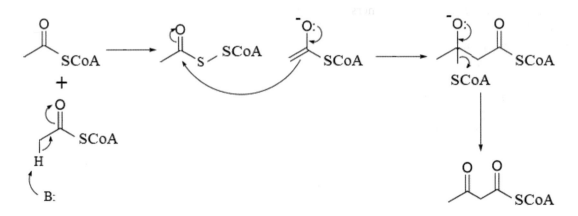

Figure 2. Isoprenoid synthesis

In fatty acid breakdown, a series of reactions is required to introduce the necessary ketone group to the beta position. Next, a thioester acts as nucleophile with an enolate serving as the leaving group. This mechanism is the exact reverse of a Claisen condensation, and the fatty acid chain is now shorter, and one acetyl CoA molecule is available to enter the citric acid cycle. This mechanism repeats until the entire fatty acid chain has been broken down to yield two-carbon acetyl CoA groups. Another form of reverse-Claisen condensation in the body is driven by hydrolysis, for example when the body must metabolize tyrosine and phenylalanine to continue cellular respiration.

Figure 3. Introduction of ketone during fatty acid breakdown

Adapted from Wu, H., et al. (2017). Oleate but not stearate induces the regulatory phenotype of myeloid suppressor cells. Scientific Reports, 7, 7498 under CCBY 4.0

1. Which of the following IR signal changes would indicate the conversion of acetyl CoA into a nucleophile?
   A. The disappearance of a broad peak at 2900 cm⁻¹
   B. The appearance of a variable peak at 3680 cm⁻¹
   C. The disappearance of a sharp peak at 1750 cm⁻¹
   D. The appearance of a medium peak at 3300 cm⁻¹

2. During the hydrolytic reverse-Claisen cleavage of tyrosine, the intermediate below is formed.

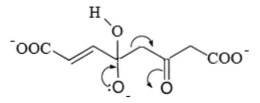

   Which molecule does the body most likely use to stabilize the intermediate long enough to facilitate the final enolate to keto protonation step?

   A. CN⁻
   B. Mg^{2+}
   C. H^+
   D. Fe^{4+}

3. What IR signal would best allow researchers to differentiate whether a eukaryotic cell is utilizing Tyr or Phe for cellular metabolism?
   A. A narrow, sharp peak at 1600 cm⁻¹
   B. A weak, narrow peak at 2700 cm⁻¹
   C. A strong, broad peak 3200 cm⁻¹
   D. A strong, broad peak at 1700 cm⁻¹

4. Which amino acid would give rise to the HNMR spectra below?

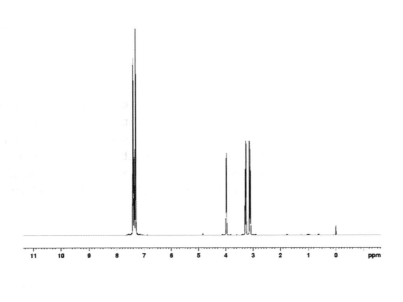

   A. R
   B. E
   C. M
   D. F

5. Students performing UV-vis spectroscopy observe that one of the isoprenoids generated by tumor cells strongly absorbs 450 nm light. What is the perceived color of this isoprenoid?
   A. Violet
   B. Indigo
   C. Red
   D. Yellow

6. On a H-NMR spectral analysis, which molecule will have the most shielding by extranuclear electrons?
   A. C_6H_{16}
   B. C_5H_4
   C. CH_3NO_2
   D. CH_3COH

7. Which of the H atoms labeled below would return the greatest degree of spin-spin coupling?

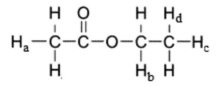

   A. H_a
   B. H_b
   C. H_c
   D. H_d

Practice Passage Explanations

During the last decade, an emerging hallmark has been added to the classical hallmarks of cancer. Lipid synthesis and lipid metabolism ratios inside tumor cells have been identified as potentially crucial factors for further tumor progression. For example, isoprenoid compounds released by human breast cancer tissue are able to suppress cytotoxic T cell responses, suggesting that isoprenoids can directly modulate the anti-tumor immunosuppressive effect.

Key terms: isoprenoid, anti-tumor immunosuppressive

Cause and effect: cancer → ↑FA synth → ↑isoprenoid synth → ↓immune response to tumor

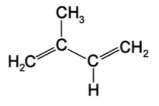

Figure 1. Isoprene unit

The biosynthesis of isoprenoid compounds begins when the α-carbon of an acetyl CoA is deprotonated to form an enolate. What follows is the Claisen condensation between two acetyl CoA molecules (Figure 2). However, when the body burns fat for energy, a related mechanism is responsible for breaking down long-chain fatty acids, one acetyl group at a time.

Key terms: biosynthesis, Claisen condensation,

Cause and effect: FA synth = Claisen; FA metabolism = similar mechanism, decreases chain by 2C/ round

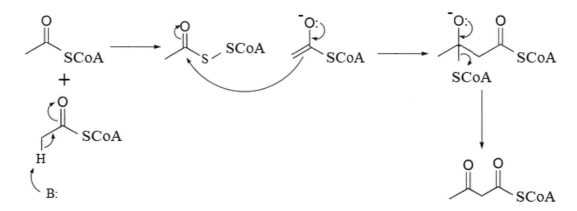

Figure 2. Isoprenoid synthesis

Figure 2 is a mechanism we should know by test day, a carbonyl loses an α–proton to become a nucleophile (enolate) and attacks the other carbonyl, leading to the elimination of H₂O and formation of an α-β-unsaturated product

In fatty acid breakdown, a series of reactions is required to introduce the necessary ketone group to the beta position. Next, a thioester acts as nucleophile with an enolate serving as the leaving group. This mechanism is the exact reverse of a Claisen condensation, and the fatty acid chain is now shorter, and one acetyl CoA molecule is available to enter the citric acid cycle. This mechanism repeats until the entire fatty acid chain has been broken down to yield two-carbon acetyl CoA groups. Another form of reverse-Claisen condensation in the body is driven by hydrolysis, for example when the body must metabolize tyrosine and phenylalanine to continue cellular respiration.

Key terms: fatty acid breakdown, reverse Claisen, hydrolysis

Cause and effect: FA break down = β-ketone formation → reverse-Claisen; AA metabolism = H_2O driven reverse-Claisen

Figure 3. Introduction of ketone during fatty acid breakdown

Figure 3 shows the initial step of FA breakdown; now the molecule is ready for attack by an RCOOSR' nucleophile as the enolate leaves

Adapted from Wu, H., et al. (2017). Oleate but not stearate induces the regulatory phenotype of myeloid suppressor cells. Scientific Reports, 7, 7498 under CCBY 4.0

1. C is correct. The second paragraph tells us that one of the acetyl-CoA groups is deprotonated in order to form the enolate, shown happening in step 1 of Figure 1. This enolate will carry a negative charge that it can stabilize via resonance between a keto group and an alkene group between the alpha carbon and the carbonyl carbon. Thus, if the carbonyl signal of the acetyl CoA is lost, it would indicate that this deprotonation has occurred.

2. B is correct. To stabilize the anions, we would need a cation. Since either oxygen atom can resonate to become negatively charged, a divalent cation would be best.

    A: An anion would not help stabilize the negatively charged intermediate.
    C: The proton is much more likely to attach to the carboxylic acid groups, or to the carbonyl oxygens to form hydroxyl moieties, rather than temporarily bind to the oxygen atoms and stabilize them.
    D: While Fe^{4+} might be able to stabilize the intermediate, this ion is not particularly stable and is far less likely to form than Mg^{2+}, or even Fe^{2+} and Fe^{3+}.

3. C is correct. The primary difference between the structure of tyrosine (Y) and phenylalanine (F) is the OH group attached to the phenyl group that is found on Y but not on F. The distinctive IR signal of the hydroxyl group is a big, broad peak around 3100-3300 cm^{-1}.

4. D is correct. The spectra shows the characteristic peaks (6-8 ppm) of aromatic hydrogen atoms. Phenylalanine (F) contains a phenyl substituent as its side chain while neither arginine (R), glutamic acid (E) nor methionine (M) contain aromatic groups.

5. D is correct. In UV-Vis spectroscopy, Colored compounds are colored because of the absorption of visible radiation. The perceived color is due to the emission of light of a complementary color, i.e. the wavelength "opposite" of the absorbed color.

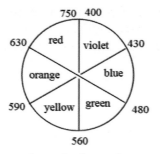

The color wheel above shows complementary color pairs, located on opposite sides of the wheel as we go from 700 nm (red) to 400 nm (violet).

6. A is correct. The level of shielding or protection afforded to a hydrogen atom on a molecule depends on the chemical environment surrounding that H atom. The more the surrounding area pulls away or delocalizes electron density, the further downfield (i.e. to the left, de-shielded) the signal will be. Alkanes, which retain almost the entire electron cloud on their H atoms, are found between 0-3 ppm.

    B, C, D: Alkynes, due to the presence of pi-bonds are more de-shielded than alkanes and are found between 2-3ppm. Nitro groups are commonly found between 4-5 ppm, while aldehyde H atoms are among the most de-shielded, returning signals between 9-10 ppm.

7. B is correct. The signal splitting, or spin-spin coupling of a proton's H-NMR signal, is caused by magnetic interactions between neighboring, non-equivalent H atoms within 3 bonds of the H atom being analyzed. The 2 H atoms on the carbon 2nd from the right has 3 H atoms within 3 bonds (n), so the signal will be split into n + 1 = 3 + 1 = 4 peaks.

    A: The 3 H atoms on the far left carbon will be visualized as a singlet, since they have no H neighbors within 3 bonds of themselves.
    C, D: These 2 H atoms will be a part of the same signal. Since they cannot both be correct, they both must be wrong. These will appear as a triplet, since they have 2 H atoms on their relevant neighbors (H_{b1} and H_{b2}).

Independent Questions

1. An organic chemistry student conducts thin-layer chromatography (TLC) on two unknown compounds using a developing solvent consisting of equal parts ethyl acetate and hexane by volume. The TLC plate, which is silica on glass, is visualized by staining with iodine vapor. The result is shown below.

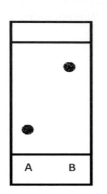

   Which of the following is most likely true of the two unknown compounds?

   A. Compound A has a greater molecular weight than compound B.
   B. Compound A is more soluble in polar solvents than Compound B.
   C. Compound A carries a net charge at neutral pH, while Compound B does not.
   D. Compound A emits light in the visible spectrum, while Compound B does not.

2. Tetraethyl lead (TEL) is an organometallic compound with the formula $(CH_3CH_2)_4Pb$. An environmental scientist wishes to test a sample for the presence of TEL. She conducts a liquid-liquid extraction using an aqueous layer and a layer of dichloromethane, which settles above the aqueous layer. If the sample contained TEL, it would be present in the:
   A. organic layer, because low-density solutes rise to the top layer.
   B. organic layer, because TEL is a nonpolar compound.
   C. aqueous layer, because high-molecular-weight solutes settle to the bottom layer.
   D. aqueous layer, because TEL is a nonpolar compound.

3. Which of the following liquids are likely to be immiscible?
   A. Diethyl ether and benzene
   B. Water and methanol
   C. Hexane and dichloromethane
   D. Water and carbon tetrachloride

4. The IUPAC name for D-tartaric acid is (2S,3S)-2,3-dihydroxybutanedioic acid. The structure of D-tartaric acid is shown below.

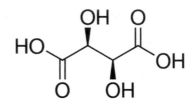

   If a solution of pure D-tartaric acid has an optical activity of –12°, what is the optical activity of a solution of pure (2R,3S)-2,3-dihydroxybutanedioic acid?

   A. –12°
   B. +12°
   C. 0°
   D. It cannot be determined from the given information.

5. High-performance liquid chromatography (HPLC) is often used in pharmaceutical chemistry to test for impurities. If a mixture of organic compounds were subjected to normal-phase HPLC, which of the following would be the most likely outcome?
   A. The most polar compound will elute first, because the column is packed with a polar solid.
   B. The most polar compound will elute first, because the column is packed with a nonpolar solid.
   C. The least polar compound will elute first, because the column is packed with a polar solid.
   D. The least polar compound will elute first, because the column is packed with a nonpolar solid.

6. A student wishes to separate two known liquids. The organic liquids are both colorless and have similar solubility profiles, but their boiling points differ significantly. Which of the following separation techniques would be most appropriate for these circumstances?
   A. Distillation
   B. Liquid-liquid extraction
   C. Gel electrophoresis
   D. Recrystallization

7. The structure of ethyl acetate is shown below.

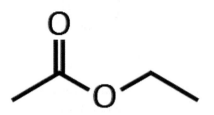

The ^{1}H NMR spectrum of ethyl acetate is expected to display:

   A. one singlet, two quartets, and one triplet.
   B. two triplets and one doublet.
   C. one doublet, one triplet, and one quartet.
   D. one singlet, one quartet, and one triplet.

8. A synthetic chemist conducts thin-layer chromatography on the crude product of a reaction and finds that it contains two unique compounds. The chemist separates the compounds by simple distillation and subsequently finds that they have different NMR spectra. Which of the following is LEAST likely true of these two compounds?
   A. They are enantiomers.
   B. They are structural isomers.
   C. They are liquids at room temperature.
   D. They have different molecular formulas.

Independent Questions

1. B is correct. The silica-coated TLC place is a polar interface, while the organic developing solvent is a nonpolar interface. Relatively polar compounds will interact more extensively with the polar interface, while less polar compounds will interact more extensively with the nonpolar solvent. In this fashion, TLC separates compounds based on their relative polarities. As the developing solvent travels up the TLC plate, the sample compounds are pulled along with it. The more polar compound will not travel as far since its movement is slowed by its attraction to the plate. Here, since Compound A did not travel as far along the plate, it must be the more polar of the two compounds. Choice C may be tempting, because charged compounds are relatively polar, but we cannot know for certain whether Compound A carries a net charge.

2. B is correct. Liquid-liquid extraction separates compounds according to solubility, a property which largely depends on polarity. Although the denser solvent does form the bottom layer and the less dense solvent forms the top layer, the solutes do not separate according to density. Instead, nonpolar compounds such as TEL are pulled from aqueous solution into the organic layer, regardless of whether that layer is on the top or bottom. (Note that TEL must be nonpolar due to its many hydrocarbon groups and lack of charge.)

3. D is correct. Polar solvents tend to be miscible with other polar solvents, while nonpolar solvents tend to mix more readily with other nonpolar solvents. Water is a polar solvent and carbon tetrachloride is a nonpolar solvent; since these two compounds differ substantially in polarity, they are likely to be immiscible.

4. C is correct. The inversion of a single chiral center in D-tartaric acid produces a meso compound because of the symmetry between the left and right sides. Meso compounds, like racemic mixtures, are optically inactive.

5. C is correct. Normal-phase HPLC features a nonpolar solvent that is run through a column packed with a polar solid (eliminate choices B and D). Since polar solutes are attracted to the polar solid in the column, they pass more slowly through the column and elute after nonpolar solutes. Note that reverse-phase HPLC is a variation on this technique that involves a polar solvent passing through a nonpolar column. If this question had asked about reverse-phase HPLC instead of normal-phase HPLC, choice B would be the correct answer.

6. A is correct. Distillation separates liquids according to boiling point; thus, it works best when the compounds involved have significantly different boiling points. Liquid-liquid extraction separates compounds based on their relative solubility profiles. Gel electrophoresis is generally used for macromolecules, not organic liquids. Recrystallization is used to purify compounds that are solids under standard conditions.

7. D is correct. Ethyl acetate contains three sets of equivalent protons, as shown below.

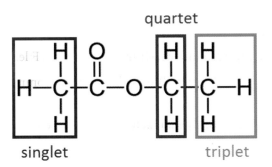

In ^{1}H NMR, each set of equivalent protons corresponds to one peak, but peaks can be split into smaller peaks by hydrogen atoms present on adjacent carbons. If no hydrogens are present on the adjacent carbon atom(s), the peak will remain a singlet, as is true for the protons on the left side of the diagram above. If two hydrogen atoms are present on the neighboring carbon(s), as is true for the set of protons on the far right, the peak will be split into a triplet. Finally, if three hydrogen atoms exist on the neighboring position, the peak will appear as a quartet. These are the only three peaks expected to be found on the spectrum of ethyl acetate.

8. A is correct. Enantiomers tend to have very similar physical properties and must be separated using special techniques. It would be very unusual for two enantiomers to separate from undergoing TLC or simple distillation.

IMAGE ATTRIBUTIONS

Chapter 1

Fig 4: https://commons.wikimedia.org/wiki/File:Single_electron_orbitals.jpg by haade under CC-BY-SA-3.0

Chapter 2

Fig 4: https://commons.wikimedia.org/wiki/File:Pi-Bond.svg by JoJan; derivative work: Vladsinger, under CC BY-SA 3.0

Fig 7: https://commons.wikimedia.org/wiki/File:Nitrate_ion_resonance_structures.png by Azazell0 under CC BY-SA 3.0

Chapter 5

Fig 2: https://commons.wikimedia.org/wiki/File:Phase_changes.svg by AnyFile under CC BY-SA 3.0

Fig 4: Phase diagram; Brews ohare; https://commons.wikimedia.org/wiki/File:Phase_diagram_for_pure_substance.JPG; CC BY-SA 3.0

Fig 5: Osmosis; OpenStax; https://en.wikipedia.org/wiki/Osmosis#/media/File:0307_Osmosis.jpg; CC BY 4.0

Chapter 6

Independent Question 1: Image adapted from: https://commons.wikimedia.org/wiki/File:Reaction_Coordinate_Diagram.png by AimNature under CC BY-SA 3.0

Chapter 8

Fig 1: https://en.wikipedia.org/wiki/Electrolysis_of_water#/media/File:Electrolysis.svg CC BY-SA 4.0

Fig 3: https://en.wikipedia.org/wiki/File:Recharged.gif CC BY-3.0

Fig 4: https://en.wikipedia.org/wiki/File:Discharged.gif CC BY-3.0

Chapter 12

Fig 1: https://commons.wikimedia.org/wiki/File:EM_spectrumrevised.png by Philip Ronan, Gringer under CC BY-SA 3.0

Fig 3: https://commons.wikimedia.org/wiki/File:1H_NMR_Ethyl_Acetate_Coupling_shown.png by T.vanschaik, under CC BY-SA 3.0

Fig 5: https://commons.wikimedia.org/wiki/File:Beta-carotene.png by Polimerek under CC BY-SA 3.0

Fig 6: https://commons.wikimedia.org/wiki/File:Hexanal_edited.gif by Vladislav Andriashvili under CC BY-SA 3.0

Fig 7: https://commons.wikimedia.org/wiki/File:Fractional_distillation_lab_apparatus.svg by John Kershaw under CC BY-SA 3.0

Fig 8: https://commons.wikimedia.org/wiki/File:SeparatoryFunnel.svg by Borb under CC BY-SA 3.0

Fig 9: https://commons.wikimedia.org/wiki/File:TLC_plate.svg by Theresa Knott and Marek M under CC BY-SA 3.0

INDEX